YOUTH MINISTRY

MANAGEMENT TOOLS

Everything you need to successfully manage and administrate your youth ministry

YOUTH MINISTRY

MANAGEMENT
TOOLS

**Everything you need
to successfully manage
and administrate your
youth ministry**

GINNY OLSON   DIANE ELLIOT   MIKE WORK

Youth Specialties

ZondervanPublishingHouse
Grand Rapids, Michigan
A Division of HarperCollinsPublishers

Youth Ministry Management Tools: Everything you need to successfully manage and administrate your youth ministry

Copyright © 2001 by Ginny Olson, Diane Elliot, and Mike Work

Youth Specialties Books, 300 S. Pierce St., El Cajon, CA 92020, are published by Zondervan Publishing House, 5300 Patterson Ave. S.E., Grand Rapids, MI 49530.

Library of Congress Cataloging-in-Publication Data

Olson, Ginny,
    Youth ministry management tools : everything you need to successfully manage and
administrate your youth ministry / Ginny Olson, Diane Elliot, Mike Work.
        p. cm.
    Includes bibliographical references and index.
    ISBN 0-310-23596-0
    1. Church work with youth. 2. Church youth workers. 3. Church management. I. Elliot,
Diane. II. Work, Mike, 1961- III. Title.

BV4447 .O49 2001
259'.23—dc21

00-043936

Unless otherwise indicated, all Scripture quotations are taken from the Holy Bible: New International Version (North America Edition). Copyright © 1973, 1978, 1984 by International Bible Society. Used by permission of Zondervan Publishing House.

Before you use any forms or tips or checklists or any other piece of advice in this book, evaluate them for their sutability to your own church and youth group, for any potential risks, for safety precautions that must be taken, and for advance preparation that may be required. Neither Youth Specialties, Zondervan Publishing House, TCS Software, nor the authors are responsible for, nor have any control over, the use of misuse of any information published in this book and CD-ROM. Neither are these resources a substitute for your own legal counsel.

Edited by Linda Bannan, Cheri McLaughlin, and Dave Urbanski
Cover, interior, CD-ROM label, and splash screen design by Left Coast
Additional design contributions by Mary Fletcher
Other contributions by Heidi Clevenger, Tom Gulotta, Lorna McFarland Hartman, and Roni Valerio-Meek

Printed in the United States of America

01 02 03 04 05 06 / / 10 9 8 7 6 5 4 3

Introduction

Part 1: Tools to help you manage yourself

Part 2: Tools to help you manage your ministry

Part 3: Tools to help you stay in youth ministry

Part 4: Forms

Acknowledgements

We, the authors, are deeply indebted to Tim McLaughlin and Cheri McLaughlin for helping us make our vision a reality. Thank you for your coaching, your encouragement, your sweat, and your inspiration. Your fingerprints are all over this thing. We also appreciate all the people who've helped us throughout our ministry careers with management ideas and tools.

From Ginny

I'm grateful for the people who coached me and gave me feedback—and taught me about management tools. Many of their ideas are sprinkled in one form or another throughout these pages. The following are just a few of them:

- Scott Pederson, Randy Black, and Saundra Hensel—my former teammates in the junior high ministry at Willow Creek Community Church. What a privilege to have worked with a group of people who value relationships, creativity, fun, administration, and excellence—and somehow keep them all in balance.
- Mark Gold, Dave Busby, and Dennis Miller—they not only believed in youth ministry but also in developing young leaders who would minister to youth. They took a chance on a rookie right out of college. I'm thankful for their guidance and for giving me a strong start.
- The youth ministry students in the Leadership and Management course at North Park University. They have been a living laboratory over the years—helping me to refine, change, wrestle with, and create many of the concepts that are present in this project. They've kept in contact with me after graduation, telling me from the trenches what works and doesn't, what to add and what to tweak. Their honesty, encouragement, and raw passion for both God and ministry often reminds me of why I keep doing what I do—and why I still love it after all these years.
- I've learned much over the years from my coauthors, Mike and Diane—especially that it's possible to combine loving God and kids with administration. What a joy it's been to work with them.
- And thanks to Julie Gnoyke, a North Park student who pitched in and made phone calls, checked sources, and dug for answers to random questions for us. She was a true servant with a great attitude.

Finally, I'd like to dedicate my efforts toward the creation of this project to the memory of my sister Julie. Her head for business was amazing, but her heart for others is the legacy that's lasted. Her life still continues to teach me.

From Diane

I'd like to dedicate this project to all the kids who've touched my life and given me the privilege of impacting theirs. Especially to Erica and Jessica—you make me want to be the hero that you think I am.

From Mike

I have many to thank for the tools and skills I have acquired over the years! My mentors—Dr. Brian Richardson, Dave Busby, Mark Gold, Warren Schuh, Rich Van Pelt, and Geoff Cragg. Thanks also to my friends with whom I've spent hours talking about ministry; my coauthors, Ginny and Diane; also Dave Shirley, Lisa Poellot, Greg Weismann, Todd Temple, Heather Heinsch, Lynn Ziegenfuss, and Jim Hancock.

I'd like to dedicate *Youth Ministry Management Tools* to my wonderful family—Patti, Jason, Brandon, and Amy—you have walked with me through all of these years of ministry. Thank you for your love and encouragement and help.

How to use this book

A vision with a task is a dream,
A task without a vision is drudgery
A vision with a task is the hope of the world.
Church Window in Sussex England, c. 1730

Many of us in youth ministry share a vision: tribes of adolescents encountering God, families healed, churches reenergized, communities rolling up their sleeves and serving each other. But since we're usually mired in a bog of details surrounding those dreams, our vision can get cloudy—or slowly dissipate altogether.

One of our goals in writing this book was to help youth workers out of the bog and get back on track with their vision. Those who're merely ankle deep in the muck can discover here fresh ideas and variations on old practices. Those who sense they're sinking fast can find a lifeline in *Youth Ministry Management Tools*. This book and the accompanying Youth Assistant / Special Edition CD-ROM will help all youth workers do more than merely survive the tasks of ministry—they'll show you how crucial those tasks are for accomplishing your vision.

Our vision as trainers is to help you succeed in all facets of youth ministry management. Our task as authors was to write a book to facilitate that success. We hope God will use our vision and our task to impact teens and their families for the kingdom through your work and your skills.

Interact with this book. Read the narrative, underline it, dog-ear it, put Post-It Notes on it. Play with the forms. Get your team to wrestle with the case studies. Ask, "How can I use this stuff?" "How can it help our ministry run better and more smoothly?" "What do I need to do because of what I'm reading?" Gobble it all up.

- *Rookie youth workers* will find ideas in *Youth Ministry Management Tools* for handling tasks that are basic to long-term youth ministry. There are case studies to get you thinking, forms you can adapt and tweak, and checklists to help you anticipate and track details of ministry.

- *Youth workers who're primarily creative* (read: "disorganization is my middle name") will enjoy systems, structures, and forms that are easily adaptable to your needs. No more creating procedures from scratch.

- *Veteran youth workers* can use this book to train interns or key volunteers, as a resource manual to dip into periodically, and as a storehouse to supplement (perhaps even reapproach) your already effective ministry practices.

Pile Management (by Diane Elliot)

I've done ministry the hard way for the last 14 years. Why? Because management doesn't come naturally to me. I'm a people person who puts projects off until the last minute, has little time for budgeting, uses the "pile method" of organization, and then hopes for the best. I still have to labor to keep my natural disorganization from hindering my ministry. But I'm living proof that giving the effort necessary to change is worth it. I firmly believe that my acquired management, leadership, and organizational skills have allowed me to succeed in ministry. In fact, as I become more proactive, think smarter, and act more professionally, I'm getting even better ministry results.

      Youth Ministry Management Tools is for those heroes who sacrifice their time, talents, and personal comfort to reach other peoples' kids for God. But I admit a selfish motive for writing the book, too—more than 40 children call me Aunt Di (a little more than half are not even remotely related to me). I've taught thousands of adolescents, and my current job is leading a Christian school with more than 80 students. It wouldn't surprise me at all if one of my "kids"—or their offspring—shows up in your youth group some day. For their sake, I want you freed up to give them your best—and to be the hero to them you're destined to be.

Cob Webs and Charts (by Ginny Olson)

Life is like a cob web, not an organization chart. – H. Ross Perot

This book was born from a need in my life. Personally I prefer "cob webs" to charts and systems. I'm drawn to the visionary side of ministry; organization does not come naturally or easily to me. I started in ministry because of God and relationships, not because of policies and procedures. But I quickly learned that if I was going to stay in ministry, I would need to acquire some basic management skills. And for years I looked for a book like this one! A one-stop shop where I could unearth quick ways out of the maze of file folders, permission slips, and camp contracts. But most of what was out there was either too vague or written by Type-A people who bled *organization* and *systems* and had no idea how to harness the right sides of their brains. It was then that I became determined to someday write a book for youth workers like me, who knew more about cob webs than organizational charts—who were just looking for a little help sorting out administrative things. I've always wanted a book just like this one—and here it is.

Having trouble with a Web site address?

Web site addresses listed in this book were current at the time of publication—which means there's no way we can guarantee that these addresses are still current. But we'll do our best to keep them updated at www.YouthSpecialties.com/YMMT. If you have trouble with an URL, and the correction isn't posted on the Web site listed above, please contact us via e-mail (YS@Youth-Specialties.com) to let us know if you've found the correct or new URL—or if the URL is no longer operational.

    avantgo.com
    ccli.com
    christianlinks.com
    churchmutual.com
    cimaworld.com
    datamasters.com
    daytimer.com
    franklincovey.com
    galescreek.com
    handspring.com
    mediashout.com
    monster.com
    mplc.com
    nino.com
    nonprofitcoverage.com
    nonprofitrisk.com
    palm.com
    pdacentral.com
    pdamart.com
    pdastreet.com
    rcmaweb.org
    redcross.org
    safetyonline.com
    sonlife.com
    swank.com
    ugeek.com
    youthassistant.com
    YouthSpecialties.com
    youthtrack.com
    YouthWorkers.net

Role juggling (by Mike Work)

As a career youth worker, I'm faced with many challenges every day. But all too often, what I come to work *thinking* I'm going to do gets pushed aside by unexpected tasks. And I'm forced to juggle. (And then there are the things I'm *supposed* to do!) I mean, I'm paid to be a devoted follower of Christ, a friend and discipler of students, a parent counselor, a staff trainer and recruiter, an event planner, a master financier, an articulate and relevant communicator, a Bible expert (and student), the source of endless, fun games, a youth culture expert, a medic, an evangelist and missiologist, plus an organizer, motivator, and—last but not least—a husband and father.

Wow! No wonder I so often feel tired and tugged in all directions. (No wonder *you* feel the same pressures.) So how do we hold it all together? How do we find what we need? These constant pressures are what motivated me to contribute to this book. My aim was to help youth workers more effectively reach students. The systems, structures, and ideas presented in the forthcoming pages are meant to quietly and effectively run in the background of your ministry. I wish I had put many of these pieces in place much earlier in my professional life. And while great forms, organized files, and efficient systems aren't the end goal, kids will feel cared for in the midst of a structure that *cares for them*—one that lifts their levels of excitement. It's my prayer that this book helps you do just that.

Register

Please register your **Youth Assistant / Special Edition** CD-ROM!

Photocopy this page (or write this information down) and send it either by fax or snail-mail
to: TCS Software
        120 W. Jackson Street
        Cookeville, TN 38501
        attn: Software Registration
        Fax (toll free): (888) 297-6496

Name _____   Church name _____

Church address _____
                      Street   City   State   Zip

Phone number _____   Fax _____E-mail_____

Register to: ❑ the name listed above   ❑ the church listed above

Date purchased _____   Signature _____

Thanks for your cooperation!

Using the Youth Assistant / Special Edition CD-ROM

Using Microsoft Word®

The forms are in Microsoft Word®95 / 6.0 format. Those of you with Microsoft Word®95 / 6.0 (or above) can open, read, and change any text on any form. Here are a few tips when working in these forms. (If you need or want more instructions, please consult the Microsoft Word® software manual.)

► Text boxes and tables

Some Microsoft Word® forms on the Youth Assistant / Special Edition CD-ROM contain text boxes or tables—some are simply text documents.

• **How to move a text box**. If you click on a text box with your mouse, a thick, light grey border will appear. To move the text box, click on the border of the text box until you see a cross-like icon (✛). Then you can move the text box. If you don't see the cross-like icon, the box won't move. You may need to double click on the border with your mouse until you see the icon.

• **How to change text in a text box**. Click inside the text box with your mouse until you see the curser blinking. If you need to make the text box bigger to fit more text, click on the border of the text box with the mouse until you see small, white squares on the border. Put your pointer on a square and drag a side of the text box to make it bigger or smaller. (For example, to make the text box longer on the bottom, click the square on the bottom of the text box border.)

• **How to change text in a table**. If you click on a box in a form and nothing happens, it's probably a table—you can change the text, but you can't move the box.

• **How to add a row or column to a table**. Either 1) click the "tab" button when you're in the last row of the table, or 2) when your curser is in the table, click on the "table" menu at the top of the screen, scroll down to "insert," and move the mouse to the right. Then select where you'd like to insert the row. You can insert a new column to a table by following #2 above.

► Changing headers and footers

Each of the Microsoft Word® forms on the Youth Assistant / Special Edition CD-ROM has a header (a black text box with the form name) and a footer (place to enter your church information). If you open a form and can't see the header or footer in grey, go the the "view" menu, and select "print layout" to see the complete form.

• **How to access the text in headers and footers**. Go to the "view" menu at the top of the screen and click on "header and footer." Then you can change text in the header and scroll down to change text in the footer. **Important**: changes to headers and footers apply to the *whole* form, not just a specific page. If you want to make changes to one page only, resave the form under another name, delete the pages you don't want, and change the header and footer.

The black boxes (that show up as grey until you enter "header and footer") in the headers are text boxes. You can change text in the text box by following the instructions given in the section above.

When you're finished making changes to the header and footer, press the close button to exit.

► Saving changed forms

After you load the Youth Assistant program on your computer's hard drive, the Microsoft Word® forms are automatically placed in a folder on the hard drive as well. If you want to save *your* version of a form on your hard drive or disk, click the "file" menu and select "save as." Be sure to save your version of the form as a different name (other than the original form name), or else you'll accidentally save over the original form!

► You are responsible...

Before you use any forms, tips, or checklists in this book or on the CD-ROM, evaluate them for suitability to your church and youth group—as well as for potential risks so you can take safety precautions. Neither Youth Specialties, Zondervan Publishing House, TCS Software, or the authors are responsible for—nor have any control over—the use or misuse of any information published in this book or CD-ROM. And neither resources are substitutes for your own legal counsel.

All forms are copyright © 2001 by Ginny Olson, Diane Elliot, and Mike Work and may only be reproduced for use in the buyer's own youth ministry. Thanks for cooperating.

► Tips for using Youth Assistant

For complete instructions on loading and using the Youth Assistant program, please see pages 62-64. Note that each screen in this program (not the Microsoft Word® forms) has a Help! menu that will help you with any questions about Youth Assisant.

► Technical support

If you need help with the Youth Assistant / Special Edition CD-ROM, please contact TYA support by e-mail at ymmt@youthassistant.com or by phone at 888/297-6495.

Tools to help you manage yourself

PART 1

The shock of lengthy lists of expectations and job requirements can make youth workers feel like they can't breathe.

- How do I keep it all balanced?
- How do I know I'm spending time on the right things?
- How do I discipline myself to do the things I don't like to do?
- Am I taking care of myself, my family, my staff, my students?
- How do I find time to adequately prepare talks, staff meetings, and plan ahead for upcoming events?

For youth ministry professionals, getting a handle on time is like trying to take a breath after coming up from a dive into icy water. (This is personal experience, mind you—a lake in the Colorado Rockies, water temperature just above freezing, me hauling myself out, can't even draw a breath I'm so chilled.)

I n Part 1 of **Youth Ministry Management Tools**— *"Tools to help you manage yourself"—you'll learn how to catch your breath by managing your time effectively and organizing your space efficiently.*

Organize your time

Youth workers often find themselves—	
	▶ Taking on too much
	▶ Underestimating the time a task requires
	▶ Unable to stay focused on a task
	▶ Feeling overwhelmed
	▶ Lacking discipline to follow through
	▶ Feeling constantly interrupted
	▶ Unable to say no.

You can conquer the ministry stress trap when you schedule it, plan it, do it, and communicate it.

In Organize your time—

1. Schedule it
2. Plan it
3. Do it

Don't forget relationships

4. Communicate it

Schedule it

Buy and use a calendar or a personal digital assistant. It's as simple—and as terrifying—as that.

Chapter preview	► Time management
	► Getting started with a planning tool
	► Low-tech calendars
	► Electronic calendars
	► **Quick Start**: Setting up your low-tech calendar

Time management

Although most of us had good elementary school teachers who made sure we understood the basics of reading, writing, and math, few of us have mastered the "other" basic skill—time management. Our efforts to organize are shaped by our personality styles, the systems of time management we use (or don't use), the environment of our churches, and our stage in ministry.

Too often our offices are littered with legal pads covered with scribbled notes, Post-it Notes, and telephone call slips overflowing onto the floor. Those precious reminders could be blown into oblivion by a small gust of wind (whether from an open window or from your door when the senior pastor bursts in with news of a hastily scheduled meeting that night—your third in four nights). You must decide on one location for your to-do list and your appointment reminders, as well as for recording phone numbers and tidbits of information.

Why put everything in one place, you ask?

► Because you can easily view an extended record of critical tasks and information at all times (especially helpful for visual people).

> **Real Life**
>
> Ministry veteran Darrell Pearson drove 90 minutes to meet with a stressed youth worker in need of time-management advice. "Can you wait a few minutes?" asked a staffer at the church. "Seems that an appointment with a volunteer just came up for Brad."
>
> An hour later, Brad and Darrel finally went to lunch, but they only had 45 minutes together. Darrell then drove the 90 minutes home. By the time he got home, he had invested more than five hours.

Personality-appropriate time management

- The creative type carries a sketch journal and a box of 64 colored pencils to draw in her days the way she wants.

- The fly-by-the-seat-of-the-pants type writes reminders on his jeans or palm (the only Palm Pilot that doesn't crash).

- The indecisive type uses 23 different versions of information-tracking—at the same time.

- The auditory learner dictates his schedule to voice mail.

- The visual learner sticks Post-its to her cubicle—a method that flunks the portability test.

- The X'er tattoos the to-do list on his arm.

➤ Because you always know where to look for important information (the best way for disorganized people to actually find things).

➤ Because you'll have a natural organizational frame-work—that means you can make plans, confident that you're available.

For your best chance at getting organized, be sure to choose a method of information management that fits your personality and style.

Evaluate

For each entry of projected dates that you place on your working calendar, ask these questions. Is there—

- ✔ a facility to reserve?
- ✔ transportation to arrange?
- ✔ a flier to design, print, and mail?
- ✔ staff to secure?
- ✔ a clear and approved budget?
- ✔ church communication pieces to which you must submit info?

Getting started with a planning tool

A number of effective products can help you get organized—Day-Timer and Franklin Covey are two of the brands you'll find at Staples, Office Depot, or other office-supply stores (and online: daytimer.com and franklincovey.com). Planners vary in style, size, and available space for scheduling. Browse the possibilities, ask friends and colleagues what they use and why, pick a style that complements your personality, and commit to using it for three months. If you stick with something for 21 consecutive days, you are well on the way toward forming a new habit. Forming effective organizational habits (as opposed to living by unsupportive, unhelpful habits) is no different. You can replace old habits with new ones.

Don't be afraid to get help, either. Never attended a time-management seminar? Find one and go to it. The investment is worth the results. (Given the complex demands on our time, managing this area of life can be hard to just figure out on our own.) Many seminars are simply careful explanations of detailed time-management systems, along with plans for integrating their systems into your life.

Worth the Time

FasTrack

1 The foundation of managing your time is finding a system that places important information in one place.

Evaluate

Buying a PDA?*
First ask yourself—

✔ Is it simple to understand and easy to use?

✔ Will it really make my life better?

✔ Does it have the features I really want and need? (Can you live without bells and whistles you'll rarely, if ever, use?)

✔ What do the product reviews say about the variety of options?

✔ What do my PDA-using friends recommend?

✔ Can I get by with a used one? (Okay, so your used PDA wouldn't sport the newest screen shape or button configuration, but often the older technology is still very helpful.)

Low-tech calendars

▶ Month-at-a-view calendars. These large, laminated wall calendars are available in many forms and varying graphic designs at most office-supply stores.

Monthly Planning page 277

Weekly Planning page 279

  ▶ Simple planning forms.

    —Monthly Planning

    —Weekly Planning

▶ 12- or 18-month calendars. Fill in simple calendar squares with the following information:

    —all major events (retreats, trips, mission projects, et cetera)

    —staff meetings and parent meetings

    —special events (outreaches, community service, fundraisers)

Expectations

Church congregations often expect youth ministers to be competent in—

▶ family counseling
▶ computer science
▶ theology
▶ graphic arts
▶ communication
▶ church history
▶ church politics
▶ sports
▶ multimedia
▶ contemporary cultural issues
▶ eating disorders
▶ music groups
▶ drugs and alcohol
▶ parenting
▶ crisis intervention
▶ budget management
▶ family systems
▶ event planning
▶ correspondence
▶ first aid
▶ death and dying
▶ marriage counseling
▶ and most likely a few other things I've left out.

(After reviewing this list, I am giving serious thought to returning to my bus driving career!)

PDAs*

Personal digital assistants are lightweight, hand-held computers designed to use as personal organizers. High-end versions have communication and Internet capabilities.

"Hold it—I'm a broke youth worker"

"I've got no cash for luxuries like this. So stop feeding me all this info...I'm resigned to using my yellow pad and the pocket calendar our church gives to new members."

If money's the only thing that's stopping you, try this nifty idea to get a PDA (or maybe even a laptop) in three easy steps:

➤ Put out the word at your church that you are looking for a PDA.

➤ Let people know you don't need a brand-new one—you want to buy a used one from someone who's upgrading.

➤ Wait by the phone. Don't worry, it'll ring.

In a typical week

A youth worker may—

➤ prepare multiple talks

➤ return calls to students and their families

➤ handwrite notes of encouragement

➤ plan upcoming events

➤ pray with worried parents

➤ wade through tons of junk mail and e-mail

➤ attend school events

➤ train staff

➤ desperately look for a fresh game

➤ replace the leg on a table on which seven freshmen sat.

Electronic calendars

PDAs (such as Palm Pilots, Royal daVinci, Helios, Casio's Cassiopeia) enable users to carry a ton of info with them or let you download *Salon* articles and *Wall Street Journal* stock prices (again, do you want a personal organizer or the Internet in your pocket?). Organize your week, keep your secretary informed of your schedule, find important numbers and addresses, operate from one schedule on multiple devices, get and read your e-mail, send covert messages across the room during boring meetings or classes—these are just a few of the things your PDA can help you do.

FasTrack

2 A planner is a good fit when it gets used and when it helps you be more effective.

A typical PDA has no keyboard, relying instead on recognition of handwritten input, through the use of special hardware and stylus-based computer software, on the surface of a liquid crystal display screen. In addition to including such applications as a word processor, spreadsheet, calendar, and address book, PDAs are notepads, appointment schedulers, and wireless communicators for sending and receiving data, faxes, and electronic-mail messages.

➤ For the latest on PDAs, browse the Web.

➤ If you're new to the world of PDAs, check them out on AOL at keyword PDA.

➤ Looking for hot PDAs? Check out handspring.com from the creators of the Palm Pilot. Or check out the Palm Pilot itself—see it at palm.com.

➤ Another brand that's received good reviews is the Nino by Phillips. Visit Nino at nino.com.

➤ Check out sites like pdamart.com to see the range of hand-held products.

➤ Prices continue to drop as the technology advances.

Quick Start

Setting up your low-tech calendar

Later in this manual you'll learn to uncover your church's ministry goals and set *your* ministry goals within that context. You'll read about taking a personal retreat where you articulate your vision for your personal life and for your ministry. "In my dreams," you retort. "I'm already four days into this month. Who can think about long-range vision and personal retreats at a time like this?" If you just want to know how to get through these next four weeks, the **Weekly Planning** and **Monthly Planning** forms will put you in action so you'll still have a job after you spend time vision making.

Monthly Planning
page 277

Weekly Planning
page 279

✔ Try using the forms like to-do lists rather than in-depth planning tools. Simply make several photocopies of each form, punch holes, and place the sheets in a thin three-ring binder. At least you'll have a place to capture ideas that come to you while you're waiting for that elusive stretch of time during which you will do serious goal setting and planning.

Priority Scale /
Time Management
page 375

✔ Another way to use the forms is to fill out the **Priority Scale/Time Management** worksheet. Instead of prioritizing one day's tasks, though, order milestone tasks or events facing you in the coming month. Complete the worksheet as explained on page 375. As you total the "votes" for each of the nine items you're ordering, list those prioritized results on the monthly or weekly planning sheet. Finally, fill in the appropriate blocks with calls, notes, or ideas that reflect your progress toward reaching the goals you've listed.

Internet resources

Trek into the PDA world at these sites:

▶ **pdastreet.com** The Internet's largest PDA information center for PDA software, Windows CE Shareware, PDA information, PDA specs, Palmtop, Windows CE Freeware, Palm Pilots, and more.

▶ **avantgo.com** Get today's paper, the weather forecast, directions to where you're headed from Mapquest™. Literally hundreds of sites to connect with and download to your PDA when you "hot-sync."

▶ **pdacentral.com** The "number one" place on the Web to find software for your hand-held PDA.

▶ **ugeek.com** Helpful info on computers, PDAs, and more. Plenty of useful stuff here.

Recommended resources

▶ *First Things First,* Stephen Covey (Simon & Schuster, 1994)

▶ *The On-Purpose Person: Making Your Life Make Sense,* Kevin McCarthy (Piñon Press, 1992)

▶ *The Seven Habits of Highly Effective People,* Stephen Covey (Simon & Schuster, 1989)

Plan it

Be aware of the things that use up your time, seemingly without your permission.

Chapter preview

- Defining a personal vision
- Determining priorities
- Sensitizing yourself to your time use
- Planning primer
- Plans
- Personal retreat
- **Quick Start**: Charting priorities

Defining a personal vision

Find yourself a yellow pad and do a brain dump: write all the words that you hope will describe you in three years and how you will be ministering then. Ask God to help you see these things. You might, for example, describe—

- personal qualities (such as *caring, focused on others, fun, real*)
- types of students you want to draw into your ministry
- how you'll prepare to develop leaders
- how you'll prepare to start new ministries
- your desired spiritual growth
- your relationships with parents of children in your group
- your professional development
- your relationship with people and organizations in your community

The stewardship of planning

You're guaranteed trouble if you come to the office without a plan for the day. Time just slides by. Ministry is not about putting our time in at the office. It's about being men and women who are good stewards of time. Not that you need to plan every moment of every day, which will only lead to frustration, inflexibility, and the end of students dropping by your office. It means being aware of the ways you spend your time—deliberately choosing the things that you will allow to use up your time.

Base this list on your values—the core things you believe and ultimately shape your behavior. Values are measured by our behavior. In other words, a careful examination of your previous week's schedule would reveal your actual values, despite what you say you value. A person can say that working out is a high value, but if he hasn't been to the gym in the past month, it's only a wish, not a value.

After you have written out your dreams, prayerfully consider ways these hopes can become realities. For each idea, list action steps you can take to move yourself toward your vision, sketch a timeline for taking the steps, list barriers you'll likely need to overcome to reach the goal, and identify people to involve in the process. The worksheet **Defining a Personal Vision** can walk you through the process.

Defining a Personal Vision page 372

Determining priorities

Stephen Covey surveyed thousands of people for his book *First Things First* (Simon & Schuster, 1994). He asked, "What is the one activity that you know if you did superbly well and consistently would have significant positive results in your professional life?" He found that a great majority of responses fall under seven key activities:

- Improving communication
- Better preparation
- Better planning and organizing
- Taking better care of self
- Seizing new opportunities
- Personal development
- Empowerment

FasTrack

3 List your personal and ministry dreams; write out action steps that will make them happen.

Look at this list and see which of these activities needs to become a greater priority in your life. If you say all of them (as I did), work on prioritizing change into your life from this list, one area at a time.

Planning primer

Once you have your planning system in place, use it! Sorry, but it's not enough to carry around your planner like all the other important people in your town. So here's how to start:

- **Plan your week before it starts.** Commit to spend the last hour on Friday mapping out the next week. Do this by filling in your schedule with standard weekly responsibilities and priorities first: staff meetings, church services, appointments, study time, taking your day off (really!), personal devotional time, Bible studies, calling new students, whatever. Then fill it in with the more flexible stuff: when you'll return e-mails and phone calls, when you'll be on campus, when you'll meet with students, write newsletters, clean up Wednesday night's mess...

➤ **Do long-range planning.** The goal here is to fill in major dates a minimum of six to 12 months out. (Yes, you heard right.) First, however, you must establish your goals. What are they, anyway? Your calendar should reflect your commitment to your goals. Fill in the following (with the help of your boss, spouse, and whoever else is affected by or helps determine your schedule): important family dates (including regular time with your significant other), vacation, long-range planning days, prep time (it's in the section above), retreats, camps and mission trips, staff retreats, youth ministry conventions, personal retreat days for your spiritual renewal, continuing education days. Don't forget to fill in standard monthly responsibilities in advance. (See "Activities calendaring and ministry values," Chapter 10, for a more complete list of things to consider in your annual planning.)

➤ **Take time to design your annual teaching plan.** Lay out your teaching curriculum a year out. Why that far in advance? Because it relieves the weekly "What am I going to teach this week?" pressure. Because it enables you to balance what you teach. Because it allows you to prepare earlier for your talks. A drama team can check your teaching schedule and plan dramas that complement your topic. The leader of your music team can plan special music. Planning way ahead gives you time to schedule guest speakers who could do a great job on a certain subject. And, last but certainly not least, because it makes people think you actually know what you are doing!

Candidates for your regular weekly schedule

➤ new student follow-up
➤ message prep
➤ Web updates
➤ staff communication
➤ newsletter writing
➤ check requests
➤ sharing prayer needs
➤ personal devotion and prayer
➤ exercise
➤ reading
➤ encouragement-note writing
➤ relationship building
➤ pastor's choice
(Ask your pastor what he or she thinks you need to schedule in each week.)

FasTrack

4 Use your last hour each Friday to calendar repeating responsibilities and then your to-do list for the next week.

Sensitizing yourself to your time use

Be aware of the ways you choose to spend your time. Be aware of the things that use up your time, seemingly without your permission. In youth ministry, we can easily fall into responding to all situations as if they're crises—even when they're not. To put it plainly, helping a suicidal student would be a crisis. Making sure you return every e-mail within an hour would not.

To take a look at how you use your time, use the following incredibly helpful tool developed by Stephen Covey to evaluate all the things you do during a week. (Use last week as an example, or use the Time Log to track your time use in the coming week.) Label each thing you do with one of the four quadrants. Be tough on yourself! Is reading through the latest catalog of spam really "Important and Urgent"? Granted, after seasons in youth ministry where everything is "Urgent and Important," camping out in the "Not Urgent and Not Important" square for awhile needs to be your first priority. Just don't settle down there!

Time Log page 377

In reality we spend too little time in the "Not Urgent but Important" square. Yet there's where our creativity is fed, our priorities ordered, and our soul nourished. This quandrant includes spiritual retreats, reading for the fun of it, and dreaming and praying over the future of the ministry (further out than tonight's lock-in). If you want to last in a youth ministry career, spend a greater proportion of your time and energy on tasks in the "Not Urgent but Important" quadrant.

	URGENT	NOT URGENT
IMPORTANT	• Crises • Pressing problems • Deadline-driven projects, meetings, preparations I	• Preparation • Prevention • Values clarification • Planning • Relationship building • True re-creation • Empowerment II
NOT IMPORTANT	• Interruptions, some phone calls • Some mail, some reports • Some meetings • Many proximate, pressing matters • Many popular activities III	• Trivia, busywork • Junk mail • Some phone calls • Time wasters • "Escape" activities IV

	URGENT	NOT URGENT
IMPORTANT	**Quadrant I: Urgent and important.** We experience the activities in Quadrant I as both important and urgent. Our normal day can have its share of unscheduled meetings with parents or students, deadlines for agendas or newsletters, and cries for help from other staff members. This square can get unmanageable, though, if we also fill it with procrastinated tasks that have achieved rush status. Back when we said we'd do these jobs, we had time to do them well and even thought they would be fun to do. But once they make the Quadrant I list, they become unwelcome clutter among the truly important and urgent.	**Quadrant II: Not urgent and important.** Quadrant II represents activities that make for quality ministry long-range planning, developing interns, professional development, and visioning. Pushing off these kinds of tasks until they're urgent means we're no longer leading; rather we're barely ahead of the pack and maybe just as clueless as they are about where we're headed. "Purpose-driven" describes the results of time spent in this quadrant.
NOT IMPORTANT	**Quadrant III: Urgent and not important.** When we catch ourselves doing Quadrant III activities, we can be sure that other people's priorities and expectations are overshadowing our goals. Like airline passengers at 30,000 feet in a plane that has blown its doors, we're sucked out of our purpose into an unchecked plummet.	**Quadrant IV: Not urgent and not important.** The final square—Covey calls it the Quadrant of Waste—feels like gulping in air after holding our breath too long. But its activities, far from helping us survive, merely help us deteriorate further. Better to spend time in true re-creation, a Quadrant II energy recharge.

Quick Start

Charting priorities

On page 375 is the **Priority Scale/Time Management** from *Management: A Biblical Approach* by Myron Rush (Victor Books, 1983). It's a little cumbersome to use at first, but once you have mastered it, it works wonderfully well. This is how you use it:

1. On the list down the left side of the page, write up to nine things you would like to prioritize for a given day, week, or month.

Priority Scale/ Time Management page 375

2. Compare item 1 with item 2 below it. Next, compare 1 with 3; compare 1 with 4, et cetera, all the way through to 9, in the first column of boxed numbers. With each comparison, circle the number of the item that's the highest priority.

3. Then move to column 2 and compare 2 to 3, 2 to 4, 2 to 5, and so on, all the way down the column.

4. After you have gone down each numbered column comparing each item, tally up the times each item number is circled and record the result on the blanks below the number chart.

5. On the lines to the right of the chart, list each item in order of priority. There are your priorities for your day. Now, complete one item at a time. What doesn't get done that day is the first on your list for the next.

Smart Tip

Bulletin Board. Create a visual reminder of scheduled appointments, events, activities by writing the names of projects on index cards and then pinning them on your bulletin board, ordered by project priority.

Recommended resources

▶ *The On-Purpose Person: Making Your Life Make Sense,* Kevin McCarthy (Piñon Press, 1992)

▶ *Management: A Biblical Approach,* Myron Rush (Victor Books, 1983)

▶ *First Things First,* Stephen Covey (Simon & Schuster, 1994)

▶ *The Seven Habits of Highly Effective People,* Stephen Covey (Simon & Schuster, 1989)

Do it

Don't be afraid to close your door, unplug your phone, and seriously focus on a single task.

Chapter preview

- Manage interruptions
- Office arrangement for focus
- Multiply your time with time beaters
- Beware of time eaters
- **Quick Start**: Guard time at the office

Manage interruptions

We all require slots of uninterrupted time to do tasks that require extended focus. So how do you deal with the inevitable interruptions to your plan for the day? Try these ideas:

- If you don't have an office door to close, make a sign: "Revival in progress. Do not disturb."

- Work away from your office—a park, restaurant, library. Leave a note on your desk or door or with a receptionist about your return time.

- If someone interrupts, let her know that you must finish what you're working on and suggest another time to get together.

- Train others to always ask, "Is this a good time for you?" Never assume someone is available just because you are!

Real Life

I was asked not long ago what it was like to do ministry in the "old days"—you know, before voice mail, computers, and e-mail. During the heyday of mimeograph machines and White-Out. When people walked to school barefoot, in the snow, uphill—both ways.

New tools certainly make it easier, faster, and more efficient to communicate with people today, but something tells me it was easier to stay focused then. I'm sure I had more time to think. I could work without hearing "You've got mail" every two minutes.

On the other hand, I can remember frittering away a lot of perfectly good thinking time and visiting around the office, distracting other people. So when we remember the good old days truthfully, we recognize the same saboteurs that derail us in the twenty-first century—the timeless human traits of restlessness, procrastination, and avoidance in the old days were as prevalent as they are today. It's just that the tools were fewer and simpler.

Guarding your time

▶ Part of a youth ministry job description is being available to spontaneously connect with people. Early on in ministry, I got the idea that I needed to be all things to all people at all times. I guess that's still a popular myth—I know of some youth workers who carry both a cell phone and a beeper so that they can be reached anytime, night or day. It's worth stepping back to ask if this is healthy and to explore the potential consequences of this habit. After years of ministry, I've concluded that I waited too long to learn how to guard my time.

Availability and boundaries

ALWAYS AVAILABLE, ALWAYS ON CALL, ALWAYS WILLING TO LISTEN Isn't this the motto of youth workers? Isn't this at least what's expected?

Motto or not, this is unhealthy if not impossible, and leads to broken lives and broken families. If your church expects your unlimited availability, polish up your résumé. Yes, students must sense your accessibility and feel how deeply you care for them. Yes, we must be available in crises. Yet we must also choose to place boundaries around our time when there's no legitimate crisis.

▶ Instead of interrupting another person with "just a quick question," write it down so you don't forget. Then when he takes a break, schedule a 10-minute meeting with him.

▶ Send e-mail instead of phoning or making face-to-face contact. That way people can respond when it's convenient for them.

▶ File questions until you can meet with the person you want to ask. When you question a receipt, a line item on the budget, or fill out a check request, for example, place the document in a file folder labeled "church treasurer." (Caveat: Never leave checks or cash in a mere file folder or in the back of a desk drawer. Make deposits daily, if necessary. Don't keep money in your office!)

FasTrack

5 Schedule regular, interruption-free time for yourself.

▶ Carry a microcassette recorder or a small notebook titled "My Brilliant Thoughts" to capture those big "a-has."

▶ When you're on task, give to that task the same consideration you give to students you counsel. Just as counselees need 100 percent of your attention (they can always tell when your mind wanders), whatever it is you're working on needs 100 percent, too.

▶ Don't read your e-mail while talking to someone on the phone. It's obvious and rude!

▶ Rather than calling or going into someone's office every time you think of something to talk over, make a "People Page" to record thoughts, ideas, conversations, and questions you need to discuss with others. Interrupting is a bad habit. Interrupting can be as obnoxious as nose-picking.

Evaluate
Managing a crisis

✔ What's your ministry's plan in case of a crisis?

✔ Who contacts whom?

✔ Does it start with the senior pastor, a board chairperson, or—

Office arrangement for focus

How you arrange your office can affect and even determine how you deal with interruptions. For instance, if you're frequently bored and feeling clueless as to what to do at work, put your desk where large crowds can gather. This will not only fill your work life with meaning, but it will also pass the time quickly. On the other hand, if you require quiet focus to accomplish tasks, situate your desk in a position where you won't be tempted to look up at everyone who passes by. Your glance invites an interruption from passersby.

Smart Tip

Rotate a pager among key leaders (both lay and paid) who take turns being Crisis Point-Persons.

Beware of time eaters

As a very young child, I was convinced that monsters lived under my bed. Only if my body was between the sheets and all bedding was tucked in tightly around me did I feel safe. If I ever sensed the monsters were about to eat me, I pulled the sheet over my head. No monster ever broke through that protective shield.

Most of us survived childhood monsters, managing to keep them secret from our friends. But as adults we're now terrorized by the monsters of poor time management. Instead of facing them down, many of us pull the sheet over our head when they threaten to eat up our time. You can tell the monsters are on the loose in your office if you're—

FasTrack

6 Use the Touch It Once strategy when a piece of paper first comes across your desk: read it, respond to it, then file it or toss it. If you don't know how to deal with it today, you probably won't tomorrow, either.

➤ distracted by a constant stream of urgent but unimportant e-mail.

➤ browsing junk mail that cries out "open me now."

➤ putting out fires (literally and figuratively).

➤ getting sucked into helping unjam the copy machine…for the third time today…for the children's ministry volunteer.

➤ having multiple unimportant-but-apparently-urgent conversations.

➤ taking phone calls when you should be writing, studying, or praying.

➤ rearranging your CD collection.

➤ wandering around and calling it a prayer walk.

➤ not planning your time and working your plan.

➤ moving piles from your desk to the top of the filing cabinet.

➤ buying your fourth Mountain Dew (before 11a.m.).

Multiply your time with Time Beaters

A Time Beater is the opposite of a speed bump—it gets you moving faster and more efficiently. People don't plan to fail, it has been said—they simply fail to plan. It can be lots of little things that keep us from planning, things that keep us from thinking clearly and purposefully about the important things. Time Beaters increase the amount of work you can complete in a limited amount of time.

Time Beater 1
Limit the amount of time you spend checking e-mail.

Nothing undermines commitment to our priorities more often than receiving a new e-mail joke that we just have to read and forward to 20 friends. Instant messaging should be renamed instant distraction. You're halfway through this week's talk (your self-imposed deadline is one hour away), and you're desperately searching online for the perfect illustration. Accompanied by a custom sound, a messaging window suddenly pops into view. "Hey, it's Julian…wonder how she's doing?" Thirty minutes of reliving college life later… If you're online with a mission, use the invisibility feature of your chat software. Go for finishing your message on time.

Time Beater 2
Schedule a time of day to check and return voice-mail messages.

Although it's okay to ignore the flashing message light on your phone, nothing eats away at your credibility like having a vox that says, "I've just stepped away from my desk, but I'll get right back to you" when the caller knows you're in Mexico building an orphanage or suspects you're still home in bed sleeping. A better message (changed daily when appropriate) lets people know when you'll return phone calls: "I'm off-site today doing some retreat prep. I'll be returning phone calls tomorrow morning between 8 and 10. If you need immediate assistance, press 0." This allows you to just say no. Don't worry—if the message is from a kid in a major crisis, someone will knock on your door.

Smart Tip

Intervene for a staff member who may need some quiet time. For instance, give your senior pastor an interruption-free afternoon by covering phone calls and taking messages.

Time Beater 3
Get out.

Take an occasional day away from the office to plan and reflect. Clear a date with your boss weeks or months in advance. After 20 years of ministry, I have found there is never time to take these types of days, but nothing has been more helpful to me. They are especially important when you're faced with significant ministry decisions (including how to tell the pastor about the bus accident, how to reimburse that family for the hole in their living room wall, how to explain to your board about your summer mission trip to Hawaii). It's amazing what comes to light when you stop to be quiet. Sit down at the beginning of the year with your supervisor and calendar several of these days (or at least half-days). Then no matter what happens when that day arrives—get away. If you take your cell phone, turn it off. Leave the pager in your dresser drawer. Don't call in and check your messages. Be unavailable. Use these days for prayer, journaling, study, reflection, evaluation, planning—and maybe, just maybe—rest. Dare to take a nap. Daydream. Go for a long walk. Who's gonna tell?

Quick Start

Guard time at the office

From cubicles to broom closets, youth workers get the strangest offices. You may be getting by with a cubicle offering limited privacy and no door to close. How can you guard time in that setting? Try this office version of the child-hood game "Red Light, Green Light." Create a cardboard stop-light with light discs attached by Velcro. Or make it out of con-struction paper and have it laminated. (Better yet, buy an old stoplight at an architectural salvage shop.) Place the stoplight outside of your cubicle, and explain to your immediate cowork-ers the meaning of the three colored discs.

✔ Green means "Come on in, and hang out."

✔ Yellow means "I'm in the middle of a project, and I'm trying to stay focused. Unless it's critical you speak with me right now, how about e-mailing me or leaving a note in my box?"

✔ Red means "I'm totally into something with a hard deadline. If you value our relationship and my sanity, don't interrupt me unless the van exploded or the senior pastor just quit."

In time your coworkers will learn to respect your boundaries.

Don't Forget Relationships

Effective time managers value relationships

How is investing in people part of time management? Because the greatest way to multiply your time is by developing leaders among your students and volunteers. While it may be possible within a few years to clone yourself, in the meantime you're charged with the responsibility and privilege of working through others—better known as delegation.

Youth ministry routinely suffers because the youth worker gets caught up in short-term demands and minor duties (Quadrant III activities—see page 26). But it's long-range planning, training volunteer and student leaders, and professional development that produce quality, long-lasting ministry. To create more time for doing what *only you can do,* hand off routine work by delegation, even though—

➤ you know you could do it better (and faster) yourself.

➤ you worry that someone else might do it so well it'll make you look bad.

➤ your controlling nature rebels at the thought.

➤ you're too disorganized to have the time and presence of mind to delegate.

➤ Fill in the blank with your personal angst.

Expand your network of relationships

This will help you to grow. Get to know the principal of the local high school, youth workers from around your city, police (for a real eye-opener, sign up for a ride-along with a cop), a therapist whose specialty is teenagers and parents, sports coaches, and others. Carve out regular time to get to know those who can help you be more effective in your ministry. Some of these people may assist you in a time of need (or you may assist them). Some of these relationships may open up significant doors of ministry in your community. Many of these people will be eager to connect with you—just be sure to give them plenty of lead time when you ask to meet. Most need one to three week's notice to fit you into their schedule.

Good delegation is rooted in the soil of good relationships. Good relationships grow when watered with plenty of frank communication and mutual esteem. Producing frank communication and building mutual esteem takes time—time that you purposefully calendar into your weekly schedule. Your schedule reflects the things you value. (Remember that you show yourself and others that you value working out by actually doing it!)

FasTrack

7 Make relationship building a priority when you schedule your week's activities.

Are you scheduling enough time to effectively delegate significant ministry tasks to paid staff, volunteers, and students? Keep a **Time Log** for one week.

Time Log page 377

Log in at fifteen-minute intervals—minimum. At the end of the week classify how you spent your time, using major categories (such as appointments, staffing, teaching, planning, studying, e-mail, office stuff). To increase time in key areas for the next week, place those items in your schedule in advance. Then delegate those tasks another person could do, with a few pointers—like purchasing a list of supplies you need for an upcoming trip or retreat. Delegation is an absolutely essential life skill. After successfully delegating simple tasks, you'll gradually learn to trust people to achieve more complex results.

Find ways each week to invest in important relationships

As a people developer, ask yourself questions like these every week:

- What have I done to encourage others?
- How am I multiplying my ministry?
- Who are the different people I (and my ministry) need to relate to: new students, long-time church kids, parents, volunteer staff, troubled teens, the pastor's kids, unchurched kids in the community, others?
- Who can help me meet the diverse needs of these groups?
- What have I done this week to work my way out of a job? (As crazy as this sounds, delegating and mentoring build job security. Yes, it takes time—you could probably do a given job quicker and better by yourself. But by taking the time to train and empower others, you slowly expand and multiply your ministry. A greater number of people have ownership and, ultimately, the opportunity to grow.)

FasTrack

8 If your volunteer staffers are convinced you're more concerned about their development than what they can do for you, you'll never have a shortage of team members.

Smart Tip

Want to figure out quickly what you really value? Use the **Time Log** for one week.

Worth the Time

Build chosen relationships by getting to know people and students well

In *Leadership That Works*, Leith Anderson reminds us that everyone needs to be paid—if not with money, then in other ways:

- Build a reminder file to help you keep up with their favorite things—foods, music, books, places, and movies.

- Mail or e-mail them notes of encouragement.

- Remember their birthdays—drop them cards and call them. Most birthdays are remembered only by one's own family. Having non-relatives celebrate birthdays with lunches, calls to wish them a great day, or afternoon snacks help make people feel special. Make a big deal out of that day (unless of course they are trying to forget their age). Business giant Harvey McKay designed his relationship-building strategy around remembering and caring for people on their birthdays.

- Request budgeted money to purchase birthday cards, lunches, and other treats for your staff.

- Share with them a helpful book or resource.

- Send them to a seminar.

- Learn to appreciate them in ways that are meaningful to them.

Is relationship building part of your job description? (and other expectations issues)

Building relationships is a staple in a youth minister's job description. The only problem is that this task is a "soft" one that defies typical quantification. It's a lot easier to report how many seats were filled in Sunday school or how many parent complaints you're getting than to describe the state of the several relationships you're cultivating.

Furthermore, just who is it that you're paid to or compelled to relate to and encourage? Students? Your adult volunteer staff? Families of your students? Fringe kids? Non-Christians? You'll need to sit down and talk with your pastor or a member of the appropriate board. Ask them point blank, "What do you expect my relationship building to look like—a coke with a kid at Burger King, Sunday school teaching, training a small group of adult volunteers to do youth ministry?" Boldly probe your pastor or board about their expectations of you until they are articulated to your satisfaction—and preferably in writing.

While it may feel at times that you have been hired to plan lessons and activities, developing people is as important a role—no matter what your ministry title. Calendaring a good chunk of time each week to invest in people helps you keep relationship-building a priority.

Smart Tip

Role 'em! Is your head spinning with all the roles you must play? No biggie. Write down all your roles. Identify the top six or seven. Number them in order of priority. Use the **Priority Scale/Time Management** on page 375 to help you think through what tasks need to happen each week in each of these areas.

> **Priority Scale/Time Management page 375**

Birthday card tips

▶ Purchase a three- to-six-month supply of cards appropriate for various people: staff, parents, students, others. Or print up your own cards. (Several software packages and many printers come with card-making software and samples.) However you acquire them, have cards on hand.

▶ Find a volunteer to help you organize birthday cards. Find another volunteer to handwrite the addresses on a month's worth of birthday envelopes and then bring them to you to sign and send in the office mail.

▶ In the corner of the envelope where the stamp goes, ask the volunteer to write the number of the birthdate so you know when in the month to mail the cards. *(Worth the Time)*

▶ Make your cards feel more personal by—

- hand-writing the address on the envelope. No mailing labels.

- putting a real stamp on the envelope instead of running it through the postage meter.

- mailing it just a few days before the birthday.

- spelling the name correctly.

▶ Block out a few hours and write a month's worth of cards.

▶ Seal the envelopes and put a Post-It Note on the outside showing when it should be mailed (ideally four days prior to the birthday).

▶ Write the birthday in your calendar.

Communicate it

Many organizational problems can be traced to communication problems.

Chapter preview

- ► Communication: Key to good time management
- ► Exiting the overwhelm vortex
- ► Communicating event information
- ► Organizing all that paper communication
- ► **Quick Start**: How to make each day run a little smoother

► Communication: Key to good time management

Think about how each of the following suggestions could help you be more organized by communicating more effectively.

► **Keep the right people informed.**

The church secretary or receptionist may be the person with the most power to make or break your reputation with others. If you bring her on your team—that is, if you give her reason to trust and support you—she will defend you with any caller. Provide her with your schedule for the whole week, if possible. At least simply stay in close touch each day. That gives her what she needs to do her job.

► **Update your voice mail daily.**

"Sorry, I'm away from my desk" doesn't do much to sooth the anxious dad who needs to talk with you about a big issue. People expect to receive a timely response from you when they call. If you take Fridays off, let people know this when they call—or on Sunday you may face an angry parent who wants to know why you didn't call back. When you are away on a retreat, mission trip, or vacation, state the date on which you will begin returning messages. Also provide the name (and phone number, if appropriate) of someone who can help them while you are away.

FasTrack

9 Effective team members communicate—through voice mail and e-mail, through informing support staff, and in meetings.

Keeping records

Good records assure consistent communication, save money on postage, and help track students who might otherwise slip through the cracks. Lead an interested person, whom you know and trust, through the entire staff application process. Prepare them to maintain accurate records on your students. Among your volunteers you may find someone who knows or can quickly learn your software to do data input.

▶ **Promptly return calls and e-mails.**

Communication etiquette teaches that we should return calls and e-mails within two days. Youth workers, however, are notorious for not returning calls. Is it because so many of our calls are from people who are upset, concerned, or complaining? I have been amazed by how many parents, staff, and students thank me when I return their calls quickly—even if they called about a difficult issue. Confront the issue quickly; you'll be surprised at how positively people respond.

I use my cell phone primarily to take advantage of my 30-minute commute to return all my calls on the same day.

▶ **Give your secretary or coworkers a copy of your weekly schedule.**

When they see that you were out last night until 11:30 p.m. running an event, they'll likely be more supportive of your late arrival at the office the next morning. Don't assume that people understand the complexities and expectations of youth ministry.

▶ **Be on time to meetings and run them well.**

Arriving late to meetings draws negative attention from others in the meeting; you might as well just tell people, "My time is more important than your time." Set the example as the leader of your team by arriving a little early so that you can confirm the room setup, check your meeting supplies, and say hello to people as they arrive.

FasTrack

10 Make it easy for team members to find and use event information—keep relevant documents in an event notebook.

Evaluate

Exiting the overwhelm vortex

Youth workers in forums and in informal conversations have expressed their need for help in managing their time. Men and women alike comment, "I need help keeping my priorities straight...I need help juggling all my responsibilities...I need more time." You're not alone if you feel too busy and in need of help. Using the principles of this section (schedule it, plan it, do it, communicate it), answer these questions:

✔ How can I regain control of my schedule?
✔ How can I regain my ministry focus?
✔ What will it take for me to listen, to pray, and to be still and hear God's voice?
✔ What can I do to make time to plan?

(Suggested answers and solutions in Quick Start, page 27.)

Communication: Event information

Wise use of time depends heavily on wise use of people's abilities—including your abilities. Much of a youth worker's energy goes into planning and doing events. The more accessible the event information is to your staff and volunteers, the fewer interruptions and dropped balls you'll have to endure.

Keep one file (or notebook) for each event. You could code the notebooks similarly to the five-drawer filing system we described earlier and store them in your event drawer when you're not working with that event. Team members will be able to find answers without using you as a go-between.

➤ The annual mission trip to Mexico is coded MS:MEX:01 (MS for missions, MEX for the location, 01 to identify the year).

➤ Your annual lock-in notebook would be labeled LI:99.

➤ Outreach events are coded blue, discipleship events receive a red code, service projects are yellow, et cetera. The value of making and keeping event notebooks is in consulting them when you plan next year's event. Don't let yourself make the same mistake twice. And don't do yourself what you can hand off to another leader.

➤ Keep detailed notes on people, places, and resources relevant to a given event.

➤ This file should contain:

Budget
page 282

Evaluation Worksheet page 286

Planning Worksheet page 303

Single-Event Registration page 395

Sample Schedule page 308

✔ Event **Budget**

✔ Event **Evaluation Worksheet**

✔ Event **Planning Worksheet**

✔ Event **Sample Schedule**

✔ Maps, brochures, or fliers

✔ **Single-Event Registration**

✔ Promotional materials, including an event flier

Event
Sample Schedule

Day of Prayer
Setting: Youth Rooms—darkened, candles

6:45   Preshow—meditative music; quotes on prayer

7:00   Opening Prayer

7:02   Scriptures on the Promises of Prayer

7:04   Song: "Be Still" by Steven Curtis Chapman

7:08   Worship

7:20   Personal Prayer—Confession

Write out confession   Quiet Music—2 min.
Kneel to Confess   Quiet Music—1 min.
7:30   Verses on Thanksgiving

7:32   Large Group Prayer—Thanksgiving
Reading on Thankfulness
Open mike sentence prayers of thanksgiving

7:40   Worship

7:52   Guided Personal Prayer
Major themes

8:00   Small Group Prayer—groups of 6

8:15   Closing Verse

Closing Song—"Open the Eyes of My Heart"

Psalm 34:4-6   Becca and Zach
Jeremiah 33:3
Matthew 7:7-8   Brian
Psalm 62:7-8   Maggie
                     Kristina
                     Heather

                     Worship Team

Luke 18:9-12
Luke 18:13-14   Sheree
I John 1:9   Tyler
"Close the Door"   Michael
                     Barb

Psalm 34:1-3
James 1:17   Chris
Colossians 3:15-17   Kyle
                     Ken

                     Heather

                     Worship team

Ephesians 3:14-19   CT

308

Organizing all that paper communication

In-boxes and out-boxes, a.k.a. "junk stackers." You know how it goes—paperwork comes into your office, overflows the in-basket, and finally guilts you into action. You wade through about the top third, throw some pieces away, deal with a few others, and mourn a missed deadline or lost money-saving opportunity. The rest goes back to the in-basket that, within a few days, is overflowing once again. Just for laughs, see what happens when you apply the following rules:

► Use the boxes as they were intended—short-term parking for items coming in and going out. Never use them as a long-term, virtual filing cabinet.

► Live by the Touch It Once strategy. When a piece of paper comes across your desk, read it, respond to it, then file it or throw it away.

► Add a few other stackers for heavy paper flow, like non-time-sensitive mail to be read.

Your desk files. As we'll discuss in Chapter 5, your desk and office area reflect your personality to those who enter. What do you want to say about yourself? Not only that, ask yourself if you like how you're treating yourself as a worker. It's important to create a work area that's comfortable and provides you with the necessary tools to complete your work easily. So what actually needs to be on your desk?

Worth the Time

Quick Start

How to make each day run a little smoother

1. **How can I regain control of my schedule?**
   ✔ Review your schedule daily, early in the day—before you miss an appointment, come to a meeting unprepared, or miss a deadline.
   ✔ Take a look at your schedule for the next day before you go to bed. That means that you must have already made an effort to...
   ✔ ...Write everything down. Neglecting to develop the habit of writing everything down means that, sooner or later, your brain won't be able to keep track of everything, and you'll spin out of control during heavily scheduled seasons.

2. **How can I regain my ministry focus?**
   ✔ Choose to be involved in activities based on your goals, not merely on whether or not you have open slots on your calendar. Speaking at a friend's camp may be fun for you—maybe even make you feel wanted and important. But if it's in direct conflict with priorities in your own ministry, let it go. This is, of course, another way of saying...
   ✔ ...Learn to say no. When people say, "Can you...?" buy some time to make a good decision by responding, "Let me review my schedule and get back to you."
   ✔ Delegate to volunteers tasks that they can do; do yourself only those tasks that require your unique ability, experience, or availability.

3. **What will it take for me to listen, pray, and be still and hear God's voice?**
   - ✔ Listen as part of a daily ritual, like brushing your teeth or showering. In fact, the shower can be a good place to be still and undistracted.
   - ✔ Pray. Without ceasing. Like breathing in and out. Pray on purpose. Pray when something happens. Pray when you have a quiet moment for reflection.
   - ✔ Be still. You'll probably have the most luck being still if you schedule a time for it the day before. But don't let that deter you from taking advantage of unplanned moments of still-ness. Sometimes wresting a still moment from the middle of bustling activity opens your eyes to insight you wouldn't be prompted to discover in solitude.

4. **What can I do to make time to plan?**

   - ✔ Create extra time by making your scheduled times count. What kinds of activities do you do other than keeping appointments, calendaring new dates, and making the most of meetings? List them and imagine how you could compress your efforts—or delegate routine tasks—and liberate some time.
   - ✔ Confirm your appointment before you leave your office to meet someone.
   - ✔ Bring along professional reading in case your appointment is late.
   - ✔ Calendar deadlines and assignments right at the time you agree to them, or as soon as you finish a meeting or conversation.
   - ✔ Read a meeting agenda in advance—that in itself may trigger planning and communicating with team members.
   - ✔ Write down informed questions before a meeting so you can get answers while the decision-makers are in the room.
   - ✔ Bring with you to meetings any materials, notes, and files you may need.

- Organize your time
- **Organize your office**

Organize your office

*Organization?!
What's up with that?
The very nature of
youth ministry seems
to defeat all attempts
to organize.*

Picture the last time you came into the office early. You are excited to accomplish a bunch of work. Your to-do list includes finishing your next three-month calendar, whipping out a newsletter, lunching at the middle school, and meeting a volunteer for coffee. As you log on to your e-mail, the church administrator calls to remind you that your budget is due tonight. The phone rings again—a parent wants to know how much money his son has yet to pay for next summer's mission trip. The custodian drops by to ask where the keys to the church van are and how much you spent on gas last week.

By this time, your e-mail has finished downloading, and you hear "You have mail." Thirteen new messages? One from the pastor reads,

> I've got to make a presentation to the board tonight, and I need some information from you on the last six months in the youth ministry. You know, attendance, finances, event evaluations, etc…I know it's last minute, but I figured you could reach into the file and grab this information quickly. Oh, and a few pictures, and maybe student comments would be a nice touch. Have a great day.

So much for an early start! Your to-do list is overrun by everyone else's crises—unless you are ready for the onslaught because you organize your space, your information, your resources, your paper, and your tasks for days just like this.

In Organize your office—

5. Organize your space

6. Organize your information

7. Organize your day-to-day functioning

Organize your space

5

Whether it's valid or not, people will make assumptions about who you are based on your office.

Chapter preview

▶ If these walls could speak!

▶ Organizing for peer pressure

▶ Office atmosphere

▶ Protecting confidential material

▶ **Quick Start**: Two tasks of space organizing

If these walls could speak!

Like it or not, the condition of your office communicates a lot about your youth ministry and how it runs. What statement does your office make about you—about your approach to ministry? The way you keep your office may communicate that—

▶ you are warm and welcoming.

▶ you want to get right down to business.

▶ being your friend would be a cozy, comfortable mess.

▶ working with you could be chaotic and life-threatening.

▶ hanging out with you would be hip and cool.

You've seen offices like these (do you recognize yours here?)

▶ **The perfect office** looks like it did on the day you started your job—and the way it will look the day after you leave. Nothing's on the desk or bookshelves—no dust, no mission trip memorabilia, no crushed aluminum soda cans, and an upright, empty trashcan.

▶ **Things could be growing in here** describes the office in which the same pizza box sits on the same crumpled sleeping bag that half covers the same partially emptied bag of potato chips that you cleared out of the rental van from the winter retreat. Is it the mildewed towel that stinks? The inhabitant of this kind of office takes quiet pride in knowing that a resourceful individual could survive for a week in there with no outside contact.

FasTrack

11 Create a work environment where you are effective and people feel comfortable.

Categories for organizing books

QUICK-GRAB SHELF

This shelf is home for books you need within easy reach from where you sit.

- dictionary
- concordance
- Bible
- thesaurus
- other books you use at least weekly, including your professional reading

GENERAL SHELF

- biography
- Bible study
- counseling
- devotional or spiritual formation
- games and resources
- history
- missions
- parenting and family
- pastoral
- programming
- small groups
- speaking resources
- theology
- youth ministry

Real Life

My first church required my desktop to be completely clean at the end of each day. Our office was in a highly trafficked part of the church and used for numerous things after hours. So I kept one desk drawer free that, at the end of the day, I could rake everything off my desk into.

- **"I know it's in here somewhere"** is the desperate assurance of the one who layers unanswered mail with new books and magazines to read. On a double dare, this youth worker could uncover checks from last summer's camp (now invalid), urgent memos from the church administrator looking for those checks, and leftover calendars from 1994.

- The **"Organized Piler"** resents being labeled *disorganized*. Neat stacks throughout the office represent a sophisticated system of organization (modeled from the movie *Tommy Boy*) that, to the uneducated outsider, appears to be merely chaotic piles. This youth worker knows exactly where things are—just give him a half-hour to find it.

Evaluate

What is your office used for?

- ✔ studying
- ✔ meeting students
- ✔ staff meetings
- ✔ Sunday school classes
- ✔ after-hours committee meetings
- ✔ other:

The working desk

This is the U-shaped work area in my office.

FasTrack

12 Organize your office space for protective privacy.

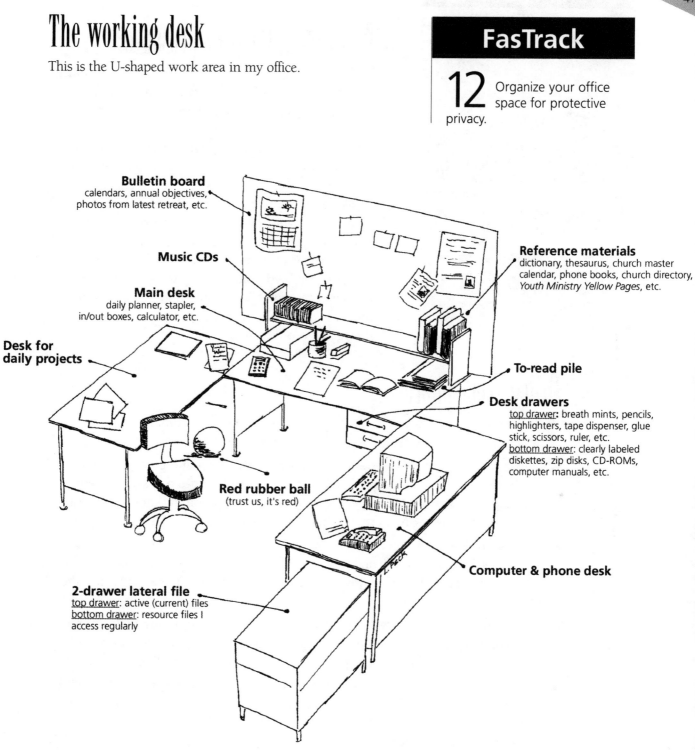

Bulletin board
calendars, annual objectives, photos from latest retreat, etc.

Music CDs

Main desk
daily planner, stapler, in/out boxes, calculator, etc.

Desk for daily projects

Reference materials
dictionary, thesaurus, church master calendar, phone books, church directory, *Youth Ministry Yellow Pages*, etc.

To-read pile

Desk drawers
top drawer: breath mints, pencils, highlighters, tape dispenser, glue stick, scissors, ruler, etc.
bottom drawer: clearly labeled diskettes, zip disks, CD-ROMs, computer manuals, etc.

Red rubber ball
(trust us, it's red)

Computer & phone desk

2-drawer lateral file
top drawer: active (current) files
bottom drawer: resource files I access regularly

Get a door with a window

If you have inherited an office with no windows, ask the facilities board to give you a door with a window in it—or have them sign a statement promising that they will visit you every week in prison. Too much privacy can put us in situations where we are defenseless against accusation. If you meet one-on-one with another person, you need to have a window in your door—for your protection and for theirs. Keep the door open until you get that window.

Organizing for peer pressure

Who else sees or uses your office? If your office gets a lot of church-staff or parent traffic, then you'll probably want to keep it in corporate, neatnik shape. If your office is in the basement or in a far-flung building that gets regular visits by only your students, you can stay with something more like mildly chaotic coziness, if that's your style. Generally speaking, the more exposure and use outside of youth ministry that your office receives, the cleaner and more organized you'd better be. The larger your church or organization, the more corporate (read, neat and organized) you must keep your office. Finally, the smaller your church or organization, the greater the tolerance for quirky, highly personalized, or blatantly disorganized office space.

Office atmosphere

Even limited or nonexistent budgets can support the creation of the right feel, given your personality and your church's expectations.

- Bulletin boards protect the walls from unsightly pin holes and gooey, dust-collecting tape remains, while earning you points with the facilities manager. Bulletin boards are easy ways to post current calendars, photos from recent events, posters for upcoming events, and artwork from your own kids.

- Chairs—dare to deny entrance to church folding chairs. These ergonomic disasters don't exactly exude warmth and welcome, either. Your four walls may never see a leather love seat, but even a lowly beanbag chair says "Come on in!" better than the folding metal chair.

- A dry-erase board encourages spontaneous communication during both planning and counseling. And in between, it invites random artistic endeavors inspired by seasonal themes, Bible verses, upcoming events, or personal feelings and wishes.

- Fun stuff to do judiciously placed around the office guarantees that students and staff members will want to stop in for an informal visit. A funky gumball machine, a dart board, Silly Putty and Sunday comics, fad toys, or even a lava lamp help make your space fun for visitors.

- Displaying items that inspire you lets visitors know something of your priorities and your interests. Paintings, carvings, photographs, hobbies, weird lost-and-found junk—all these can express at a glance what it would take an hour for you to explain (And who would listen anyway?)

- Music as ministry or mood setter—you'll never have a shortage of it given today's obsession with sound and rhythm. Invest in secondhand speakers for your computer, or find a garage-sale boom box with a CD player. Internet sites such as christianlinks.com provide links to Christian music and music video sites.

- Posting photos, of course, tells stories about who you love and what you value. Student pictures (enlarged to poster size if you have room and cash), your spouse, siblings, pets—students and others enjoy viewing these slices of your life when they drop in to see you.

- Books on shelves say a lot about the resident in that office. How many you have, what titles you've selected, the systematic (or unsystematic) way you shelve them or loan them out—all these are clues about you.

Smart Tip

Learn your church's office standards. This is strategic reconnaissance, not brown-nosing: Peek inside your supervisor's or senior pastor's door for a glance at his or her desk, for its unspoken guideline for how much or how little clutter will be tolerated in your own office. You could do this during a meeting—maybe even ask the pastor to show you his filing system. Whatever gets you in.

Protect confidential material

You likely work hard to communicate that your door is always open. When students, staff, or volunteers stop by, though, will their trust in you be undermined because they discover a confidential memo on your chair, an updated résumé on your desktop with an addressed envelope (oops!), or an open e-mail on your screen? How do you guard confidential files like staff applications and counseling forms? A person inclined to entrust you with personal revelations is forming an opinion about your trustworthiness. Ask yourself—

- is my office used by others quite a bit or seldom?

- where can I safely file confidential counseling info? Medical release forms? Staff applications?

- is there a way to lock my files?

- when people open my desk drawer to look for a pen, envelope, or a flier, will they find confidential materials?

Real Life

A youth pastor hung on his office wall a photograph of himself sitting in one of the toilet stalls at the church reading the newspaper. He thought it was hilarious. The parents who commandeered his office for a meeting one night, however, were not amused. He never did quite understand the message he was sending.

Keep or toss?

Two basic questions regarding historical records:

▸ How much should you keep?

▸ How long should you keep it?

Find out your church's policy for retaining records. If no policy exists, you're at the mercy of your personal preference for either storing everything indefinitely or tossing everything immediately. Paper products generally multiply in the cabinet. The only known cure is the garbage can. Bible quiz team records from the late '70s should be given either to your church's museum or the participants themselves. And there's always the rummage remedy—sell old files, photos, and fliers to sentimental church members at the annual rummage sale. Really, check with others (who, unlike you perhaps, have a long history at that church) before loading all the junk into a dumpster. Your junk may be someone else's prized posessions.

Evaluate   Your organization's expectations

Ministry environments have differing expectations, different standards. Some expectations are expressed as written rules and some as unstated, assumed rules.

✔ What level of orderliness does your organization expect?

✔ Can you incur the wrath of some person, institution, or committee for keeping a messy office or using the "pile" system instead of a file system?

✔ What are the cultural expectations for a youth worker's office?

✔ Can you find what you need quickly? Can you lay your hand on the forms to reserve the church van?

✔ Do you know where to find out what information to request from event participants so that your insurance will cover accidents?

✔ Do you even know whether you have a certain piece of information in your file system?

✔ Could someone else figure out how to find it?

✔ If you're not in the office, do other staffers know where to file a brochure about a new camp, how to locate last year's budget figures, where to find student contact information or event details?

✔ Is there a common filing system among the staff so that everyone knows where to look for things? Do you file things the same way?

Quick Start

Two tasks of space organizing

1. Sort the stuff in your office

Sort everything into four boxes—quickly! Don't read beyond the header. Don't take anything to the place where you're going to put it. Don't get comfortable. Think "hot potato"—pick an item up and send it to one of four boxes before it burns your hands:

✔ Label box 1 **Stuff to File**. Fill it with forms, old pictures, archive files, anything paper-ish that you need to keep.

✔ Label box 2 **Stuff to Read**. Fill it with magazines, brochures, fliers, youth ministry mail.

✔ Label box 3 **Stuff to Give Away**. Fill it with ministry T-shirts (keep one for the archives), free books you'll never read, old books you'll never read again, two-thirds of the pens you've accumulated.

✔ Label box 4 **Stuff to Throw Away**. Fill it with anything not covered by boxes 1-3. You think I'm joking! A deciding question to ask yourself when in doubt: Can I find this information somewhere else if I throw it away (for example, on the Internet, in a book)? If the answer is yes, toss it.

2. Go through the boxes

✔ Box 1: Label each item in the box with a Post-It Note giving the name of the folder in which the item belongs. Then invite an assistant or a volunteer to file each one.

✔ Box 2: Use Post-It Notes to identify any article you wish to save. Invite an assistant or volunteer to rip out or photocopy necessary articles, toss the rest of the magazine, and file the articles.

✔ Box 3: Give yourself one week only to find a home for all your "good junk." After that, retire it to box 4.

✔ Box 4: Empty it into the dumpster.

Don't hyperventilate! You'll have the opportunity for more detailed organizing later.

Volunteer

Cleaning your office

From the moment you step into your ministry role, people are lined up to meet with you and already-scheduled events need attention. No wonder office organization is a low (or very low) priority for youth workers. Even so, carving out time to get supplies and clean your office will make your job a lot easier. (Start with at least a half day; those of us with low attention spans can take an hour each day during a week.)

Supplies needed for your first-pass office cleaning

➤ (colored) (hanging) file folders, folder labels

➤ Post-It Notes

➤ 4 cardboard boxes

➤ 2 huge waste cans (for recyclables and unrecyclables)

➤ a paper shredder (for notes from the staff meeting where you proposed firing the church secretary)

Quick Start (above, left) describes the steps to bring order to any level of office chaos you've inherited or descended into.

Organize your information

Taking the time to think through and implement a good system will pay you back many times over.

Chapter preview

6

- ► Filing system basics
- ► Five drawer system
- ► Drawer 1: Events
- ► Drawer 2: People
- ► Drawer 3: Resources and organizations
- ► Drawer 4: Topical teaching resources
- ► Drawer 5: Messages, studies, lessons
- ► **Quick Start**: Contents of staff files

Filing system basics

We've all used filing cabinets to hide things, make messes disappear, store Doritos and Dr. Pepper, or even lose things. A user-friendly filing system, however, is vital to your ministry. Here are a few ideas to help you develop your filing system.

► **Event files**

Keep one file on every event (Fall Retreat 2003, Project Mexico, et cetera). At the conclusion of that event, place all the important event documents in that file—such as **Planning Worksheets**, **Budget** worksheet, fliers, signup lists, schedules, **Evaluation Worksheets** (filled out!), great pictures, important addresses and phone numbers. Staple the event **Notebook Checklist** in front of the file folder.

> **Event Forms**
> **pages 282 to 326**

► **Student files**

Using the **Student Profile** worksheet, start a file on each of your students. Keep anything and everything you come across relating to that student in that file. When they graduate, you'll have some great things to create a memory book for them, as well as to track their spiritual progress.

> **Student Profile**
> **page 396**

What to keep

Keep only those items that will make your job easier next time. Place in a properly labeled folder, for instance, every relevant flier and materials list for the annual "Gut Bomb Strobe Light Pillow Fight." Then ask yourself, "Will what's in this file help me more easily do the event next time and remind me how to avoid this year's mistakes?" If so, file it in the event drawer. If not, empty the contents into the trash can and recycle the folder.

➤ **Archive files more than one year old in a less-convenient location.** In other words, before the file drawer explodes move older files out.

➤ **Keep a tickler file in your desk.** A tickler file consists of 12 folders—one for each month of the year. When a piece of paper crosses your desk that's relevant to July and it's only February, place it in the folder named with the month in which you need to take action on it. The key is to review the contents of the folder at the first of each month. For example, you need to order new basketballs in November. Put a note in the November file to order basketballs. When that month rolls around, you'll be reminded (if you open the file, that is).

Five-drawer system

Here's an example of how to coordinate your files. You create five categories that encompass your ministry in order to more easily find things (should you forget a name of a file). You can move and expand certain sections without moving the whole file. Also, it allows you to lock your confidential files separately from the file contents that other staff may need to access.

Use the following folder-tab guidelines to give your system uniformity that makes it easier to use.

✔ Use one color of plastic tabs per drawer.

✔ Type all labels in a uniform font and size.

✔ Place tabs in a uniform place on the folders (that is, the left side of the folder).

✔ Insert folder tabs for hanging folders in the front of the file.

Drawer one: Events—Red

F ile event folders alphabetically by your ministry's name for that event, an abbreviation for the age group, and the year the event occurs. Here's an example: E/ FALL RETREAT – JH – 2003.

✔ E/ indicates "EVENTS" category

✔ "FALL RETREAT" is the event name

✔ "JH" represents the age group

➤ JH junior high

➤ SH senior high

➤ CO college

✔ "2003" is, of course, the year

Once you've planned your year calendar, ask a volunteer (student or adult) to write out a file label and set up a folder for every event on the calendar.

> ### Smart Tip
>
> As you spend more time online, build an extensive, organized, and helpful bookmark list in your Internet browser for sites related to both drawer-three and drawer-four issues.

Volunteer

Drawer two: People—Green

I f you don't have a locking file for your PEOPLE files, get one today. You can be held liable for invasion of privacy unless you protect these files. This drawer contains confidential information that should not be available to the general public—even to other members of your volunteer team. This information should be available only on a "need to know" basis. Staff applications, references, counseling notes, and student profiles are not public documents. It's your responsibility to protect them.

Create three distinct filing areas in this drawer: event forms, staff information, student information. Event forms include permission and medical forms filed by specific events.

> ### FasTrack
>
> **14** Screening and record keeping on adult volunteers is not an option but a requirement. (See Screening Volunteers on page 175)

These folders are in the back of the file with hanging tabs on the right side of the folder. Next, in the middle of the drawer, are staff folders with the tabs in the center of the folder. Finally, place student files in the front of the drawer, with the tabs on the left side of the folder. This will keep each grouping together, and the distinct tab placement makes it easy to see the three sections in your drawer.

Contents of student files

Keep one file for every student in your ministry. Every student has unique needs and information to track as your ministry expands. Each file on a student in your ministry should contain at least the following:

- Hard copy of database info. (You can print updated reports from The Youth Assistant.)
- Copies of relevant **Incident Report** forms
- **Parent Information**
- Photo
- Photocopy of student **Authorization for Medical Treatment**
- **Student Profile** form

You can file student folders in one large alphabetical file, or group them in the following categories:

- Inactive students
- New students
- Regular students
- Invite a volunteer to label empty folders with a "P/" for "People," followed by each student's last name, first name, and their year of graduation from high school: P/ SANCHEZ, BRANDON, 2008. This enables you to easily find all the student files for a certain grade and label the folders only once—unless a student flunks a grade. And when groups graduate, you can easily locate those files for archiving.

Volunteer

Drawer three: Resources and organizations (catalogs, brochures on organizations)—Blue

I n these files you'll store mailers, brochures, faxes, scraps of paper—anything that identifies vendors or organizations you use in youth ministry.

Drawer four: Topical teaching resources—Yellow

I n these files you'll store illustrations, quotes and funnies, borrowed sermon or lesson outlines, news articles, seminar handouts—anything that you might use in developing talks or curriculum.

Smart Tip

Release forms. Group them together by event identification. Plan to archive about five years of forms in carefully labeled and sealed envelopes. Place the envelopes in a hanging folder marked with the event information:
P/FALL RETREAT FORMS 2004

Drawer five: Messages, studies, and lessons—Orange

This is the place to put those messages you agonize over. You worked hard to prepare these messages. (Okay, you stole from your friend. Whatever.) After you go to all of that trouble, place in the folder your outline, your study notes, the feedback you received, and anything else helpful to developing the message. On the inside of the folder, write the date and location of where you gave the talk. (When you become a famous speaker, you'll need to remember who has already heard it!.)

Real Life

Once while cleaning my files I found clipped to the back of a totally unrelated event file a missing personal gift certificate—just two weeks after it expired.

Guidelines for file management

▶ Keep your system simple. Categories to avoid: THINGS, STUFF, MISCELLANEOUS. The five-drawer system is a basic foundation on which to build your information storehouse. Small, portable files can keep your system flexible.

—Transport files needed for weekly meetings.

—Store attendance information at special events.

—Bring to events necessary staff information, event fliers, and standard forms.

▶ If you hate filing, and could potentially damage or destroy your filing system, enlist a volunteer to come each month to complete your filing.

Volunteer

▶ If you are too lazy or have a hard time with the alphabet, create a TO FILE bin for items to be filed. Ask a volunteer to come in once a week and file the contents.

Volunteer

▶ If your filing cabinet overflows, use those uniform-sized, cardboard boxes with lids to store files. Carefully label multiple sides of the box to identify the contents.

Quick Start

Contents of staff files

Keeping good records on the people on your team is essential. You need to demonstrate that you carefully screen and keep good records on all adults who work with minors. Screening involves an application, interview, references, and a background check.

Include the following information for each paid or volunteer team member:

- ✔ **Staff Orientation Process**

- ✔ **Staff Application** (Keep staff applications for the length of time required by your state—perhaps up to 10 years.)

- ✔ church membership information

- ✔ disciplinary discussions (dated and stating action taken)

- ✔ **Driver Application** (if an approved driver)

- ✔ **Incident Report** forms as needed

- ✔ **Staff Reference Check** and background check

- ✔ signed ministry covenant

- ✔ volunteer staff evaluation

> **Volunteer
> Staff Forms
> page 399 to 420**
>
> **Driver Application
> page 400**
>
> **Incident Report
> page 380**

Volunteer

Invite a volunteer to label empty folders with P/ for people, the name of the staff person (last name first), followed by the age group with which they work, and finally the word STAFF: P/OWENS, MARK - JH STAFF

Eventually, you'll need to divide the contents of the drawer into active and inactive staff as people move on from your ministry. Consult an attorney to learn how long after staffers' departure you need to keep their files intact. (In some states it will be at least five years after they leave staff.)

Organize your day-to-day functioning

Effectively tracking whom you know, where you go, and what vendors you use pays dividends in the currency of time—even cash.

Chapter preview	
►	Organize your contact management system
►	Organize your student database
►	Organize your e-mail
►	Organize your computer and software
►	**Quick Start**: Get started with The Youth Assistant

Organizing your contact management system

So how do you effectively track contacts? In the absence of technology, you can always default to an alphabetical card file. However, a respectable number of commercial contact management software packages can serve the computer-savvy youth worker.

► Many word processing programs come with templates useful for contact tracking.

► Off-the-shelf database software often has templates for contact management: Filemaker Pro, ACT from Symantec, Microsoft Outlook, Microsoft Access.

► Calendar systems like Day-Timers also make programs that integrate your schedule and your contact database. Some will even interact with your personal digital assistant (make sure it does before you buy).

FasTrack

15 Create a 3x5 card file or an electronic file capturing pertinent information for each vendor or organization you use.

Cultivate contacts

▶ Among the forms in the appendix of this book is **Contact Numbers / Worksheet**—where you can list about 30 phone numbers that you'll likely need to be safe and supplied in youth ministry. (In fact, you'll discover even more the longer you minister.) Before you freak out about not having time to look up all the numbers, consider finding a parent in your ministry with the gift of helps. There are people in your church who would consider it genuine ministry to fill out this list for you. Check your parent interest forms for likely candidates. Ask them to take the list home and look up and write out the phone numbers for you.

▶ As you develop relationships with each of these organizations or people, keep notes in the file to remind you of contact persons or things you need to remember about each name or organization. It's helpful to develop a good relationship with the manager or a key staff member of organizations or businesses you frequently use. Ask them to place your tax identification number on file, note their office hours, request them to bill your church if you fill out a credit application (clear this with your church administrator first).

Organizing your student database

Maintaining good records on all students and their families from day one—no matter how large or small your group—saves time, reduces stress, enhances professional credibility, and just makes good sense. The CD-ROM that comes with this book is The Youth Assistant / Special Edition (TYA / SE). Unless you're reading this on your first day in your new position, you probably have at least address-label information for most of your regularly attending students and their families. The Sunday school superintendent may even have student lists with information on parent work phones, cell phones, and emergency contact information. That's enough to quickly create a set of records for those students. If you just can't wait to start building your student database in YTA / SE, turn ahead to the Quick Start for this chapter and go to it!

> **Student Profile page**
> page 396
>
> **Contact Numbers / Worksheet**
> page 264

Organizing your e-mail

Start by recognizing that you have to do something with all that e-mail.

✔ When e-mail arrives, read it and then…

—respond to it and throw away the original e-mail.

—respond to it and file the original e-mail for future reference.

—throw away the e-mail after reading because it requires no action and is worthless.

—file it away for future use.

✔ Establish an e-mail file system similar to the paper-based file system described earlier in Chapter 6 (page 53).

—Event files

—People files: staff, parents, networking, students

—Resource files: camps, speakers, helps

—Teaching files: illustrations, quotes, stories

✔ If you feel swamped or are distracted by incoming e-mail, create two files in which to place any incoming communications.

—response needed (for example, a request from your pastor to explain missing furniture from his office)

—no response needed (for example, weekly update from Youth Specialties)

✔ Keep e-mail in your "response needed" queue until you are ready to reply.

✔ Allocate time in your schedule to handle e-mail. Read your e-mail at a time when you're free to take action: answer, forward, file, or act (write letter, make call, design proposal).

✔ Answer e-mail in one to two days, depending on the source.

✔ Use your auto-reply function (do you even know if you have one?) when you're away from the office for extended periods. People appreciate knowing you're away and not checking e-mail. See the computer expert in your ministry to check this feature out.

✔ Forward e-mail to the appropriate person when necessary. Do not save the original copy. Instead, set your program's preferences to automatically save all your outgoing e-mail. That way you will have a record of all your out-going correspondence.

✔ After reading an e-mail for which no action is required, yet you need to save, file it in the appropriate computer folder. Don't leave it in either of your two incoming folders or your electronic Inbox.

✔ Keep e-mails that need further action in your Inbox until you have time to complete an action. For example, you might have long e-mails requiring additional reading time, you may need to record an event on your calendar, or you may need to compile additional information before you are ready to respond.

✔ Finally, remember this statistic (which may or may not be accurate but is worth thinking about): 80 percent of what you file will never be looked at again.

Software

If you need software for any of the following tasks, here are some winners:

► accounting: Quicken, Excel

► Bible helps: Logos Library System, Navpress Lessonmaker

► contact management: ACT The Youth Assistant

► database: Access, Filemaker

► graphics: QuarkXpress, Pagemaker

► presentation: PowerPoint, Kai Power Tools, MediaShout.

► Web Development: Dreamweaver, FrontPage

► schedule management: Outlook, Day-Timer

► word processing: Microsoft Word, Word Perfect, Appleworks

Made for youth workers

MediaShout, an exciting new presentation software package developed by veteran youth workers, allows you to display text, graphics, Bible text, video clips, and song lyrics. It also plays sound files. MediaShout delivers audio and visual media for worship services, Bible studies, seminars, retreats, and special events, from start to finish—every cue, screen, Bible verse, song, message point. Everything. Check out their cool website at mediashout.com.

Database software

► The Youth Assistant / Special Edition (TYA / SE), you have in the back inside cover of this manual, is a "lite" version of N•Spire, a contact management system for church workers. TYA / SE provides the interface for editing the youth ministry management forms from this book. Visit www.youthassistant.com for more information—or open up your CD and follow the Quick Start directions at the end of this chapter.

► A growing number of database programs specifically target youth ministry. YouthTrack is one such program—check it out at www.youthtrack.com or call 888/476-7325.

► The database software should track not only your students and their families, but also should offer fields for tracking information unique to business contacts. Try a simple download to gain a greater understanding of the software before buying.

Organizing your computer and your software

No matter what system of organization you choose, the most important factor for success is that you use the system. One youth worker organizes his computer files like this:

Top-level folders

► Applications

► Church general files

► General youth ministry folder

► High school

► Internet

► Middle school

► Old youth ministry files from previous churches

► Personal folder

Another idea is to add a folder called "Five Drawer" and follow the same format as your filing cabinet.

Quick Start

Starting out with The Youth Assistant / Special Edition CD-ROM
(TYA / SE is the youth ministry portion of N•Spire, a database written by experienced programmers with the assistance of seasoned ministers.)

Filing in a student database means more than capturing information—it's a tool to enhance relationships between you and your staff and students. The principle function of The Youth Assistant / Special Edition is to organize student and staff data, freeing you to put more energy into relationship building than into administrative tasks. As you build your database you'll easily find information such as phone numbers, addresses, and emergency contacts. You can identify what small groups students attend, what grade they're in, what schools they attend, and what events they've signed up for. In the note field connected to each name in the database, you can comment on their spiritual development, who their mentor is, the name of their best friend, or any information helpful for ministering to individual needs.

✔ **Here's how to install The Youth Assistant / Special Edition—**

1. Insert your TYA / SE software into your CD-ROM drive.

2. In Windows, choose Start | Run.

3. In the dialog box that appears on the screen, type d:setup.exe for the CD installation (where D represents your CD drive).

4. Follow the instructions that appear on screen as The Youth Assistant / Special Edition installs.

5. Continue to follow the prompts on the screen until the software completes installation. *Note: Once the software has been installed, you will not need to insert the disk each time you want to use the program. The installation will put a short cut in your* Start *menu to open TYA.*

Your first view of TYA will be a mostly blank screen with menu bar and five buttons at the top. Clicking on the first button on the left opens up the student database. If you have a question about any button, hover your cursor over the button for a tool tip.

✔ **Before entering your first student record, set up the list of schools your students attend—**

1. In the View Individuals screen, click on the Utilities drop-down list on the menu bar at the top of the screen.

2. Choose Schools.

3. A data screen appears—Setup Schools for Youth Ministry. Click on the image of the blank sheet of paper to insert the name of a local school.

4. A data entry screen opens and asks for the school name and contact information. On the right side you click a checkmark into the box beside each grade represented at that school, then click the green checkmark to save and close that record.

5. You can add any number of schools to this list in the same way.

6. Now click the blue arrow to close the schools list and return to View Individuals.

✔ **Here's how to enter your first student record—**

1. Click on the Insert button—the image of the blank sheet of paper in the left half of the screen.

2. Start inputting Individual Info. *Note: Generation is the cell where you write in Jr. or III for those family names.*

3. As you enter the student's grade level, the school cell will be filled with one of the schools you entered that offers that grade level. If it's the wrong school, click on the arrow beside the cell for a drop-down list from which you can select the correct school name. *Note: If you didn't take the time to fill in your Schools list from the Utilities menu, no school names will be available to choose. To avoid reopening each record later to enter school names, exit the the Individual Info screen and follow the steps described in the first section of this Quick Start.*

4. Change screens to enter Address, Contact information, and Dates (for birthdays) by clicking on one of those tabs. Then double click on the highlighted word or phrase to open up the dialog box where you are prompted to input specific information.

5. Inputting information in the Events and Small Groups tabs calls for a little advance preparation. Use the software documentation on the CD to get all the details.

6. When you've filled in all you know about an individual (except for School, Events, and Small Groups), click the green checkmark to save and close that record.

Click on the name of the student you entered earlier. Then choose the middle image—the blank paper and a pencil.

✓ **Here's how to print reports and mailing labels—**

1. At the View Individuals screen, click on the printer image below your list of names.

2. A report/label wizard opens up and walks you through a report-making process. You can choose which individuals you want included in the report.

3. You can select the Report option and choose from several kinds of reports—Birthday, Contact, Individual Directory. Or you can select the Label option and choose Address Label.

4. From the Address Label report screen, click on the printer image for a list of default labels or to design a custom label with the help of a wizard.

5. Once you select a label style using the green checkmark at the bottom left of the screen, you'll get a preview of what will be printed. To print, click on the printer image in the upper left corner of the window.

6. If you choose the Report option from the Reports screen, and then select Individual Directory, for instance, you'll get to name your directory when you click the printer image. Then click the green checkmark to see a preview of your directory.

Worth the Time

Once you've made the Quick Start, you'll have the basic know-how for using all functions of The Youth Assistant / Special Edition. Treat yourself to some interruption-free time to explore other options the software offers. Administrative tasks have never been so painless.

Tools to help you manage your ministry

PART 2

So you've thumbed through Youth Ministry Management Tools, and you're sufficiently inspired to leap into managing your ministry.

But have you first organized your own time and work space (the subjects of Part 1)? Trying to manage your ministry without first harnessing your own, pell-mell energy to a defined and purposeful mission is like leaping off a bungee tower without a bungee cord—"Real TV" material, for sure. Splats make for great ratings.

Part 1 of Youth Ministry Management Tools introduces you to tools for personal visioning, for balancing your schedule, for purpose-powered planning, and for making a space conducive to working well. Since you guide the rudder of the youth ministry, you need practice in looking ahead, balance, living purposefully, and creating a supportive space. I've been in youth ministry for more than a few years, and I can assure you that it's less embarrassing to practice those skills on yourself before you start writing youth ministry mission statements and engineering an outreach event with a team of volunteers.

If you've browsed Part 1, you may have photocopied or printed a few forms that have helped you define a personal vision, prioritize personal tasks, impose order on your desk and shelves, and set yourself up to accumulate and communicate information.

N*ow you're ready to put some of those skills and forms to work for you—*

- *as you provide leadership for your organization's youth ministry.*

- *as you manage ministry resources (people, time, money, and other stuff).*

- *as you work with a team to plan and carry out activities and events.*

Calendaring

It's that time again. Your next calendar has to be mailed by the end of this week.

- What meetings, activities, events, and programs are you offering?
- When is the best time to offer them?
- What scheduling conflicts might you encounter?
- How many activities a week should you plan?
- How do you balance types of activities with the diverse target student community?

In Calendaring—

Visions and values

"By revealing a purpose statement, you'll take away the mystery of your ministry. A clear purpose statement will help you make sense of your programs, utilize your volunteers more effectively, and provide direction for your students' spiritual maturity." (Doug Fields, *Purpose Driven Youth Ministry*, Youth Sp/Zondervan)

Chapter preview
- ► Harmony of visions
- ► The power of shared vision
- ► Starting the visioning process
- ► **Quick Start**: Visioning for the visual person

Harmony of visions

The answers to these questions unfold as you plan ahead, plan wisely, and know where you're headed. Without a clear direction and purpose, you can become a Christian activity planner for teens—much like what many of our communities already have. In a perfect world, you would come into a ministry where a visionary board spells out for you the church's philosophy and priorities, giving you a clear picture of where the church has been, where the church is, and where the church is going. On this foundation you would develop your philosophy and strategy for working with the youths in the church.

In reality, however, many churches cannot or do not articulate their ministry visions, philosophies, and strategies. Don't let that hold you back, though. You may be able to spur on your church leadership team to put into words a ministry vision and to help plan strategies to bring that vision into reality. The direction of your ministry must be in harmony with the feel of your church. If it isn't, it's only a matter of time before you're at odds with key leaders in your ministry.

Top five leadership lessons

- The mission comes first. For churches, the mission is changing lives.

- The function of management is to make the church more church-like, not more business-like.

- An organization begins to die the day it begins to function for the benefit of the insiders and not for the benefit of the outsiders.

- Know the value of planned abandonment—that is, you must decide what not to do.

- Focus on opportunities, not on problems.

Important Lessons from Peter Drucker, Bob Buford (Net Fax July 7, 1997 Leadership Network)

FasTrack

16 Assign your best resources to your ministry opportunities, not to your problems.

The power of shared vision

Much has been written about purpose, goals, and vision. Bottom line—to be an effective youth leader you must have a good idea of what you believe, where you are headed, and how you will get there. You also need to be able to paint a picture of the future for others to see. A picture that your church—your volunteer leaders, students, and parents—can grasp and share with others. Here are two images that demonstrate the power of shared vision.

- **A map.** On a recent backpacking trip through the Boundary Waters canoe area, a group of friends were delayed a full day from their return home. Both the hikers and those waiting for their return felt anxious. When the travelers showed up the next day, they explained the cause of their delay—the outdated map they had used to navigate their trek led them to a trail that had been recently removed.

  Navigating ministry treks also requires a regularly updated map. A purpose statement—which is simply a clear statement about where you are headed—can be like a map. Periodically, however, you need to test it against the overall direction of your church.

- **A compass.** Stephen Covey began a seminar by asking everyone to respond to a simple instruction after giving it careful consideration. In a room with no windows, he asked the audience to stand and, on the count of three, turn toward the north. As you can imagine, people turned to every direction imaginable. Which directions would members of your staff face if you turned them loose to minister?

  If your staff can't identify true north in your organization, how will the youth ministry ever make headway? A purpose statement, like a compass, helps get everyone headed in the same direction.

Begin each day with a plan

You're almost guaranteed trouble if you come to the office without a plan for the day. It's amazing how time slides by and, to your dismay, you discover you haven't accomplished anything close to six hours' worth of results from your day's activities. Ministry is not about us simply putting our time in at the office. Ministry is about being men and women who use time well. Not that you need to plan every moment of every day. (In fact, that kind of rigidity leads to frustration and the kind of inflexibility that keeps students from dropping by.) Take the following into consideration as you plan:

- How important is a given item in the youth ministry, as well as in the more comprehensive ministry of the whole organization? If you can't answer this question, talk through items one at a time with your supervisor or a mentor.

- How do various activities show up on Covey's time grid (see page 26)? Let the labels guide you in prioritizing activities.

- When does this item really need to be completed? Most of us figure out the deadline, and then we work to complete the item an hour before it's due. But imagine how you would feel if you finished your talk and handouts for an upcoming seminar a week ahead of time!

- Don't assign priorities based primarily on your likes and dislikes. Maybe you love to make calls but hate to write thank-you notes. Guess which activity generally turns out to be a higher priority? If valuing people is important to you, then make writing those notes a priority.

Evaluate
Have you given serious consideration to—

✔ the culture in which you minister?
✔ the culture in which your students live?
✔ the needs of your students?
✔ the basics of adolescent development?

Qualities of a vision

Leaders help develop, clarify, and articulate vision through a process that includes solitude as well as teamwork among trusted people. Bo Boshers writes, "It's difficult to give how-to's in creating a vision statement, because it starts in quietness with you and God" (*Student Ministry for the 21st Century*). He identifies some qualities of vision that can assist you in developing your mission statement:

- Vision must come from God. You can't manufacture a vision; you need to be quiet and listen to God.

- Vision must answer the questions: *Where are you going? Where do you ultimately want to be?*

- Vision can be exclusive; it may not always be shared by everyone.

- Vision inspires.

- Vision attracts leaders and students to a cause.

FasTrack

17 Using time well means choosing to act based on predetermined priorities.

Try this

If you believe everyone agrees on the purpose of your ministry, over the next few days, ask students, your volunteers, parents, board members, and other members of your church's staff to answer the question: "What is the purpose of our church's youth ministry?" Said another way, "Why do we exist?" When you compile the answers, you'll most likely discover such perceived purposes as—

▶ to teach responsibility

▶ to help confirm students' beliefs

▶ to keep kids out of trouble

▶ to reach and disciple young people

▶ to have fun

▶ to get to know God

▶ to keep kids from going to another church in town

▶ to share the Good News

▶ to fight drugs and crime

Starting the visioning process

If your ministry doesn't currently have a purpose statement, carve out a day to spend with your leaders to paint a picture of the future of the youth ministry. Work to establish a purpose statement and a vision. Your overall goal for this workshop is to define why your ministry exists in a short, memorable statement. A book that does an excellent job of walking you through this process is *Masterplanning: A Complete Guide for Building a Strategic Plan for Your Business, Church, or Organization* by Bobb Biehl (Broadman and Holeman, 1997). Be aware that vision is not something you can copy from someone else or from some other organization. Copying means it won't be uniquely yours.

Start the visioning process in solitude by doing a "brain dump" on a yellow pad. Jot down all the words you hope will describe your ministry in three years (five is too long). Ask God to help you see these things.

▶ List qualities that will characterize the youth group (such as caring, others-focused, fun, real, et cetera).

▶ Describe the types of students you hope will attend.

▶ Picture how many leaders you'll need.

▶ Imagine new ministries.

▶ Describe the spiritual growth you anticipate for students.

▶ List types of outreach you hope to perform and the growth that will result.

▶ Name service and missions trips you would like to run with your students.

▶ Describe the kind of relationship you'll have with parents.

▶ Dream about your professional development.

▶ Describe your group's relationship with the community.

After dreaming, list how these wishes can become realities. For each idea, list action steps, a possible timeline, barriers to overcome, people to involve, and a projected budget. Prayerfully consider the right people with whom to share your dreams. Pray. See what God does.

Evaluate

What if...?

"Vision gives hope," writes Leith Anderson. "Vision answers the 'what if' question." (*Leadership That Works*, Bethany House, 1999)

✔ What if your ministry did what you dream about— you know, lived out your vision?

✔ What if your staff were trained?

✔ What if students became fully devoted followers of Christ?

✔ What if the gospel was regularly shared?

✔ What if parents were equipped with parenting skills?

✔ What if students took ownership in the ministry?

✔ What if prayer was really a priority?

✔ What if students cared for the needs of the poor?

Quick Start

Visioning for the visual person

Write down what you will see, hear, taste, touch, and feel in your ministry three years from now.

✔ Describe what your team will do (gathering in groups to pray, eagerly welcoming newcomers, going on campuses, conversing with community leaders).

✔ Describe what you hear when the group is together (students laughing, affirming each other, praying out loud for each other).

✔ Tell what you taste (espressos, lots of Coke and pizza, potluck foods).

✔ Describe what you smell (sawdust from the new youth center being built).

✔ Tell what you feel (the hand of a small child that you've met on a mission trip, the wood of the pulpit for the new church the youth ministry helped build).

Providing supportive leadership

Supportive leadership • Pools skills and resources • Divides the labor • Motivates • Generates ideas • Informs members • Encourages each participant
(Individuals and Groups, A.A. Harrison, 1976)

Chapter preview

► Conducting a successful meeting
► Brainstorming
► Sensitizing yourself to your time use
► Five essentials for leadership meetings
► **Quick Start**: Plan your next meeting

Conducting a successful meeting

I t takes practice, skill, patience, self-confidence, and flexibility. Meetings don't often turn out exactly as you expect. We've all been in meetings (and led some) that never should have been. Unclear roles and undefined outcomes promise nothing but bumpy, frustrating, and unproductive meetings. Even well-planned meetings can take unexpected turns, however, because they're all about people, different personalities, and uniqueness. But those skilled in leading meetings use the inevitable side trails to their advantage.

To lead a well-run meeting—

► **Know your goals and outcomes.** Clearly define goals and expected outcomes prior to the meeting.

► **Send out the agenda in advance.** Provide participants with their agenda several days in advance (especially if you expect them to prepare prior to the meeting). Include the projected goals and outcomes of the meeting where possible.

So what is a meeting, anyway?

► Dictionaries say it's "a coming together…a junction, an encounter…an assembly or gathering." In *Meetings, Meetings*, Winston Fletcher describes a meeting as a gathering of three to 20 people, lasting 15 minutes or more…regular, formalized, structured, usually with a chairman and other functionaries (William Morrow & Company, Inc.,1983).

► For our purposes, a meeting is a gathering of two to 20 people with a specific goal and a common purpose to plan, develop, organize, or strategize.

▶ **Start on time.** Sound like a no-brainer? It's not. If you set a precedent of starting 15 minutes late, committee members will learn to come 20 minutes late. Set the example you want your team to follow. Arrive a little early so that you have time to say hello to people as they arrive. Come to the meeting prepared—make sure the room and any props, handouts, or equipment are ready to go. Start on time, and don't interrupt the meeting to brief latecomers on what they missed. They'll learn to be on time or miss out on important information. All you owe them is a quick "thanks for coming, this is where we are now," 15-second intro—and keep moving.

▶ **Define meeting etiquette or protocol.** Defining protocol by *Robert's Rules of Order* is appropriate for ministries that want to be corporate. Even if you don't follow RRO, you'll still need to define some simple rules prior to leading a meeting, or you may lead the members to come up with a set of rules at the beginning of the meeting. Rules may relate to confidentiality, respecting one another, no negativity or inappropriate sarcasm, et cetera. You know your group. Do what you need to do to keep it on the topic and productive.

▶ **Invite questions.** Dedicate a time for questions and answers in your staff meetings. This avoids interruptions by those who may not be taking notes and assists them in focusing on the business at hand.

▶ **Keep things moving.** Before discussions bog down, call for a time by which you will bring an issue's discussion to an end. Acknowledge that the group might not be able to resolve the issue in that time frame, and place the topic on the agenda for the next meeting. Or if you anticipate that a particular issue could monopolize the meeting, write into the agenda a time limit for discussion of it. Some issues are better resolved after a curing time, anyway.

Sometimes it's a person, not an issue, that bogs down the discussion. Avert that danger by letting the group know at the start of the meeting that there are only 10 minutes (or 30, or 60) for discussion on any given topic. If someone goes on and on, give him a three-minute warning before you request him to stop speaking. If you have to, gently intervene with a request for others to share their opinions. If people regularly disrupt meetings in this way, talk to them afterwards, and individually. Let them know their input is important, but ask that they respect others' needs to offer input as well.

FasTrack

18 Read the agenda *before* a meeting and come prepared with insightful questions and any materials, notes, or files you may need.

Make meetings fun and creative. Even Robert's rules don't require that a meeting be stuffy and boring. People are more likely to pull themselves away from their dinner tables if your meetings are fun and creative. Take the meeting outside on a nice day. Put some little hand toys or art supplies in the middle of the table and encourage team members to use them. Things like Silly Putty®, Play-Doh®, crayons, and colorful magic markers help people to get their brains thinking creatively. Offering food and drink helps members let down barriers among themselves and makes room for them to shift their focus to your meeting. Even background music might have a place for part of the meeting. (Sadly, you probably won't have much luck recommending these kinds of ideas for church board meetings. And you won't get any points for bringing your Game Boy or Walkman to meetings you attend.)

Smart Tip

Lead tangent-free meetings.
Tape a piece of newsprint to the wall. Designate it the "parking lot." Whenever someone (including you) comes up with an idea that takes the group on a tangent, ask the group if they agree that it needs to be discussed right now. If not, put the ideas in the parking lot. At the end of the meeting, revisit the parking lot and answer any questions. You'll be amazed at how many of the tangents have been addressed during the course of the meeting—and you were even able to end early!

Define action points. Throughout the meeting, state the action decided upon and assign individuals to each action point. In other words, keep track of meeting decisions. Transfer deadlines and assignments from your meetings to your calendar, either during the meeting or as soon as it is finished.

Schedule the next meeting. If another meeting is needed, schedule a time for it before you complete the current meeting.

End on time. If you say your meeting will end at 8 p.m., end at 8 p.m. No exceptions. Like a good counselor, keep track of the time so the end of the meeting won't surprise anyone. At 7:55 p.m., for instance, say something like, "It looks like our time is almost over. Let's wrap up with…," or "We can pick up here next time." If you don't end on time, people won't want to come. Let the group know the meeting is officially finished when you reach the predetermined time. Assure them they can stay on and chat or finish off the snacks, but that the meeting is officially ended. People then understand that their obligation is complete, and they won't feel imposed upon.

Provide follow-up notes. After the meeting, print out notes and send or give them to each person. Follow up with attendees who have tasks to complete before the next meeting. Help them be successful committee members.

Brainstorming

The overall goal of meetings is productivity. If your meetings have no goals, no stated purpose, and are not productive, hire a band and call it what it is—a party! Assuming you want the meeting not the party, consider using the discussion technique of brainstorming. In a lively group it can almost feel like a party. Here are few rules for fruitful brainstorming:

- There are no bad ideas. (Ideas are not meant to be evaluated at a brainstorming session.)

- Be kind when someone comes up with a really bad idea. (Assure them you're not laughing at them; you're laughing with them.)

- Keep the brainstorming session long enough to get good ideas, but short enough to maintain energy.

   To kick off a brainstorming session, gather a group of creative, free thinkers around a table for a specified amount of time. They may be a mix of leaders, students, and even some artistic folks who aren't part of your ministry—yet. Before your group arrives, tape plenty of newsprint to the walls and place colorful markers (that won't bleed through to the wall) on the table. Spread across the center of the table small toys like Slinkys, Silly Putty, TinkerToys, and Play-Doh. Giving people something to occupy their hands frees their minds for creative thinking. Offer snacks and drinks if you can.

- **1. Begin by thanking the attendees for coming.** Invite them to play and eat.

- **2. Restate the focus for the meeting.** (Since you've sent the agenda in advance, this will be old news to some—unfortunately, not the majority.)

- **3. Precede the brainstorming session with an activity or question that catches the group off guard**. For instance, if your focus is the theme for a retreat, ask them to draw a picture of what a retreat looks like to them. Laughing at each other's pictures breaks the ice and readies the planners to think outside of traditional lines.

- **4. Shift gears into actual brainstorming by writing on the newsprint some of the crazy ideas that surfaced from the opening activity.** Assure everyone that no idea is too bizarre to be recorded on the newsprint. You never know when a ridiculous idea becomes the gateway to a great idea! Like the time in our ministry when a comment about pirates and Peter Pan led to planning a retreat that was a weekend-long scavenger/adventure hunt for cabin groups. We exchanged the pirate part for more of an Indiana Jones feel. The kids loved getting close with their small groups, felt challenged by thinking through clues, and enjoyed competing. All this from a comment about Peter Pan.

Five essentials for leadership meetings

W hat sets the novice youth worker apart from the veteran? Paying attention to five essential planning ingredients as you put together meetings, and answering the questions or completing the tasks related to each ingredient. Quickly answering the questions listed can put you well on your way to a successful meeting.

Leadership Meetings

Determining goals	
Purposeful planning	• What is the goal of the meeting? • What is the desired outcome? • Who will participate? How many? • How long does it need to last? • Where is the best place to meet? • When is the best time for this meeting (based on above answers)? • What resources will I contribute to the meeting? • Do I need to receive anything from the participants (either before or during the meeting)?
Designing details	
Coordinated details	• How are my goals best accomplished? • When and how do I deliver the meeting agenda to participants? • Will there be any costs? • What do I need to do ahead of time to secure and make the most of the location? • What food shall I offer to attendees? • What materials do I need to prepare ahead to bring?
Getting out the word—inform and energize participants (Tailor promotion to the group size, make up, and the personality of the occasion.)	
Directed promotion	• Use one or all of the regular avenues of communication in your church: phone calls, memos, E-mail or snail-mail invitations, announcements, one-on-one invitations, et cetera
Purpose-driven content	
Focused programming	• Provide the agenda in advance • Start on time • Define meeting etiquette or protocol • Keep things moving • Use creativity to make meetings fun • Define action points • End on time • Provide follow-up notes
Prayer	
Trust in God	• Ask for wisdom, flexibility, and growth

► **Purposeful planning**

Like just about every other aspect of youth ministry, meetings are easy prey to the activity trap. They regularly degenerate into just one more treadmill session.

"To begin with the end in mind," writes Stephen Covey in *The Seven Habits of Highly Effective People*, "means to start with a clear understanding of your destination." Purposeful planning on your part raises a meeting above the level of "mere activity." In fact, the very phrase "conducting a meeting" conjures up the image of a symphony orchestra arrayed on stage, moving from the start to the climactic finish of a complex piece of music—all under the direction of the conductor.

Okay, maybe the orchestral metaphor is stretching it. And maybe you're more likely to have to pay people to come to your meetings. Still, you can communicate to the participants the purpose for meeting and describe the results the group will produce. Set up your meeting room to energize the group toward that purpose. Know the score if you expect to lead them and the ministry to reach full potential.

► **Coordinating details**

There's no shortcut for the planning stage of a successful leadership meeting. Although many youth workers prefer generating ideas to executing those ideas, this pre-work smoothes out your meeting and generates enthusiasm among attendees. After sketching out your meeting, start a to-do list with all the steps that will make the meeting a reality.

► **Directed promotion**

Meeting promotion can generally be handled through phone calls and memos. These are most successful when you allow enough time for people to plan ahead and then follow up with a reminder closer to the meeting date. The most effective method of getting people to meetings, however, is keeping them informed and excited about what's happening in the ministry as a result of previous meetings. Through spoken and written words we try to give as much information as they need to catch the vision.

► **Focused programming**

Programming a meeting means designing each part of the meeting to support your goals for the meeting and describing specific desired outcomes of the meeting. Clearly state your meeting purpose on the agenda you send out. Set up your meeting environment to encourage communication among participants. Choose activities and props that generate creativity and a spirit of fun. Conclude the meeting by reviewing what the group accomplished, listing tasks generated by the meeting, assigning members to tasks, and setting a date for task completion.

► **Trust in God**

Prayer is the power that drives any ministry. From the time you know you'll be leading a meeting, invite God to be an integral part. Pray that God's wisdom will influence your thoughts and ideas, and that you and your team will be open to God's leading and direction.

Quick Start

Be the conductor at your next meeting

Using the questions from the "Five Essentials" table, tune up your next meeting a step or two above the last couple meetings you've led. With each meeting, add extra elements of purpose, design, participation, and prayer. (And have some fun while you're all at it.)

✔ **Determining goals: Purposeful planning**

What is the goal of the meeting?

What is the desired outcome?

Who will participate? How many?

How long does it need to last?

Where is the best place to meet?

When is the best time for this meeting (based on above answers)?

What resources will I contribute to the meeting?

Do I need to receive anything from the participants
(either before or during the meeting)?

✔ **Designing details: Coordinated details**

How are my goals best accomplished?

When and how do I deliver the meeting agenda to participants?

Will there be any costs?

What do I need to do ahead of time to secure and make the most of the location of the meeting?

What food shall I offer to attendees?

What materials do I need to prepare ahead to bring?

✔ **Getting out the word: Inform and energize participants**
(Tailor promotion to the group size and make up and the personality of the occasion.)
Use one or all of the regular avenues of communication in your church: phone calls, memos, E-mail or snail-mail invitations, announcements, one-on-one invitations, et cetera

✔ **Purpose-driven content: Focused programming**

Provide the agenda in advance

Start on time

Define meeting etiquette or protocol

Keep things moving

Use creativity to make meetings fun

Define action points

End on time

Provide follow-up notes

> **Meeting Planning Worksheet page 373**

✔ **Prayer: Trust in God**

Ask for wisdom, flexibility, and growth

Activities calendaring and ministry values

Plan for activities that appeal to many types of students in your ministry as you create your calendar.

10

Chapter preview

- Creating a master calendar
- Annual church/ministry calendar
- Community schedules
- Denominational commitments
- Season schedule
- **Quick Start**: Instant planning for activities

Creating a master calendar

Don't rush the process of designing an appropriate ministry calendar. And don't take a shortcut by developing the calendar on your own. Allow adult leaders, parents, your pastor, and key student leaders to go through this process with you. If you try the shortcuts, you'll likely fill your ministry calendar only with stuff you like to do or that the ministry has always done.

You have many options to guide your master calendar creation:

- Continue doing what the group has always done.
- Repeat activities you did at another church.
- Adapt calendars from other churches and model your ministry on them.
- Ask the kids what they want to do; add to the calendar every single idea they give you.
- Find a calendar. Fill up every day with something. Run like crazy. Quit after nine months.

FasTrack

20 Once you have clearly established the vision and purpose of your youth ministry, transfer your vision to reality by planning your master calendar.

Balance of events

► One challenge of building a ministry calendar is providing diverse opportunities in which a variety of kids—in a variety of spiritual growth stages—all can feel excited about being involved. Youth ministries characterized wholly by intense discipleship and seriousness that minimize play or simply coming together for friendship can leave out a large percentage of students. How can you reach and challenge the wide variety of students who have been entrusted to you?

After selecting one of the previous options, use a process like this:

► Begin with a blank calendar.

► These are out of your control, so place them on the calendar first:

✔ church- or ministry-mandated dates

✔ community or school conflicts to avoid

✔ significant sporting events, locally and nationally

✔ family dates: birthdays, anniversaries, vacations

✔ major holidays

► Examine your purpose, values, and goals as created by your ministry team and approved by the church leadership, senior pastor first.

► Establish the *why* behind all the events you're considering.

► Examine your tentative plan for good balance among the following activities:

✔ outreach and evangelistic events

✔ service projects (including local tasks, missions events, and trips)

✔ opportunities for students to develop relationships and have fun together

✔ opportunities for growth (Bible studies, small groups, teaching)

✔ leadership development opportunities

✔ worship and prayer events

✔ staff meetings and training

✔ parent meetings

Take time to study your community. Meet with a diverse group of representative students. Ask about popular social hangouts, radio stations, musical preferences, how they experience peer relationships—including sexual standards, local rites of passage, perceptions of illegal substances—their views of local churches, work habits, and family relationships. Effective ministry strategy aligns with the needs of your community.

FasTrack

21 To be a good planner, you must first become a good student of your church calendar, your various community calendars, and your students' calendars.

Annual church or ministry calendar

Most ministries establish significant dates 18 to 24 months in advance as they book speakers, plan community programs, and schedule guest missionaries. Fill in your working ministry calendar with your church's established ministry dates first (senior pastor's birthday party cruise, all-church picnic) Ask the pastor to be specific on his or her expectations regarding your or students' participation in:

- Special worship and prayer services

- Choir and musical performances (especially Easter and Christmas)

- Church membership classes

- Church staff retreats

- Holiday services

- Missions conferences

- Vacation Bible school

- All-church picnics

- Denominational events and retreats

Don't discount traditions that your church expects you to be a part of. If you want to change the expectation, first present an alternative (in much the same way that we earn the right to be heard with our students). You won't earn this right by planning a major retreat during the annual church missions conference. But you will earn major respect and trust by sitting down with church leaders to discuss these issues before you start your planning.

Real Life

Learn about the significant events and holidays in your community. Fishing and hunting dates, fairs, rodeos, music festivals, parades, seasonal farming rhythms, performing arts events. Is there an expected role for your church or youth ministry in any of these events? The smaller the church, the more closely tied to the community you likely are. If you are new, sit down with someone from the community who can brief you on the community's traditions and expectations. Subscribe to the local community paper. Contact the mayor's office.

A youth worker in Minnesota recently learned the hard way the lesson of checking the community calendar before planning a major youth ministry event. He planned a significant outreach activity, bringing in a band and speaker on a Wednesday night in early March—the week of the state hockey tournament. Two of his major campuses were involved in a final playoff game that very Wednesday night. Needless to say, he couldn't even pay kids to come to his outreach!

Community schedules

▶ **School.** Unfortunately, complete school-year calendars often aren't released until August. Ask the school to put you on their mailing list or find a parent to be the expert on a certain school. Put the main secretaries from your local schools on your "gotta know" list. Buying a cup of coffee for or sending flowers to the main secretary in the school office may reap rewards for months to come. Often an experienced school secretary can share with you subtle scheduling issues before the school calendar is released. Ask in particular about these important dates:

- ✔ captain's practices
- ✔ homecoming
- ✔ fall break (in some areas)
- ✔ Christmas break
- ✔ Spring break
- ✔ President's Day and Martin Luther King weekend
- ✔ state or city holidays
- ✔ major testing periods
- ✔ school start and end dates
- ✔ sports and band schedules (beginning in the summer)
- ✔ prom
- ✔ major concerts, plays, debates
- ✔ graduations, baccalaureate services
- ✔ SAT, ACT, and PSAT tests

▶ **Events and concerts.** Take advantage of major concerts, Christian music festivals, and citywide Christian events. Bring your staff to the event training offered, encourage your students' parents to come to hear the speakers, and expose your students to strong events that give them a sense of being part of the broader body of Christ. Seek out the "connected" people in your area who seem to always know about upcoming events. Consult the Web.

▶ **Sports.** Are there sporting events that "own" your community? If so, don't plan a retreat on a tournament weekend (unless your team hasn't won a game in the last five years). Check the band and Future Farmers' schedule! Consider both men's and women's and recreational sports schedules. Their importance varies by community: football, basketball, skiing, baseball, volleyball, swimming, hockey, soccer, lacrosse, track, golf, and tennis. Also check major dates for college and professional sports, (Superbowl, World Series, Final Four, World Cup, Stanley Cup, NASCAR Racing, X-Games, and the Olympics).

By the way, many of these sporting events provide natural themes for your programming. So instead of avoiding activities on these dates, you might capitalize on them. Ask questions and determine how sporting events can help or hinder your ministry.

Danger!

▶ Planning by the old adage "Better to ask forgiveness than permission" is fun, can cause a few laughs, and actually often works well. But the lifespan of a leader who lives by this rule varies from place to place. If your ministry has a three-strikes policy (that is, screw up three times and you're out), then don't waste a strike by surprising the senior pastor or other church leaders. Ask their permission while you're in the early planning stages.

Denominational commitments

If your church is part of a denomination, make an appointment for an honest, heart-to-heart talk with your pastor about denominational expectations.

▶ What are the expectations regarding denominational events and camps?

▶ Is there a denominational network monthly or yearly gathering you are expected to attend?

▶ What traditions must be continued and which are up to your discretion? If the choice to attend a denominational event is up to you, ask these questions before making a decision to leave traditions aside:

▶ What was the feedback from the last denominational event of this kind?

▶ What do the old-timers on your youth team think?

▶ Whom would you offend if you pull out of this event?

▶ What do other youth workers you respect say about it?

▶ How could you and your students benefit from attending the event?

Although creating your own events might make you look better in the eyes of your kids, your denominational event may have a lot more going for it than you realize. If you're new to the denomination, participate in a few events with an open mind. Those events that aren't all they could be might benefit from your contribution to event planning. If your church isn't part of a denomination, a number of quality organizations and even some denominations will invite you to participate with them. Ask other youth workers in your area about upcoming events, retreats, and great camps near you.

Seasonal schedule

E vents may need to be planned around weather and culturally supported seasons.

▶ Does the expected weather support your ministry event? It's hard to play broomball when it's 40 degrees outside, and picnics are no fun when it's cold and rainy.

▶ Based on your ministry environment and the culture in which you minister, determine what times of year are best for initiatives in specific areas. September and January, for instance, are months when students in the United States are more open to new things, fresh starts. Some churches use the following timeline:

✔ Summer is for relationship building.

✔ Late summer suits volunteer recruitment.

✔ Fall supports outreach and forming new relationships.

✔ Winter is the season for personal growth, building deeper relationships, and student leadership development.

✔ Spring is a good time for celebration and preparations for summer missions activities.

Get your dates out

O nce your calendar is approved through the necessary channels (student leaders, parent advisors, volunteer staff, and your boss), print it. With as much cultural static as we have today, people have to hear about something from seven to nine times and in different ways before they become aware of—much less interested in—what you're doing in your ministry. Say it often and say it loud. It's the youth worker's job to "wave the flag" of youth ministry in your church. Invite others to wave the flag with you.

▶ Don't assume that people know what's happening in your ministry. Communicate through a published calendar (handed to kids and mailed to all sets of parents).

▶ Place your activity information in the church newsletter.

▶ List your events in a "This Week in Youth Ministry" section of the Sunday bulletin.

▶ Cleverly design and strategically place a youth group bulletin board.

▶ Put a Web page up with the most current ministry information. (There are at least a couple of kids in your group who can do this for you.)

➤ Acquire a dedicated information phone line where people can call for your youth ministry details.

➤ Prepare a weekly, monthly, or daily E-mail with ministry info, spiritual encouragement, et cetera.

➤ Provide youth updates in worship services.

➤ Publish well-written newsletters following major retreats, camps, mission trips, and other significant events.

Smart Tip

Give your calendar to a proofreader who hasn't been a part of developing the calendar. Instruct him to mark information that seems incomplete and to carefully review your calendar for mistakes.

Quick Start

Instant planning for activities

Use a timeline tool to keep deadlines in front of you (see page 134 in the Event Planning chapter for a complete guide). To create a timeline, start with the actual date of a particular event and work backward, tracking and dating the steps you need to take in order to bring off the activity. A timeline uncovers often-forgotten issues like the following:

✔ Event clean up. Do you really want to do that job alone one more time?

✔ Staff responsibilities—day of event. Staffers want to feel needed and part of the team. You can make them feel needed by giving them (in advance) a real job, a staff shirt or cool I.D. tag, and a radio communicator.

✔ Transportation. Know how you'll get there—plane, train, bus, van or car; know where you're going—mark an accurate map with an address and directions; know how long it really takes to get there.

✔ Church checks or cash you'll need for an activity. Learn to ask for money from your business office far enough in advance of the event that the office has time to run the check request through their usual channels.

✔ Promotion. To effectively market your activity, you may use any or all of these methods: fliers, Web site, phone calls, E-mail, community announcements, et cetera.

✔ Staff. In advance, contact parents and other adults who may be willing to help. Given plenty of lead time, people often gladly lend a hand.

✔ Supplies you'll need and who can get them. Your goal? Prepare someone else to do the shopping.

✔ Reserving the room or place where you're conducting the activity—'nuff said!

Recommended resources

➤ *Purpose Driven Youth Ministry*, Doug Fields (Zondervan, 1999)

➤ *Student Ministry for the 21st Century*, Bo Boshers (Zondervan, 1997)

➤ *Reaching a Generation for Christ*, Rick Dunn and Mark Sente, eds. (Moody Press, 1997)

➤ *Changing Lives*, Dennis Miller (CD Books, 1988). Out of print, but worth looking for.

➤ *Sonlife Ministries Training. 526 N. Main, Elburn, IL 60119. (630) 365-5855. www.sonlife.com*

Ministry finances

For those of you who live by the motto "Don't sweat the small stuff," managing finances can seem a menial chore.

That kind of youth worker would rather be off with students at a retreat, blissfully ignorant of the fact that the church accountant is home biting her fingernails and awaiting the bad news about the retreat's financial shortfall. If this sounds like you, then we have good news and bad news.

➤ **Good news.** You *can* manage your ministry's financial health successfully. Financial management is largely a matter of training, practice, and systems to get and keep your finances in order.

➤ **Bad news.** It takes time and diligent effort to learn how to establish and maintain healthy financial habits.

In this section we'll look at ministry finance philosophies, creating and managing general and special event budgets, managing cash flow, soliciting donations, and looking at sure-fire fundraisers.

So—sit yourself down, grab a legal pad, and let's make a plan to keep your ministry afloat financially.

In Ministry finances —

11. Basic finances for youth ministry

12. Budgets and why you need them

13. Donations and income

Basic finances for youth ministry

Successful ministry starts with keeping a close eye on ministry resources and learning to utilize the resources without expending them.

Chapter preview

- ► Resource management
- ► Foundations for financial health
- ► Personal finances
- ► Avoiding temptation and suspicion
- ► Case studies in finance
- ► **Quick Start**: Basic finance startup tasks

Resource management

Y ou have a lot of resources at your fingertips and perhaps don't even know it. Resources come in two major categories: relational and physical. You know the old saying: "Love people, use things." That's also the case with resource management: people are meant to be loved, things are meant to be used.

► **Relational resources**

Much of what I know about managing relational resources I learned from Jolene. Even before we met, her son told me that she was a "relational animal"—and he was right. Every year our student ministry organized a huge fundraiser, and fortunately for me, Jolene was on our team. She was amazing at finding the right people for the right tasks and helping them to feel great about serving. She also openly showed genuine gratitude to those who helped. I believe that's why she was so successful. A lot of people and ministries ask for help, but how many take the time to meaning-fully thank the volunteers after the job is completed? Jolene did, and it kept people coming back again and again.

Relational resource management also includes providing administrative support for your ministry team. You support the quality of their assistance by being pur-poseful about where and when they volunteer. For instance, assigning an accountant to make posters wouldn't make the best use of your resources, unless that is the most pressing need of the hour. Jolene taught me to plug in volunteers in ways that honor and energize them. Then balance your use of volunteers, avoiding both overusing and under-using them. Place them where they're needed and where they thrive.

FasTrack

22 Financial management is all about knowledge, creativity, imagination, and persistence.

Physical resources

Funds, equipment, space (buildings, rooms, et cetera)—the goal of managing these "things" is to use them to help create a more efficient and effective ministry. If using a thing takes a lot of time and produces few results, eliminate it (or at least quit using it).

For example, take using a computer for word processing or desktop publishing. Computers and software products are meant to make humans more productive. For those who are not already computer literate, the huge learning curve might scare you away from tackling a level of proficiency. But when you consider how your productivity will skyrocket once you learn basic skills, you may decide it's worth the effort.

On the other hand, if you consistently waste valuable time fixing a physical resource over and over again, you may decide to get rid of it and do your work another way. Or you may push for the purchase of a new piece of equipment. When your photocopy repairman suggests you buy stock in his company, perhaps it's time to use the machine for your youth group's "Smash It" fundraiser. By charging a buck a swing, students could raise a fair amount of cash before the old photocopier is rubble.

The point is, analyze each physical resource to see if it still does its job, and if so, how efficient it is. Keep each physical resource in the best shape possible. Consistent maintenance increases the lifespan of the equipment and stretches your youth ministry budget. A car is an example of the value of regular maintenance, as well as of the wisdom of getting rid of things that you're investing too much time and money in.

Share resources with other ministries—either in your own church or with other churches in the area. One youth worker said, "Often I purchase a youth ministry need, only to find out later that the music or education ministry already has those supplies. With other youth workers in your area, list resources you could share. The list can include everything from the best bus company to use to a French chef caterer for the senior banquet.

Smart Tip

If you master these financial skills for your ministry, they'll serve you in your home or in other small businesses.

Foundations for financial health

T hree principles make a solid foundation on which your ministry can stand:

► **Control your finances or they will control you.** Financial management is one area where not making a decision is making a decision. The longer you wait to get a handle on ministry finances, the harder it will be to recover damage done from neglect.

Finances need to be a high priority or you will stifle the growth and development of your ministry. Here's the rub: most of us youth workers want to be making an impact on kids' lives, not sitting in a stuffy office poring over boring numbers that sometimes don't make sense. Or you can look at it this way—understanding those numbers means that you recognize a retreat is too costly (and will exclude some of your kids) in time to change the location to an affordable site.

Do you need to beef up your financial skills?

A healthy and thriving ministry that's going to last for the long haul must demonstrate successful money management. By diligently managing ministry finances, you set yourself up to affect this generation of students for Christ. Whether you have a large or small budget, careful and consistent money management can make a dramatic difference in your effectiveness.

Evaluate

Take the following quiz to see if you're up for the challenge.

✔ When you come face to face with the church accountant, does she duck into a doorway, snicker as you pass by, or shake her head and mumble, "Too bad, he was such a nice guy"?

✔ When you attend the elder meetings, do they laugh out loud when you request a budget increase?

✔ Did the phrase "laundering money" take on new meaning when you discovered you not only washed your jeans after the last retreat, but you also washed 10 checks?

✔ Are you surprised when you see how much or how little money you have in your youth ministry account at the end of the month?

✔ Have you ever put your personal money and ministry money in the same pocket and then wondered which was which...and never really figured it out?

✔ Have you ever borrowed ministry money to use for personal expenses?

FasTrack

23 Finances are merely one of the most obvious resources that need to be managed.

If you answered yes to any of these questions, you might need some help managing your ministry's finances. Take heart—this section is designed for you. Put its suggestions to work, and your ministry will thank you for it. And even the experienced youth worker will find some tips here for staying healthy and on the right track.

▶ **Bring in (or keep) more money than you spend.** Again, and a little louder: To get ahead, you need to bring in more money than you spend. (If that's the only idea you internalize and live by, the price of this book has been worth it.) The moment you spend more money than you bring in, you begin a slide from which it's enormously hard to recover. Our country's credit-card debt shows that most Americans overspend—we've honed an instant-gratification society in which we're allowed to have it now. Only spend what you have budgeted (and spend less if you can). That new stereo system (on sale!) would be great in the youth room, but it's not in the budget. Where will the purchasing price come from? Downscaling the mission trip? Skipping the traditional gift of new Bibles to the confirmands?

The smallest cost of spending more money than you have is regrets. The greatest cost? We've all had nightmares about that, I'm sure. Ministry finances can slide down that same slope, and churches tire of bailing out an overspending ministry.

FasTrack

24 A youth ministry won't be successful if the leader doesn't understand and take control of her resources.

▶ **Do the work to maintain your financial health.** Careful money management means that you know how much money your organization has budgeted to the youth ministry and that you spend it realistically. Be able to tell the difference between your personal wish list for ministry and actual ministry needs. Focus budgeted monies on what your ministry truly needs to be effective. That means spending money on purchases that best support ministry purposes and goals, rather than purchases that reflect merely your personal preferences. Keep the greater good of the ministry in mind when making all your financial decisions. *What is the focus of your ministry? Where do you touch the lives of students? Are Sunday mornings a big deal for your students?* Put a good share of your resources there. If you're involved in campus ministry and forever transporting groups of students, a larger, more reliable vehicle may be the best use of your ministry money. (If, on the other hand, you're just looking for an excuse to get a four-wheeler, give it up. Get the picture?) Practically speaking, keeping in mind the greater good of the ministry may also mean buying inexpensive office supplies that will do the job, rather than spending ministry funds on cool-looking stuff.

Real Life

I used to dabble in interior design. I learned how to walk into people's homes, discover their stylistic likes and dislikes, and counsel them about enhancing their home. I was stronger with some styles than others. Clients' style preferences occasionally stretched my consulting skill, and I found it difficult to give good advice. I was forever trying to throw in personal favorites, unrelated to their styles, and it never worked. I had to labor at leaving my personal preferences at home so I could listen to and understand my clients' needs and then look for products or ideas that I thought they would like.

Students and finance

Invite selected students to learn about this seldom-seen side of ministry. Use students in a limited way, however, and offer close supervision (for their protection, as well as the ministry's). Students who are good with numbers, for instance, might attend finance committee meetings. These students could express to the committee the views of the youth group, as well as informing the planning done by the youths who provide leadership in your ministry.

▶ **Keep integrity first, last, and always.** Finances are an arena of spiritual warfare. Financial management, although admittedly only one small part of an effective ministry, is among the most critical of ministry tasks. Yet often we let lapse with finances the moral code to which we hold ourselves in other areas of life and ministry. We put the water park money in the same pocket as our own and don't realize it when we come out with an extra ten at the end of the evening. Or we're short twenty dollars for a date that night and figure the ministry can loan us some. (After all, haven't we been working every night for the past week?) We'll pay it back on Monday—or is that "someday"? Satan would like nothing better than to trip us up in the area of finances. But we snatch away his victory when we stay spiritually and financially strong. So roll your sleeves up and get to work.

Real Life

I didn't care at all about numbers until Leslie, a business friend of mine, offered me a more supportive perspective over lunch. I was telling her of my woes in my fledgling ministry—how the financial details were driving me crazy. I was fishing for advice on how I could pass the financial management to someone who could do a better job than me. She said that the foundation of successfully managing a small business (or ministry in my case) is for the CEO to get a good grasp of the finances, then personally and watchfully manage them.

I squirmed. "I'm not good with numbers," I whined, "and besides, I would rather be in real ministry with the students."

"If you're managing your ministry finances well," she replied, "you *are* doing real ministry. Rather than hiding from responsibility, you're taking your rightful role as the ministry leader. God put you in this place at this time, and you need to grow into your leadership role. This doesn't mean that you have to fill out every check requisition or personally keep the books. But it does mean that you need to see, approve, and keep a mental record of every dollar that goes in or out of your ministry. That's the only way you can know that your ministry is on track."

For me, financial leadership means that I double check and pay close attention to the work done by my bookkeeper. Yes, it takes time and effort, but it has been worth the work.

Spending policy

As ministry leader, you are the financial gatekeeper. If you have a hard time saying no, you better start practicing because the gatekeeper's job includes calling for a temporary spending freeze if your finances get out of control.

► The gatekeeper is the one who closes credit-card accounts if they're draining the ministry.

► Personally strong enough to keep the ministry's best interest in mind, gatekeepers don't have the luxury of feeling crushed when someone disagrees with them or decides not to like them.

Especially in ministry, you can't please everyone all the time. Satisfy yourself that you've heeded wise counsel from several sources, made a wise decision to the best of your experience, and acted on your decision consistently and fairly.

On Baths & Bucks

Managing finances is like maintaining the water level in a bathtub. If the drain is open, you can still maintain the water level if you have an equal amount of water flowing in from the faucet. However, if you're losing more water than is coming in, your tub will soon be empty.

Personal finances

How are you doing on your personal finances? It's likely that if you are good with personal finances, you will be good with your ministry finances, too. But the door swings both ways. If you struggle with personal finances, you'll likely have ministry finance troubles, too. Perhaps it's time to put the spotlight on your personal accounts to see what you need to do to get them in order.

Fred E. Waddell addresses some of the psychological issues underlying a person's handling of finances in *Money Mastery in Just Minutes a Day* (Dearborn Financial Publishing, Inc., 1996). Unlike many cerebral financial manuals that present difficult-to-grasp concepts, Waddell helps readers analyze their own financial baggage and offers practical ways to reprogram their thinking where necessary. He suggests six simple steps to take control of your personal finances.

FasTrack

25 Overspending is the cardinal sin; continual disregard for responsible handling of finances won't be tolerated by your organization. *The goal with ministry finances is to balance the inflow and the outflow of money.*

► Track your expenses.

► Have a written spending plan.

► Reduce your dependence on credit cards and other credit.

► Pay off the entire balance of your credit cards each month.

► Save some money each pay period.

► Balance your checkbook.

Learning to manage finances is a lifelong journey. It's well worth the effort to follow this plan.

Avoiding temptation and suspicion

I n a conversation with some veteran youth pastors, one commented that he was more likely to fail because of a financial indiscretion than a moral one. Not surprising, points out veteran youth worker Tiger McLuen (director of Minneapolis-based Youth Leadership). In the first year out of college, more cash will pass through a youth pastor's hands than any other graduate's. Think of collecting money from students paying for retreats, mission trips, camps, and overnighters. And then there are the fundraisers. Handling cash with little accountability can tempt even the most honest. I mean, how wrong can it be to take a short-term loan from the retreat food cash and pay it back next week? Or maybe there's some left-over pizza money, and you've been working a lot of unpaid overtime. How bad can it be to take your family out to lunch? On a grand scale, this is called embezzlement. At the very least, it's sloppy and dangerous financial management practice.

The following simple principles can help you wisely manage your money so you don't end up feeling guilty—or sleeping behind bars.

➤ **Keep yourself accountable.** Make it a priority to inform your church accountant, treasurer, or supervisor about your ministry finances. Youth workers often have little supervisory accountability. Being unsupervised might feel fun for a time, but for those who don't make themselves accountable it can be disastrous. Invite a mentor to train, develop, and challenge you in the area of finances. If you already know you're susceptible to temptation by money, tell someone that you trust and have him or her keep you accountable—if only to let you know that you forgot to deposit the retreat fee.

Before you buy . . .

Let several people know what type of item you are looking for and ask them to pray with you about acquiring the item for your ministry. If they agree the ministry needs the item, then fortify yourself for wisely acquiring it by asking yourself these questions:

➤ Do we really need this item?

➤ Is there any way we could locate someone who will donate this item?

➤ If not, where can we buy it?

➤ How much time is it worth to shop around for the best price?

After investigating, wait 24 hours before making a decision, and ask someone (who knows something about the item) whether you're looking at a good deal.

Smart Tip

Never use a ten-dollar bill as a torch to find nickels in the snow. (*A Goal Is a Dream with a Deadline*, by Leo B. Helzel and Friends, McGraw-Hill, Inc., 1995).

► **Don't mix personal money with ministry money.**
Amazingly enough, this no-brainer is usually learned the hard way. One youth worker put his family in debt because he foolishly used his personal credit card for some large ministry purchases, then lost the receipts. He couldn't request reimbursement from the church, and his wife was furious. Not a satisfying way to make a donation. Keep ministry money totally separate from personal money. Don't borrow from the retreat money to buy lunch for yourself and expect that you'll remember why you're $5.23 short when you turn in the retreat fees. Keep the money in separate, marked envelopes.

FasTrack

26 Three important financial principles: take control of your finances; take in more than you spend; do the work to maintain your financial health.

Real Life

I once entered a ministry that owed a lot of money to vendors. Aside from the financial mess the debts created, owing so much to so many was a terrible testimony. Some bills were more than a year past due. One account hadn't been settled in more than five years.

Settling the five-years' overdue account required more than 40 hours of reconciling statements against receipts, and the final cost to the ministry exceeded $4,500. About 15 hours into the process, I closed the delinquent account. By hour 20, I was mentally phrasing a letter requesting a salary increase. After 38 hours of this tedium, I was ready to kick my dog (but didn't). By hour 40 I got on the phone and closed every open account that the ministry had. We began to operate on a strictly cash basis and offer reimbursements only for preauthorized expenses. I was not popular with the staff during that time, but by the end of the season (and in spite of the year's early financial blunders), we came out ahead. (And yes, my popularity ratings soared.)

► **Switch to a checks-only policy.** Stay away from cash as much as possible. Cash is not only easily mixed up wit-personal money, but it's difficult to track. Over the course of several events, we received registration forms but could find no associated money. The students claimed they had left cash with the form. We never did figure out where the cash was going, but someone's wallet got well padded. When we went to the no-cash policy, the stealing stopped; but we had already lost several hundred dollars. State on all brochures and fliers your policy of requiring that all event payments or T-shirt purchases, for instance, be made by check (or credit card if your church has that capability). The only time you should see cash is for small events costing less than five dollars per person.

Word of experience: Just make sure you take the checks out of your pocket before you do your wash. Unlike cash, the ink on checks disappears in the rinse cycle.

► **Establish checks and balances.** Evaluate how the money flows in your ministry and create checks and balances to keep others honest. For example, it's not a good idea to have only one person count the offering. By having two people who are not related to one another sign off on counting and depositing the money, you've instituted a safety precaution. Checks make it harder for a person to be dishonest, but use two people anyway—a counter to fill out a slip recording income received and a depositor to verify and sign it.

➤ **Don't be personally in charge of the petty cash.** Select a detail-oriented administrative assistant or volunteer to take charge of the petty cash. Keep a set amount of cash on hand—$100 to $200, depending on the size and scope of your ministry. When someone takes cash out for an expense, replace it with a marker that tells who has how much. They need to return receipts and or cash equaling the amount of money that was taken. When the cash gets low, have your assistant or volunteer write all the transactions on one piece of paper and attach all the receipts to it. Turn it in to the accounting department and request that amount in cash to refill the petty cash fund.

➤ **Dedicate a credit card for ministry use.** If you don't have a ministry credit card, you may want to get a personal credit card that you use only for ministry expenses, and pay it off every month. Use it when you need to make large purchases and don't want to carry cash or bother with preauthorizing a check. When the bill comes, attach all receipts and a completed reimbursement form to a copy of your statement. Turn them in to the bookkeeper and ask him to pay your credit-card company directly. Submit all the information to the accountant as soon as you receive the statement, and follow up with a phone call to make sure that payment is sent within a week. After all, it's your credit on the line if the payment is late! You may need to get this approved by your church administrator if your church's policy is to have purchases over a certain amount approved by a supervisor.

Remember where the money comes from. Money in ministry is peculiar—the source of the vast majority of it are people who have given up a better car, a nicer family vacation, or dining out for a ministry they believe in. You're spending money that was contributed as a sacrifice to God. Don't forget that!

FasTrack

27 Avoid temptation and suspicion by: a) keeping yourself accountable to your ministry's financial officer, b) keeping ministry money separate from personal money, c) maintaining a checks-only policy, d) establishing checks and balances to keep others honest, e) putting someone else in charge of petty cash, and f) putting ministry expenses on a credit card dedicated to ministry use only.

What's the difference between a physical and fiscal year?

► The physical year, often called calendar year, runs from January 1 through December 31.

► The fiscal year varies depending on the decision of the corporation. In many ministries, it parallels a school year, running from August 1 of one year to July 31 of the next year. Check with your church to see how it defines its fiscal year.

► Although you will provide reports to the board based on the church's fiscal year, you may choose to track your income and expenses according to when you mark the beginning of your ministry year.

Test your financial skills

1. It's your first year at a new church. You need to manage a budget for a retreat that has been done each year for the last five years. What do you do?

   ❑ Use the same numbers that show up on last year's retreat budget.

   ❑ Study budgets from the past five years, and base your event budget on the average expenses in similar categories.

   ❑ Because you are pressed for time, simply pick a number that sounds good for each category.

   ❑ Look at the last two years of retreat budgets. If the event finished in the black, use those numbers for your base budget. Then call the retreat facility, the transportation provider, and other expensive vendors to get current prices. Adjust your budget.

2. You sponsor a concert on campus. Because of high attendance, you finish with a $500 surplus in the event account. What do you do with it?

   ❑ Put it into the ministry's general expense account.

   ❑ Put it into a savings account for future use.

   ❑ Refund the money to your students.

   ❑ Purchase a new computer the ministry has wanted.

   ❑ Take the staff on a weekend retreat.

   ❑ Any of the above.

3. After a mission trip, you learn that you're $4,500 in the red. Your ministry budget is in its last month, and you have a deficit of $1,500—so there's no reserve to draw on. You are a total of $6,000 behind for the whole year. What do you do?

   ❑ Pack your bags and get out of town.

   ❑ Put it on your personal credit card and repay it from next year's budget.

   ❑ Write a letter to all your students parents saying that you were financially short from the mission trip and they need to pay $200 more.

   ❑ Make an appointment with your church treasurer to bring him up to speed, beg forgiveness, and get suggestions on what you need to do now.

4. Each time you collect money from your students for an event or outing, you come up shorter than your estimations. What should you do?

   ❑ Take a close look at your collection team to see if anyone is wearing a new leather jacket.

   ❑ Double-check your estimations to see if you are estimating correctly.

   ❑ Require students to pay with a check instead of cash so you can track the money.

   ❑ All of the above.

Creating a paper trail

Picture 10 crisp, new, $100 bills. (What? You've never seen one? You must be a youth worker.) Anyway, let's say you're managing your ministry on a strictly cash basis, and $1,000 is your budget for the year. You keep those $100 bills in one big envelope in your office safe. (Because you wouldn't leave it in your top, right-hand drawer, would you?)

When you need to purchase something, you grab your big envelope in the safe and place one of the bills in a letter-sized envelope marked "Youth Ministry Cash." After you purchase the item, you replace the cash spent with a store receipt and put the change back into the little envelope. Anyone who wants to find out the financial status of the youth ministry could take out the contents of the envelope, add up the cash and the receipt totals and get a total of exactly $1,000. Your cash and receipts should always total the amount you start with. That is a paper trail.

Paper trails get complicated when there's too much money to keep in an envelope, so you open a checking account (more paper) or a savings account (still more paper) and pay with checks or a credit card, generating even more paper. But this is good (except for the poor trees, of course) because regardless of how complicated the system, your paper trail always shows where the money comes from and where it goes.

Quick Start

Basic finance startup tasks

✔ Make and use a tax I.D. card.

Not-for-profit, 501(c)(3) organizations are exempt from sales tax on purchases in line with their primary purpose. Tax-exempt purchases can include office supplies, furniture, building materials, automobiles, some restaurants (generally not fast foods).Your organization should have a tax I.D. letter, like the one on the left, stating its nonprofit status.

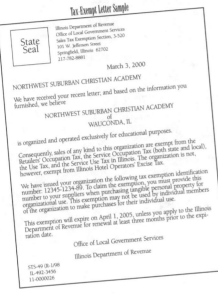
Tax-Exempt Letter Sample

This exemption is given to individuals purchasing supplies only if they show a copy of the tax-exempt letter to the vendor. To be sure you always have the letter with you, photocopy and shrink the letter to 4" high by 3" wide. Type or write the tax number in bigger print wherever there's white space so that it is easy to read. Fold the paper in half from top to bottom so the card is 2" high by 3" wide—part of the letter shows on the front and part on the back. After it's folded, laminate it, carry it in your wallet, and use it.

Give each of your staff members this card, and mention that your church won't reimburse for tax. One ministry set this policy. If a staff person chooses not to use the card, the ministry reimburses authorized expenses and thanks them for paying the tax. It was only one or two times before everyone got the hang of using the card. Over the next year, the church saved several thousand dollars. It was exciting to see how one little card could make such a difference. A little bit goes a long way.

✔ Store all your receipts in a labeled clasp envelope.

It's illegal for your church to reimburse you for expenses without a receipt. Asking your church to make an exception for you puts it in a precarious position: if the church is audited, they could receive penalties.

The simplest way to track receipts and petty cash is to have one envelope that contains your cash, your church's tax I.D. card, and your receipts. When you purchase something, write on the receipt the name of the activity for which you purchased the item—fall retreat, mission trip, whatever. Then each week fill out and turn in a reimbursement form attached to your receipts. Use the Reimbursement form if your church doesn't have one. Some church policies state that if a receipt isn't submitted within a month, they won't reimburse you. Check with your church administrator. It's simple if you keep up with it; it's a nightmare if you don't. Bottom line: Keep good records in an organized and logical order. If you insist on using a shoebox, make sure it's for a big pair of shoes!

✔ Set up a simple reporting system.

At least monthly you'll need to report your income and expenses to your financial officer. To get yourself started, choose one or two reports from among these—**Monthly Expense Report**, **Summary Balance Sheet**, **Budget & Monthly Report**, **Profit & Loss Statement**—whichever one captures the information you need right away.

Monthly Expense Report
page 338

Summary Balance Sheet
page 344

Budget & Monthly Report
page 333

Profit & Loss Statement
page 341

Reimbursement
page 342

✔ **Plan out your financial calendar.**

The simplest way to make sure you don't come up short at the end of the year is to take your total yearly budget and divide it by 12—for each month of the year. This will give you guidelines for where your regular spending needs to stay.

Recommended resources

▶ *Money Mastery in Just Minutes a Day,* Fred E. Waddell (Dearborn Financial Publishing, Inc.1996)

▶ *Church Administration Handbook,* Bruce P. Powers (Broadman & Holman,1997)

▶ *Organizing for Accountability,* Robert R. Thompson & Gerald R. Thompson (Shaw, 1991)

▶ *Management: A Biblical Approach,* Myron Rush (Victor, 1983)

▶ *Business Management in the Local Church,* David R. Pollock (Moody Press, 1984, 1991, 1995)

Budgets and why you need them 12

A ministry budget is as important as an overall vision for the ministry. The finances are the part of the equation that help the vision become a reality.

Chapter preview

- Creating a budget
- Asking the right questions
- Viewing a sample budget
- Managing a budget
- Keeping your financial paperwork in order
- **Quick Start**: Determining per-person cost for an event

Creating a budget

A budget is a financial plan. Just as a builder works from a plan to avoid construction chaos, you need to work from a budget to analyze ministry needs, prioritize finances, and manage money. That is the way of financial health for your ministry. One easy way to start creating a budget is to find out what has worked in the past. Get copies of what the financial committee has approved in the past. It will give you an idea how open it is to new ideas and programs

Starting a budget from scratch isn't that difficult, as long as you don't leave out significant expenditures. You'll need to monitor fixed, variable, and one-time expenses.

> ## FasTrack
>
> ## 28 Plan your work, work your plan. Manage, manage, manage.

- **Fixed costs are like a mortgage.** You pay about the same amount every month, at the same time, month after month. Other fixed costs include electric, utilities, Internet services, et cetera. These costs are generally fairly easy to predict and plan for.

- **Variable costs might include things like educational materials, which may vary from year to year by type and quantity**. Gasoline is another variable cost, depending on oil prices and your amount of business-related travel. Estimate variable costs to the best of your ability—it's often no more than a guessing game. The way to play is to always estimate on the high side. If you spend less, you're a hero. If you low-ball your estimate, you may wind up short at year's end.

The short story on budgets

▶ Hire or recruit a competent bookkeeper, or take an accounting course.

▶ Evaluate the ministry's financial history.

▶ Assess the ministry values.

▶ Project large expenses for the next year.

▶ Assess the ministry calendar to project financial needs.

▶ Form ministry activities into broad categories—for instance, operations, staff development, curriculum, miscellaneous expenses.

▶ Add specific items to each category.

▶ Assign a projected dollar amount needed for each category.

▶ Total the numbers and see if the budget is realistic. Add or subtract to make the budget add up.

▶ Assign management numbers to each category, if needed.

▶ Develop simple monthly financial reports.

▶ **One-time costs generally cover big-ticket items—** like a piece of equipment, a computer, or a copier— that you pay out only once in a great while.

Asking the right questions

When you join a new ministry, you'll operate under its current budget system and funding. Briefing yourself on the church's and the youth ministry's budget history lets you know how things worked in the past. By the time the next fiscal year rolls around, however, you'll have the chance to reevaluate the current budget and make some changes. To do that you need to be aware of the philosophy of financial management for both the youth ministry and the larger organization. The budget should reflect the philosophies, not drive them. Allocation of ministry money is directly linked to your values and goals. If you're handed a budget for which the majority of the money goes toward laser lights and smoke machines, but you value relationships built through small groups over big events, then you'll allocate the money differently than the other youth pastor did.

When you develop the budget, you and your team determine where to allocate money by answering questions like the following:

What does the church value?

▶ Where does the church invest its resources? (Find out by browsing the last few annual reports.)

▶ What is the church's spending philosophy? Does it buy the best of a particular item, knowing that it will last a long time, or does it get the cheapest possible item that will do the job because it doesn't have a lot of cash on hand? Is youth ministry spending in line with the philosophy of the larger organization?

▶ Is youth ministry a critical part of the church or is it a small part? (Find out by examining the percentage of the total budget dedicated to youth ministry. If it's less than the sandbox allotment for the preschool, you're likely in for a struggle if you want to increase your budget.)

Potential expense categories

➤ Salaries, travel, vehicles, gas, maintenance, rental equipment, continuing education, staff development, seminars, conventions, educational materials, supplies, phone, research, administration, promotion, printing, advertisement, brochures, mailings (including stamps and shipping), liability insurance, vehicle insurance, events, food or hospitality, repairs, purchased equipment, music, musical equipment, and miscellaneous for those unexpected expenses.

➤ What has the financial committee approved in the past for youth ministry programs and equipment? You'll get an idea of how flexible it is—how open to ideas new to the church.

What does the youth ministry value?

➤ Of all the good things on which we can spend ministry money, which things, programs, and people do we value most? How will our spending reflect those values?

➤ How important is environment to your ministry? Do you need to appropriate funds to make your ministry area more student-friendly?

➤ How important is staff and staff development?

➤ Do you have experienced staffers, or do they need a lot of training and development?

➤ Do your staff members need a lot of encouragement? A lot of resources?

What is the financial history of the youth ministry?

➤ What was the annual budget?

➤ Where does that money come from?

➤ Where has the majority of money gone (outreach events, small group materials, van rentals)?

➤ What brought in the most money (fundraisers, mission trips, service or work projects)?

➤ Have you inherited any debt? What debt can be carried over and what debt must you immediately clear up?

➤ What needs to be carried on and what can be disposed of?

➤ Are there any annual events you need to finance—denominational gatherings, the annual junior high or senior citizen putt-putt golf tournament?

What are the mechanics of the financial process?

➤ Does your church tell you to get what you need when you need it, or does it require you to work the purchase into next year's budget and to make do with what you have for this year?

➤ Does your church have predetermined vendors for curriculum, sound equipment, retreat sites? Or do you determine from whom to purchase?

Do you get parental financial support, or are you solely

FasTrack

29 Finances need daily attention or they become problems to your ministry.

The bottom line on budgets

▶ The goal of a budget is to keep the ministry financially healthy. Developing an accurate budget, managing it well, and maintaining tight controls on spending will help you and your ministry to finish the year strong—maybe even with money left over. If you can pull that off, congratulations—you've finished in the black. (Old adding machines and typewriters had either black or red inked ribbons. Black was used for positive numbers, red for negative numbers. If your ministry overspends—oops! You're in the red.)

▶ If at the end of the year your ministry is in the black, you'll need to do something with the remaining money. Some churches and ministries have strict policies about that. Check with your Chief Financial Officer or treasurer. You may be asked to give back any surplus to the governing body for redistribution. It's hard to give up what you count as your share, though. After being thrifty all year, it's tempting to spend the leftovers during the last two weeks of the fiscal year just because you don't want to give any back. Some ministries let departments carry their surplus over to the next year as an addition to their next year's requested budget. Another likely scenario is working within a budget where your expenses must match your income.

▶ dependent on money allocated from the church general budget? What role do your ministry fundraisers play?

▶ When do you need to turn in your budget proposal to the administration?

▶ When is the budget decided, and are midyear changes allowed? If so, what's the procedure?

▶ Can you raise additional funds if needed? Do you need approval for that?

What financial standards are in harmony with your community?

▶ In what socioeconomic area is the church located and in what way is that population reflected in your group? (If your church is primarily populated by upper-middle-class members, you can probably request a bigger budget. If your congregation is financially tight, you will have fewer available resources and ministry finances. Study how your church's socioeconomic makeup affects your ministry finances.)

▶ Do you have transportation available to you for ministry outings, or do you have to rent vehicles?

▶ What things need upgrading over the next year—for student safety?

▶ What must you purchase to make the ministry more student-friendly?

▶ What items must be purchased in order for you to continue your development ministry? List in order of priority and find out the approximate costs of each item.

▶ After you've answered these questions, you'll be able to develop a budget that reflects your values.

Viewing a sample budget

L et's say, for example, your church allocates a blanket $10,000 to spend on youth ministry needs in any way you choose. What do you do?

- Answer all the above questions.
- Determine your broad income and expense categories.
- Determine what percentage of your money you will allocate to each category.

A list of categories might include staff development, outreach events, Sunday school, small groups, administrative, summer activities, and miscellaneous. Show on a money wheel, like the one below, how much of your $10,000 you set apart for each category. This will let you see how your spending reflects your priorities.

Here's how you do it. List the percentage allocated to a category, then multiply your total budget by that percentage to translate the percentage to a dollar amount.

Staff development	10%	($10,000 x .1 = $1,000)
Outreach events	40%	($10,000 x .4 = $4,000)
Sunday school	20%	($10,000 x .2 = $2,000)
Small groups	5%	($10,000 x .05 = $ 500)
Administrative	10%	($10,000 x .1 = $1,000)
Summer activities	10%	($10,000 x .1 = $1,000)
Miscellaneous	5%	($10,000 x .05 = $ 500)
	100%	$10,000

You can also draw a wheel that shows desired spending compared with actual spending. You'll plainly see where you need to put more dollars and where you're overspending.

Budget Categories

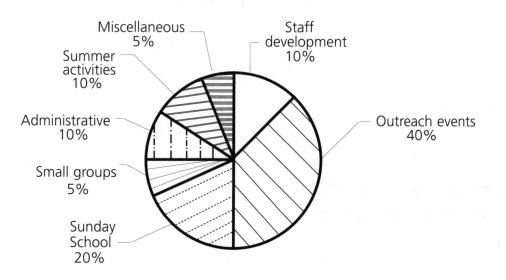

Some ministries, after having their budget approved, receive a lump sum that they use like a savings or checking account. The money isn't designated by line items; rather, spending is at the discretion of the youth pastor. As long as he or she doesn't spend more money than is in the account, it works fine.

On the other hand, some churches can't afford to disburse money in one lump sum. Instead, they approve budgets and then depend on regular giving by their contributors to keep a positive cash flow. Individual ministries within the organization receive small amounts of money as needed (and if there's money available in the bank). In other words, these ministries have both income and expenses throughout the year.

Given a choice, receiving a lump sum is the way to go. On the other hand, living by cash flow requires a special kind of faith. In either case, accurate and consistent tracking of income and expenses is vital. Be sure that there's money in the bank before you spend.

Managing a budget

Managing a budget is like taking a shower—if you don't do it every day, people start to notice. Sometimes you can get away with neglecting to shower for a day or two, but when your closest friends start backing away from you, you know there's a problem. Financial tasks (reports, recording receipts, handling income) are also a daily necessity. But stacks of paper, piles of receipts, or months of statements that need balancing are ominous signs of finance mismanagement.

What type of daily (or weekly) management keeps finances manageable?

FasTrack

30 Keep the budget as simple as you can while giving as much detail as you need.

➤ **Read your monthly (or weekly) reports as soon as you get them.** Be sure you understand what they say. If you do not understand them, ask your accountant or bookkeeper to explain them to you. Use these reports to keep track of where you are in your fiscal year, and how much money you have left to spend.

➤ **Be willing to say no.** Knowing where you are financially—at all times—gives you the freedom to say no to expenditures. Don't shy away from the difficult conversations. Someone should be keeping you accountable, and you should keep your staff and volunteers accountable.

➤ **Keep the paper flow moving.** If you get a check requisition from a staff person, decide within two days whether to okay the expense, and then pass the paper on. If you're keeping up with your monthly statements, you'll know if you can afford the expense or not.

Smart Tip

If you still don't understand the finances, ask.

► **Offer timely reimbursement.** Within two days of a request for reimbursement, either send it back for more information or sign and put it in the financial officer's box. (For some reason, staff people who don't receive timely reimbursement get agitated.)

► **File your documents.** At the end of the paper trail, file each document in the appropriate spot. Keep your files updated, and always add new paperwork to the appropriate file. Add each document to the front of the file—the most recent document will always be on top of the pile.

► **Hold your receipts for reimbursement until you have $100 dollars in receipts, or 10 receipts, whichever comes first.** Keep all your receipts in one place in your wallet, then one place in your desk. Then, fill out your check requisition form and turn it in to the appropriate staff member. Never hold receipts longer than 30 days unless you have a good reason. Receipts that are held too long or reimbursement requests that have no proper documentation sometimes don't get paid.

► **Ask questions.** Ask the head of the technology team, "Why do we really need a new video projection unit right now?" Ask the accountant, "What exactly do you need from me? Do you have a sample format you can show me?" To the pastor say, "Yes, I know I overspent the budget, and we still have two months left, but do you really think it is fair to punish the students for my mistake?" (Well, maybe not the last one!)

Real Life

When giving financial reports, more is not necessarily better. At staff or board meetings I always gave a very detailed financial report. At one meeting I realized that I gave the members more information than they needed, because when I looked up, I saw ministry visionaries staring blankly at me through the financial report. They were confused by so much information. I now prepare one or two simple reports that give the ministry's bottom line. Everyone understands, it saves us time, and I get to leave earlier. Win-win!

On the other hand, when you meet with the CFO of your organization, bring every number you ever crunched because he or she will ask for it. CFOs not only want to see the end result, they want to see how you got there. Schedule enough time to answer all the questions. You might even get lunch out of the deal.

Keeping your financial paperwork in order

Simple is better.

Monthly reports and statements

The notebook method of preserving financial reports is a winner—the contents are easily accessible and portable. Section off a red, two-inch binder based on the kinds of reports and statements that cross your desk each month. Review each month's statement and file it in the notebook with the most recent one at the front of the appropriate section. In the very front of the notebook, place a copy of your annual budget. Create similar binders to store check requisitions (using dividers organized by line item number) and another for miscellaneous, one-time reports and statements.

> ## Smart Tip
>
> "Year-to-date" describes financial records from the beginning of the budget year (whether calendar or fiscal) to the date the report is printed.

Report formats

Simple and concise reporting is the rule of thumb. Reporting too much information and irrelevant information makes it impossible to determine if the ministry is in debt or just hit the Lotto. Your church might have some standard reports that work for you. If not, try using our **Budget & Monthly Report** and **Profit & Loss Statement**.

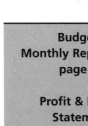

Budget & Monthly Report
page 333

Profit & Loss Statement
page 341

Reimbursement page 342

Whichever report form you choose, be certain it effectively communicates where the ministry is financially at any given time. A monthly budget report shows your annual budget allocation and shows what you spent in the previous month in each of your categories. A monthly profit-and-loss statement shows how much money came in within the last month and where it came from, and how much money went out in the last month and where it went. These one-page forms, covering one month, show where you are year-to-date.

Reimbursement form

For the sake of whomever writes the checks, reimbursements should be submitted no more than once a week or even once a month (whatever works for your ministry). Reimbursements are made only upon receiving completed documentation. Those submitting receipts must circle the applicable expenditures on the receipts and sign them. They must also complete the reimbursement form so you know the following:

✔ How they paid for items

✔ What items or types of items they purchased

✔ The purpose of the purchase

✔ The budget number for their purchases (unless you prefer to assign budget numbers yourself)

They must attach all receipts to the Reimbursement form and put it in your box.

After your careful review, sign it and put it in the bookkeeper's box for a check to be written. Turnaround time for reimbursement should be no more than one to four weeks, depending on when the form is submitted and how often checks are cut. Provide to all those who make purchases the procedures for reimbursement. That ensures properly submitted receipts and timely reimbursements. Remember to give all purchasers a tax-exempt card and remind them of the no-tax-reimbursement policy.

Case studies

► They know what they're doing, right?

It's your first week on the job in your first full-time youth ministry position. The ministry is well established, with a good track record. Although you haven't yet seen the budget figures, the ministry seems to be financially sound. A volunteer who has been handling the retreats for the last two years asks you to approve a large expense for the upcoming retreat. What do you do?

► Better programming needs better funding.

You've been at a ministry for just under one year. Money is always tight, but somehow you've managed to squeeze by without overspending. You dream of doing so much more, but you feel held back by a lack of money. It's almost time to prepare next year's budget, and you want to recommend budget figures that will support new strategies for building the ministry. What steps do you take to make your dream a reality?

► I'm still in control, I'm still in control...

You're one week out from an event for which you've planned, budgeted, and already collected student money. You've tracked the finances carefully up to this point, but a whirlwind of last-minute expenses and program additions have thrown you off track. Several staff and volunteers are out making purchases, and you have a feeling that they're overspending—but you can't be sure. You really want this event to be great, so you don't want to inhibit their creativity by raising red flags; but you can't overspend either. What immediate steps do you take? How do you handle future events differently?

► **Uh, honey, about that credit-card bill…**
You're busy. So busy, in fact, that it's difficult to find time for your husband. At least four nights a week he doesn't even see you before he goes to bed. You're building a volunteer base to take some of the ministry burden off your shoulders, but there just isn't enough time in the day to do everything that needs doing—let alone train and plug in volunteers.

Then, in your rush to get everything done, you can't wait on a check requisition to cover urgently needed supplies. So, you decide to charge several hundred dollars to your personal credit card. When you finally get around to requesting reimbursement, you can't find the receipts; and you know the church won't reimburse you without receipts. You're afraid to tell your husband because you know he'll be angry. But he's going to find out soon anyway because the credit card statement will likely come in this week's mail. What do you do?

Quick Start

Making a simple budget

To create a budget, answer the following questions on one of those columnar accounting pads—

► 1. Where does the ministry income currently come from? Make a list of the sources under the column heading "Income."

► 2. Are there other sources of income you will tap in the coming year? This is a subcategory called "Projected Income" and lists fundraisers you're adding, promised donations, additional funding from the larger organization. Be realistic.

► 3. Where does the ministry money currently get spent? On another columnar sheet under the heading "Expenses," list all the things ministry money bought in the last year. If you don't have accurate records to guide your list making, look at what you have in your office or in the youth rooms. What looks new? Look at old newsletters to discover which activities generated expenses. A simple budget that does not account for payroll will have at least the following categories:

- ✔ administrative and office
- ✔ advertisements and mailings
- ✔ postage
- ✔ travel
- ✔ books and materials
- ✔ sports and game equipment
- ✔ small-group materials
- ✔ research
- ✔ food and hospitality

(If this or any other expense category is large, break it down into subcategories: staff meals, gifts, student meals, pizza socials).

✔ janitorial supplies

✔ utilities—phone, water, heat

✔ transportation

✔ fundraising

✔ miscellaneous

A more complex budget might include—

✔ payroll expenses (bonuses, employee insurance, dental and health insurance)

✔ facilities (repairs, contract labor, cleaning, building maintenance)

✔ mortgage

✔ utilities (trash, phone, water, sewer)

4. What other areas do you anticipate funding in the next year? This subcategory is "Projected Expenses," and lists anything you believe will be a necessary expense to maintain and improve the youth ministry.

Budget
page 282

Trip Budget
page 347

Single-Event Registration
page 395

Financial Accountability Worksheet
page 288

Determining per-person cost for an event

Finding your stride in creating a budget for an entire year of youth ministry comes after you experience the rhythms unique to your location, kids, and style of ministry. Rather then pulling numbers out of your backpack, you may want to model last year's budget. After working eight to 12 months with an organization, you'll most likely want to make changes.

So for a Quick Start, look ahead on your ministry calendar to an event you'll ask your students to pay for—a weekend retreat, a two-day visit to a theme park 100 miles away, an adventure night with a lock-in. Working from the **Budget** (or the **Trip Budget**), the **Single-Event Registration**, and the **Financial Accountability Worksheet**, determine the per-person cost of the event and then track your collection and deposits of registration fees.

Case studies solutions

They know what they're doing, right? (from page 115)

Before approving the expense, look at the budget for the past retreat to see if what the volunteer says rings true. Then ask the church treasurer if the youth retreats have paid for themselves in the past. If you sense a go-ahead based on your research, approve the expense. If you find inadequate records or if the records show that retreats usually draw on budgeted money, work with the volunteer to modify the request. With any luck, the volunteer is requesting enough in advance to allow time for your investigation. If, through lack of planning or bad timing of your arrival on staff, you feel pressured to make a snap decision, resist it. Never let someone else's urgency force you to take shortcuts that could cost you in the long run. Always do the homework before approving expenses.

Better programming needs better funding (from page 115)

- Reevaluate your current budget and spending to determine if it reflects ministry values.

- Decide if you can cut some expenses and put the money saved toward your ministry dreams.

- Meet with the ministry team to brainstorm how you can put feet to your dream.

- Settle on sacrifices you can make up front that will get you closer to your dream.

- Meet with the treasurer and pastor to describe your vision. They might direct you to sources for extra funding or other help.

I'm still in control, I'm still in control... (from page 115)

This is a tough case. Whether you track spending on a computer or a yellow pad, update income and expenses daily. Request purchasers to daily turn in or fax their receipts. Daily completion of your financial homework is your best bet for staying in touch with the event balance sheet. Don't let your paperwork start piling up.

Uh, honey, about that credit-card bill... (from page 116)

Books have been written that offer advice to someone in this position. Any way you cut it, this one's gonna hurt. Check your health insurance policy and hope it covers marriage counseling.

Donations and income

13

Whether you receive cash donations, money from fundraising activities, or equipment, make it worth the donors' efforts by helping them see how their gifts enhance the youth ministry.

Chapter preview

► Definitions
► Donation basics
► Donation letters that work
► **Quick Start**: Writing donation receipts and thank-you letters

Definitions

We've talked a lot about expenses and how to budget them—yet it's all irrelevant without an income or donations.

► Donations are for ministry use, usually tax deductible, and require a receipt, if one is requested by the donor. Usually the ministry organization tracks donations and sends out year-end receipts to donors.

► Income is paid as a fee-for-service—such as retreat registration or a New Year's all-nighter—or money paid to the organization so the youth worker can purchase something like concert tickets or entrance to a water park for a group event. The fee charged to sign up for the event covers (or mostly covers) the expense for the individual attending the event.

Honorariums for speaking or leading workshops are also income—whether the income is yours or should be turned over to the church is a matter of policy. Typically, if you are speaking on church time, you need to pass the honorarium on to the church (otherwise you're double dipping—getting paid twice). If you're speaking on your own time, however, you can keep the money. But when in doubt, ask.

Smart Tip

"In-kind donation" is when an individual or company, in lieu of a cash donation, gives you a "thing" instead—like a computer, for instance. You can provide them with a receipt for the item as a tax write-off. (More on in-kind donations later in Chapter 13.)

Fundraisers
The key to successful fundraising is to be selective.

▶ The reward needs to be worth the work. In other words, don't expend a lot of time and resources on fundraisers that promise minimal returns.

▶ Sponsor a few choice, well-done fundraisers a year rather than many minifundraisers. Concentrate your effort where you can reap the most rewards.

▶ Enter into the fundraiser whole-heartedly, plan it well, drum up a lot of support among your organization's leadership and extended membership, and motivate the students.

FasTrack

31 Donations—whether to the larger ministry or to the youth ministry—fund your budget: ask for specific amounts with a proposed budget in mind, take what you receive and use it wisely, and always say thank you in a meaningful way.

Donation basics

There are two major forms of donations: cash and in-kind donations. **Cash** donations are the easiest to handle. Cash can come in the form of a check, actual dollars and cents, or a credit card (if your organization is equipped to accept them). **In-kind** donations are things—equipment, furniture, vehicles. Both in-kind and cash donations have their place in ministry, but they both need to be solicited and tracked differently.

▶ **Develop a donor database.** Keep your donors informed, interested, and motivated. Avoid badgering potential donors; instead help them to see the value of your ministry as evidenced by the results you're getting. People want to give to worthwhile causes. Show them the difference your ministry makes in the community, how their gifts can sustain and expand effective ministry.

▶ **In-kind donations build your resources and supplement your finances by providing directly an object or service that you would otherwise have purchased.** Some items arrive unsolicited (like the computer a youth worker found on her desk one morning, donated anonymously), but usually you must make your need known to the right people at the right time in hopes that they can use their connections or resources to help you out.

Many people would give in-kind donations if they knew what to give. Giving money is not an option for them, but they happen to have the ability to offer certain goods or services. You'll do best to solicit in-kind donations from your closest donors. It's like letting your family know what you need or want for your ministry. Be specific about acceptable quality and quantity of the items you request. Give specific directions on how and when donors can transfer ownership of the items to you. Inspect each item as it comes in, and accept or reject it at that time. (There's nothing worse than being given an item that you will have to pay to get rid of in the future.) Give the donor a tax-deductible receipt for the item. The donor is responsible to assess the presumed value of the item.

▶ **Keep a wish list of things your ministry needs.** Send it out to your families occasionally, or just keep it handy in case someone asks. My own ministry has a lot of self-employed parents who regularly upgrade their office equipment. Their throwaways are better than anything I have, so I welcome their donations. (Since they have probably already depreciated the item over time, and since the donation becomes a write-off for their company, it's as good a deal for them as for you.)

▶ **Research your organization's accepted way to raise money.** Your organization most likely has guidelines for receiving cash donations. Since you need to follow the plan, check with the finance officer before you hand out any fundraising letters at the Sunday morning service. The guidelines may vary for your personal fundraising, corporate ministry fundraising, or fundraising for special projects (like mission trips).

Special event budgets

▶ These contain many of the same elements as general budgets, but they focus on specific events. Very small events, of course, may be lumped into the general books, but you'll mange larger events more effectively if you track them separately. Larger, more complex events have multiple sources of income and expense details. When the event is over, transfer to your general budget one number for income and one for expense. (See Chapter 16 for specific information on budgeting for events.)

Donation letters that work

If you are allowed to solicit donations, the traditional donor letter is a good way to start. The most effective fundraising letters are concise, well-written, specific, need-driven, and written from the heart. Your mission is to paint a picture to which the reader can relate—and that motivates them to respond by giving to your ministry.

Statistics prove that if you include a return envelope with your letter, you will receive more responses. And if you take it one step further by placing a stamp on the return envelope, you will receive slightly more. (You'll have to experiment to learn if that extra expense of the stamp is offset by increased returns on the mailing.) Another tidbit—handwriting the addresses on the envelopes is a sure way to get people to actually open the letter in the first place. People respond more readily and generously to the personal touch.

FasTrack

32 Fundraising and direct contact requests for donations must follow protocol for your organization.

Donation letters that bring responses—

- are well written—no spelling or grammatical errors.
- paint a moving picture of the need.
- give a specific vision of how you're going to meet the need.
- tell the reader what you want them to do and by when.
- are short—no more than one page.
- are written with heart and conviction.
- have the personal touch.
- look clean and neat.
- have a handwritten address on the envelope.
- include a self-addressed envelope (with or without a stamp).
- are timed appropriately.
- are covered with prayer.

The last word on donations

Follow up all donations (no matter how small) with a tax-deductible receipt and a heartfelt thank you. People will only give once if they feel their gift wasn't appreciated. Many organizations request donations from your pool of donors. Thank your donors lavishly and often to keep them coming back.

Tips for the newcomer

"It's my first day on the job. What do I do now?"

First week:

- Request a copy of the current budget and last year's budget.
- Schedule a meeting with the person familiar with the youth ministry budget.
- Ask for training on the current procedures for tracking income and expenses.
- Ask what ways of handling finances have worked in the past and what trouble spots you should be aware of. (Keep an eye on the trouble spots during the next few weeks.)
- Unless the finances are in crisis, keep to the system currently in place. Change and improvements can come when you have more knowledge of and experience with the ministry.

First month:

- Study and understand the budget. Get a feel for how it's been used in the past—what worked and what didn't.
- Talk to anyone who's had experience working with the youth ministry budget.
- Talk to the church treasurer to see what has worked well with the youth ministry and what hasn't. Also ask if there's anything that can be done differently to help to the treasurer.
- Work on patching the financial holes. If necessary, call a temporary spending freeze until you get a handle on the finances.
- Meet with the pastor or treasurer to discuss—
  - ✔ the church's philosophy on spending, corporate and personal fundraising, and ministry money management.
  - ✔ what things are set in stone and what things are negotiable.
  - ✔ what the current systems are for bill paying and reimbursements, and when you have to submit the paperwork to receive timely payment.

➤ Investigate how youth ministry petty cash, donations, fees, and expense reimbursements are handled and evaluate if it's successful or not. Try to assign someone else to handle the petty cash (administrative assistant, financial volunteer). If needed, change the system so that every bill, check, donation, petty-cash receipt, and dollar goes across your desk. You need to know how every penny is being collected and spent. That's the only way you'll ever get a handle on the ministry finances.

First six months:

➤ After understanding, observing, and personally monitoring the budget for at least six months, you can delegate to a staff person or trusted (experienced) volunteer some of the routine procedures. Request weekly or monthly reports from your volunteer so you can monitor any major income or expense (perhaps more than $25 or $100, depending on the size and scope of your ministry).

➤ Reevaluate the budget and adjust it according to your ministry needs.

➤ Never assume. Always check and double-check numbers.

➤ If at any time you creep into the financial danger zone—overspending a monthly budget, losing money on an event, unable to account for some expenses or the reason you're finding checks or cash in your drawer—notify the church's treasurer or CFO and get assistance ASAP. CFO's don't like surprises and are more forgiving if you come forward sooner rather than later.

Quick Start

Writing donation receipts and thank-you letters

Start off on the right foot with donors by using the sample letter on the next page. The main thing is to write the letter on organization letterhead, include the date of the donation, the donor's name, the amount given, and a word of thanks. The IRS views a letter with the above information as a receipt. You may also include an actual receipt, if your church already has one. Or you can enclose the **Donor Receipts** form with your letter.

**Donor Receipts
page 336**

NASCA NORTHWEST
N SUBURBAN
CHRISTIAN
ACADEMY

September 24, 2000

Marty Babcock
1234 N. Ridge Rd.
Vista, NC 03214

Dear Marty,

We would like to thank you for your thoughtful gift of $150. Your generosity allows us to continue our mission to provide a quality education and train a generation of children to serve God!

May God return to you the blessing you have so generously given to us. We appreciate your continued prayers for our school, as we depend on the Lord's strength and provision every day.

Sincerely,
Liz Fedor

Northwest Suburban Christian Academy • 15348 NW Martin Blvd. • Mitchell, South Dakota 23456

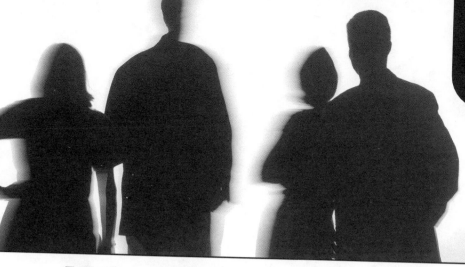

Managing events

Youth ministry, by its nature, cycles all year through the stages of event management. You're always planning an event, in the middle of one, completing it, or evaluating it.

This section coaches both the detail-conscious and the organizationally challenged to—

▶ Acquire basic skills for planning events.

▶ Discover five ways to build success into every event.

▶ Master tools that help you coordinate and manage events, retreats, camps, or mission projects.

▶ Get a handle on what tasks you personally need to do and be responsible for, and what tasks you can delegate.

Although event managing is hard work, it gets easier with practice. Living the event in your head several times over before you ever board the bus, for instance, prepares you to put on an event that will be memorable for the right reasons. (Forgetting a student at a rest stop is not a memory you want people to talk about. And running out of gas in the middle of the desert with 12 junior highers is not as cool a time as your anecdote cracks it up to be.) Your goal through the process is to repeat successes and avoid pitfalls.

In Managing events—

Planning events with a purpose

Putting time and effort into planning and executing a well-run event saves money and time, and produces impact.

Chapter preview

▶ Five essentials for planning events with purpose:
1. Purposeful planning
2. Coordinated details
3. Directed promotion
4. Focused programming
5. Trust in God

▶ **Quick Start**: Making a simple event timeline

Five essentials for planning a purposeful event

E vents flourish when you apply the five essentials. The trick is to keep the big picture in mind while you focus on the details that will make your event a reality.

Event Planning

Determining goals	
Purposeful planning **Planning Worksheet page 303**	• What outcome do you want? • Are your ministry goals in harmony with this event? • Who will participate? How many? • How long will it last? • Where is the best place to meet? • When is the best time for this event (based on above answers)? • Do you need to receive anything from the participants (either before or during the event)?
Designing details	
Coordinated Details **Task Master page 312** **Site Inspection page 310**	• Describe how your purpose is best accomplished. • Outline the event schedule. • Determine budget. • Determine needs for facility, transportation, housing, food, meeting space, contracts, printed materials.

Getting out the word—inform and energize participants (Tailor promotion to group size and makeup and the personality of the occasion.)	
Directed promotion **Marketing Strategy** **page 290**	• Develop a marketing strategy well in advance of the event: posters, mailings, announcements, video clips, word-of-mouth invitation. • Allow enough time for participants to respond to the promotion.
Purpose-driven content	
Focused programming **Task Master** **page 312**	• This is when event managers focus their vision and goals into a theme that will attract participants. • Storyboard the event: play out event goals through general sessions, small-group times, meals, activities, games, work projects, and so on. • Develop an event timeline. • Develop contingency plans.
Prayer	
Trust in God	• Ask for wisdom, flexibility, safety, and growth.

What is an event?
The dictionary describes it as something that happens—an incident of special interest.

For youth ministry purposes, an event is a gathering of people who have a common goal or who unite around a common theme, often with activities containing the elements of entertainment, excitement, education, and fun. A small event would serve under 100 people; more attendees qualify an event as "large."

Purposeful planning

The detail work invested in the event-planning stage sets apart the novice from the professional youth worker. The five essential ingredients we reviewed in the chapter on leading meetings apply in event planning as well—even though an event is different in character and scope from a meeting. These ingredients are woven throughout the event section to help you track with the big picture while you focus on the details that will make your event a reality.

Coordinated details

There's no shortcut through the planning of a successful event. Although many youth workers see tracking details as grueling punishment, in reality this pre-work makes your event smoother and more enjoyable for all concerned—especially you.

After sketching out your event, sit down with a yellow pad and list all the steps needed to make the event a reality. If the complexity of the event takes more time and skills than you have, delegate to staff and volunteers.

► Successful delegation begins by thoughtfully matching the right staff person or volunteer with the right task.

► The next step is to clearly communicate instructions, expectations, and deadlines.

► Once they understand what has to be done, support them while they do the job. Providing support to a volunteer, or even a staff member, is essential until you know the person is able to complete the task. Following up with volunteers can be trickier than with staff since they are not on site, and they may be scheduling your tasks around their work hours and around other projects for which they've volunteered.

► Finally, demonstrate to both volunteers and paid staff your appreciation for their efforts. Your support should be heavy on appreciation and making sure that they feel they are an essential part of the team and that you're counting on them.

FasTrack

33 Purposeful planning opens doors to sites too costly to use in season.

Why put time and effort into planning and executing a well-run event?

► **Saves money.**
If events are driven over budget, it's typically because of crisis management or mismanagement. Overlooking needed materials or services means you acquire them at the last minute. You can forget price checking or shopping the deal.

► **Saves time.**
Close your eyes and roughly calculate the time you've spent scrambling to save an event that's falling apart at the last minute. Now tack about half that amount onto the beginning of the planning process, and you'll save yourself the rest of the time and all the associated stress. As they say, if it's worth doing, it's worth doing right the first time.

► **Gives impact.**
Well-run events are more likely to equip students to grow up in their faith—or to find faith. Last-minute events generally don't motivate teens, no matter how good we are at flying by the seat of our pants. In fact, the larger and more complex the event, the more likely our shorting the planning process will produce mistakes that negatively affect the event's overall impact.

Directed promotion

How you promote an event largely depends on who and how many are coming. The larger the event, the more you and your team need to develop a workable marketing strategy. Over a period of weeks (or months) do a media roll-out to promote the event and develop interest. Use many promo methods creatively for best results: posters, mailings, announcements, video clips.

▶ Probably the most effective method of promoting an event is a personal invitation from staff and students. The media blitz sets the stage, but the personal invite is what gets students to cross the line. The key to getting the leaders and students to buy into the event is to keep them informed and excited. Through spoken and written words we try to give as much information as kids need to catch the vision.

▶ Another key to event promotion is giving students enough time to respond. In mass marketing, statistics show that it takes approximately seven contacts through written or spoken words for a person to take action. You want to give students as much time as possible to get used to the idea of the event and to hear about it in unique and creative ways. Event promotion should reflect the event's personality. As the first snapshot that students see of the event, it should be fun and inviting. It's that picture that creates energy and excitement about the event before it happens.

Smart Tip

Give parents a copy of a simple event schedule, stating the event location, address, phone number, and emergency phone numbers. On the back of the schedule, spell out the code of student conduct and draw a map to the event location. That way, if disciplinary action is taken, parents are fully aware of the consequences (like receiving a call in the middle of the night to pick up Johnny because he raided the girls' sleeping quarters).

Real Life

Our winter camp theme was *Mission Impossible*. The movie by that name had come out the previous summer, and students could still get excited about the theme. We created our brochures, promotions, and curriculum around some of the catch phrases and video clips students were familiar with. Woven into the promotion and the fabric of the event was the message that God has a mission for each of us, and it's our job to discover it and take steps toward accomplishing it.

Focused programming

Programming—the heart (or content) of an event—is the art of fashioning general sessions, small-group time, meals, activities, games, work projects, and so on. Focused programming means designing each of those components around your event goals. Focused programming means describing specific, desired outcomes for each component. Either by yourself or in a planning group, ask questions to help define the theme and general tone for a meeting or event.

► What is the purpose of the event?

► Who is the audience?

► What will participants walk away with after the event?

► What key principles will participants learn?

► What is the best way to communicate this information to them?

► What environment best encourages communication of and receptivity to the information?

► Who would best communicate this information?

► What activities will help accomplish meeting or event goals and objectives?

After answering these questions, you're prepared to develop your theme. That means you condense your vision and goals into a contemporary theme that students can get excited about. Long before the event, with a handful of creative people, storyboard the event. The person directing the event (probably you) usually leads the meeting of staff and select volunteers who can contribute creative and wacky ideas. The overall time frame for the event is written on colored 3x5 cards pinned (or taped) to the walls or to fabric-covered foam boards). The planning team then walks through the event, coming up with ideas to make it fun and exciting for students. Each suggestion, no matter how crazy, is posted on the storyboard (usually with a point person's name on it). The general sessions are slotted, but the actual moment-by-moment cue sheets can be completed at a second meeting dedicated just to general sessions. As the storyboard fills up, your program will start to unfold.

Before you run over to the storyboard to start filling it up, you and your team need to make sure you're all on the same page by developing a rationale or purpose statement: the why and what for the event. Sometimes the program director comes into the meeting with the rationale. Other times it's developed at the first meeting. Whatever the case, with the rationale clear in everyone's mind, the team maps out the specifics. At this meeting, life is breathed into the theme. The event's environment is carefully constructed to creatively and effectively communicate God's truths to students. Your goal is to influence students with the life-changing message of God through creative communication. Maximize that impact in every moment of the event—in other words, create a purpose-driven event.

Developing a theme and storyboarding put the content of the event in a context, a form that is easy for students to assimilate into their lives. A catchy theme makes a retreat or event more tangible. Themes inspire sound bites that will stick with the students long after the event is over. It also gives the programming team more to work with. Even a mission trip benefits from a theme by unifying your group—base the theme on a verse or brainstorm with the students for a motto that expresses their hopes or goals for the trip.

Following the programming meeting, use the **Task Master** to work out more details and assign tasks. Beside each action point, place the name of the person responsible, the date by which the task needs to be done, and a list of all the equipment needed to accomplish the task.

> **Task Master**
> **page 312**

Finally, the team lays out contingency plans for potential problems. It's not a waste of time, either. More often than not, one or more contingency plans have to be implemented at the last minute. With smaller groups it's easier to be flexible and to get away with last-minute changes. The larger the group, however, the more difficult it is to flex with emergencies. Planning alternative options can be a lifesaver.

Smart Tip

Timing is everything in event planning. Did you know that you save money using a facility during its off season? During the middle of summer, every good lakeside camp is packed. But come late fall or early spring, they're usually begging for business.

Ski resorts are screaming for business during their off-seasons (or "shoulder seasons" or "slush seasons"): between fall and winter and between ski season and late spring. If you're flexible with your time schedule and creative with your programming, you might be able to land the deal of the century.

FasTrack

35 Purposeful planning increases the chances for a well-attended event.

General Session Cue Sheet
Event

sample

6:30 - 6:45 pm	Sound check in general session auditorium
6:50 - 7:00 pm	Background music
7:00 - 7:05 pm	Solo by Chris Smith
7:05 - 7:15 pm	Welcome by emcee - Introduce himself - Purpose for the retreat
7:15 - 7:25 pm	Worship and praise
7:25 - 7:30 pm	Video clip
7:30 - 7:33 pm	Speaker introduction
7:33 - 8:05 pm	Main speaker
8:05 - 8:10 pm	Closing song
8:10 - 8:15 pm	Closing announcements and prayer
8:15 - 8:30 pm	Walk-out music

289

Trust in God

Prayer is the power that drives any ministry—including events. In the ever-changing student world in which we minister, we work hard at staying relevant and on top of our game. Prayer transcends cultures and connects our hearts to students. Here are just a few of the areas where we need to focus our prayers:

FasTrack

36 Purposeful planning informs your event programming early enough in the process to support unique touches that make for a memorable occasion.

Wisdom

From the time that you calendar an event, invite God to be an integral part of it. You and your team need wisdom and discernment to carefully and creatively design an environment where God will be glorified and his principles taught. Pray that God's wisdom will influence your thoughts and ideas. Pray that you and your team will be open to God's leading and direction.

Flexibility

When the event occurs, no matter how much planning went into it, unexpected glitches require flexibility among the planners. Pray that people and programs will be able to flex if needed. When a portion of a program gets cut at the last minute, for instance, its contributors can feel frustrated and hurt and lose sight of the fact that the changing or axing of their idea is not an indicator of its quality or value. Pray that God will keep you and your team humble and flexible.

Safety

Never take this for granted. Continually do your part to keep your students safe, and leave the rest up to God. Pray that God will keep your students safe from the time they step onto your campus to the time they open their own front door.

Growth

You and your team plan, program, create, and labor to build an environment in which students will grow. No amount of effort on your part will touch the hearts of students, however; that job is God's alone. Pray that God will significantly affect your students' lives, as well as your own.

FasTrack

37 Purposeful planning, energized by prayer, assures leaders that God's presence pervades the event.

Quick Start

Making a simple event timeline

Starting with the actual date of the event, live the event through in reverse, making notes as you go. (Leave space between each category to add related items and potential volunteer assistants as they come to mind.) That way you'll consider those nonglamorous issues that are often forgotten until the last moment:

✔ **Event cleanup.** Do you really want to do that job one more time—alone?

✔ **Staff responsibilities the day of event.** Staff feel needed and part of a team when you entrust to them a real job to do in advance, give them a staff shirt or cool I.D. tag, or assign them a radio communication device.

✔ **Transportation.** Knowing how you'll get there—plane, train, bus, van, or car. Know where your "there" is—accurate map and directions for all drivers. Know how long travel time will be—including different legs of the trip.

✔ **Checks needed for the event.** The business office may not have signer(s) on site to cut you an emergency check on the day (or night) you leave.

✔ **Promotion.** Fliers, Web presence, phone calls, E-mails, community announcements, word of mouth—leave yourself plenty of time to populate your event with kids who would like to come…if only they had known about it.

✔ **Staff.** It's amazing who offers to lend a hand when you contact people well in advance of the day you need the help—parents (site inspections, sign-up monitors, promotional pieces), the church's women's groups and men's groups (prop making, sewing, food preparation, setup and cleanup), community organizations (see if the Boy Scouts will cook your send-off barbecue), local retailers (sponsor ads, donate goods or services, use of parking lot or warehouse), et cetera.

✔ **Supplies you'll need and who can get them.** List supplies early, and someone else can shop for them.

✔ **Reservations at the room or place you're having the event**—'nuff said!

For each category on the list you've created, detail the related tasks. Beside each task write two or three names of people who might help complete the task. Assign a date for when the task ought to be completed, based on the date of your event and on how long it takes to complete. Another thing to keep in mind—some tasks can't be started unless a certain other task is completed, or at least begun.

Once you've done all of this prethinking, start calling to find those who will form a core event leadership group. Set a first-meeting date, and go for it.

Tools for event management

Using management tools can walk you through the maze of producing a quality event.

Chapter preview

- Using professional event planners
- Tool 1: Critical path management
- Tool 2: Master timeline
- Tool 3: To-do list
- Tool 4: Event notebook
- Event notebook contents
- Small off-campus events
- Small on-campus events
- **Quick Start**: Choosing the right event location

Using professional event planners

Basically four variables determine the complexity and drive the management style of an event:

- number of people involved
- time length of the event
- complexity of event goals and objectives
- distance to the event location

FasTrack

38 For a particularly complex event, let a professional event planner handle logistics.

But even for the detail-oriented, event management can seem overwhelming. If your event is large and complex enough that you wish to hire a professional event planner to manage logistical details, then your responsibilities shift from things like facilities, transportation, and food to primarily programming.

Christian meeting planning professionals can help with site selection, contract negotiation, registration, and on-site management. Especially if you select a hotel as your event site, hiring an event professional (who is trained and experienced in providing the level of detail hotels require) is a good way to go. Many times, the meeting planner negotiates a better fee with the hotel—not only because they do it all the time, but because they bring the hotel so many other clients that the hotel wants to give them the best deal.

Meeting planner fees vary based on the amount of responsibility you delegate to them and on the facility you desire to use. In some cases, hotel facilities work with professional meeting planners on a commission basis. That means the planner won't charge you at all for finding the facility and negotiating the contract. (For more information regarding training or potential meeting planners look at the resources at the back of the chapter.)

EVENT MANAGEMENT TOOL Critical path management

The critical path of an event is the sequence of critical activities that connect the event's start with the event's conclusion. Knowing the critical path of an event helps you prioritize tasks that have no leeway in their timing, letting you see exactly what needs to happen and when to keep your event planning on schedule. Most tasks in event management have some slack, and you can delay them some without affecting the event itself. If you delay critical tasks, however, you jeopardize your event. Some tasks that at first aren't on the critical path move onto the critical path if you procrastinate.

Your first entry on the critical path map is the date your event is to occur. Once you've established that, move backward to assign dates to tasks that must be completed the day before the event begins, the week before, the month before, and so on. This is how it works in simple form:

- **On July 10, at 7 p.m.**, you want to play a game of cards on your back porch with a few friends and serve them ice cream. That means that by—
- **July 10** you must have pulled out the cards, put chairs on the deck, set the bowls and spoons on the countertop.
- **July 9** you must have cleaned the house.
- **July 6** you must have bought the ice cream.
- **July 1** you must have invited a few friends to come over.

House cleaning must occur as scheduled—by July 9 —or it won't get done in time for the event. It's already a critical task on the path since there's no room for delay. (If you're not a clean freak, of course, you can always skip this step.) You can't have the party without ice cream, though. That means buying it is already a critical task, and you've built in some slack time to cover yourself for emergencies (or procrastination). If the ninth rolls around, and you still haven't bought ice cream, however, that becomes your number-one priority on the critical path.

How the event actually pans out can look very different than your critical path map. Here's one scenario:

FasTrack

39 Track your event planning progress on a master timeline.

- **On July 1** you could only reach four of your seven friends. Two were out of town and won't get their messages until after the July fourth holiday, and one must not have been paying attention to her call-waiting feature.

- **On July 3** you finally remember to call the one back, and she can't come. You start to think of who can finish out the second foursome.

- **By July 8** you've finally got seven yeses and you go buy the ice cream.

- **July 9** starts with your car breaking down and ends with you buying paper plates because you still haven't had time to do your dishes, let alone clean the house.

- **On July 10** your friends show up at 7:20 and apologize for being late—and for bringing three extra friends. You improvise partners for the card game and everyone gets a little less ice cream, but hey! It turns out to be a fun evening just as you'd hoped when you planned it.

EVENT MANAGEMENT TOOL Task Master

The **Event Planning Worksheet** can guide your preparation for your first team meeting. Use the **Task Master** to prompt you to send out assignments to team members after the first meeting.

The critical path is your map for event planning. Based on your map, you fill in your **Task Master** and start making your to-do lists.

- Visualize your desired event—how the space will support your goals, what activities will happen and in what order, who will provide leadership for small groups, et cetera.

- Describe in a list as many steps as you think are required to make the event happen.

- Put the steps in order according to which steps need to happen before other steps can happen, and according to which steps take the longest time to accomplish or the longest lead time to get the desired results.

- Assign each step a deadline and a person to be responsible for the task.

- Track your progress, and don't slack on the details that need to be completed early in the process. If you go off schedule early on, you'll be playing catch-up all the way through.

- Although your critical path map started with the day of the event and worked backward, your timeline should start with today's date and work forward toward the event date.

EVENT MANAGEMENT TOOL To-do list

Generate a master to-do list. Include tasks from your **Event Planning Worksheet**, your **Task Master**, and action steps brought up at your team meetings. The master to-do list is a catch-all place for any job, no matter how simple, that you have to do to make the event happen. (You can use the **Monthly Planning** and **Weekly Planning forms**.) Instead of naming complex jobs on the list, break them down into parts and list each part. To the left of an item, record the date you entered it; to the right jot down the task's deadline.

At least weekly skim your master to-do list for tasks that must be done (and can be done) the next day, or on each day in the next week. Transfer those items to daily to-do lists that you keep in this section of your event notebook. Don't write down more tasks than you can actually do on a given day—and then do them.

EVENT MANAGEMENT TOOL Event notebook

Tracking event details can swamp even the most organized of leaders if they have no one place to keep all the papers in order. After planning hundreds of events, professional meeting planner and senior partner of Conferences Inc., Linda Daniels, recommends keeping an event notebook—one three-ring binder per event, with at least 12 section markers. An event notebook helps keep your event-tracking smooth and organized. The sections may include—

**Event Forms
page 282 to 326**

➤ To-do list

➤ Meeting notes

➤ Schedule

➤ Budget

➤ Facility

➤ Transportation

➤ Housing

➤ Food

➤ Meeting space

➤ Contracts

➤ Printed materials

➤ Miscellaneous

Smart Tip

When you negotiate the facility contract, bring in a similar schedule from a prior event. The representative will get a better idea of the type of space you need and of your program requirements.

On the cover of your notebook write the event name, your church name, and your name. That way if it's misplaced during the event, it can be returned to you.

Event notebook contents

The notebook holds all your ideas, logistical information, maps, original copies, et cetera—a one-stop-shop for everything you need to manage your event. Keep a three-hole punch handy so you can add fliers and other written materials. Insert some blank pages for meeting notes and clear-pocket page holders for originals, room keys, and miscellaneous items. When a piece of paper, idea, or detail comes your way, immediately file it in the proper section of the notebook. That way, things will always be at your fingertips. The notebook will evolve into a tool that you can't live without. Following is a partial list of the items that can be kept in each section:

FasTrack

40 Browse your master to-do list at the end of each week to set up daily tasks for the next week.

Event Notebook Checklist

- **Timeline**. Keep a current copy of your **Master Timeline**, with its adjusted dates and assignments, at the front of the notebook.

- **To-do list**. Build a list based on your timeline that tells you what needs to be done today or in the next few days.

- **Meeting notes**. Keep a copy of all meeting notes, including your **Planning Worksheet**. Record assignment changes, action items, and other vital information to the appropriate sections of your notebook as well. Choose one team member to take notes during your planning meetings, then type them up and E-mail them to all the team members. Your copy can make its home in your event notebook.

- **Event schedule**. Make up two event schedules—one that gives details necessary for planning, and the other a **Simplified Timeline** for student, parent, and staff use. On your final, detailed schedule, show meeting room assignments beside each entry.

- **Budget**. In this section keep at least a copy of the general budget. The **Financial Accountability Worksheet** and the **Budget** would go here. If you do your books manually, keep your expense sheet in this section as well. Place unprocessed receipts in a clear sheet-holder within this section. It's best to have another folder and envelope for processed receipts, or the event notebook gets too bulky.

- **Facility**. Once you have the big picture of the kind of even you want to do, record in your event notebook specific details of the kind of facility you need to accomplish your goals. Sometimes budget determines facility; sometimes facility determines budget. If your group has been using a certain retreat center for the last bazillion years, for example, then the facility cost will drive the budget. If on the other hand you're looking for a new facility, check out several to find an affordable one that works for you. Record your search results in your notebook on the **Site Inspection** form.

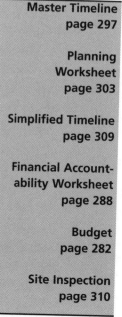

The facility category in event planning includes maps, rules and regulations, general facility schedule, snack bar hours, lake front hours, et cetera. Place at the front of the section a list of the phone numbers or extension numbers of individuals on site who work with you: meeting planner, facilities manager, banquet manager.

► **Transportation**. Pull from your office filing cabinet information on transportation companies in your area. Start calling. Keep notes on your phone calls in this section, and when you select the company to use, photocopy their flier or brochure and place the copy in your event notebook. You can file a copy of the contract with your selected company in this section as well.

► **Housing**. The more people attending your event, the more that housing concerns can make or break your event. The facility generally provides a grounds map or hotel floor plan that specifically shows sleeping rooms. Request a sales packet with housing-specific information. Find out the type of bed setup in each room: king, queen, double/double (two double beds), or two singles. Hotels also list what amenities each room offers.

► **Food**. Your food service choices depend on the type of facility you select. Some retreat centers offer no options. Upscale retreat centers and hotels give you lots of choices, and only your budget limits your cuisine. In this section you can put menus, lists of meals needed, and any choices that you're offered.

► **Meeting space**. Keep in your event notebook floor plans of the meeting spaces you've reserved on your **Meeting Space Setup Worksheet**. Facility-provided diagrams generally show room footage and possible room arrangements. Your staging plans affect the number of seats you can set up. Since you might use one room in several ways, sketch out the details of your set-up needs—along with the dates and times for each set up. They like to have your exact schedule two-to-four weeks in advance.

AV equipment, flip charts, screens, and sound systems (other than the "house" system) generally cost extra. Renting AV equipment through a facility can be expensive. It's usually cheaper to bring in rented equipment. House systems rarely work for youth ministry events—the quality is poor and the capacity is limited.

► **Contracts**. You make several contracts as you progress with your event: facility, speaker, transportation (if you use busses), and perhaps a meeting planner. Keep the clean, signed original in your notebook and a copy in your office file drawer. During an event, you will refer to the contracts several times. Especially if there are issues that need clarifying.

Programming the purpose-driven event

► Once you have determined your event's purpose, budget, and location, you know what you have to work with for programming the event. Programming is an expanded version of the event schedule. It encompasses general sessions, small-group time, meals, activities, games, work projects, and so on. From another perspective, the schedule is the synopsis of the program.

FasTrack

41 Keep a notebook in which all material related to the event is accessible.

▶ **Printed materials**. Keep with you in a clear page holder any originals of schedules, study notes, PR and registration brochures, logo, et cetera. You never know when you'll need to make just one more copy of whatever. Put a Post-it Note , on each sheet saying "Original."

▶ **Miscellaneous**. As you live out the event, note things that work and things that don't. Write out what you would change if you could and what you would never do again. In a clear sheet-holder, collect any incident reports or other items that don't fit any notebook category.

Once your notebook is organized, so are you. It will be well worth the time you spend setting it up and keeping it up. The next time someone asks you a tough question about the event, you can turn to your notebook and give the right answer in a moment.

Small on-campus events

On-campus events typically are easier, less expensive, and less cumbersome than off-campus events. Following a few guidelines will keep you in favor on your home turf.

▶ **Be a good neighbor.** Some churches have systems in place for facility and vehicle requests that you need to follow. Be a good neighbor to the other ministries in the church by sharing the rooms and the van throughout the year. One large church took vehicle requests for one full year, starting on a specific date late in the spring. Different van-dependent ministries would write out 10 to even 100 vehicle requests and turn them in the first day of "open season." Good for the ministry, but bad for being a good neighbor. Other ministries that weren't as proactive were left without transportation, even if they requested six months in advance. Working together with other ministries for resources is part of being a good neighbor. We work for the same boss, and no one ministry is more important than another.

▶ **Respect and value your facility.** Not only must you treat the facilities respectfully, your staff, volunteers, and students need to be taught the same respect. Waterlogged bathrooms or paint-splattered walls discredit your ministry.

What you need to know about contracts

▶ Read and understand every word of the contract before you sign it. A contract serves two purposes: clarification and instructions.

▶ Ask another person to read a contract before you sign it—the fine print can be devastating.

▶ A contract is meant to be changed until both parties sign it. Before you sign, let the service provider know if you're uncomfortable about something in the contract. After the contract is signed, you have to live with it.

▶ A contract often bounces back and forth several times before it's usable. Make sure that you sign only the edited and clean copy of the contract. You will be referring to the contract several times throughout your event and need to be able to read and understand it.

▶ Be prepared to live and die by the contract. Don't assume anything. Put it in writing. If they say they can do this or that, ask them to write it into the contract. If it's not in writing, it's considered hearsay and not legally binding. Food services can say that you'll have 14 meals a day per person, but if the contract says you'll get only one meal, you'll go hungry.

Small off-campus events

Some of the greatest events are simple ones where a youth worker and few volunteers take a van full of students on a weekend retreat at a cabin. Even though most of you may have to sleep on the floor, your time can be rich and memorable. Events don't have to be huge to have impact. Smaller events can effectively build and develop the personal relationships that can drive growth.

▶ **Facility.** Depending on your group's size, you might use anything from a tent to a cabin in a retreat center. Many retreat centers or camp facilities accommodate small groups. Scheduling facility use for small groups is easier and can be done even at a later date because a small group can often use a facility at the same time as larger, previously scheduled groups. A living room or conference room can serve as your meeting room. Meals can be on campus or at the local McDonald's. Your event can be more spontaneous and flexible, but some planning is none the less important.

▶ **Transportation.** Small groups can use a van or two, along with some other leaders' vehicles. Remember that transportation is as important to the event as housing, speakers, or breakout sessions. Your event starts the moment your students show up at the church doors and ends when they step into their parent's car.

A small group traveling a moderate distance can recruit parent drivers and personal vehicles to transport students. Bus and van rental, of course, remains an option. If your group is large enough for several buses and if you're traveling a substantial distance, investigate chartering through a large transportation company. In addition to increased comfort and bathroom facilities, chartered buses offer separate storage for luggage.

▶ **Housing.** Although you secure your facility very early in the planning process, you'll assign rooms or cabins only one week before the event. That way you only do housing assignments once. If you assign housing too early and a few more students join, you end up having to redo the assignments.

More on contracts

▶ While on site or just prior to the event, state in writing mutually agreed upon additions or changes to the contract and add them to your contract. Keep good notes.

▶ Honor your contract. If it says that you need to pay X amount by Y date, then make sure that you do. Don't jeopardize your event by tardy payments.

▶ Keep the original of each of your contracts in your event notebook for quick reference. Keep a copy in your office.

▶ You must have a contract for any service provider that you pay: facility, speaker(s), musicians, transportation. Spell out in the contract any specifics related to the service—fees, special circumstances, benefits, and anything else you want the service provider to be accountable to fulfill.

▶ Investigate putting in a clause for Christian arbitration in case of a dispute. Seldom, if ever, would you actually need it, but should problems arise, it's a lifesaver.

FasTrack

42 Put everything in writing, at least; at most, put everything in writing in the contract.

Small retreat programming ideas

- Use a video series for your program and spend time in discussion.

- Choose a small book to work through and have the students read through it before the retreat.

- Choose a book of the Bible to work through.

- Talk about one or two characters in the Bible and make it relevant to your students' world.

- Choose a curriculum and spend time working through it.

▶ **Food.** No matter what facility you select, you'll have to select menus. If you've purchased a prepackaged meal deal, request complete menus so you're certain the food is appropriate for your group. Simple is best, and large quantity is mandatory. After all, you're bringing in growing kids with healthy appetites. Quality is tricky to judge accurately for a group of students. Request well in advance additions or changes necessary for any student's special dietary needs.

FasTrack

43
Keep your contact at the facility informed about meeting space use.

Ask if you can supplement the food offered. Some facilities don't allow you to bring store-bought snacks or to call out for pizza, but you can bring homemade goodies. Others might let you bring packaged snacks, like candy bars or sodas, only if you're selling them at break times. Most facilities let students bring their own snacks for their own rooms.

▶ **Meeting space.** Appropriate meeting space for a small event is determined by your programming plans. Are you always going to meet as one big group? Do you need breakout rooms? If so, how many and when? Talk through your schedule with the facility manager, noting group size and kind of activity for each time and room. Hotels require your exact schedule in order to work around the needs of other groups. Retreat settings are usually more flexible. You can even have a 24-hour access to your main meeting space.

Smart Tip

If another group uses your chosen facility at the same time, place a copy of their schedule in your notebook so you plan with the other group in mind.

Quick Start

Choosing the right event location

Event planning is not quite like real estates sales—location, location, location—but you must use a thoughtful and complete selection process when choosing the appropriate location for your event. The **Site Inspection** form walks you through consideration of facility distance from your home base, facility flexibility, room sizes and usability, eating area and recreation facilities, and other facility issues that affect your event experience.

Before your first event planning meeting, open up a copy of the form in your word processor and read through the lists of questions. Add in questions about location that relate to the general kind of event you have in mind. Maybe you want to include a sleep-out under the stars one night. Write that criteria in question form under "General facility flexibility." Just browsing the list will spark ideas for other inquiries about event facilities and help you to quickly focus your location search.

Site Inspection
page 310

Innocent negligence

Handling copyrighted materials

Just in case
(hint, hint, hint)

Check with your umbrella organization or your denomination to see what copyright licenses you may already be covered by.

An often overlooked—even intentionally ignored—area is copyright infringement. Although I'm sure that section 110 of the Copyright Law of 1976 {17 U.S.C. 110(3)} is on your recreational reading list this year, let me relieve your suspense regarding its content.

Without fear of breaking the law, churches may—

✔ perform nondramatic literary or musical works and religious dramatic and musical works.

✔ display individual works of a nonsequential nature (17 U.S.C. 101).

This means that during worship, you may—

✔ perform contemporary songs, regardless of the owner.

✔ show any still image, regardless of its source. You may even show frames of a film, if they are not in sequence. You may show scanned images of any sort, including newspaper headlines, periodicals, and pictorial books.

Here's what churches may NOT do during worship, according to Section 110(3):

✔ Play any non-live-performed recording of a musical work—whether on CD or audiocassette.

✔ Reproduce lyrics in any fashion from a copyright-protected musical work, including displaying lyrics within projected graphic images and printing the lyrics in bulletins or other handouts. Section 110(1) applies the same rules for media use in nonprofit educational environments, as well.

Outside of worship and classroom, legal use of copyrighted works (including posting works on the Internet and selling works to other churches or individuals) is not as clearly defined. Much is made of the exemption in the copyright law for fair use (NUGGET). As a rule, never make blanket use of fair use.

Keep in mind the following guidelines for claiming fair use of a copyrighted piece:

✔ The more creative the work, the less likely that it's covered by the fair use clause.

✔ Although no specific percentages apply, the more of a work you use, the less likely that your use is covered by fair use.

✔ The more fair use decreases a work's market value, the less likely that you can claim fair use of it.

The only activities qualifying for blanket fair use, according to standard interpretations of the First Amendment, are news reporting, research, and criticism. Evaluate all other uses on a work-by-work basis.

Parodies may violate copyright protection.

Fair use of copyrighted works for parodies may allow use of prerecorded music with original dramatics, such as in a skit or video version of a sketch or TV show. To be sure you're not in audio-visual copyright violations, however, check with a copyright lawyer on a case-by-case basis.

Non-home showing of rented videos requires a license.

By law, as well as by intent, prerecorded videocassettes and videodiscs available for rental or purchase are for home use only. You must have a license to show them in any other setting. Rentals or purchases of home videocassettes do not carry with them licenses for nonhome showings.

These rules are stated in the Federal Copyright Act, Public Law 94-553, Title 17 of the United States Code. Any institution, organization, company, or individual wishing to engage in nonhome showings of home videocassettes must obtain a special license to show video materials. Among other rights, the Copyright Act grants to the copyright owner the exclusive right "to perform the copyrighted work publicly" (Section 106).

Obtaining a license for nonhome use of copyrighted materials.

Licenses to show motion pictures at a church meeting and to display song lyrics are available through the following businesses, as well as through other channels:

✔ Motion Picture Licensing Corporation, P.O. Box 66970, Los Angeles, CA 90066. 800/462-8855. The MPLC offers an umbrella license for a number of studios whose films are already available for rental. They charge an affordable yearly fee. mplc.com.

✔ Swank Motion Pictures, 201 S. Jefferson Avenue, St. Louis, Missouri 63103-2579. 800/876-5577, swank.com. Swank offers copies with license for public showings of films not yet available for rent.

✔ Criterion Pictures, 800/890-9494

✔ Christian Copyright Licensing International (CCLI), 17201 N.E. Sacramento St., Portland, OR 97230. 800/234-2446 or ccli.com.

Event budget, facilities, registration, and evaluation

Although sometimes difficult to estimate and time consuming to develop, accurate budgets are essential to a financially successful event.

Chapter preview

- ► Budget criteria
- ► Getting at the per-person cost
- ► Event facilities
- ► Facility negotiation
- ► Registration
- ► The measure of success
- ► Case studies
- ► **Quick Start**: Customizing your event sign-up sheet

Budget criteria

The estimating process for retreat budgets—or large events where a fee is charged to students—includes many of the same questions that you need to ask regarding a general budget (see the finance chapter page 95). Basing a budget on specific, accurate prices is critical to the budget's effectiveness. There are a lot of variables to consider.

First, determine your budget criteria. Your socioeconomic area, for example, directly affects how much you can charge your students. Determine the most that you can charge the students for the activity and not exclude potential attendees. Then ask if you should—

- ► charge your staff to attend the event. If so, how much?
- ► charge your volunteer staff to attend the event. If so, how much?
- ► have scholarships for your students. If so, how do you determine need?
- ► pay your hourly staff when working at an event. If so, how much?
- ► cut expenses for the event to lower the price. If so, what would you cut out completely? What would you trim to save money?

Based on your answers to the budget questions—and keeping in mind your event purpose and group size—you can get a good sense of your budget. Your budget then informs your facility choice. What accommodations can the group afford and still accomplish the event's purpose: tents, rustic camp, retreat center, or hotel?

Retreat centers

▶ Typically, camps and retreat centers give you one, all-inclusive price per person for the entire event, and the prices are more affordable than hotels. However, you get what you pay for. You might be expected to do anything from table setup to cleaning your own bathrooms. Many retreat facilities offer administrative and setup staff only during daytime hours. Double check to make sure your needs will be met for setup and for emergencies.

Smart Tip

To avoid pricing your students out of an event, slightly overprice less costly events to make a small percentage of money to subsidize more costly events.

Getting at the per-person cost

To select categories to include on a retreat budget, think through what will occur during your event. List all the areas, with their associated costs. Some costs start as per-person costs, and some are bulk costs that have to be translated into per-person costs.

▶ **Per-person costs**

- housing (what the location charges for a person to stay there)
- food (what the facility charges per meal, per person)
- transportation (tickets)
- materials (what will be provided to each individual)
- activities charged per person (any addtional entrance fees)

▶ **Bulk costs**

- meeting space (reserving a hotel meeting room or other space where the whole group gathers)
- sound system (rental or purchase)
- staff costs (counselors, speakers, chaperones)
- hospitality (snacks, door prizes)
- decorations (for tables, walls, stage)
- registration
- office supplies

After totaling the bulk cost for a given expense, translate your bulk costs to per-person costs by dividing the total cost for one category by the number of attendees. For example, if renting a 50-passenger bus costs $500 and 50 students are signed up, the cost per person is $10 ($500 ÷ 50 = $10). What if only 40 students sign up? Then your cost per person for transportation goes up to $12.50 per person ($500 ÷ 40 = $12.50). The **Event Budget** form leads you through the process.

FasTrack

44 You want to charge the least amount to your students (so that as many students as possible can participate), but you can't regularly lose money on your event or you jeopardize future ministry or events.

Event facilities

Y our facility is your home away from home and needs to be comfortable and appropriate for you, as well as for your students. If it's 20-below, and you're staying in a drafty barn, your students won't catch anything but a cold. Conversely, if you're thinking of shutting high-energy kids in with hanging chandeliers at the Hilton, you'll only drive yourself out of ministry.

On first contact with a facility, ask them to check their calendar to see if they have available space on your selected dates. If not, check alternate times that could work for you. If you can plan enough in advance, you can offer several date options to facilities. If they're booked on all the dates you have available, ask them to send you an information packet for future reference—and keep dialing.

Before making your final selection, always conduct site inspections of facilities under serious consideration. (See the **Site Inspection** form.) Even if you've conducted dozens and dozens of site inspections and feel like you're really good at it—take good notes and answer all the questions on the form. Some facilities wine and dine you, and others merely give you a quickie tour. If you fill out the **Site Inspection** form, your recollection of the facility will be more objective. (Just don't let the T-bone steak with mushroom gravy weigh too heavily in your thinking.) At least tour the sleeping rooms, general session room, and meeting spaces. Take time to envision what the rooms will look like when they're full of your students: *Is there enough space in the halls? Will you be staying too close to other guests? What's the worst damage that could occur? What might it cost you?*

Dollars and cents will probably weigh heaviest in choosing your event facility. Be sure you compare apples with apples. Although it's difficult to compare a retreat center to a hotel, in the financial midrange, upscale retreat centers compete with the lower-end hotels. Each kind of facility has its pros and cons. Make sure you know all the costs involved before you choose which way to head.

Event Budget
page 282

Site Inspection
page 310

Hotels

▶ In general, hotels cost more. They charge per room (leaving you to decide how to divide the cost per person), and they charge per person for food costs. Hotels vary in service quality, but in most cases are much more service-oriented than camps and retreat centers. When they say they'll do something, they do it. Hotels are often more open to negotiating details.

For example, the more sleeping rooms you take, the less they charge you for your meeting space. Also, hotels make their gravy on food and beverages. That means, crazy as it sounds, that it's sometimes less expensive to eat more. As your food dollars go up, your meeting space charges go down. In essence, you pay the same dollars but get a meal for it.

▶ Hotels come with three major downsides:

1) They charge you for every add-on—sleeping cots, extra snacks, et cetera, which can kill your budget.

2) If you break it, you buy it.

3) Student noise and behavior can disturb other hotel guests.

Smart Tip

Although hotels are generally more work on the front end, it usually pays off with the service on the back end.

The savvy negotiator

▶ You never want the facility to give up everything in the first round of negotiations. Going straight to their rock-bottom price won't leave any room for favors. The first time at the table, you may negotiate only until the facility manager gets a little uncomfortable. To know where they draw the line, you might push them until they say no.

But don't push them in every area. You might get a lower sleeping room price and but not push them on the food prices. Later—when you recognize you'll need an additional night snack, some vegetarian plates not mentioned in the meal plan, or a change in setup here or there that wasn't originally in the contract—you can ask them if they'll throw it in for you at no additional cost.

If you pull out of them in the beginning what you believe is every little detail you need, they'll end up charging you for every little change that you make after the contract is signed. Believe me, you don't want that.

Facility negotiation

The rule of thumb on negotiation is to keep working the numbers until both you and the facility representative are happy. You want to walk away knowing that you received a fair deal and that your needs will be met. A reputable hotel lives to serve their clients and will bend over backward to do so. A nonreputable or lower-end hotel, however, will be an annoyance to you every step of the way. Choose carefully. Also, be aware that hotels can often feel like they nickel-and-dime you to death. There are hidden costs that can kill your budget—and you won't know about it till the event is over.

Retreat and camping facilities vary greatly with respect to fees and in management structures. Investigate the management. Get to know the person who will be assisting your group with logistics. That person can make or break your retreat. Know him by name, and keep in frequent contact with him. Retreat facilities generally negotiate less on the per-person fees than hotels, but offer more flexibility on the programming side. Be very specific about your needs and your expectations so you're not surprised. For example, hotel staff is available 24/7. At a retreat center, the staff often go home at a certain hour.

The fine art of negotiations is a book of its own. These few tips will be helpful, but not close to thorough. If you are facilitating a large group and are using a hotel property, your best bet is to use a professional meeting planner to do the negotiating for you. In one author's experience, she has saved literally thousands of dollars just because of the professional planner's expertise. In general, the larger the group, the more room for negotiation. The smaller the group, the less flex the facility will agree to. Retreat properties negotiate little. It's best to ask them up front what their best price is and then live with it. If the experience is successful and you wish to use the facility again, come back to the table ready to talk about possible cost reduction or extra amenities. Sometimes they'll work with you to get your business back.

FasTrack

45 You'll always cover your expenses if you follow this basic formula: Divide all expenses by the lowest number of students that might attend the retreat. That way, if you only meet your minimum student attendance, you'll still make your budget.

Registration

From the moment students arrive at the event, they should experience the energy of the planning your team has done. The theme and purpose of the event can begin its trek into their hearts, even during registration. Set the stage for what's ahead by making registration festive and inviting. Easily overlooked as unrelated to the "real" event itself, registration can take an unexpected chunk out of your event time if it's done haphazardly.

Disney World is the master at moving masses of people efficiently. Use that model to lay out registration. Leave open spaces. Spread tables out. Train more staff than you think you need. Form follows function. Think logically about what needs to happen when, and set up your registration accordingly.

➤ Students arrive to register.

➤ They put down their luggage. (Where?)

➤ They pick up their registration packets. (How will they locate them?)

➤ They turn in their permission forms. (How will your team verify them? Where will they file them?)

➤ When they pick up their packets, they'll find out if they owe money. (What is the process for them to pay off their accounts?)

➤ Students with special medical needs go from registration or finance to the nurse's table to register their meds or discuss their medical needs. (Does this require a private setting?)

➤ Students return to pick up their luggage and head for the bus that's marked with their corresponding numbers. (When and how do they learn which bus they're on? What if they want to trade buses to ride with friends?)

➤ A couple of students may have made arrangements for a friend to pick them up around the corner of the building to take off for the weekend and show up again when you unload the buses. (Will you know that they are gone? What supervision is in place to be sure students actually leave on their bus?)

➤ Parents pick up an information brochure providing the name, address, and phone number of the facility and a map showing how to get there. Include contact information for the leadership team at the event in case of an emergency. (Who is available to answer their questions?)

Meeting space set-up

You'll need to answer these questions for each room you use, both for general sessions and breakouts.

➤ Do you require staging? If so, what size and what height?

➤ Do you want chairs? How many? Set up in which way?

— *Theater*: chairs in rows, all facing front.

— *Classroom*: narrow tables with chairs behind them, all facing front.

— *Rounds*: round tables for 6-10 people each (good for discussions; bad for lectures).

— *Cocktail rounds*: round tables for 3-4.

— *Table square*: Four or eight tables set in a square. Participants sit around the outer edge of the table facing each other.

(Generally you are not charged for chairs or tables.)

➤ How many tables and where? Do you need numbers on the tables to indicate where students sit?

➤ Do you need information tables?

➤ Do you want the tables skirted?

➤ Do you want water service in the meeting rooms?

➤ What audiovisual equipment do you need?

➤ Is there a Green Room near the staging area for the musicians and speakers?

Event insurance

➤ On occasion you may take out an insurance policy in addition to your standard coverage. The additional insurance would cover unavoidable accidents, mishaps, or cancellations. One company that deals with not-for-profit event insurance is located at galescreek.com. You can check out their policy and coverage there.

The measure of success

We've looked at what it takes to program and execute an event. These three questions can help you to measure its success.

➤ Did students and leaders show any movement of growth toward God?

➤ Did you meet your event goals and measure up to your expectations?

➤ From a logistical standpoint, did you create a God-honoring event that you're proud to identify with?

FasTrack

46 Facility representatives expect you to negotiate every offer they make—don't disappoint them.

Base your evaluation on the totality of the event—in particular, how effectively students' hearts turned toward God as a result of your efforts. If you can look back over your event and answer yes, you've had a successful event. Every event has potholes and bumps along the way. If you see marks of spiritual growth, if you met your goals, if no logistical difficulties overshadowed it, then you have hit the mark. Well done!

Smart Tip

You don't know what the best price is until you have negotiated a "no."

Tips for the negotiator

➤ Always come to the table with a kind, friendly attitude.

➤ Act in a professional manner.

➤ Think smart.

➤ If you don't understand, ask.

➤ Come across as the decision-maker, but if you're feeling pressured to sign something, don't hesitate to use your boss as an excuse to buy yourself some processing time. ("It looks good to me, but there are a few things that I would like to run by the senior pastor before I sign." Or say, "I need a few days to think about it. I'll get back to you then.") (See "What You Need to Know About Contracts" page 141.)

➤ You're not ready to finish the deal until you feel good about it.

Real Life

I once had a high school group that added $1,000 to its bill with breakage. On top of that, we ended up paying another $1,000 to pacify unhappy guests in the rooms next door who either had to be moved or had left the facility because of our noise. (One of the disgruntled guests was Keanu Reeves. I guess I would be irritated, too, if a group of giddy, screaming high school girls was chasing me.)

Case studies

▶ **Mission trip mania**

It's December and you're starting to make plans for taking 30 students on a mission trip over spring break. Your destination is any distant country where your kids can experience another culture, as well as develop a heart toward service. What are your options for effectively planning, preparing, and executing a mission trip in the next three months?

▶ **Making the most of little**

You lead a small youth ministry with a dozen students and one volunteer. As a part-time youth worker finishing up seminary, you don't have a lot of time to plan an event. Your students don't have much money to put toward an event, either. What should you do?

▶ **Wrestling with tradition**

You're the new kid on the block in a ministry that has been using the same summer camp for the last half century. Parents say things like, "I got saved at that camp back in 1961, and I want my kids to have a good camp experience, too." Although steeped in tradition, the camp is not well maintained. In some cases, it's literally falling apart. During your site inspection you felt compelled to ask, "When was the last time you had the camp inspected by the fire marshal, and did it pass?" You'd like to see your group go to a better facility—one that has flush toilets, say, and lights that are actually attached to the ceiling rather than hanging by the wires. What do you do?

▶ **The best laid plans…**

You're directing a huge, weeklong event that's one week away. It's crunch time. You've signed up 300 students, 50 staff, and a big-time speaker. You've verified the facility, double-checked the transportation. Your staff is trained, and you've even completed your housing lists. Then, you receive a phone call that no leader ever wants to receive—your speaker slipped a disk in her back and must cancel. What do you do?

Registration time savers

▶ Waiting in long lines can leave a bad first impression. Shorten the process by preparing ahead of time as much of the registration process as possible.

▶ Clearly mark the areas where students sign in and strategically place volunteers to assist and direct when needed.

▶ Lay out your floor plan to leave plenty of space for all activities to be done in an orderly fashion. Traffic should always move in one direction when there are multiple stations.

▶ Place trained volunteers at each station for efficiency. Plan for enough staff to handle the most congestion possible, and then you'll be able to meet your time deadlines.

▶ Place in one large envelope completed name tags labeled with group and room (and transportation) assignments. Include curriculum, an event schedule, and any other instructions for participants.

▶ Divide the retreat roster into manageable, alphabetical chunks (2-4 groups). You might end up having three tables labeled A–F, G–L, and M-Z.

▶ Designate one table as a solutions table, where a student can receive help from a trained volunteer without clogging up the system.

▶ At events where registration occurs before travel, number all the buses so that students easily recognize which bus they are to ride. Have a roster for each bus leader to verify, both coming and going, that each student is on board.

► **Snow im-mobile**

It's 5 p.m. on the Friday evening of the winter retreat, one hour from departure. You've already paid a nonrefundable $3,000 deposit for the facility and bus fees of $800. At one end of the parking lot, four buses are warming up their engines for the 150-mile trip. At the other end, 175 students are eagerly lining up to complete registration. You've been listening to the weather report all day, and six to eight inches of snow have been predicted for this evening. Anxious parents are now hovering around you as the first snowflakes begin to fall. What do you do?

❑ Cancel the trip and send the students home.

❑ Keep on schedule and pray that the snow doesn't affect the trip.

❑ Cancel the trip and have an overnight lock-in instead.

❑ Having prepared for such a contingency, forge ahead with your original plan.

FasTrack

47 Evaluate the *total* event—neither berate nor congratulate your event management on the basis of one or two of its pieces.

Real Life

The crisis in "Snow im-mobile" (left) actually happened to me—but the stakes were even higher. About 550 students, 12 motor coach busses, 75 staff, and thousands of dollars of nonrefundable fees already paid weighed in on our decision whether to brave the snow or do a lock-in. What did we do? We forged on with our original plan and drove to he retreat center.

Here's why: In the planning stages of the retreat, we prepared for this possibility. We upgraded our busses from regular school buses to motor coaches so that weather wouldn't adversely affect our travel. We also laid out a plan to comfort concerned parents—we left voice mail on our office phone with hourly updates. Also, three parents in their personal vehicles tracked the buses to keep an eye on the situation and to make sure that, in spite of the snow, the students were safe. If the snow had made the roads impassable, we would have pulled over into a rest area until it was safe to travel. In addition to counselors, every bus had a competent leader in charge, with a cell phone. Each bus leader had an envelope with parent permission forms for all their students, just in case.

We made it up to the retreat center, in five hours (not the normal three). After adjusting our schedule by cutting out several programmed activities, we kicked off the retreat with our first general session at 11 p.m. on the night we arrived. The students loved the late hour, and the retreat was a success.

For the record, nonrefundable fees should never be the most important consideration in a case like this. At the contract-signing stage, you may request the facility to write in some safeguards for emergencies. At least contact the facility to ask if you can reschedule if weather conditions change your plans. You may have to eat the deposits. No dollar amount, however, is worth risking the safety of your students. That is nonnegotiable.

Quick Start

Customizing your event sign-up sheet

A much less complicated but necessary part of event registration is the pre-event sign-up. Event facilities want to know one or two weeks ahead of time exactly how many are coming to the event. That means you need a list of students, adult leaders, and speakers or entertainment who have committed to be there. For speakers and entertainment you have their contract to assure you. Students need to pay their registration fees before you can count on their participation. So before you give a final count to a facility, use the **Single-Event Registration** to track attendees and their payments. Open the form in your word processor and fill in the event information in the page header.

Some ministries have several event sign-ups going on at the same time. Use the **Multiple-Event Registration** form to minimize paper shuffling at the sign-up table. Be sure to note which participants have turned in their medical release and/or permission forms. If you don't have one already, check out the **Authorization for Medical Treatment** on page 391.

Single-Event Registration page 395

Multiple-Event Registration page 393

Authorization for Medical Treatment page 391

Recommended resources

▶ *Conferences Incorporated, senior meeting planner,* Linda Daniels (P.O. Box 100, Wheaton, IL 60187)

▶ *Religious Conference Management Association (RCMA)* Indianapolis, IN, 317/632-1888. rcmaweb.org. (member benefits, training conferences)

▶ *International Conference Center Association (ICCA)*

▶ Portions of this chapter are printed with permission from the event chapter of *Camping and Retreating,* Bo Boshers (Zondervan,1998)

Tools to help you stay in youth ministry

PART 3

Sometimes it seems youth workers use the revolving door of the church more than any other church staffers. (When was the last time you heard of someone looking up their old youth pastor from a decade ago and finding that she's still at the same church?)

What we can't understand is why youth workers burn out when they get to lead exhausting lock-ins with really bad pizza and generic soda, sing never-ending choruses, and play a hundred games of Uno during *loooong* bus rides, sleep on dirt floors during weeklong mission trips, and run sparely attended fundraisers. (Then again, maybe we *can* understand why.)

Perhaps youth ministers can survive five and 10 and 15 years in the same church when they experience a synergy of—

- ▶ team support among staff, administrators, and parents.
- ▶ personal maturity that affects how they manage the risks inherant to youth ministry.
- ▶ practical preparation to pursue their calling.

A **strong team** doesn't happen by accident. It takes intentional recruitment, careful screening, discerning when to say no to certain people and yes to others, and lots of prayer. It takes knowing when it's time to bring on an intern

A safe ministry is founded on planning ways to protect your students from injury and ways to manage the crises that get past your protective grid. Even though we know God is in control, and we pray for his protection over our ministries, as the responsible adults, we're obligated to manage potential risk and prepare ourselves, our staff, and our students for both the avoidable and the unavoidable mishaps—even tragedies.

A career in youth ministry may be born in your passion, but it matures as you go through the process of seeking a job, evaluating available positions, and leaving a ministry gracefully so you're free to move into a new position.

Part 3 **provides both tools and *wisdom learned firsthand*** to help you make a career of ministering among teens.

Team building

It's 3 p.m. on a Sunday afternoon. You're standing in the church parking lot with a smelly sleeping bag, a half-empty bag of Doritos, and the insides of a couple of cans of shaving cream.

You've just sent the last kid home from the retreat, and you look around at an exhausted group of volunteers. Somebody suggests heading out for burgers and you think, "Bed or burgers?" You know in a second what your decision will be—as bone tired as you are, you want to spend just a little more time with this group of people to hear their stories and to celebrate the weekend.

Because that's what it means to be part of a team with members who are committed to each other.

Being a team member is about standing up at each other's weddings. It's about getting up before sunrise in order to get to the hospital to pray together before one of you has surgery. It's about bringing over red Jell-O with mandarin oranges to a home whose cook is ill, or green beans with cream of mushroom soup and little crunchy onion rings when a baby is born. (In fact, you may want to make cooking a qualification for being on your team.)

Team building is about creating community together. It's about doing ministry together.

In Team building—

17. Building a healthy team
18. Recruiting volunteers
19. Life cycle of team members
20. Developing interns

Building a healthy team

17

"It's difficult to work in a group when you're omnipotent."
Q, "Star Trek: The Next Generation"

Chapter preview
- ► Why you need a team
- ► Make way for volunteers
- ► Roles for volunteers
- ► Expectations of spiritual maturity
- ► Lifestyle expectations
- ► Participation requirements
- ► Relational expectations
- ► Expectations of length of service
- ► **Quick Start**: Identify spiritual gifts and arenas of interest

Why you need a team

V arious needs of both adolescents and the adults who work with them make team ministry essential.

► **The need of this generation.** Whereas adolescents used to have all sorts of adults with whom to connect—parents, grandparents, Scout leaders, teachers, coaches, Sunday school teachers—these days those connections are fewer and disappear faster. Students have much more coming at them, but they have fewer places to talk about what's going on in their lives. (Perhaps that's why so many of them are turning to chat rooms.)

► **The need for multiplication**. Experience shows that a person can develop only a limited number of relationships in the limited amount of time available. That means you have a choice—you can pour your life into 15 kids, and at the end of the year you'll have affected 15 kids. Or you can spend your time developing five or 10 volunteers (and five kids on the side because that's why you're doing this in the first place), and those 10 volunteers in turn nurture five or 10 kids each. At the end of the year you'll have reached anywhere from 30 to 105 kids and five to 10 adults.

Worship team

▶ **Worship team leader.** Gives direction to the team, both on a personal and a performance ministry level. *5 hours a week*

▶ **Band members.** Guitar, drums, keyboard, et cetera. *4 hours a week, includes rehearsal time*

▶ **Drama leader.** Develops a team of students to perform once a month. *10 hours a week*

▶ **Script writers.** Students and adults who write scripts that minister to high school students. *5 hours a week*

▶ **Drama team members.** Students and adults who perform scripts to minister to high school students. *4 hours a week*

▶ **Director of a student arts festival.** An entrepreneurial type who understands the importance of the arts in communicating the gospel to this generation, who knows how to organize and promote a festival, and who can coach a team of volunteers to assist in the development. *Varying time commitment*

▶ **The need to use our gifts.** Youth workers do everything from designing brochures to reserving buses to counseling kids in crisis. In other words, we spend a lot of energy doing things that pull us away from what we're good at because of what Charles Hummel calls the "tyranny of the urgent." Volunteers can help out by bringing their gifts and passions to the team. If one of your weak areas is graphic design, for instance, and yet you find yourself spending hours designing camp fliers, pray and search for someone in your church who has a background in design. He may have never have thought about volunteering with the youth ministry because he's scared to death of having a conversation with a high schooler. But he'd love to help out with designing fliers (and the camp T-shirt). The task gets done in a third of the time and looks ten times better. You're freed up to prepare the messages, and he's using his gifts for the kingdom in a way he hadn't realized he could.

▶ **The need to use common sense.** Wherever two or more are gathered, there is more protection than if there was just one. Youth ministry tends to be both relational and risky. No youth worker these days should lead an overnighter with students and without another adult. No new volunteer should lead a group without first shadowing a veteran to watch and learn. No veteran volunteer should squeeze 10 kids into her five-seat car. The wise youth worker—and the youth worker determined to stay at one job more than two years—thinks beforehand about the consequences of scenarios like these.

> ## FasTrack
>
> **48** Unless our youth ministries are only going to consist of five kids, we're going to need some help.

> ## FasTrack
>
> **49** Your requirements for volunteer time commitment must be long enough to form relationships with students and short enough to appeal to volunteers.

Make way for volunteers

Before recruiting volunteers, take time to lay the groundwork. A strong foundation minimizes future errors. Granted, not many people ever see the foundation, but they can sure tell whether or not you had one as soon as the first major storm hits (and the storms will hit).

- **Describe the roles.** List all the roles (both existing and potential) for volunteers in the youth ministry. Let your imagination run wild. What have you been dying to see happen in the ministry but don't have the time or perhaps the ability to pull off? Jog your vision by thinking in categories, such as area of service or time required to do the service.

- **Define expectations for volunteers.** Code your phone DO NOT DISTURB, or head out to the local coffee shop with your laptop. However you can, get some uninterrupted time to write out your expectations for volunteers in youth ministry—expectations for spiritual maturity, lifestyle, and participation.

What would you do?

Julia, hired to oversee kindergarten through senior high ministries, set as her first priority getting to know those already working with the kids. She learned that one of the grade school Sunday school teachers was a white witch. It had happened this way: During the past few years, this woman's husband and child had become Christians. She was curious about what they believed in, and decided to check out Christianity. The pastor's sermons were over her head, she told Julia, and she didn't quite follow what went on in the Bible study her husband attended. She did understand the stories and lessons in her child's Sunday school class, however; so she started to help out there. She ended up teaching.

Question: Should Julia let her stay or ask her to stop teaching? Why or why not?

Small groups

- **Adult leaders.** Adults who meet with a group of 3-8 students on a weekly basis for Bible study, prayer, and discussion. *4 hours a week*

- **Student leaders.** Current members of the high school ministry who desire to test their leadership skills by leading a small group of their peers. *4 hours a week*

- **Coach.** An adult volunteer who helps shepherd the student small group leaders. *4 hours a week*

Hands-on team

- **Greeters.** Parents who make new students feel welcome, gather permission slips, and hand out fliers. They also connect with other parents who may have questions. *2 hours a week*

- **Hosts.** Parents who provide both food and a place for small groups to meet, either on a regular basis or for special occasions. *Variable time commitment*

- **Drivers.** Parents who chauffeur the middle schoolers to various ministry events. *4 hours a month*

- **Office help.** Parents with an administrative bent who can organize and maintain a student database, send out mailings, call on event details, follow up on explanations on medical release forms, maintain the ministry computer. *Variable time commitment*

Specialty teams

- **Light and sound.** A team of students who run the sound system on retreats and special occasions.

- **Technology.** Includes an adult or student who can put your messages on PowerPoint or other presentation software and a Web-site designer who works with the promotion team to put the latest news and information on the Internet.

- **Graphic design.** Either a student or an adult with a strong graphic design bent who can put together newsletters, ministry brochures, fliers, posters, banners, birthday cards, welcome cards, and so on.

- **Games.** Adults or students who run weekly competitions or monthly events, like three-on-three basketball tournaments for outreach, the Valentine's Day parent-student 10K run, or the annual senior-citizens-versus-the-senior-highers sand volleyball competition.

- **Fundraising.** Adults with marketing, accounting, and entrepreneurial experience to run several fundraisers—or one large fundraiser—each year. Make sure they work with your church treasurer to stay within the ethical and legal boundaries of fundraising.

- **Public relations.** Calls for someone with a strong marketing background or who can creatively communicate to a large group. This may require only a minimal commitment, so team members can also serve as leaders in other areas.

- **Special events and projects.** Adults and students who develop service projects, mission trips, parent-student events.

- **Driving.** Adults who help transport students. To screen drivers use the **Driver Application (page 400)**.

One youth pastor's solution: Julia made the call to let her stay—provided that the woman serve in an assisting role only—helping to set up art projects and treats. She could have no direct relationship with any of the kids. The other teachers in the classroom knew the boundaries and accepted the woman in the role of helper. Two years later the woman was baptized after becoming a Christian.

P.S.: Julia had quite a few years of experience in ministry and was able to set firm boundaries for her volunteers when she had to. Her decision, of course, is not recommended for all similar situations. But considering who Julia was, who the volunteer was, and their common situation, the arrangement worked.

What would you do?

A 30-year-old man you interview for a volunteer position with your youth group states that he had been involved in several homosexual relationships in college. Although those experiences happened several years ago, he admits to having struggles with old desires during the past six months. Since he didn't want to repeat the homosexual behavior, he joined an accountability group. He says everything is fine now, but he just wanted to be up front with you about his personal history.

Question: Do you bring him on board or not?

One youth worker's solution: The youth pastor decided to bring him on board with the following stipulations:

- He must remain in the accountability group.

- For the first six months of volunteering, he must take a job offering no direct contact with students.

- The situation will be reevaluated at the end of the six months.

What would you do?

Y ou've just come off a weekend retreat, and the volunteers decide to go out for pizza to celebrate and tell stories. You offer to wait at the church for the last kid to be picked up and then meet up with them. Thirty minutes later you arrive at the restaurant. While you're still outside, you notice through the window a pitcher of beer on the table. The ministry has a well-known policy of no alcohol at church-related gatherings. What do you do?

❑ Turn around and go home. You could use the sleep anyway.

❑ Let it go. After all, this isn't strictly a ministry event since the volunteers initiated it.

❑ Go in and confront the team.

❑ Go in and hope that this is just someone's idea of a practical joke.

❑ Other:

Relational expectations

S upport your volunteers by clearly describing what kind of relationship you expect them to have with students. Without guidance the extroverts will try to build a life-changing relationship with every kid in the group, and the introverts will merely show up and sit in the back. Okay, that's an overgeneralization—but volunteers do want to know if they're to meet with students only during the scheduled meeting times, or if you expect them to contact students outside those gatherings. Are weekly phone calls an expectation? Do you want your small group leaders to get the students together for an activity once a month? Or would you be thrilled if a leader does it once

Smart Tip

One youth worker uses the Instant Messaging feature on her online service to carry on conversations with several kids at the same time.

Expectations of spiritual maturity

What level of spiritual maturity are you looking for in volunteers? Is it okay for some of the volunteers to be new believers? Seekers? Or do they need to have major portions of scripture tattooed to their forearms before you'll even consider them?

A good rule of thumb: Volunteers who have direct and regular contact with students (a small-group leader, for example) need a well-developed faith that they can easily articulate. A behind-the-scenes volunteer who does data entry or acts as the sound technician can be a new or nonbeliever. The main objective of your youth ministry is probably not evangelization of adult volunteers, though. Make sure you keep your main thing the main thing.

We like to make a distinction between our private and public lives and say, "Whatever I do in my private life is nobody else's business." But anyone trying to live a spiritual life will soon discover that the most personal is the most universal, the most hidden is the most public, and the most solitary is the most communal.

(**Henri Nouwen**. *Bread for the Journey*. HarperCollins Publishers, 1997)

Lifestyle expectations

Think through the following lifestyle concerns. What is your personal view on each one? What are your organization's expectations regarding each lifestyle for its staff and volunteers?

Alcohol

What is the view of your church or organization about Christians drinking alcohol? What is your view?

Does your church have a policy about alcohol being served at church events?

If volunteers must sign a ministry covenant of any sort, does it include a statement regarding alcohol?

Drug use

How long does someone need to be "clean" before he can work with students?

Can someone attending a 12-step program also minister among your students?

Clothing

Different cultures, subcultures, and regions have different standards of appropriateness in dress. How can you be culturally sensitive without being legalistic or scandalous?

What reasons are there for and against providing guidelines for what clothing you and your church consider appropriate for your culture for a given activity?

Sexuality

What is the view of your church or organization about homosexuality as a lifestyle for Christians? What is your view?

Does your church have a policy about people who are homosexual serving in leadership positions?

Can someone who has acknowledged having homosexual experiences earlier in life minister among your students?

What is the view of your church or organization about having had premarital or extramarital relations once? About living together unmarried? What is your view about these things?

If volunteers have sex outside of marriage or with a partner other than their spouse, what are the ramifications for their ministry with the youth? Counseling? Removal from ministry? A probationary period?

a year? If initiating extra activities with students is among your expectations for volunteers, consider offering a small stipend to cover expenses—fast food, gas, et cetera.

What expectations do you have of a volunteer's relationship to you? Do they need to meet with you on a regular basis? It's important that volunteers can regularly have access to you, one-on-one, to share their joys as well as their frustrations. Set up regular evaluations where they can evaluate both you and the ministry. Remember, you're there to serve them as they serve God through ministering to kids.

Smart Tip

Keep the culture in mind

For volunteers who believe that spending time together is more important than starting on schedule, a 6 p.m. meeting won't start till everyone has informally traded news and enjoyed a few munchies. For volunteers who live by their Palm® organizer, a 6 p.m. meeting that doesn't get rolling until 6:15 p.m. frustrates and discourages them. By placing on the agenda crucial, relationship-building activities like eating and socializing, you honor both styles…and even keep to the schedule.

Quick Start

Identify spiritual gifts and areas of interest

Many tools for discerning spiritual gifts are currently in use in churches. Find out right away if your church offers workshops or adult classes on spiritual gifts. Prospective volunteers who have taken the classes may already know that youth ministry suits their interests and abilities.

You can use the following questions to help volunteers identify their areas of interest and discern the most appropriate area in which they might serve.

Area of service

Find out what triggers a person to dream and plan and take action. That arena is where she'll find most satisfaction and where you'll get her best work.

- What keeps you awake at night (beside too much coffee)?
- What do you find yourself pounding the table over?
- What would your friends say is a recurring theme in your conversations?
- What topics do you find yourself drawn to read about?
- What Web trail do you find yourself following—music, movies, youth culture, counseling?

Spiritual gifts and natural abilities

Sometimes these overlap; sometimes not.

- What activities brought you joy, energy, or success in early childhood? In grade school? Middle school? High school? College? As a young adult?
- What are the recurring themes of your memories?
- What verbs do you find yourself using—organizing, creating, discussing, building, performing, writing?
- What patterns do you discern?
- What insights have you gained in spiritual gifts workshops (like Network or Life Keys) or from sermons or Christian teaching?

Participation requirements

What level of participation do you expect from team members?

- Do you require church membership and worship attendance? Can it be at another church?
- Do all ministry roles carry the same expectations for participation? Is the head of the drama team expected to be at Sunday school, for instance, even though she has no responsibilities during that time?
- Must volunteers attend both the Wednesday night Bible study and Sunday school?
- Must they attend weekly prep meetings? Quarterly volunteer training day?
- Do they need to attend all retreats, mission trips, and camps?
- How often do you expect them to meet one-on-one with you? Every month? Every other month?
- How long do you expect them to serve?

Expectations on length of service

Many people hesitate to volunteer for fear they're signing up for an unending commitment. Write into the job description how long you're asking them to serve. Some ministries require commitment for one school year: leadership training and development in mid-August, ministry kick-off in early September, and ministry closeout in early June. A summer team of interns comes in from June through August to allow the regular leaders to take the summer off to relax. One ministry that used the school-year commitment had leaders who stayed an average of three years. The leaders started with a group of sixth graders and stayed with them until they went to high school. The summers off allowed them to recuperate and come back eager to serve.

It's a good idea to add up the amount of time you expect volunteers to give each week. Also chart how many ongoing meetings they need to attend. You may begin to see why you have difficulty recruiting people. Adults generally won't give up two nights a week to be at church.

Schedule as many "crossroads" meetings as possible. If the team is going to be at church on Sunday morning anyway, for instance, can you provide early morning donuts and Starbucks Coffee and have your weekly prep or check an hour before church starts? Can team members come an hour before the Bible study starts on Wednesday night for training, rather than making a special trip on Saturday?

Spiritual gifts

From the following list, choose those spiritual gifts you feel you already use. (Some of these gifts are alluded to rather than named in the Bible.)

    Administration

    Creative communication

    Counseling

    Discernment

    Encouragement

    Evangelism

    Helps

    Hospitality

    Leadership

    Listening

    Mediation

    Mercy

    Shepherding

    Teaching

In what way have those close to you (who are honest with you) affirmed those gifts?

Smart Tip

The Cocktail Party Principle
In case you haven't figured it out yet, food always helps motivate people to get to a meeting. Besides that, people tend to talk more freely when they have food or a drink in their hand. No wonder eating and parties show up so often in the Bible.

Recruiting volunteers

Let volunteers feel that they will be shepherded, cared for, built into, developed.

Chapter preview	
	► Create job descriptions
	► Generic components of job descriptions
	► Leadership development opportunities
	► Insurance coverage
	► Develop an application
	► Uncovering potential volunteers
	► Screening volunteers
	► **Quick Start:** Plugging in a volunteer

Create job descriptions

O nce you've determined the roles you need filled and your expectations for those different roles, you're ready to create job descriptions. A person who doesn't know his purpose for being there won't stick around. Worse yet, it will be next to impossible to ever get him to consider coming back to the youth ministry. So before you challenge people to consider being a part of the team, know what you're going to ask them to do.

Another reason for a job description is to help you screen applicants. By clearly articulating what you expect from a volunteer, you establish what is known as bona fide occupational qualifications, or BOQs. In case an applicant wants to take legal action against you or the ministry because of the information you're requesting for screening, the BOQs help protect you. They help ensure that you are not arbitrarily asking questions or discriminating. If a volunteer will work with young children, for example, you have a legitimate reason to inquire about their history in working with minors (*RiskFacts: Screening Staff and Volunteers: A Guide for Action and Caution*, Nonprofit Risk Management Center, Washington D.C.).

FasTrack

50 One of the quickest ways to de-motivate people is to inspire them to volunteer and then neglect to tell them what to do.

Generic components of a job description

Job title. Head the job descriptions with a one-to-three-word phrase that sums up the role and describes the job focus—Small Group Leader, Games Team Member, Newsletter Designer.

Ministry mission statement. Write a one-sentence description of the ultimate purpose of the youth ministry—"To glorify God and enjoy him fully through serving middle schoolers and serving the team that works with them…To assist students in the development of their Christian faith…To challenge the students at Second Church to seriously consider the claims of Christ and to act on those claims."

Mission statement for that role. Write short description of the purpose of the job—"The sound and lights team does our job with excellence so that the gospel can clearly be understood…A small-group leader challenges high school students to grow closer to Christ through conversations and activities."

Mission statement essentials

In *The Path: Creating Your Mission Statement for Work and for Life*, Laurie Beth Jones writes that there are three simple elements to a good mission statement:

1. A mission statement should be no more than a single sentence long.

2. It should be easily understood by a 12 year-old.

3. It should be able to be recited by memory at gunpoint.

Job essentials. List essential tasks for a given role—"Small group leaders build loving and supportive relationships with students, lead group discussions, develop the group's identity, support the students' families, guide students, and help build the larger ministry team through encouraging other leaders, supporting ministry efforts, and networking to recruit new leaders."

Gift areas. Names spiritual gifts or natural abilities essential to handling this role—"A small group leader is gifted to teach or to shepherd teens…An office team leader is a gifted administrator…The game director is gifted in teaching and leadership (is there a spiritual gift of "fun"?).

FasTrack

51 People want to be wanted. Qualified individuals may not be ready to say yes the first time you explain to them why you think they would be an asset in the youth ministry; but when they are ready to make a move, they'll remember your conversation. Check in periodically to see how they're doing.

Support system. Describe the number of people they'll be responsible for. Tell whether they'll be students or adults Who will support this volunteer—you or someone else? If it's someone else, make that clear. They may be wanting to join the team to spend time with you. If the interview is the only conversation they ever have with you, they'll feel disappointed—and disappointed volunteers can infect others with their frustration.

Weekly responsibilities. Describe what they would do in a given week. A small-group leader, for instance, needs to be at all Wednesday night prep meetings (1 hour), as well as at the Bible study (2 hours). They also must contact all the regularly attending students in their group by phone, postcard, or e-mail (2 hours). One hour of personal preparation on the Bible study is also expected. Total hours: 6.

Other responsibilities. Let volunteers know what activities, other than regular meetings, that they need to be at. Do they need to be at all retreats? Do they need to attend the quarterly staff training days? What is their role at the annual mission trip fundraiser?

Costs. Also, let them know what it will cost them to attend required events. Are they expected to pay for their ticket to the water park? Do they have to pay the same amount to go on the winter retreat as the students do?

Typically the ministry pays for a good portion of the event fees, and those leaders who are financially able chip in extra or insist on paying their own way. Think about it: You're asking them to give up a weekend with their family and pay $120 for the privilege. Raising the student fee by $10 helps you offset the leaders' fees.

Leadership development opportunities

What can volunteers expect to receive from the ministry? If you want a team that stays around for a long time, make them feel like they're getting more than they're giving. When you support them and help them develop their leadership abilities, they have more to give to their students, their families, and their jobs. Schedule periodic training (beginning of the school year, a midseason retreat, a six-week Sunday school session), and bring in experts to talk about a variety of topics: a panel of social workers, police, and other youth workers to talk about local gang issues; a counselor who specializes in teens with eating disorders; or kids who deal with attention-deficit or hyperactivity disorder (ADD or ADHD).

Smart Tip

Recruiting tip. Be proactive—go after those who are qualified and would be an asset to youth ministry. Over coffee describe your passion and vision for youth ministry and explain how you see them making significant contributions to the ministry.

Develop an Application

You *must* have an application on file for *everyone* who volunteers with the youth ministry, including Sunday-school-teaching institutions who helped build the church with their own hands. We'll say it again: *Everyone needs to fill out an application.* Keep applications in a locked file, along with notes from the interview and any notes dealing with disciplinary action.

You may find the **Staff Application 1** covers all the information you require to start an applicant into the process. These categories and fields must show up in some form on a ministry application:

▸ **Identification**—name, address, phone numbers: home, work—can you call them there?—cell, pager, and when is the preferable time to reach them?

▸ **Qualifications**—education, training, licenses (including driver's license)

▸ **Job experience**—positions held, current workplace name and address, years they've been at their jobs

▸ **Ministry experience**—current and past positions, along with the name of the ministry, dates of service, names and phone numbers of supervisors.

Asking about ministry experience gives you a feel for an applicant's readiness and suitability for serving in your youth ministry.

✔ You learn about their previous youth ministry experience, if any.

✔ Based on your knowledge of their tenure in past ministry jobs, you can discern their level of perseverance. If they've jumped from ministry to ministry after only a short tenure in each, find out why during the interview.

✔ You receive contact information for previous ministries. It's worth checking to see if the applicant's story of why he left jibes with the ministry's story. You learn whether she is currently working with other ministries. If your calls reveal the applicant's former church heavily relies on her, you may want to recommend that the applicant and her previous supervisor talk before you consider her application. This prevents conflict between ministries.

▸ **Family**—On the application make it clear to applicants that their response to this section is optional (this lets you avoid charges of discriminatory hiring): marital status (single, married, separated, divorced, or widowed). If married, spouse's name. If children, names and ages.

Honor an applicant's desire to leave these questions unanswered. Yet they're still worth asking, if only for getting a feel for the applicant's season of life. Those with small children who need a lot of hands-on attention may spend their time better at home than at youth group. Someone who's recently separated may be in an emotionally intense season of life, and may be better served by focusing on their personal growth for awhile before checking out the youth ministry.

Items to include in an application packet

(see **Staff Application Checklist**, **page 415**)

• Introductory letter explaining the process

• **Staff Application Process Letter**
                                page 416

• **Staff Application (1 or 2)**
                        page 408, 410

• **Staff Expectations**
                                page 417

• Church's statement of faith

• **Reducing the Risk of Physical and Sexual Abuse**
                                page 383

• **Letter of Reference for Staff Applicant** (3 copies)
                                page 402

• Health form

• Child registry (if required by church policy or state law)

• Fingerprinting (if required by church policy or state law)

➤ **Information considered to be private**—Don't include questions about age, height, weight, or personal physical information other than necessary medical questions. Don't ask about race, ethnicity, or ethnic association. Don't request a personal photo. These are not acceptable practice in the marketplace and will send up yellow flags for some people filling out the form.

➤ **Faith and accountability**—childhood church denomination (if any); year they became a Christian; years they were discipled; current small-group involvement; name and phone number of current small-group leader or mentor. (Discussing their responses is a good way to start the interview).

➤ **Church involvement**—what church; member or regular attendee; which church; how long; level of involvement in adult Sunday school or small groups. (You'll confirm whether they're receiving spiritual encouragement elsewhere. Although spiritual growth occurs among active youth leaders, they must not look to the youth ministry as their primary source of spiritual challenge.)

FasTrack

52 Honor other ministries in the church by not stealing volunteers. Talk to the people running the other ministries to make sure you have the green light to pursue a possible candidate.

➤ **Self-description**—In this section an applicant describes how she sees herself. It's a convenient checking tool to use with the references: Does the reference describe the person in the same way? You can design this section as short essay questions, as a "word salad," or any other creative way to assist the applicant to talk about herself.

➤ **Short answer essay questions**—What are your strengths? What are your shadows? How would your closest friends respond if we asked them the same questions about you?

➤ **A word salad**—Ask the applicant to circle words that best describe him and to cross out words that least describe him.

trustworthy, dependable, active, compassionate, reliable, self-starter, punctual, laid-back, flexible, quick thinker, spontaneous, decisive, night owl, teachable, team player, big tipper, humorous, thoughtful, solitary, leader, cautious, risk taker, patient, reflective, quick tempered, organized, creative, disciplined

► **A spiritual gifts assessment**—If the applicant has taken part in your church's gifts identification program, ask what he discovered about his spiritual gifts and passions. Invite him to identify the areas in which he's currently growing and how that could affect his ministry to youth.

► **Background**—Any accusations of child abuse or neglect, convictions for serious criminal or motor vehicle violations. (As with any legal area, check with your church lawyer to be sure you don't overstep your bounds in any questions you ask or background checks you request.)

► **References**—Ask applicants to list three non-related people who can identify their character weaknesses and strengths and who can speak to their ability to work with adolescents. For each reference, request an address, work or home phone number, and relationship to the applicant. You will fax or mail copies of the **Letter of Reference for Staff Applicant** to each reference. (See how to follow up reference checks on page 170.)

► **Waiver or consent**—Include on the application a line the candidate signs indicating the information given is accurate and true, and authorizing the ministry to confirm any information given. Also include a statement for signing that the applicant waives rights to confidentiality and authorizes the ministry to perform criminal background checks, reference checks, and employment or education verification. Have your church's attorney okay the waiver/release form for your use.

FasTrack

53 Because recruiting volunteers is typically difficult, we tend to lower our standards and allow most anybody to help out.

Uncover potential volunteers

Meet the new people who are looking to get involved in your church. Request copies of the interest form new members fill out during their new member class. There's usually a question like "Do you have any interest or experience in these areas: media development, musical instruments, graphic design, school counselor, Web-site developer?" (If there's not, request that it be added.) Use the information to recruit for specific roles in your ministry.

► Ask your students what adults in the church they'd like volunteering in the ministry. My students once suggested a vibrant woman in her 70s. (When I asked her if she would be interested, she had to decline because she was already leading a third-grade Sunday school class!)

Smart Tip

Recruiting tip
White-collar workers respond better to a challenge—"Make a difference in a teenager's life." Blue-collar workers respond more to encouragement—"I believe that God has gifted you to reach teenagers, and I want to help you succeed."

Check out who's worked with the current students in their younger years. Sometimes a fifth-grade Sunday school teacher really connects with a group and would like to continue into middle school with them. You'll never know unless you ask.

➤ Invite potential volunteers to a certain event or regular meeting to check out things and see how they might fit in. Let a few students and leaders know about the visit, and encourage them to introduce themselves and converse with these potential volunteers. Schedule time afterward for visitors to ask questions of you, other volunteers, and a few key students.

➤ On a Sunday right after church, hold a church-wide ministry fair that highlights opportunities for adults to help out the youth ministry. Serve lots of food.

➤ Lobby for students and leaders to speak about youth events from the pulpit as often as possible. Help the speakers plan what they'll say. Listen to them rehearse—in the auditorium, using the mike, when possible. Include stories from students about how their leader made a difference and from parents about how a leader went out of his way to reach their kid. Throw in a few slides or video clips, too. Stories can be the best motivators of all.

Screening volunteers

If a new youth pastor makes a career-limiting move, it'll likely be in volunteer screening—specifically, not doing a thorough job of it. In our passion to create programs that have an impact on kids, we may bring on a volunteer after having little more than a casual conversation with her and an usher's assurance that she's in church every week. Look at the ripples this mistake creates:

➤ **The potential for damage becomes immense.** Adults who want to harm children and adolescents really do target youth ministries. We're sticking our heads in the sand if we don't believe it.

➤ **That church's youth ministry develops the reputation of being *easy*.** People are drawn to serve where high standards characterize the ministry and where being involved carries a certain distinction.

➤ **It's difficult to get rid of someone once you bring them on board.** Saying no right up front is easier by far.

Volunteer use

Here are several ways interested people can support your ministry:

Find a person in your church with the gift of helps. These are candidates for completing simple tasks, requiring little more than *time,* that would make for smoother ministry—tasks that when tacked on to your to-do list either never get done or are just more pressure points in an already demanding schedule.

➤ Compile vendor and emergency phone numbers.

➤ Buy event supplies.

➤ Label file folders (see pages 54 to 57 for a system).

➤ Select cards for the grads.

➤ Come in weekly to file everything in your In basket.

➤ Clip (or photocopy) and file magazine articles you've flagged.

➤ Request subscribers of selected magazines to copy and label news or magazine articles relevant to a list of topics you post.

➤ Send your magazine home with a volunteer to skim the contents and photocopy and label articles for you to review.

The screening process is meant to screen out those who are not a fit, either because of a mismatch in mission, personality, giftedness, season of life, or because they pose a possible threat. Once you have an applicant who makes it through the screening process, ask yourself these questions:

▶ **Would I want my children to be in this person's small group?** Would I feel comfortable letting them be alone with him or her?

  If the answer to either of these is no, don't bring person on board.

▶ **Am I bringing this person on because I see latent potential instead of actual skills?** If the answer is yes, am I willing to take the time and energy to develop this person, or might he be better developed in a less kid-intensive ministry?

▶ **Are there any lingering questions that won't go away no matter how much I probe?** Pay attention to your intuition. In all my years of interviewing volunteers, I have never regretted paying attention to that still, small, doubting voice. When I've ignored it, however, I've deeply regretted it.

Quick Start

Plugging in a volunteer

✔ Identify the need.

✔ Get to know potential volunteers—their story, their journey, their availability.

✔ Once a person shows interest in working with the youth ministry, start a **Volunteer Staff Orientation Process** form for them.

✔ Cast the vision—including specifics of the job you have in mind for them.

Staff Orientation Process page 419

✔ Screen them—interview, do reference and background checks.

✔ Involve them—train, support, encourage, excite.

✔ Develop them—give evaluative feedback, both encouraging and constructive. Challenge them to explore new areas of ministry and personal growth. When they achieve mastery in some area, help them learn to develop other workers.

✔ Appreciate them—find out what says "I appreciate you" in their love language. Is it gifts, time, recognition, greater opportunity?

Lifecycle of team members

Proceed in the application process only with qualified candidates whose applications you've thoroughly reviewed.

Chapter preview

Lifecycle phases:
- Beginning the application process
- Reference checks
- Interview candidates
- Background checks
- Observation
- The decision
- Developing the team
- Letting a team member go
- **Quick Start**: Learn to interview

LIFECYCLE PHASE 1

Beginning the application process

Schedule interviews only with applicants who have 1) observed the ministry in action, 2) filled out a **Volunteer Staff Application**, and 3) read all the written information distributed. Additionally, 4) interview only those qualified candidates whose applications you've thoroughly reviewed, and 5) whose references you've checked.

- **Observing the ministry in action** informs potential volunteers. Some people expect youth ministry to look like it did 20 years ago when they were high schoolers. Finding out that you don't bob for leeches anymore may drive them out of the process right away. Rule of thumb: Assign observers to veteran volunteers who're doing what they are interested in doing. Don't leave any observer unescorted in the ministry. Would you let a stranger roam freely around your home? Then don't allow it at church.

> **Volunteer Staff Application page 408, 410**

- **A completed staff application** answers questions about their ministry experience and their faith that help you plan more effective interviews.

- **The written material** should be read before candidates turn in their applications. What they learn from their reading may end the process before they go to the trouble to apply. (The readings include **Reducing the Risk of Physical and Sexual Abuse**, church and ministry statements of belief, **Staff Expectations**, your philosophy of the youth ministry, et cetera.)

Getting to know you

You want to know about the applicant's—

- expectations of the ministry
- reasons for wanting to be involved
- attitude toward students and families
- ability to handle crisis and conflict
- special abilities and gifts
- legal or criminal history
- areas of growth
- spiritual commitment to Christ.

Remember to take notes, date them, and keep them on file. You may think you have a great memory. You don't. Especially after the third interview that day.

▶ **Review the applications**. This potential stopping point can clue you in to unqualified applicants before it costs you too much time.

▶ **Wait until you receive their references** before setting dates for the interviews.

Information you learn from applicants' experience of observing the group and from these documents may stop the application process or help redirect applicants. For example, you'll find out if they regularly attend your church, and if so, for how long. If they're applying to be small-group leaders or cabin counselors at camp, for instance, and have only been attending the church for two months, they wouldn't be good candidates. Potential volunteers need to become more familiar with the church and better known to the church community before they actively lead in a ministry.

FasTrack

54 A staff application process protects you from inviting unqualified or potentially dangerous volunteers into your ministry setting.

FasTrack

55 A thorough staff application process assures families and team members that you have in mind the safety of the students and the best interests of the volunteers.

LIFECYCLE PHASE 2

Reference checks

A non-negotiable element of the screening process, the reference check needs to be done thoroughly and done for each applicant consistently. (See **Letter of Reference for Staff Applicant**.) If you check one person's references, you must check everyone's. Make sure you insert a sentence in your reference letter that gives the reference an opportunity to request a phone call from you. (For example, "If you are uncomfortable answering any of these questions in writing, or if you wish to discuss an issue over the phone, check this box and write in your phone number and the best time to reach you.") People appreciate the option of expanding on the referral, even if they rarely use it. Remember to keep notes on all your references: date sent out, date returned, date and essence of any follow-up phone calls.

Use the **Volunteer Staff Orientation Process** form to track your steps in bringing in new volunteers. Put all the information you gather in the applicants' file folders.

Letter of Reference for Staff Applicant page 402

Staff Orientation Process page 419

LIFECYCLE PHASE 3

Interviewing applicants

▶ **The environment.** Meet in a place with minimal distractions, private enough to discuss personal issues. Avoid inadvertently putting the applicant at a perceived disadvantage, like sitting in the taller chair, facing the applicant into the sun—in other words, you want a comfortable and confidential setting.

Ideally, two people interview an applicant—you and someone who doesn't know the candidate well. It's easier for a relative stranger to ask the difficult questions. Select a perceptive interview partner who can keep the interview confidential. Furthermore, the burden of evaluating the candidate rests on more than your opinion (an especially good idea if the candidate is married to the head of the elder board).

▶ **The preparation.** When you make the interview appointment, let the applicant know who will be present, where it will take place, and why it's important. Ask him to set aside about an hour to an hour and a half, and let him know that you'll ask some intense and possibly very personal questions. That gives the applicant a heads-up and, if he's uncomfortable with that, the chance to pull out of the process.

FasTrack

56 Flow with give and take in an interview—help everyone present feel comfortable both asking and answering questions.

Be familiar with the role the candidate's applying for. Bring to the interview the candidate's application, as well as a notepad—recording the interview or typing your notes into a laptop is intimidating.

▶ **The interview.** Help the applicant feel at ease by introducing other interviewers and explaining why they are there. Then explain the interview process: getting to know each other, discussing how the ministry works, responding to the applicant's questions.

You'll ask questions about the applicant and then answer questions from the applicant. If after this first part you're satisfied that the applicant may be a good fit with the ministry, take time to describe in some detail—

- your philosophy of ministry

- what it's like to work with adolescents in your ministry

- the details of the candidate's desired role

- what you expect of volunteers (read **Staff Expectations** so there are no surprises)

Placing ministry descriptions after the discussion of the application avoids influencing the applicant's responses to the interview questions and possibly providing an inaccurate picture of the person. Plus, if he's plainly not a good fit, you can end the interview at this point.

At the conclusion of the interview, if you've discerned reasons for stopping the process, let him know that and explain why. If you believe he is a good fit, let him know what happens next—an interview with the rest of the team, an assignment for ministry, any training required, follow-up appointments, and so on.

Getting to know you, the sequel

The applicant wants to know from you—

How confidential will this interview be? Only those present at the interview will know what is said, *unless you ask permission* to share the information with another person or board. For example, say in an interview you learn that the applicant was convicted of drunken driving charges four years ago, before she became a Christian. Since that time she's been active in a 12-step program and has had no recurrences. You ask her permission to talk this over with your supervisor. If she doesn't give you permission, you will tell no one—and, depending on how significant it is that you discuss this with your supervisor, she may have chosen to not be part of the youth ministry.

How did you end up in youth ministry? Especially in a larger church, the applicant may be unfamiliar with your journey into youth ministry. *Briefly* tell him your story— why you're involved and what you do. Hearing your anecdotes can help put him at ease before he starts answering questions.

What would you do?

My youth pastor was interviewing a woman to be a small-group leader. She had been a Christian less than a year, but was actively pursuing her faith. Everything seemed to be a fit. At the end of the interview, the youth pastor asked her if there was anything else she needed to know. After a pause she said, "I'm living with my fiancé right now. I moved in for financial reasons. We're not having sex. I'd make sure he'd never answer the phone, so if students were to call me, they would never know. Could this be a problem?"

You're thinking, *I'm desperate for volunteers. Do I trust that she's not sleeping with him and say yes? Do I say that it's okay because they're getting married anyway (even though no date has been set)?*

One youth pastor's response. "When you're a small-group leader in our ministry, you're modeling the Christian life, not just by what you say but by what you do. Let me ask you a question. Are you modeling the kind of decision that you would want a student to imitate?"

That question put the applicant's choices into perspective. As a result, she and her fiancé did some serious thinking and praying. Their deepening faith led them to get separate living situations until they were married.

LIFECYCLE PHASE 4

Background checks

The law requires that you exercise "reasonable care" in selecting staff (*RiskFacts: Screening Staff and Volunteers*. Nonprofit Risk Management Center, Washington, D.C.) How detailed your check is depends on what position the person is applying for. However, anyone on the team who will be unsupervised around minors should be screened through the following agencies:

➤ **Child abuse registries**. Check with your state's department of child and family services (or an equivalent organization).

► **Driving records**. Available through your state's Department of Motor Vehicles for a small price.

► **Criminal history records**. Check with your state's criminal justice system agency. They will be able to tell you how to access this information, if it's possible in your state.

Your church lawyer will be able to tell you what information is available in your state and how to go about obtaining it.

Additional methods for background checks include a national FBI record check or hiring a private company that performs background checks for you. The costs of each can range from free to more than $50 for a comprehensive check. (*RiskFacts: Criminal History Record Checks*. Nonprofit Risk Management Center, Washington, D.C.)

Make sure to put any information you receive in the applicant's file (which is kept in a locked drawer). Remember that these are not fail-safe tools. You still need to check references and perform an interview. An excellent tool to guide you through screening staff is the *Staff Screening Tool Kit: Building a Strong Foundation Through Careful Staffing* by John C. Patterson (Nonprofit Risk Management Center).

LIFECYCLE PHASE 5

Observation

Invite potential workers to observe the ministry for anywhere from one to three months. Hook them up with veterans who have the gift of discernment. What you may miss in a one-hour interview they may pick up during the one-month observation. If you have high ministry standards, you'll find that the other volunteers get pretty protective about who comes near the students. They want to uphold the reputation and level of care as much, if not more, than you do.

At any point during this time, either side can pull out of the process. Make sure you do not assign them any responsibilities dealing directly with students—that's a sure way to create difficulty if the process ends in a no. Also make sure that the team and the students know this person is merely observing and that he or she is not an official team member.

Tips on interview technique

- Order the questions to go with the flow of the conversation.

- Supplement them with any of your questions raised by their application.

- Help the applicant articulate how he will deal with conflict by using situational questions, such as, "What will you do if a student in your group consistently disrupts the discussion?" or "How will you handle a parent who comes up to you right before a worship time and says she thinks the songs you're playing are compromising Christianity and that you must stop using them?"

- Stay away from questions that can be answered with a simple yes or no.

- Remember to listen. Don't get so excited to talk about ministry issues that you lose track that this is an interview.

FasTrack

57 Background and reference checks benefit all parties—even the prospective volunteer; it's not too much to ask of someone into whose care you're entrusting your kids and your reputation.

No more solo volunteers

No adult in your ministry should ever be alone with a student (of the same or other gender) or alone with students in an isolated place. As team supervisor, you always need to have access to observe any group. That means that the Bible study that meets in the janitor's closet needs to have the door left open if there's not a window in the door. That means that if there's a sleepover, there are two ministry-approved adults participating. That means anyone who idolizes the Lone Ranger cannot be part of the youth ministry.

FasTrack

58 Whether they're raw recruits or saavy veterans, your team members need your constant feedback.

LIFECYCLE PHASE 6

The decision

Okay, you and the applicant have completed steps one through five: They've filled out the forms, you've checked all their references and done a background check, they've spent a month observing, and you've checked in with them and their host during that span. Now, it's decision time.

If you both decide to say **yes**—

▶ Welcome them to the team by officially introducing them to leaders and students, as well as sending them a letter.

▶ Keep a high level of contact with them the first few weeks. Be available to answer any questions and help them get their feet on the ground.

If your answer is **no**—

▶ Be as specific as possible about why they're not a fit with the ministry at this time. Give them constructive criticism only if they request it.

▶ Don't back down from your decision. If necessary, discuss it ahead of time with your supervisor and request her support.

▶ Suggest other avenues of service if you've truthfully observed that their gifts may be better used in another ministry. However, do not try to push unhealthy people into another ministry just because you don't want to deal with the situation.

▶ If this is not a permanent no, suggest ways for them to develop in the areas that will bring them up to your standard for volunteers—such as getting into a small group or seeking counseling. Let them know that you will be willing to consider them again in the future.

Interview scenarios

To train those who help you interview and to sharpen your skills, role-play the following situations with an interviewer and an "applicant." Give the applicant a piece of paper describing her situation. It's up to her to reveal as much or as little as she wants to. If you're doing this in a group setting, the interviewer can pass to someone else if he gets stuck. Let the group know what the situation is, but not the interviewer. You're trying to sharpen his interviewing skills.

A single parent exploring Christianity. You're a divorced dad or mom who has custody on weekends of your seventh-grade son. You want to spend some more time with him, so you thought you'd volunteer for his Saturday morning youth group. You've been going to the church for two months, since the time your divorce was final. You're in the process of exploring Christianity, but you haven't made a commitment to Christ yet.

A school teacher in love.
You're a 24-year-old school teacher who's engaged to be married this summer. You've been a Christian for six months and are excited to work with senior highers. You just bought a townhouse with your fiancé and since you're getting married in a few months, you decided to move in together to save money and get ready for the wedding. He sleeps on the hide-a-bed in the living room.

An architect with a past.
You're a single architect in your late 20s. You've been a Christian for more than five years and have spent the last three years in a spiritually intense, coed group. One of the group members is getting married and another is moving out of state, so your group is disbanding. You thought you'd try youth ministry to keep the small-group accountability. You had a couple of homosexual encounters as a college student but have not pursued anything since then.

Do as I say, not as I did. You're a recent college graduate who grew up at the church. Your high school and college years were marked by heavy partying, but in recent months you've turned your life back over to God. You want to work with students so that you can stop them from making the same mistakes you did.

Good intentions. Good idea?
You're in your mid-thirties, and you're chairing the church board which oversees the youth ministry. You think that it would be a good idea to volunteer in the youth ministry so that you can have a better idea of what's going on in the ministry. You've never worked with kids before in your life.

Following the role-plays, use these questions to debrief the group.

For the interviewer:
- Where did you find yourself getting stuck?
- Was there any time when you felt uncomfortable? Why do you think that was?
- What do you wish you would have done differently?
- What lingering questions or doubts do you have?

For the applicant:
- Was there any time when you felt uncomfortable? Why was that?
- What questions do you wish you had asked that you didn't?
- What advice do you have for someone who's performing an interview?

LIFECYCLE PHASE 7

Developing the team

Once you have a team in place, spend time developing them. Invite brand-new volunteers to "shadow" either you or a veteran so they can get a feel for the ministry, and so you can get a feel for how they operate. As they meet the challenges you give them, you can ease back on direct supervision and coach them more from the sidelines—asking them questions, posing case studies.

Constantly offer feedback. When they do something well, tell them in detail why it was effective. When they find themselves at a loss in a given situation, offer constructive comments—or ask them to critique themselves as you discuss the experience. Eventually, they'll need less direction from you, but every volunteer always needs feedback. Even if you delegate projects with complete confidence (and very little direction) to team members, they still need to receive both encouragement and feedback from you.

Here are some topics you can develop for part of your team development. Many of these ideas were suggested by veteran youth worker Les Christie in his book *How to Recruit and Train Volunteer Youth Workers* (Zondervan/Youth Specialties, 1987, 1992).

How-to skills

- Leading small groups
- Building relationships with students
- Leading students to Christ
- Giving talks
- Leading discussions
- Creating a community
- Integrating creativity
- Basic counseling skills
- Training on prevention of sexual abuse or molestation
- Working with parents

Ministry behavior and expectations

- Cover the ministry's policy on sexual abuse or molestation.
- Go over appropriate touch boundaries with students.
- Never be alone with or give a ride home to a student of the other gender.
- Don't touch areas that would normally be covered by a bathing suit.
- Give nondemanding signs of affection (side hug, shoulder squeeze, et cetera.— never a full-body hug).
- There must always be two adults at any event outside the church (especially at sleepovers).
- Don't give piggyback rides or let students sit on your lap.

- Go over appropriate discipline boundaries with adolescents.
- Never use physical punishment.
- Never withhold food or sleep.
- Never shame students in front of their peers.
- Always contact the parent immediately if a student has been asked to leave the ministry for any length of time.

Philosophy: the whys behind the how-to's

- The importance of youth ministry
- A philosophy of youth ministry
- The basics of adolescent development
- Analyzing adolescent culture

Personal needs

- Characteristics of an effective youth worker
- Time management
- Prayer and spiritual journey
- Getting into the Bible
- Family
- Self-image

> **FasTrack**
>
> **59** Let go of volunteers who don't develop themselves in team ministry by acting on feedback, learning from experience, or maintaining moral uprightness.

> **Smart Tip**
>
> **Pay volunteers**. Not, of course, with money. People eagerly participate in a ministry that gives back to them with training that they can use in their daily lives, challenges and encouragement that push them to grow, and opportunities to make a significant difference in someone else's life.

LIFECYCLE PHASE 8

Letting a team member go

When a team member isn't working out in a ministry, typically we defer to grace—"They just need a little more time." In reality, however, you need to let them go. Or as a colleague puts it, "Free them up to succeed elsewhere." Before you let someone go, however, you need to make sure you've done three things:

- **Consistently given feedback**. Part of your team development is observing team members in action and talking with them about what you observe. If someone isn't working out, she should be aware of it well before it comes time to let her go. Ask yourself, is this a ministry issue (she wants to implement liturgical dance), an attitude issue (she sporadically follows up on commitments, she shows up to meetings and refuses to participate), or a moral issue (she's sleeping with a student in the ministry)? If it's one (or both) of the first two, you can take some time to work with her on the difficulty. If it's a moral issue, fire her immediately and let your senior pastor or supervisor know as soon as possible so he or she can advocate for you should there be any repercussions.

➤ **Made sure that his failure is not related merely to job position**. Sometimes, if someone's not working out in the job he volunteered for, the job might be wrong for the person. Think about moving him to another position.

➤ **Documented the conversations leading up to dismissal**. Note the date, the person, and the gist of any disciplinary conversation that you have with a team member. Also record any steps recommended for change and whether or not he followed those steps.

If you address the behavior or attitude and see no change in the volunteer's performance, you need to let the person go. If you don't, you drain the morale of the team, the ministry, and yourself. Here's how to let someone go:

➤ Pray for wisdom.

➤ Get your facts straight. Go over your notes.

➤ Think through all the consequences carefully before you take action. Don't give a knee-jerk reaction. Sleep on it. When in doubt, call a therapist, or talk it over with another youth pastor.

➤ Get wise, confidential counsel from someone who can help you sort out the issues from the emotions.

➤ Dismiss a person face to face, not over the phone or in a letter. Find a neutral location where you won't be disturbed.

➤ Do it with a loving and caring attitude.

➤ Be clear and honest without being mean. Bill Hybels has a saying: "Have the courage to say the last 10 percent." By that he means that too many of us shy away from saying what really needs to be said. We'll say the 90 percent that's easy. But it's usually the last 10 percent that's the most powerful and important information for the person.

➤ Point out positive contributions as well as reasons for dismissal.

Suggest alternative places of ministry (if appropriate).

➤ Don't ask her to stay on until a replacement is found.

➤ Talk about a plan of action to tell the other volunteers or students.

➤ Keep confidentiality even if the other party doesn't.

➤ Remember that most volunteers will be relieved. They generally know at a gut level when it's not working.

Once you've let someone go, check in with her that week to see how she's doing or to see if anything needs to be clarified. Also let your supervisor know about the decision and the process; he needs to be your advocate.

Recommended resources

To develop your team, periodically use resources such as these:

▶ **Your local police**—gang issues, personal safety, violence in the community

▶ **Social work agencies**—current family trends, dealing with families on welfare, abuse issues

▶ **Therapists**—dealing with crisis, working with kids who have ADD/ADHD, identifying a kid in pain

▶ **Park district workers**—recreation options in your area, developing a philosophy of play

▶ **Events that train and equip youth workers**—It's a huge perk for a youth ministry team when the church pays their way to training seminars or conventions.

▶ **Denominational resources**—low- or no-cost training in the form of video rentals or seminars on tape, special speakers, leader retreats, and books.

▶ *Equipped to Serve: Volunteer Youth Worker Training Course* by Dennis "Tiger" McLuen (Youth Specialties, 1994). If you don't already have this videotaped course with accompanying workbooks, order it from Youth Specialties. In six sessions you can ground your volunteer team with practical skills and knowledge.

Quick Start

Learn to interview

If you're new to a youth ministry position, practice interviewing by asking some of the following questions of those who have been holding down the fort until you got there. You could ask them in the past tense—"Why were you interested in working with the youth ministry?" Or you could phrase them with the future in mind—"Are you interested in continuing to work in your current role?" Comments about the purpose or value of the question is in parentheses at the end of each question.

Two copies of this form are included in the appendix (**Prospective Staff Interview Questions**, page 404, and **Prospective Staff Interview Worksheet**, page 406). One version includes the commentary, the other leaves space for taking notes during an interview.

Developing interns 20

One of the greatest legacies of youth ministry is developing people who love God and love kids. It takes time and sweat and prayer, but it's a lot of fun.

Chapter preview

- ▶ Building a healthy team
- ▶ Preparing the internship: Determining the type
- ▶ Preparing the internship: Job description
- ▶ Preparing the internship: Recruiting the intern
- ▶ Preparing the internship: Interviewing the intern
- ▶ Developing the intern
- ▶ Ending the internship

Building a healthy team

You've just come off your third all-day event this year. You did everything— designed the fliers, collected registration money, drove the bus, and cleaned up. The volunteer team was great during the event, but they all left 15 minutes after it was over. As you're sitting around waiting for the senior pastor to come pick up her daughter (again), you think to yourself, "Boy, it would be nice to have some help I could count on, some kind of partner in this craziness." Then, in your semi-slumbering state, you have an epiphany. INTERN blazes across you mind. You vow to pursue this as soon as you're fully awake, along with confronting the pastor about consistently forgetting what time events end.

As you begin this process, ask yourself these questions:

- ▶ Do I have a clear job description with measurable goals?
- ▶ Do I have enough experience to develop another youth worker? What will an aspiring youth worker learn from spending time with me and this ministry?
- ▶ Do I have the time to develop and guide another youth worker? (Youth pastors quickly realize that supervising an intern to do a task always takes more of their time than doing it themselves.)
- ▶ Is my church or organization supportive of it?

▶ Is the church willing to provide financial compensation to the intern? (This can be room and board and a small stipend, tuition credit to a college or a seminary, or a salary.)

▶ Does it believe in developing future leaders for ministry, and is it willing to take on the accompanying risks? (The internship is a step in the intern's discernment process. It may be that during the internship, it becomes clear that ministry is not the right direction for this person. Is the church willing to take that risk?)

▶ Does the church staff understand the job description of a youth ministry intern? (Or will the church secretary expect an intern to stuff envelopes? Might the janitor expect he can delegate the Sunday school room set up to the intern?)

▶ Is my church willing to let this person fail as well as succeed? (Interns are rookies. As they try out their ministry legs, there are bound to be messes as well as successes. Is the church willing to extend grace?)

Preparing the internship

Determining the type

In youth ministry an internship means introducing someone to ministry by exposing him to short-term, real-life experiences and then helping him constructively reflect on those experiences. It's guided supervision, where interns can learn from both their successes and failures. It's a time to discern whether full-time youth ministry is the path the intern should follow. All of this is done with a supervisor who is committed to the internship process.

An *internship* is a process of preparation and discernment before someone enters youth ministry as a professional. An *internship* is *not* a source of cheap labor, a chance to give the pastor's kid a summer job, a way to get a substitute so you can have the summer to travel and speak and have time off.

An undefined internship can force you to wrestle with the VBS director or any number of other staff members and volunteers to win your intern's time. Like the punch line of a bad Dilbert cartoon, people tell her, "After all, *you* are the intern. What else are you going to do with your time?" Before seeking an intern, determine what kind of internship you're offering.

Shadow internship. The intern follows the supervisor around and watches what she does. There's minimal hands-on participation. Constant debriefing of every major experience exposes the intern to the supervisor's motives for making choices, the rationale for handling a situation in a certain way, and other available options and why they weren't used.

Situations where a shadow internship is appropriate:

- A high school junior thinks God is calling her into youth ministry. She also thinks that you have the easiest job in the world—give a talk on Wednesday night and spend the rest of the time going out to McDonald's with students. She needs to see behind the curtain.

- A younger high school student wants to be a counselor-in-training at your camp. He's not old enough nor does he have enough experience to handle the job. Capitalize on his eagerness by inviting him to "shadow" a veteran counselor for a week or two.

"Gopher" internship. For churches that view interns as inexpensive ways to add support staff for those clerical jobs, errands, and tasks—stuffing envelopes, copying curriculum, inputting data—that can be done well by a conscientious student with few expenses. Although not likely to be wholly satisfying, the intern does get exposed to ministry.

Situations where a "gopher" internship is appropriate:

- A junior high student is eager to be more involved in ministry because he thinks God is leading him into full-time ministry.

- A college student, home for the summer, is working the late shift at the Dairy Barn. However, she has mornings free to come in and help out in the church.

Project internship. Focuses on a special project that you're eager to get going but for which you just don't have the time. Voilà! The intern takes it on. The project can be anything from jump-starting a middle school program to reworking the confirmation curriculum. Interns can experience a lot of pride in taking an idea from creation to implementation. The danger is that when they start as the solo youth pastor next summer, they quickly realize that, although they know how to design a great fundraising program, they have no idea how to run a parents' meeting or how to counsel a kid in crisis.

Situations where a project internship is appropriate:

- A college student who's grown up in the church and is now double-majoring in youth ministry and theater. He'll be home for the summer and would love to help you fulfill your dream of having a college and high school drama team that would perform both in the youth ministry and the larger church.

➤ You're looking at your twelfth annual week at camp at the end of July, and you have no energy or creativity to put toward it. You recall that as you interviewed one of the interns, she said that one of her dreams is to work at a camp. Too good to be true!

Associate internship. Interns explore all the areas of youth ministry—a final step before heading into full-time ministry. Along with overseeing a wide variety of tasks and challenges, they're exposed to staff meetings, church leader meetings, budget development, crisis counseling with students (when appropriate), and conflict resolution.

Situations where this internship would be appropriate:

➤ A youth ministry student at a college or seminary.

➤ A volunteer from your team who's taking steps toward a mid-life career change.

FasTrack

61 An intern may shadow a youth worker to observe and learn, provide services to regular staff, focus on a special project, or thoroughly explore all areas of youth ministry.

Preparing the internship
Job description

Once you know the type of internship you desire, you're ready to develop a job description. This will eventually be supplemented by a learning contract with the actual intern. Before you pull out a job description to White Out *volunteer* and write in *intern,* sit down and begin answering these questions:

➤ Who will be his or her supervisor?

➤ How long will the internship last?

> *Is it full-time during the summer? Part-time for a year? Does it run concurrently with school, or does the intern commit a block of time (for example, one year before starting seminary)?*

➤ How many hours per week will he or she be working?

> *Does the internship pay enough to live on, or will the intern need a part-time job to supplement her income?*

> *If the internship runs concurrently with school, how many hours a week is it feasible for the intern to work? Is the church willing to be flexible when finals roll around?*

➤ What age group will the intern work with?

> *Middle school? High school? College?*

➤ What program will the intern work with?

   Vacation Bible school, day camp, small groups, worship ministry?

➤ Will there be a salary or stipend? Will room and board be provided? If so, with whom will they live? Will they need a car? Will there be reimbursment for travel and entertainment expenses? Will they be covered by insurance? Will Workers' Compensation cover any injuries that may occur?

➤ What knowledge objectives will they achieve by the end of the internship?

Write out objectives out as an informal learning contract between you and the intern. Here are some ideas:

➤ By the end of this internship, the intern should be able to—

   —begin to formulate and articulate a philosophy of youth ministry.

   —identify the key characteristics of adolescence, as well as the impact of family, society, and church on adolescents.

   —explain the rationale behind the model of youth ministry the church uses.

   —articulate the demographics of the community and the services available through the local community.

   —describe the importance of the youth minister, whether professional or volunteer, in effective leadership of adolescents and their families.

➤ By the end of this internship, the intern should be able to—

   —write and lead a Bible study appropriate for senior high students.

   —initiate exploratory conversations with parents and with several subcultures of adolescents.

   —develop and produce a worship service.

   —put together a three-month program that includes a variety of events and topics geared toward adolescents' felt and real needs. It may include Sunday school, confirmation, and weekly activities.

   —develop and manage a youth ministry budget.

   —run an effective meeting.

   —recruit and interview potential volunteers.

► By the end of this internship, the intern will have experienced—

  —weekly church staff meetings in order to better understand how the whole church operates.

  —a weekly Bible study as both an observer and a leader.

  —participating in the organization and leadership of a week-long missions trip.

  —producing a variety of communication tools: fliers, church and youth ministry announcements, calendars, permission slips.

  —participating in planning and strategy meetings.

► During this internship, the intern can expect—

  —weekly or biweekly meetings with the supervisor.

  —exposure to the full scope of the ministry, including administrative areas (budget development, hiring and development of volunteer staff, church staff meetings, congregational meetings, and counseling appointments when appropriate).

  —timely payment of a salary or stipend.

  —medical insurance.

► During this internship, the church can expect that the intern will—

  —show up on time to all meetings or responsibilities.

  —dress appropriately for the ministry situation.

  —maintain a model lifestyle during the internship.

  —immediately inform the supervisor of any areas of concern or conflict.

Preparing the internship

Recruiting the intern

Here are several ways to recruit potential interns:

- **Look within**. Is there a student within the larger ministry who is trying to discern his or her call to ministry?

- **Look at local colleges and seminaries**. Christian colleges with youth ministry majors or minors usually post job openings. Send yours to the chairs of the departments, as well as to the career counseling offices. (Often students interested in going into youth ministry major in another field.) You may even want to post your internship with local community colleges or universities.

- **Look at your denominational seminary**. If you have a strong denominational affiliation and are looking for several interns, sometimes it helps to actually recruit live on a campus. "Cold call" students are more likely to consider your ministry's internship if they have a conversation with you.

- **Look at other youth ministries**. Are there colleagues who have students who might be potential interns in your ministry? I advise students to avoid doing an internship at their home church—it's usually too difficult to be seen as an adult. Perhaps some intern-swapping might work in your local network.

Preparing the internship

Interviewing the intern

Thoroughly interview prospective interns. Hire in haste, repent in leisure. Check all references. (See **Letter of Reference for Applicant**.) Be aware of your biases as you interview him. You may think this guy's incredible based on his résumé and his youth pastor's recommendation, so you don't really pay attention to his resident assistant's comment that he's been involved in some questionable behavior. You imagine that merely means college pranks. Ignoring that reference means you fail to find out that he's been accused of stealing CDs from other rooms in the hall. You realize that you should have paid better attention after he's discovered pocketing $150 from the mission trip.

> **Letter of Reference for Applicant**
> **page 354**

For best results, have the intern interview with several people in the church—several parents (who can be advocates for him and help break the ice), the senior pastor (so she remembers that you're bringing on an intern this summer), and some of the students (so they're familiar with the intern before he arrives).

Developing the intern

FasTrack

63 Build into your internship clear goals, expectations, an evaluation process, and a grace-full way to conclude an internship.

Step 1: Develop goals.

► Stephen Covey says, "Begin with the end in mind." Revisit the job description with the intern and talk about what she wants to accomplish or experience by the end of the internship. Talk about what you would like to see accomplished in the ministry. How will both parties be different because of this experience?

► Develop goals in the areas of knowledge, skill, and character qualities.

► Make sure you look at each person's time, abilities, motivations, resources available, and so on.

Step 2: Clarify expectations.

► Is church membership an expectation?

► What meetings must interns attend on a regular basis?

► What meetings should interns attend once or twice for the experience?

► When do you expect interns to be in the office? What about days off?

► What is acceptable dress in the church? What about when interns are with students?

► How does the intern gain access to resources—secretarial help, church vehicles?

► How will you deal with conflict? (It's always better to be proactive than reactive on this one.)

► How can the relationship be terminated if things don't work out as planned?

Step 3: Set up an evaluation process.

Self-Evaluation page 356

Supervisor Evaluation page 358

► How will success be determined? If the intern just finishes the task? Level of excellence?

► Who will perform the evaluation? The supervisor? A lay person? And how will it be done? Formally in a meeting or informally in the hallway? (See intern **Self-Evaluation** and intern **Supervisor Evaluation**.)

► The evaluation should be both result-oriented (what happened?) and learning-oriented (why did it happen?)

Ending the internship

O fficially conclude an internship through evaluation and celebration. Even if the person stays on, make sure it's in another capacity.

➤ **Meet to debrief the internship.**

—Discuss the objectives set at the beginning of the internship. (This should be the conclusion of an ongoing discussion and shouldn't have any surprises.)

—Ask what suggestions the intern has for future interns.

➤ Fill out any paperwork required by the academic institution evaluating the intern, as well as the church.

➤ **Celebrate.** Let the ministry and the church celebrate this person's season with you through a party or through special acknowledgement at a church service.

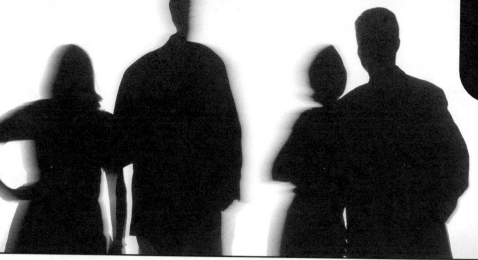

Risk management

We had played the game a month ago with no injuries. This time, though, because of the number of students playing, we adjusted the rules just a bit—and we didn't foresee that those slight modifications would make a huge difference in the safety factor of the game.

Within 15 minutes, three students injured their legs and one received a head injury. And because there were several game stations, the danger wasn't apparent until after the game was over. Too little knowledge, too late in game.

Our mistake cost us. Of the four students, one ended up having knee surgery that took over a year to heal. Bad? Yes. But it could have been much worse. Needless to say, we didn't play that game again. The fun wasn't worth the risk.

Risk management is a critical and essential part of youth ministry. Unfortunately, no matter how well you manage risks throughout your career, sooner or later, you will still have to deal with tragic or unfortunate situations. Perhaps it will be a freak accident and no amount of safeguards and preparations will have helped you avoid it. More likely, it will be an accident whose consequences can be less drastic with adequate planning and preparation. In any case, as the responsible adult, you have the obligation to manage potential risk and be prepared for both the avoidable and the unavoidable.

This section equips youth workers to do ministry without putting students at risk of injury. Yes, God is in control and we need to continuously pray that he will lead, guide, and protect our ministries. At the same time, we must avoid unnecessary risks and be prepared if the worst should happen.

In Risk management—

21. Safety first
Insurances and vehicle safety
22. When accidents happen

Safety first

Effective risk management identifies threats, controls loss (preventing loss and reducing the severity should a loss occur), safeguards against unauthorized use of funds, protects against injury, and takes appropriate action to ensure legal compliance.

Chapter preview

➤ Safety first: Who needs it and why?
➤ Provide adequate event preparation and planning
➤ Understand risk management
➤ Negligence
➤ Sample safety guidelines

Safety first: Who needs it and why?

If you have spent any time in youth ministry, you know of youth workers who have dealt with disasters. Within a five-year period, youth workers I knew faced the tragedy of a student's brutal murder, a student's accidental death, a student drowning on a ministry rafting retreat, another student killed at a kiddy park while at an overnight lock-in, and a student who threatened to blow up her parents and her home. One ministry lost several students in a bus accident. For the one chance that these tragic disasters could have been avoided, preparation is priceless.

Youth workers in these cases were sometimes on the sidelines lending support; others were involved in the nitty-gritty details of funeral preparations and legal battles. Although preparation won't make you invulnerable to problems, the tools you find here can prepare you and your ministry for the expected and the unexpected.

Everyone agrees that leaders in ministry have to provide a safe environment for learning and growth. However, people have different interpretations of the meaning of "safe." Youth workers who are risk takers have an exciting, cutting edge, cool reputation. Their life motto is "It's flesh; it'll heal." Although they generally bring the group home safely, they may or may not have an actual head count. But they have most of the kids' phone numbers…somewhere. They are, of course, on a first-name basis with ER personnel. But hey, if it takes kids to the edge of challenge and growth…

FasTrack

64 Risk management includes anticipating problems before they happen and recognizing situations to avoid.

Only a start

This chapter is not intended to replace professional legal advice or consultation with your ministry's insurance agent. You must understand and comply with the laws where you live. Laws change and are different from state to state, even city to city. What you read here is only a start—a good start, but a start nonetheless. When you're finished reading here, get legal advice appropriate to your state and city.

Other youth workers have grown up in overprotective families and now share that spirit of overprotection with teenagers. An action game to them is Four on the Couch. They have notarized release forms for all events—filed in multiple places. Staff-to-student ratio at events is always 1:2, and group members all have whistles, laminated IN CASE OF EMERGENCY cards, and snake-bite kits slung around their necks. And they saw a film on whitewater rafting once.

Of course, the middle ground allows kids to be stretched through various experiences without placing themselves at unnecessary risk. So the big question is this: *What qualifies as necessary risk?* Before a problem drives you into an emergency meeting with your senior pastor and church chairperson, find out their perception of acceptable risk and what activities your church insurance covers.

In other words, be proactive.

Provide adequate event preparation and planning

Youth leaders need to demonstrate to parents, leaders, and students that they have planned and prepared for a safe event and are consistently executing that plan. That means you have chosen to be the adult.

Welcome to the real world of youth ministry—the one where you have to make the tough choices and provide the voice of reason.

Diane remembers the first moment she thought about that:

> I was in the midst of a heated discussion with three high school seniors and not at all appreciating that I had to put the lid on their indoor water park. I would much rather have joined them in their only slightly destructive merry making. Instead, all I could think of was, *Who's going to clean up this mess?* and *Am I ever in trouble with the janitor!* Not to mention *How long until the running, slipping, and sliding students hurt themselves?*

She had joined the ranks of responsible adults. Then there was the time she watched helplessly while one of the students—on stage—swallowed a live goldfish. (Sushi was probably invented at a youth retreat.) Funny? Perhaps. A liability issue? Most

Smart Tip

The legal gloves are off—churches are no longer sanctuaries from lawsuits. Hundreds of lawsuits are brought against churches every year—many of which could have been prevented. (Adapted from *Business Management in the Local Church*, David R. Pollock, Moody Press, 1995).

certainly. Fortunately the whole episode blew over with only one scathing, "That *will not* happen again on my watch" speech to the staff. Again, we were lucky. What if the student had come down with a rare goldfish disease? Or what if animal-loving parents got really upset and called it goldfish murder? The outcome could have been very different. A seemingly harmless and funny thing could have blown up in our faces.

FasTrack

65 We often find ourselves balancing a fun ministry that students want to join with a safe ministry to which parents repeatedly entrust their children.

You're the adult in charge, you're the youth worker—and so you are the one whose task it is to think through possible contingencies, weigh the problems versus the benefits, and decide whether an activity is worth the risk. That's because *you* are the one who has to live with the consequences of your decision—right or wrong—before the ministry staff, the students, the board, the pastor, the parents, and perhaps even the community and media.

Understand risk management

Risk management provides strategies, techniques, and an approach to recognizing and confronting any threat of harm faced by an organization in fulfilling its mission. Whereas insurance covers you after a loss, risk management deals with *avoiding* problems (losses) and with being prepared to deal with them if they do happen.

Your organization's policies regarding many issues in managing risks may already be addressed in a policy manual—be sure to read policies with which you are expected to comply. Here's a four-step management process that will help your ministry to better protect itself:

Acknowledge and identify risks that you take while managing your ministry—

➤ Adults forming inappropriate or abusive relationships with children or youth.

➤ Physical injury to staff, volunteers, students, and guests under normal operating conditions.

Safety Grid

Test ideas through a safety grid. Using the questions below, talk your new idea through with a partner before trying it out.

➤ What can go wrong?

➤ If something does go wrong, what would we do?

➤ How much could a mistake cost?

➤ What is the worst thing that could happen if this doesn't work?

➤ Who has done this before, and what was their experience like?

➤ What do parents (who know all the details) think of this idea?

➤ Would parents let their kids do this if they were here?

➤ Does this activity need the permission of our pastor?

➤ Are the people we're hiring to take or lead our group really qualified to do this? What about their safety record? Who regulates them?

Sample guidelines for travel

When you are away from home with your group, do you know—

- How to provide safe food and water for your group?
- The location, phone number, and directions to the closest emergency medical facility?
- Dangers that you may face in a given location (such as flash flooding, animals, insects)?
- How to contact family members?
- How to facilitate an emergency medical evacuation?
- Accurate bus or van lists and which vehicles students and staff are in?

Travel considerations—

- Are the vehicles you're driving really safe? Who says?
- Do you have a backup plan for dealing with worse-case scenarios?
- Have you enlisted a staff person to handle issues such as kids who come late, get sick, have discipline needs?
- Do you have a vehicle to transport your group in case of a sudden need? Who has the keys? If you only have the church bus or van, your options are limited.
- Do you have access to a cell phone or radio for communication?
- Have you trained your staff how to respond in the event of an emergency? What if you are injured?

- Physical injury to staff, volunteers, students, and guests under risky conditions—like whitewater rafting, bungee jumping).
- Damage to items such as cars, buildings, office equipment.
- Loss of your tax-exempt status (501(c)(3) not-for-profit corporation status) due to litigation or improper fundraising practices.
- Loss of reputation due to litigation prompted by inappropriate behavior of staff members or adult volunteers.
- Loss of funds due to embezzlement by staff members or volunteers.
- Loss of funds due to litigation by a former employee claiming violations of his civil rights.

From *Risk facts #2* (Nonprofit Risk Management Center, Washington, D.C.).

Evaluate and prioritize risk. Determine how vulnerable you or your ministry is, then outline appropriate cautions to implement.

Decide how to manage your risks. Determine what needs to be done and document it. The plan should include these four basic strategies for controlling risk:

- **Avoidance**. Don't offer that activity as an option. (No more goldfish-swallowing contests.)
- **Modification**. Change the activity to minimize the chance of harm. (Give the students padding when playing a physical contact game.)

Smart Tip

If kids have access to your ministry computers, install whatever controls, filters, or safeguards your Internet browser offers. Be sure students can't access pornography. Make a policy about allowing students to visit chat rooms.

► **Retention**. Accept all or a portion of the risk, then prepare for the consequences if the worst happens. (If you play Capture the Flag on asphalt, for instance, have Band-Aids and Bactine on hand for the inevitable scrapes. If you're deciding whether to let thirsty kids drink unsafe water in Mexico on your next mission trip, first read up on the long-term effects of amebic dysentery on human intestines.)

► **Sharing the risk**. Along with the general liability insurance that covers your organization, purchase event-specific insurance that will cover you for higher-risk activities. Contract with another organization to provide leadership for the risky activities, like rock climbing, rappelling, or whitewater rafting.

FasTrack

66 Know what your insurance covers—and what it doesn't cover. Ignorance is not bliss—it's stupidity.

High-risk events

Does your church allow—and your insurance company cover—the activities listed below? (Your insurance policy generally spells out exclusions. Read the policy carefully.) If you are free to choose the following types of activities, carefully evaluate the fun in context with the accompanying risks. Also provide qualified adults to supervise your group's event. Consult with your supervisor and insurance agent first. Safety is the #1 priority.

Bungee jumping

Trampolines

Spelunking

Scuba diving

Boating events

Rock climbing

Parasailing

Skiing and snowboarding

Hayrides

Snowmobiling

Whitewater rafting

Drag racing in the church parking lot

Negligence

The church and the minister are not immune from legal responsibility for their actions because they are in the religion business. Anyone related to the activities of the church is responsible for the care and protection of people.

A church may be called upon to provide compensation for anyone—members, visitors, employees, or others outside the church—when there is negligence resulting in any loss or damage. The act of negligence may result from doing or not doing something that a reasonable person would do or not do in a similar situation.

Permission slips for trips away from the church are helpful, but they cannot be used as an excuse for negligence. The church should make every effort to keep from being negligent as well as to provide adequate insurance coverage for protection from unforeseen situations. Maintain workers compensation insurance coverage for employees and public liability insurance coverage for property and vehicles in significant amounts.

From *Church Administration Handbook* by Bruce P. Powers (Broadman & Holman), page 209.

Sample guidelines for a camping event

- Bring staff experienced in outdoor camping.

- Require a member of your camp staff to become trained in first aid and CPR.

- Designate a contact person at home who knows where you're camping and when you'll return.

- Find out how to get help when you're at your destination campsite.

- Obtain current road and trail maps.

- Bring supplies necessary for the kind of camping—tent, cabin, wilderness.

- On your **Medical Release** form, specifically ask about special medical needs of students relevant to the kind of camping—poison oak allergies, hay fever, bee stings—especially those needs that affect their level of participation in selected activites.

- Ask a professional outfitter to review your route, supplies, and meal plans.

- Bring a weather radio to warn you of significant weather threats, such as thunderstorms and tornadoes.

- Well ahead of the event, provide a training program for adult leaders for preventing sexual abuse.

- No swimming without a certified lifeguard.

- No use of the ropes course without trained staff supervising.

- Male and female students and staff will not share the same sleeping facilities.

- Youth will not share tents with an adult other than their own parent.

- Coed overnight activities require both male and female leadership from qualified members of your staff over 21 years of age.

- No alcohol, tobacco, or controlled substances permitted (applies to students and adults).

- Set a curfew—all campers in their sleeping quarters by 11 p.m.

- Preview the camping facility to be sure you planned for adequate supervision. Note places and situations where supervision is difficult and prep your staff.

- Provide the camp director with a list of students participating in an event, accompanied by a **Medical Release** form. Be certain that the form tells you whom to contact in case of an emergency. It must contain all important medical information about the student

- Only those adult leaders who have completed the driver screening process may provide transportation to the event.

Sample guidelines for water events

Swimming

- Is there a certified lifeguard watching your group?

- Is the diving area deep enough?

- Have you assigned a buddy to each swimmer?

Boating

- Are there enough Coast Guard-approved life preservers?

- Is the boat driver qualified to drive the boat? To haul skiers?

- Have you limited the number of boat riders to what the boat safely holds?

- Have you confirmed that the weather is safe for boating?

- Have you confirmed that the boat is equipped with other safety measures?

    —whistle

    —drinking water

    —paddles

    —fire extinguisher

    —two-way radio

- Have you informed your contact person onshore where you're going and when you'll return?

Sample guidelines for retreats

When using a retreat facility or hotel, do you know—

- Where everyone is (room assignments)?

- How to evacuate everyone safely in the event of a fire?

- How to make sure everyone is accounted for in the event of an emergency?

- How to summon medical or police help and how long it will take for them to arrive?

Recommended resource

For a more complete guide to risk management, get the book *More Than a Matter of Trust* by White, Patterson and Herman, 1998. Published by The Nonprofit Risk Management Center in Washington D.C. To order, visit nonprofitrisk.org.

This book covers risk management fundamentals, understanding legal liability, using liability shields wisely, and 10 keys to mentoring risk management.

Insurances and vehicle safety

Guidelines for safe group travel

Passenger rules—

- No standing while the vehicle is in motion.
- No smoking when students are on the bus.
- Keep arms, feet, and hands inside the vehicle.
- No throwing things while in the vehicle.

Other safety rules—

- Don't allow the driver to deal with discipline.
- Appoint a staff member.
- Keep doors closed when moving.
- Never lock the emergency door when passengers are on board a bus.
- Never transport more than the posted number of passengers.
- Keep children out of the back row of seats, except when the bus is filled, to protect against injury in case the bus is rear-ended.
- Make smooth starts and stops.
- Because of fire hazard, fill the fuel tank only when there are no passengers on the bus. *Never* travel with a gas can or other flammables. Never.
- Keep packages, coats, and other objects out of the aisle.
- Watch for clearances (bridges, overpasses, et cetera).
- Pick up and drop off students in such a manner that they are not required to cross streets.

How much insurance is enough?

Only your insurance agent knows for sure. Check with your church or ministry business administrator to see what kind of insurance you have and what it covers. Then after talking to a good insurance agent (and an attorney), you can determine if your ministry needs any additional coverage.

Remember that insurance is only a safety net. It doesn't remove your responsibility to do what is "reasonable" under the law. If you ever have a situation in which the law could cast doubt on the reasonable safety you provided, you're already in trouble. If you err on the side of doing more to promote safety than what is considered "reasonable," you don't have to worry.

Words to know

Call your ministry's insurance agent and ask the significance of these three words in relation to youth ministry: *care, custody,* and *control.* Your understanding of the responsibility you possess as a youth leader will move to a new level.

It's time to sell the church bus when . . .

Fifty junior highers packed into our church's 20-year-old bus and headed to the fall retreat. Just over half way to the camp, the steering mechanism dropped out of the bottom of the bus. Literally. Our driver somehow safely pulled over to the side of the road. Thankfully, no one was injured.

"I don't care how much we save in the future," the shaken driver muttered as he stepped off the bus. "Risking injuries or killing kids is never worth it."

Be prepared in case of an accident

W rite up your own travel emergency procedure and distribute it at the organizational meetings for all church activities. Place a copy of the procedure in the first-aid kit that travels with you. That way everyone knows what to do in case of an accident or injury, and the victim will receive help as quickly as possible. In case of serious accidents, even a few minutes can be critical.

Here's a sample of an emergency procedure—

- Make the injured person as comfortable as possible. *Do not attempt to move the injured person.* Keep him or her warm. Administer first aid *only* if you are certified to do so.

- Without leaving the injured person unattended, send someone to call for help.

- Call 911 or ask a bystander to call. Give your location clearly and distinctly.

- Move uninjured passengers to a safe area away from danger. Get them away from the highway.

- Get the names and telephone numbers of any witnesses.

- The driver involved in the accident may be, understandably, upset. Don't ask the driver to call the families of the injured. To avoid undue panic, call the pastor (or another designated person) and allow him or her to explain the status of the situation to the injured person's family.

- Cooperate with police and fire department investigators. If you are a witness, you can answer questions about the accident. Provide investigators with your list of witnesses.

- As soon as possible after the injured person has helped and a preliminary investigation has been made, inform your insurance agent of the accident. Tell what happened, simply and factually. Provide the names of any witnesses. This will facilitate fast, equitable settlement of claims for those injured.

FasTrack

67 Ask yourself what would be considered "reasonable" planning and protection in a court of law. Picture yourself standing before the jury and saying, "Yes, I was the only leader on the bus with the 25 kids, and it was my decision to let 17-year-old Eric drive."

Insurance coverage

W hat coverage does your ministry provide to those who volunteer? Before you skip over this section, realize that volunteers are increasingly being named in lawsuits, according to the *Chicago Tribune* ("Watch Your Step: Protect Yourself from Lawsuits in Volunteer Work," Friday, June 28, 1996.) Make a note to talk to your church's insurance agent to see what insurance you need to provide for volunteer protection and ask the agent these questions:

▶ What insurance coverage does our organization offer to volunteers?

▶ Does our policy include medical reimbursement, personal liability insurance, or excess automobile insurance?

▶ Do we have a commercial general liability (CGL) policy? If so, can we add volunteers as additional insureds?

▶ Does the CGL include or exclude travel between their home and the church or event?

▶ Do we have accident insurance and what does it cover? (In case a volunteer is injured during the course of a ministry event.)

▶ Do we have volunteer liability? (If volunteers cause damage or are negligent, they may be sued. This protection helps if financial judgments are rendered.)

▶ Do we have excess auto liability? (This is coverage over and above the volunteers' own coverage as required by state law. See page 213 for more on vehicle safety and insurance.)

▶ Do we have coverage for volunteer/employee dishonesty? (To protect the ministry in case a volunteer steals money or destroys property.)

This isn't a complete list, so you need to meet with your church's insurance agent—and your senior pastor, church administrator, and church lawyer—to discuss this further. Do not assume that it is being taken care of by another staff person at the church. Don't stop asking until you have an answer. For more on insurance, see the *Legal Defense Handbook for Christians in Ministry* by Carl F. Lansing (NavPress).

(Thanks to The CIMA Companies, Inc., for its help with this section. For more information, call 800/468-4200 or see its cimaworld.com site and click on "Volunteers Insurance." CIMA specializes in insurance coverage for nonprofit organizations and volunteer workers.)

Risk management gold mine

One of the best resources for researching insurance for volunteers (as well as the whole area of screening volunteers) is the Nonprofit Risk Management Center at nonprofitrisk.org (202/785-3891). Among their many excellent products is *Risk Facts*, a binder of about 30 short, extremely practical articles dealing with risk management in a nonprofit setting—child abuse, selecting an insurance expert, criminal history checks, liability basics. If you've ever asked the question "Can we be sued for that?" or "Are you sure we're covered?" you need to get in touch with these people.

Evaluate

Regarding insurance. Meet with your insurance agent as soon as possible. It can be costly to assume you have adequate coverage. And don't assume that your church administrator completely understands all the issues. Go to the insurance source. Ask questions. Protect yourself, your staff, your students, and your church.

- ✔ Who do I ask when I have questions about our church's insurance coverage?
- ✔ Who is the insurer?
- ✔ Who is covered by our insurance?
- ✔ What crisis procedures does our insurance company use?
- ✔ What insurance coverage is in effect at the facility to which we're going?
- ✔ What kind and amount of insurance will protect volunteers with my group?
- ✔ What level of driver training does our policy require of volunteer drivers?

Insurance and safety guidelines

Parents will be your best supporters—until you put their children at risk through unwise choices. You will create and keep the trust and respect of parents by carefully thinking through the risks you face with students. Use the following safety check up to evaluate activities sponsored by your ministry:

- ▶ Do your staff members understand their overall roles and responsibilities?

- ▶ Do you have enough adult leaders for this activity?

- ▶ Do they understand their roles for this event? Have you given them clear assignments? Rule of thumb—that is, the younger the kids, the more adults you'll need.

- ▶ For junior highers you'll want one sponsor for every eight students; senior highers require a one-to-10 ratio. The number of sponsors needed is also influenced by the type of activity.

- ▶ Have you clearly spelled out to both adult leaders and students the guidelines for student behavior for each event?

Real Life

We stopped for lunch on our way to a week of ministry in Mexico. For some reason, I walked around inspecting the van and trailer while everyone was eating. I noticed that the back bumper was precariously hanging off. "Hmm, this doesn't look right," I thought. (I have a keen grasp of the obvious.) Taking a closer look, I noticed that the trailer hitch had been welded to the bumper. We were only one weld away from losing our supplies and clothes for the entire trip and from setting a vehicle loose to potentially strike and kill someone else.

Vehicle safety

According to Church Mutual Insurance Company (churchmutual.com), 50,000 deaths due to transportation accidents occur each year. Until we experience an accident firsthand, we often don't take precautions to protect ourselves and our group.

► Select your drivers carefully. Screen them with the **Driver Application**. Make sure they have received the necessary training and have experience with the type of vehicle you're asking them to drive.

► Use a maintenance routine before heading out on any trip. If you're driving a church-owned vehicle, make sure it is being regularly maintained by a professional mechanic. It should have thorough, semiannual inspections. Check the file for yourself.

**Driver Application
page 400**

► Always inspect the vehicle(s) your group uses prior to leaving. Walk around the vehicle to check tires (pressure and tread wear), all lights, and any sign of leakage under the vehicle. Check fluid levels, brakes, wiper operation, and fuel level.

Practice defensive driving

► Keep your eyes moving.

► Be courteous to other drivers.

► Use caution.

► Plan ahead.

► Maintain proper following distances.

► Be prepared for the unexpected.

Think through carefully the wisdom of driving your group all night:

► Reaction time is affected by illness or fatigue, highway hypnosis, anger or preoccupied thoughts, effects of alcohol or other drugs.

► Set a maximum time for driving—no more than eight hours per 24-hour day

► Have a number of qualified drivers for longer trips.

► Respect visibility issues.

► Acknowledge wet pavement.

► Be extra careful in ice and snow.

FasTrack

68 Along with regularly inspecting and maintaining vehicles, write up travel guidelines and emergency procedures.

Practical steps for providing safe transportation for your ministry

> Don't assume your insurance coverage is adequate or in effect. Check with your church business administrator and your insurance agent.

> Check out the driving records of your staff. Don't skip this step. Use the **Driver Application** form to screen potential drivers.

**Driver Application
page 400**

> Don't let students drive. Period. Adult leaders should be at least 21 years old to drive.

> Tell your staff drivers that you expect them to obey all traffic laws. (Seriously!)

> Don't put more people in the car or van than it is designed to handle. Counting seatbelts generally lets you know how many you can legally transport. Don't exceed that number—ever.

> Check with your insurance agent regarding insurance coverage. Your church can be held liable for the damage and injuries caused by its employees or volunteers using their own vehicles or vehicles that the church rents or borrows for its operations. If your church uses vehicles owned by staff or volunteers, you should consider purchasing non-owned or hired auto liability coverage.

> When you leave for an event, make sure someone knows who went, where you are going, how you're getting there, and when to expect your return. Leave trip details and a list of participants and staff at the church office.

> It's generally safer to rent or lease a vehicle than to borrow. Any problems with the vehicle are the responsibility of the rental company. Plus, insurance coverage is more clearly defined.

Real Life

Live and learn.

A person volunteered to drive her van with a load of people for a staff retreat.

"We better drive carefully," she said offhandedly, "because I don't have any vehicle insurance." I chuckled. Nice joke, I thought. Later, while preparing this chapter, I found out she *really didn't* have coverage. It could have been disastrous if we'd experienced an accident. Next time, here's what I'll do differently:

- Check the driver's insurance coverage before counting on her to drive. No coverage, no driving.

- Check the driver's previous accidents or violations. More than two accidents or moving violations within the last two years disqualifies a person.

- Check the driver's health for obvious problems. The same driver who had no vehicle insurance is diabetic and has fallen into diabetic convulsions recently, so she shouldn't have been driving anyway. Because of my neglect, I put everyone at risk. Fortunately, there will be a next time—but not for this driver.

When accidents happen

Be prepared to deal with accidents and injuries at your event—and hope they're not headline disasters. They'll change your life forever—and no amount of preparation changes that.

Chapter preview

- Establish general emergency procedures
- Designate a crisis manager—a Top Dog (TD)
- Qualities of a TD
- Emergency procedures for the TD
- Permission slips: When and why
- Follow-up accidents with an **Incident Report**
- Claim management
- What to do when the worst happens
- Case studies

Establish general emergency procedures

Every youth leader should have a *written* emergency procedure policy for all general ministry activities.

- Provide each staff member a written manual, including emergency procedures.
- Verbally explain procedures at new-staff orientation.
- At each event assign an emergency or crisis manager (you or another staff person) who knows procedures. Larger ministries who retain a doctor, nurse, or EMT may place that professional in the manager position.
- Staff and leadership need to specifically know who is the crisis manager on duty (sometimes called the Top Dog or point person). In an emergency, speed is important, clarity is critical, and teamwork is essential.
- Make sure that several members of your staff have taken basic CPR and first-aid training courses. Clear thinking in a medical crisis comes with proper medical training.
- Keep a well-stocked medical kit easily accessible.

The well-supplied medical kit

Assuming you call an EMT immediately when you have a serious injury—and a hospital is readily accessible—your medical kit should be filled with these medical supplies:

- Band-Aids
- instant ice packs
- hydrogen peroxide
- rubbing alcohol
- tweezers
- aspirin or non-aspirin medication such as Tylenol (for you and other adults—don't give to students without written permission)
- surgical (rubber) gloves
- thermometer (the small, plastic disposable ones are handy)
- antibiotic ointment or cream (such as Neosporin)
- antibacterial or antiseptic spray (such as Bactine)
- bug bite cream or lotion (such as Cortaid or Cortizone 10)
- gauze
- medical tape

You also may need to keep a biohazard kit on hand in case of bleeding (available in janitorial supply catalog or visit safetyon-line.com for links to suppliers). In addition to surgical gloves and medical supplies, you'll need a chemical that absorbs blood spills and sanitizes the area. If you need a more extensive medical kit (remote location, international travel, special-needs kids), and consult with trained medical personnel.

➤ Have additional staff who have received advanced first-aid training, if possible.

➤ Get to know doctors, nurses, Certified First Responders, and EMTs in your ministry. In case you have an emergency, however, do not rely on them as a substitute for calling 911. Instead, rely on them to provide assistance until help arrives. Make yourself aware of liability related to using off-duty medical personnel.

Your church leadership must establish a comprehensive crisis plan to deal with a number of emergency situations your church could face. Resist the temptation to come up with this plan alone. Ask for help. Some experts in this area may already attend your church.

First, good communication can defuse a crisis—cell phones and radios are an asset (especially in the case of large events were your staff are spread out). Before the event starts, decide on a central meeting place in case of a crisis where staff can learn pertinent information. Assign a point person. Store emergency supplies in an accessible but secure place. Keep a procedure notebook with the supplies that spells out what to do in case of an emergency.

Depending on your geographic location, you'll need to prepare for specific emergencies:

➤ **Fires**. How quickly can you evacuate your building? Do you have a way to account for everyone? Identify a meeting place if ever you're forced to evacuate.

➤ **Earthquakes**. Where is the safest place to go?

➤ **Tornadoes**. When a warning siren goes off, where are people supposed to go?

➤ **Missing students**. If you discover a student missing from an event, what steps should you follow?

➤ **Acts of violence**. If one of your students is assaulted at a ministry event, what would you do?

➤ **Suicide.** If you've learned of a suicide in your community or group, what should you do?

➤ **Bomb threats**. If a caller threatened to bomb your church, how would you handle it?

➤ **Floods**. Is your church in a flood zone?

Designate a crisis manager— a Top Dog

In the event of a crisis, every ministry staffer needs to know their own roles—as well as others' roles. We recommend having one crisis manager—one Top Dog (or chief, captain, head honcho, director, bigwig, protector, "the person in charge in case of emergencies").

Realistically, you'll need to equip several people to act as Top Dogs, as well as to handle other, more specific tasks. The main criteria for the TDs' other tasks is that they are flexible enough to drop if they're called to manage a crisis. For example, the TD shouldn't be the only judge at a sporting event. Because if the TD is needed for an emergency, the whole event will come to a halt. Parents are often qualified candidates for the TD role and are happy to help.

Real Life

In the middle of the service on a normal Sunday morning at church, the fire alarm went off. One usher ran to the back of the building and said to me, "How do we shut this thing off? It's disturbing the service!" Another staff member countered, "We've got to get everyone out of the building. I think something is wrong."

The person in the pulpit said, "Let's pray."

For a moment, no one took charge.

Several of us knew the alarm system well. We instructed the ushers that the alarm must be treated as signaling a real emergency until we could determine otherwise. The children's ministry had rehearsed this scene many times and was already evacuating kids. All totaled, 1,600 people lined up outside the building. Was there a fire? Was the evacuation really necessary?

We checked out the alarm system and learned that a sensor had malfunctioned; there was no fire. We gave the all-clear, and everyone came back into the building. We learned several things that day—

- In an emergency, people need direction from leaders.

- Plans developed in advance remove pressure.

- When in doubt, respond to the alarm as if a real emergency is occurring. In a real fire, seconds matter.

Emergency tools

The most valuable emergency tools today are—

- a cell phone (with a charged battery).

- an emergency plan and training.

- a first-aid kit.

Kids are kids

Teenagers tend to play down their physical ailments in front of their peers. "I'm okay—really! I was only out for a few seconds. I feel fine." Don't be fooled. Do you really want to take responsibility for that student when she collapses 20 minutes later because her brain is bleeding? Leave accident assessment to medical professionals. For clearly minor injuries—or injuries that could escalate to serious—contact the parents and transfer the care responsibility to them. If parents leave it up to you, seek medical attention.

FasTrack

69 Prepare for emergencies by writing out procedures—for general as well as specific emergency situations.

Accompanying a student to medical facilities

The staff person assigned to the student by the TD should have the **Medical Release** form, which contains emergency contact numbers, all medical conditions, allergies, and medications. The staff person assigned is the parent's representative and should remain with the student at all times, if possible. Without being in the way, this staffer should persistently request to be included in the decision-making process for treatment.

Once the parents arrive, the staff member brings them up to speed on what has occurred so far, and then slides into a support role for the parents. Once the crisis is over, or when the parents no longer require assistance, the staff person reports to the TD about events at the medical facility and fills out an **Incident Report**.

Qualities of a Top Dog

▶ **Experience in successful crisis managing.** The Top Dog needs to be a trained and accomplished leader who's shown the ability to act when a crisis arises. Use a trainee TD in an apprentice role with a current TD. Only after proving themselves should trainees be appointed sole Top Dog. Although the job is a "hurry up and wait" type position, when they are needed, Top Dogs must always be at their best. It's a bummer to find out in the middle of a problem that the adult in charge doesn't handle crisis well.

▶ **Equipped with basic medical training.** TDs need at least a certification in first aid and CPR—not that the job of the TD is to diagnose or treat the injured, but rather to assess what the next course of action should be and to lead the team in that direction.

▶ **Calm and cool-headed.** Even though most injuries are minor and only minimal treatment is necessary, the TD needs to be able to remain calm under pressure.

▶ **Available.** The TD must be accessible and available. On a retreat or extended event, several people may act as the TD at different times. That way your crisis manager is always ready and refreshed. You may equip the TD with a communication tool to make the TD more accessible. At a retreat use a walkie-talkie, a pager, or an air horn. Try different things to see what works.

▶ **Supported by the rest of the leadership team.** Once the TD determines the course of action, the staff needs to support the decision. A crisis is not the time to debate issues; it's the time for the leader to lead and the followers to follow. If the stakes are high, the lines of authority must be clear and everyone has to do his or her job.

The TD shouldn't accompany the injured to the hospital, if hospitalization is required. The TD needs to stay with the group in case there are other incidents. The TD should pick a staff person or two to accompany the injured to the hospital until parents arrive. The accompanying staffers should be responsible people, preferably of the same gender, and with whom the student feels comfortable.

▶ **Good adult communicator.** The TD discusses the incident with the staff member who accompanied the injured person and reviews the person's written incident report.

Emergency procedures for the TD

1. One staff person attends to the injured party's needs.
2. Another staff person immediately contacts the TD. (In a dire emergency, if the TD can't be located expediently, the staff in charge proceeds with the next steps while sending someone to find the TD.)
3. TD assesses the situation.
4. TD determines if the individual can be assisted locally. If so, the TD assigns an appropriate adult to assist the injured. The TD also determines at this point whether to notify the parents or apply a Band-Aid and call it good.
5. If the situation requires trained medical assistance or transportation to the hospital, TD asks a leader to call 911 to request paramedics and an ambulance. The caller needs to know the status of the injured person and the specific street address or location of the injured. The caller needs to remain on the phone to assist the dispatcher as long as necessary.
6. TD sends a staff member to the entrance to guide the paramedics.
7. TD assigns another *calm* staff person to contact the individual's parents and advise them of the situation. If the person is being transported to the hospital, the parents should meet them at the hospital.
8. The TD and any other needed staff member stays with the injured individual. All other staff assist the TD by keeping students and other onlookers away from the victim and out of the emergency team's way.
9. A staff member brings the student's **Medical Release** form to the TD.
10. The TD appoints a staff member to accompany the student to the hospital and gives her the form.
11. After the student is transported, the TD assigns someone to clean up the accident site. If there is blood involved, use a biohazard kit for cleanup.
12. The TD determines what, if any, explanation needs to be given to the remaining students or if the scheduled activities needs to be adjusted or cancelled.
13. The staff person who accompanies the student to the hospital checks in with the TD once they arrive at the medical facilities, and again when there is any news. (Remember that cellular phones cannot be used inside hospitals.)
14. The TD and the leaders involved fill out an **Incident Report** and, if necessary, a **Damage Report.**
15. The following day, or as soon as possible, the TD distributes copies of the reports to the appropriate recipients.

What a Top Dog must know

➤ Location of phone(s) and how to dial out

➤ How and where to find trained medical help (especially if the group is in a remote location)

➤ Address, directions, and phone number of the nearest medical center

➤ Location of the first-aid kit

➤ Where staff and students are rooming

➤ How to reach the facility director (camp, hotel, retreat center)

➤ Location of medical release forms

➤ Where a designated emergency vehicle is parked and who has the keys

➤ Special medical or physical conditions of the participants as recorded on the medical release forms. TD must communicate these special needs to the rest of the staff.

Incident Report
page 380

Damage Report
page 378

Transporting the injured

If students need transportation to a hospital, rather than take them by car, call an ambulance.

Transportation by ambulance offers consistent, quality care for the injured person and more protection for you from lawsuits. It's cheaper to take responsibility for the cost of the ambulance trip than to assume liability in the event something goes terribly wrong. You also may be unaware of additional, unseen injuries that may cause greater damage if you try to transport the person yourself. Let trained medical professionals take the responsibility.

Permission slips: When and why

Always require student participants to fill out **Medical Release** forms. Permission slips provide emergency contact information, instructions about a student's special medical or physical needs, and let medical personnel start helping your student right away.

Ask a legal professional to check out any legal document—including the ones offered in this book. Permissions and medical forms must be signed by a parent or *legal* guardian. Baby-sitters, sisters, and grandparents don't count. Some ministries request every student to submit a signed medical release at the start of every year. Staff bring copies of those forms to all ministry events throughout the year. Yes, it's a lot of work, but I can tell you from experience that it's worth it when you face the inevitable emergencies.

FasTrack

71 For liability purposes, *if at all possible* send an injured student to the hospital by ambulance. Call 911 first.

- If you are transporting students off site for anything, you need permission slips.

- If you conduct an overnight at your church building, you need permission slips.

- If a small group of students go with a youth group leader *anywhere*, you need permission slips. (Gone are the days that the youth worker can pick up a group of students at school and go out for a Coke without getting permission from their parents. Plan ahead and make sure you have at the very least, verbal permission from a parent directly to you—not through the student. *Never assume.*)

Real Life

My friend and I were galloping on horseback when I was awkwardly thrown. I was badly injured and in severe pain. Although I've known my friend my whole life, this was the first time we had to endure a physical crisis together. She is good at many things; I learned that day that she is not good in a crisis. There I was, rolling around on the ground in pain, and all she could do was sit on her horse and laugh. "You looked so funny flying off the horse," she explained.

Next time I'm near death I'm going to call 911. Although I love my friend, I would never place her in the role of TD. Some people just aren't made to be a TD. Be sure to pick one who is.

Follow up accidents and injuries with an Incident Report

An incident report is written documentation of incidents, accidents, or mishaps involving people in your ministry. Injuries *will* happen. Giving careful thought to the process of crisis managing before it happens protects staff and students, saves precious time in a crisis, and avoids confusion.

Submit copies of the **Incident Report** to the various individuals who need to know what happened. Record in your emergency procedure manual the pastors or ministry supervisors who should receive an incident report. Contact your insurance company. Deal with the incident report in an objective manner. State the facts as completely as possible. It's not your responsibility to assess blame but to collect and record the facts as accurately as possible. Your report should include what you and other witnesses heard and observed. Given today's legal environment, if a student is injured, assume you will be sued. Document everything. Be proactive in following up with the parents.

What to include on an incident report.
All vital information needs to be documented.

- **Who** was hurt, who else was involved, and who was in charge at the time of the injury?

- **What** happened to whom, what exactly was the injury (not the diagnosis but the symptoms)?

- **When** did the incident occur? Include the date and time.

- **Where** was the group? Where was the injured person?

- **How** did the injury occur?

What to include on a Damage Report

Document all vital information about the damaged items.

Who was involved and who, if anyone, was in charge at the time the damage was done?

What happened to what equipment? Take a photo if at all possible.

When did the damage occur? Include the date and time.

Where was damaged item at the time of damage, and where is it currently?

How did the damage occur?

Additional comments: Include contact information for eyewitnesses and other pertinent information. Note if people were injured in the accident, and if so, attach a copy of the **Incident Report** to the **Damage Report**.

Smart Tip

Seek counsel from your ministry's attorney prior to facing an accident. Do not use the information in this book as the replacement for professional legal advice. In fact, call and set up that appointment today!

Additional comments. Also include names and contact information of eyewitnesses. Record the specific diagnosis if professional, medical personnel label the injury. Who stayed with the student? Was an ambulance called? Or was the student driven to the hospital in a private vehicle? Who drove? If property was damaged in the incident, attach a copy of the **Damage Report.**

Legal Counsel

Go to the senor pastor regarding legal issues. When he says, "We're fine and need no help from a lawyer—God can take care of us," write back something like this:

Dear Pastor,

Thanks for speaking with me today. From our conversation I understand that you don't want me to seek legal counsel regarding our current youth ministry situation. So, based on your advice, we will continue to allow students to stand on top of the bus while driving to events.

A copy of this letter will be in my permanent file.

Have a good day.

Susan
Your dedicated youth pastor

knowing that it is not the job of you or your staff to analyze the situation; you must objectively state what happened. Offering your opinions or conclusions about the diagnosis or case is inappropriate at this time. The insurance investigator will check with the medical records for the diagnosis.

Claim management

Once an injury has occurred, someone must follow through with the management of the case. Check with your pastor or ministry supervisor to learn who manages the paperwork and claims. A file should be started. It is impossible to over emphasize how important accurate and detailed records of incidents and damages are. Accurate documentation by numerous parties is critical to legal treatment of a case. You can jeopardize yourself and your ministry with sloppy documentation.

If a student is filing a claim through her own insurance company (sometimes damage to property is covered on personal homeowner's policies—again, check with your agent), all she might need is a copy of your incident report. If there is an investigation on behalf of the insurance company, you or your staff may be interviewed. Attend the interview

FasTrack

72 Document and place in the file every step that you or your staff take during and after the crisis.

Real Life

No kidding, this one really happened.

A youth group was doing a scavenger hunt at a local mall. Carrying a list of things and people that they had to find, the students scattered into the mall. One of their tasks was to find their disguised youth pastor. He had dressed as an old woman being pushed in a wheelchair by a staff person dressed as an older man.

Trying very hard to look like an old woman and not succeeding, the youth pastor was stopped by the mall security and questioned. When he said that the group was doing a scavenger hunt, the officers told him that was illegal and they arrested him. After cuffing him, they escorted him out of the mall and drove him to the police station. Unfortunately, he had the van keys in his purse. The stranded students began calling home for help.

What would you have done differently? (Improving your disguise is not an option.)

What to do when the worst happens

It's normal not to seek help until you need it, but it's wise to be prepared for the worst. No one knows when a tragedy will strike. The responsible leader prepares the youth ministry staff and the youth of the church for fatalities—not only accidental deaths, but also suicides and disabling injuries.

Jack Crabtree, in *Better Safe Than Sued* (Group Publishing), tells a chilling story of an accident on a youth group trip resulting in the death of a student. Although no preparation is honestly adequate to equip someone to deal with that magnitude of disaster, Crabtree suggests ways to recover from such a trauma.

- **Take care of yourself.** You need rest, friendships, and time to deal with such a life-altering event. Cling to a trusted friend or partner. Restore your personal balance by putting yourself in a healing place: the mountains, the ocean, your garden, among friends, alone.

- **Help the family and friends** emotionally by listening, being supportive, spending time with them, being patient with them, and by asking what they need you to do for them.

- **Help your group process the tragedy.** Take time to process the recent events. Provide counselors who will meet with those students who are deeply affected by the event. Don't expect people to recover at your speed—some require less time, some more.

Case Studies

- **Climb, climb up Sunshine Mountain**
  Your new, middle school staff person (who won't have any idea that Sunshine Mountain is a Sunday school chorus) wants to take a small group of students on an overnight, rock-climbing trip. Although he has climbed before, he's never taken students before. What do you do?

- **School crisis**
  Thursday morning in your office you're listening to music on the radio while you prepare your Sunday morning talk. You have a full agenda, with several meetings scheduled throughout the day. An announcer interrupts the music to say that a local high school bus has been in an accident. There are serious injuries and some fatalities. Dozens of your students attend that school. You pray none of them was on the bus. The bulletin concludes by naming the hospitals to which the injured students are being taken. What do you do?

▸ **Game dilemma**

One of your staff wants to lead a game that you're not familiar with at youth group. After listening to him describe the game, you have some reservations about it. What do you do?

▸ **And your name is…?**

A parent calls four days after your youth meeting to report that her son was injured at your church and request that the church pay his medical bills. The mother also says it's possible that her son will need ongoing treatment. You don't know the student or the parent and assume he may have been a visitor. What do you do?

▸ **Choose your own ending—car trouble**

You are beginning a two-week summer trip and retreat that has you driving more than 1,000 miles with 27 students and five leaders. Of your three large, borrowed vans, one is eight years old. On a two-lane rural highway the older van starts to overheat. No gas stations, no McDonald's, and no convenience store for 20 miles in either direction. What do you do?

    ❑ Leave all the students, take two leaders, and go to get help.

    ❑ Take as many students as you can fit in the other vans, leave a few students and leaders with the old van, and go to the nearest gas station.

    ❑ Go to the nearest farm and ask for help.

    ❑ Call AAA on your cell phone and wait with everyone for help.

    ❑ Call AAA on your cell phone, take all the students you can fit in the vans, and go to the nearest town where there is fast food.

▸ **Tired of waiting**

Only one student remains to be picked after an event ends. That student is the opposite sex from you. The other staff already went home. It's just you and the student at the church. What do you do?

    ❑ Don't get caught in this situation. Always have two staff (preferably one male and one female) stay until all students are picked up. Ask the student to call his parents—even if he's called before—and leave a message stating that he is the only student left, that the youth worker is waiting with them, and where he is to be picked up.

    ❑ If possible, wait outdoors or in the entrance hall with the student until the parents come.

    ❑ Talk to the parent when he arrives and encourage him to be more punctual next time.

    ❑ Delegate the job of waiting on late parents to parents. Recruit a married couple with kids in your program to handle these situations.

    ❑ All of the above.

Recommended resources

RESOURCES IN TRAINING TEENAGERS

First Aid, Lifesaving, and Safety, Irving, Texas: Boy Scouts of America

To order by credit card—call BSA operators toll-free, 800/323-0732.

or write to—Direct Mail Center
P.O. Box 909
Pineville, NC 28134

PRINT RESOURCES

➤ *Better Safe Than Sued,* Jack Crabtree (Group Publishing, 1998).

➤ *More Than a Matter of Trust,* Melanie L. Herman, John Patterson, and Leslie T. White (Nonprofit Risk Management Center, 1998).

➤ *Legal Defense Handbook; For Christians in Ministry,* Carl F. Lansing (NavPress, 1992).

➤ *Business Management in the Local Church,* David R. Pollock (Moody Press, 1995).

➤ *Church Administration Handbook,* Bruce P. Powers (Broadman & Holman, 1997).

➤ *Management: A Biblical Approach,* Myron Rush (Scripture Press, 1983).

➤ *Avoiding a Crash Course,* Pam Rypkema (Nonprofit Risk Management Center, 1995).

➤ *Organizing for Accountability,* Robert R. Thompson and Gerald R. Thompson (Shaw, 1991).

➤ *Guide to Safe Scouting* (Irving: Boy Scouts of America,1996)

➤ *No Surprises,* Charles Tremper and Gwynne Kostin (Nonprofit Risk Management Center, 1993)

WEB RESOURCES

Church Mutual Insurance Company has a number of resources on their Web site to assist you. Check them out at www. churchmutual.com. They are available free by mail or can be immediately downloaded.

Information brochures available from Church Mutual:

Church Safety Begins with People
Helpful information and tips you can use to make your church a safer place for all who gather there.

Fire Safety for Your Church
A checklist of practical steps you can take to help prevent a fire (including arson) in your church. The United States Fire Administration (a division of FEMA) has distributed 307,000 copies of this booklet!

Crime-Proof Your Church
Easy ways you and your congregation can minimize the threat of serious crime through a church crime-prevention program.

Make Activities Safer at Your Church
Potential hazards among your many church activities are highlighted, with suggestions on how to minimize risks.

Maintaining Safety Away from Your Church
Guidelines to assist you in planning safe trips for groups of all ages—highlighting precautionary and supervisory tactics.

Protecting Your Church Against Cold-Weather Damage and Energy Loss
Important tips on energy conservation and cold-weather precautions, designed to supplement your regular winterization procedures.

The Road to Safer Transportation
Problems that can occur when transporting a group of people, and how you can help avoid them.

Recognizing Your Church's Liability Risks
A revealing glimpse at the many exposures facing your church today, offering a broad understanding of the civil justice system and how it affects your church.

Make Your Camping Activities Safer
A checklist of safety precautions that you and your congregation should take before a camping trip.

Safety Tips on a Sensitive Subject—Child Sexual Abuse
Advice on how to help prevent the problem, and if it does occur, how to better cope with it. Our most popular booklet.

Severe Weather Protection for Your Church
Tips on precautionary measures against a variety of different storms to help protect your church and congregation.

Insuring Your Church—Points to Consider
An explanation of the protection that insurance can give your church. No matter what precautions you take, some accidents will happen for which you need a well-tailored insurance program.

Youth Safety and Your Church
Filled with useful information that will help you identify and prevent risks in areas such as camping, transportation, winter sports, water activities, weather hazards, sexual abuse, and more.

RED CROSS

Check out the Red Cross at redcross.org for resources and local training in—

First aid and CPR

HIV and AIDS awareness

Disaster services

Baby sitter training

EVENT INSURANCE

For the larger event you might want to get some additional coverage than the standard church coverage. Check with your churches insurance agent or you can contact Gales Creek for more information (galescreek.com).

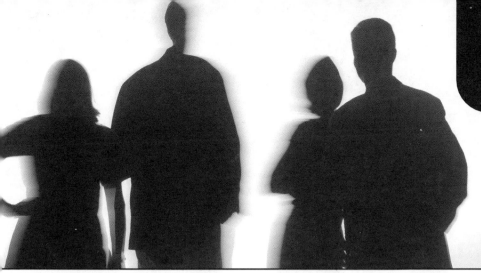

Getting a youth ministry job

If you can do anything else in life besides youth ministry, do it. Youth ministry requires a strong sense of calling from God, powerful passion, and a good dose of vision—especially midway through a lock-in when you've just discovered a group of sophomores tagging the church sign outside.

The answer to the question, "Should I go into youth ministry?" may wind up being a yes or a no; but the journey to the answer winds through family, friends, and acquaintances and follows the hills and valleys of your life. Here's a list of questions to ask yourself and your friends and family to affirm your direction:

• What else in my life agrees that I'm cut out for professional youth ministry?
• Does my ministry supervisor concur with my decision to become a youth ministry professional?
• What does my former youth pastor think about me doing full-time youth ministry?
• What experiences make me believe I'm making a good decision (volunteer, camp counselor, intern)?
• Have I "shadowed" a youth pastor and seen a cross-section of programming—everything from midweek Bible studies to weekend retreats to parent meetings? Have I observed mundane as well as crisis times?
• What does my family (spouse, parents, children) think about my desire to do full-time youth ministry?
• How much time have I spent listening for God's guidance?
• Is there anything about me—sins I don't give up or impossibly annoying personality traits—that would make it difficult for me to be in full-time ministry?
• Have I discussed my professional direction with a career counselor?

In Getting a youth ministry job—

How to get a great youth ministry job

The simple reality of the workplace is that to get a job you must generally look for one.

Chapter preview

- A career in youth ministry
- What a résumé should look like
- What a résumé should say about you
- The cover letter
- Youth ministry jobs—finding one

A career in youth ministry

The dream has kept you awake nights. As you've talked with friends, you've caught yourself pounding the table about the importance of working with adolescents. Your journal entries underscore this passionate theme. Whether you're an upper-level student considering your first full-time position or in your thirties and considering a midlife career switch to youth ministry as a full-time profession, this chapter will start you in the process.

Veteran youth workers offer these tips on discerning if youth ministry is the right direction in which to move:

- Look for a place to volunteer that has people who can help you become a better youth worker. Suck their brains clean of everything they know about youth ministry. At the end of the season, ask them to act as references.

- Kids who want to get into a great college figure out in high school what it will take to get accepted. Yet, too often, potential youth workers fail to do this. If you're thinking about entering the youth ministry field, figure out what experience and knowledge you can get *now*.

- A helpful practice for me was reflecting on my life and thinking about experiences when I was really energized. I realized what those experiences had in common: when I was organizing groups of people to do things, when I was creating community, and when I was discussing ideas with people—especially when those ideas pertained to God.

Real Life

During a recent search for candidates to fill a youth ministry position, I received 100 résumés. Out of those 100 responses, I received 10 phone calls. Of those 10 callers, only three candidates knew how to handle the call. Two candidates were clearly clueless, and the remaining five callers were almost rude in the way they followed up on their applications: "I called to find out where the process is," and "So when can I expect to hear from you?"

If ministry is primarily about relationships, learn how to come across as a relational person as you look for a ministry. Don't just sit by the phone waiting for it to ring—do your part: pray, write your résumé and get it out there, meet with people who can help you sharpen your interviewing skills, make follow-up calls. If you're serious about moving to a specific area, go there—fly, drive, run, walk—and meet with churches.

By the way, just in case any of your contacts decide to call you, you may want to change the message on your voice mail. Do you really want potential employers hearing you imitate Bart Simpson or make weird sounds?

➤ Getting youth ministry experience early on in your decision-making process and making time to reflect on your experiences can undergird your confidence in your decision to either enter into or turn away from ministry among adolescents.

What a résumé should look like

The same rules apply for a youth ministry résumé as for a résumé for other professions. A well-done résumé is primarily a tool to get your foot in the interviewer's door. A poorly prepared résumé will get recycled.

FasTrack

73 Ask several people to proofread your résumé. If no one is available, read it backward. It slows you down and you're more likely to catch any errors. Many résumés get tossed after the first reading because they have too many typos or other errors.

Even though youth ministry allows for a lot more creativity and freedom than most professions, you should still be fairly conservative with your résumé unless you know the organization really well. Your résumé should be—

➤ **No more than one page long**. The exceptions: If you've been in youth ministry for 10 or more years or if you're making a midlife career switch, you can stretch the résumé to no more than two pages.

➤ **Printed with black ink on white, ivory, or gray paper**. Head to an office supply store and buy résumé paper with matching envelopes. Use a heavier, high-quality paper, not what you find in your laser printer or copier.

➤ **Printed in a legible font**. Using serif fonts makes for the easiest reading because the tags, or serifs, naturally draw the eye to the next letter. (This is a serif font; this font is without serif.) Chose a font that draws attention to your experience, not to the font itself. Stay away from funky, unless you're applying for a job that places a high value on creativity. Besides, your basic funky fonts tend to look cheesy rather than hip.

➤ **Have at least a one-inch border all around**. Resist the urge to cram the page full of information. Give the gist of what you want to say and leave plenty of white space. It looks sharper and more professional.

➤ **Without typos or grammatical errors**.

➤ **A personal Web page.** This can work. An easily navigable site may graphically convey your ministry philosophy, demonstrate your creativity, and show that you're technologically astute (at least you can fake it). Keep it simple and clean in design. Don't make yourself bigger than you really are. Looking too good to be true is a turn off.

➤ **Need help?** Head to Kinko's or another copy shop. They have the hardware, software, resource books, and paper to do the job right. Don't scrimp on quality. You're selling yourself. Show that you care.

Smart Tip

Develop a personal board of directors you can tap when you're making critical decisions. These are people whose discernment, discretion, and insight you value. They may not all be close friends, but they are familiar with your life. They could be mentors, former youth pastors, relatives, college professors, or best friends.

What a résumé should say about you

Real Life

I received a résumé that listed incorrect phone numbers. I had to ask why would I trust this person with the lives of high schoolers if he couldn't manage to get the right phone numbers for his references.

Tons of books on creative résumé writing line the shelves of bookstores, and a wealth of Web sites will reveal the fine points of résumé writing—monster.com for one. Remember that a résumé is a jumping-off spot for conversations in the interview. You only want to give the church a taste of what you can do, not overwhelm it with the whole smorgasbord. Arrange your résumé according to your strengths and weaknesses and according to the job you're applying for. If you're a recent college graduate with minimal job experience, for example, include leadership positions you held in school, such as resident assistant or newspaper editor. If you've been out of school for awhile, put your experience first and your education at the end. A youth ministry résumé should include these basic components (not necessarily in this order):

RÉSUMÉ COMPONENT 1—
Biodata

At the top of the résumé, include—

➤ Your name

➤ Phone (with area code)

➤ E-mail address

➤ Home address

➤ Any temporary addresses (for example, "From May 23 to August 14 I can be reached at Camp of the Blue Frogs.")

RÉSUMÉ COMPONENT 2—
Personal objective statement or long-term goal

Focus your résumé with this statement—make it specific enough to land you the right interview, but avoid too narrow a focus if you're interested in related jobs, as well. If you write, for example, "I am seeking a position in a drama ministry that will allow me to use my skills in acting, directing, and scriptwriting," you've disqualified yourself from being considered for directing extended care programs for latchkey kids—which could have a drama component. Your personal objective statement lets the potential interviewer know if you could be a right fit for the available position.

Sample objective statements

"I am seeking a position as a high school pastor that would allow me to use my gifts and abilities to reach high school adolescents for Christ."

"My objective is to use my passion and experience in ministering to teens as a director of a growing student ministry."

"I am seeking a one-year internship in the area of youth ministry in a town-and-country church setting."

"My goal is to find a challenging youth pastor position in an urban church that has a desire to reach adolescents in the community."

"My goal is to continue my career in youth ministry."

RÉSUMÉ COMPONENT 3—
Educational background

Here's where you describe your formal education—courses taken at universities, seminaries, community colleges. (Save the mention of training taken at seminars or conferences for later.) Name the schools you attended, the degrees you received (and the dates you graduated), and your major and minor areas of study. Don't even think about fudging. Many churches will check your credentials. If you didn't graduate with a degree in youth ministry, you may also want to list courses you took that are applicable to youth ministry, such as counseling, adolescent psychology, public speaking, small-business management, curriculum development, practical theology, methods of biblical study, or small group dynamics.

RÉSUMÉ COMPONENT 4—
Experience

Experience can include both professional employment and volunteer leadership experience.

▶ List your most recent employer or ministry and position first, and work backward.

▶ Include the dates of your employment or service.

▶ Depending on your experience, you may want to exclude certain jobs that don't pertain to your objective. Just make sure you don't leave any large, unexplainable gaps in your employment history. People who read résumés are smart. They read between the lines. Literally.

➤ Summarize each job experience. You can use full sentences, phrases, or bullet points, depending on your style preference. When writing up your experience, use active words like *designed, selected, developed, evaluated, coordinated, planned, led, facilitated, envisioned, organized, executed, implemented, managed, assessed, oversaw, created, supervised,* and *maintained.*

➤ As you describe the job, emphasize the skills that you've exercised that are applicable to youth ministry: organized groups of people…led and coordinated projects…resolved conflict between employees…set up procedures and practices…maintained a buget… coordinated a team…developed a curriculum…created a new program.

➤ Be truthful. Don't fall for the temptation to exaggerate. The youth ministry world is not that large; if your story doesn't totally add up, it's likely you'll be find out.

RÉSUMÉ COMPONENT 5—
Honors, special achievements, memberships and activities, additional education

You want to use common sense in filling out this section. Is it really important, for instance, that the church knows you were elected "the student with the best manners"? (Well, maybe it is.) In this section, highlight areas of notable achievements as a means of offering insight into who you are as a person. Emphasize activities that communicate leadership and teamwork.

Here's where you include any youth ministry-related seminars, conferences, and workshops, such as Youth Specialties Resource Seminars and Youth Worker Conventions, SonLife seminars, membership in the National Network of Youth Ministries.

> **Smart Tip**
>
> If you are replying to someone by e-mail, follow up right away with a good old-fashioned letter.

RÉSUMÉ COMPONENT 6—
References

To make your résumé as flexible as possible, write "Available upon request" in the reference section instead of listing names and phone numbers. This way you may offer different references for different positions. For example, if your high school youth pastor was the college roommate of the senior pastor at the church that's hiring, it may (or may not) be a good idea to include his or her name. People move, after all, and area codes change; you don't want to have a wrong number on your résumé.

➤ Create a sheet of references to send out when they're requested. Include names, positions, organizations, phone numbers, e-mail addresses, business addresses, and relationship to you.

➤ When choosing whom you'll ask to be a reference, consider former employers, youth pastors, professors, and mentors. You want people who can give testimony to both your character and your abilities. (Don't include your mother or your baby sitter in third grade.)

➤ Talk to your potential references ahead of time. Ask, "Do you feel that you know me well enough to be a reference?" This gives them an easy out if they don't think they can be a good reference.

➤ If they agree to be references for you, get permission to use their names and find out where they prefer to be contacted (at work or at home). Let them know the position and the organizations or churches to which you are applying.

Youth ministry résumé double speak

Facilitated a study in biblical literature in the original language.

(Led a Bible study for junior high guys using the King James version.)

Visionary implementer of change.

(Repainted the youth room in the church basement.)

Directed a team of creative entrepreneurs.

(Oversaw the babysitting fundraiser for confirmands.)

Thrive on challenge.

(Drove a bus for four hours with 35 high schoolers and one chaperone who had all gotten food poisoning at camp. What else can you throw at me?)

Skilled in conflict management.

(Separated two girls fighting over the bathroom mirror at the retreat.)

► If your job search takes more than one year, call your references to give them a heads-up on your job search process. If it's been more than three years since you've talked with them, they're probably not the best choice for a reference any more.

Cover letter

Whether you send your résumé by e-mail or snail mail, include a cover letter to introduce yourself, explain how you heard about the position, and highlight relevant experience or skills you especially want a potential employer to notice in the résumé. You may also want to include a sentence saying that your present employer does or does not know you are seeking a new position, thus alerting them to the level of confidentiality needed.

FasTrack

74 Include on your professional résumé biodata, long-term goals, education, experience, honors, and references.

► Make sure you personalize the letter to every situation. Call the church and get the correct spelling of the pastor and of the church. Type the address on the outside of the envelope—don't hand-address it.

► Name the position for which you're applying and where you can be reached (in case the cover letter gets separated from your résumé). End by thanking this person for her consideration and letting her know that you will be following up in the next two weeks. This way, you keep the ball in your court and don't have to sit around waiting for the phone to ring. Just make sure you actually do call. That communicates initiative and follow through.

► When you call, know exactly what you want to say. Don't just call to chat, but don't read from a script, either. And don't make the potential employer feel uncomfortable or pressured. It's not the time to say, "Gee, I really thought you would have called by now," or "Where are your priorities?" or "Am I in the top 10?" Start the call by saying something like—

"I'm following up my letter from last week…"

"I wanted you to know that I am very interested in discussing the position with you…"

"I would really appreciate the chance to talk with you further about this ministry opportunity. You have my contact information if you think I might fit the profile of the person you are looking to lead this ministry…"

"I know you are busy, thanks for taking my call and for your time. I look forward to hearing from you…"

Youth ministry jobs—finding one

Where do you begin to look for a youth ministry position? Here are a couple of ideas to help you in your search—

- **Denominational offices**. Denominations usually keep a list of churches that are looking for youth pastors. They may also be able to tell you a little bit about the history of each position (why the last person left, for starters).

- **Network**. Talk to youth workers in your area to find out who's thinking about moving, or what currently open positions they're aware of. Also, contact the National Network of Youth Ministries (www.youthworkers.net), an organization that specializes in linking youth workers together.

- **Youth Specialties' Web site** (www.YouthSpecialties.com). Youth Specialties maintains an area for individuals, churches, and organizations to post open positions.

- **Publications**. Several magazines (*Christianity Today*, for one) list job openings in their want-ad sections.

- **Local colleges or seminaries**. Contact local Christian colleges or seminaries to find out what churches and organizations have posted job openings with them. Talk to their career counselors, as well as to those in their youth ministry or Christian education departments.

- **Youth ministry conferences**. At some conferences or conventions you can post your résumé on a community bulletin board.

A résumé should not . . .

- Have anything handwritten
- State a salary expectation
- Contain personal information like weight, height, age, race, physical health, place of birth, or marital status. Do not include photos, number of pets, children, or spouses. These are factors that can cause a future employer to be accused of discrimination. Rather than take the chance of being accused, they may toss the résumé. (Besides, it looks very unprofessional.)

Recommended resources

- *Red Light, Green Light: Discerning the Time for a Change in Ministry*, John Cionca (Baker). Out of print, but worth finding. Although geared toward senior pastors, this book is very transferable to youth ministry. It helps assess different signals that let you know when it's time to make a move in ministry.

- *What You Do Best*, Bruce Bugbee (Zondervan 1995)

- *Please Understand Me: Character and Temperament Types*, David Keirsey and Marilyn Bates. (Prometheus Nemesis Book Co. 1984)

- *What Color is Your Parachute?* Richard Nelson Bolles (published annually by Ten Speed Press).

Interviewing for a job in youth ministry

A good interview follows good preparation: know the church, know the community, know yourself.

Chapter preview

▶ Preparing for the interview

▶ The interview

▶ Critical questions you need to ask

▶ Responding to inappropriate questions

▶ Follow-up

Preparing for the interview

So your stellar résumé prompted the longed-for call and—good news—you got the interview. But before you book your plane flight, make the following preparations—otherwise your blind date might end up a horror story rather than an anniversary tale.

1. Familiarize yourself with that particular church or organization. Find out as much as you can about the ministry with which you're interviewing. That way, you walk in primed to ask key questions and to explore the significant issues. There are a couple of ways to do this:

▶ The formal way is to request annual reports, denominational information, mission statements, and informational brochures. Also, check out their Web site, if they have one. Look not only for what they say, but what they omit. How often does the youth ministry get mentioned? What percentage of the whole church budget is dedicated to the youth ministry?

▶ The informal way differs with each situation and must be approached delicately. You may want to call former youth pastors, counselors, the church secretary (a gold mine of information), or students in the group. State the purpose of your call and then listen.

Career-limiting moves

• Condoning food wars of any kind in the church sancuary.

• Letting a student use your church Internet account for personal e-mails.

• Getting permission to use the pastor's office as a breakout room for your junior high event, and then leaving 12 unattended boys there while you run out to buy Cokes.

• Revealing the password for the church's computer network.

• Borrowing cash from the offering.

• Covering the bull's-eye on your office dartboard with your pastor's photo.

• Exceeding your youth ministry budget—again.

Caveat: Resist digging up dirt on the ministry by instead asking questions like—

—What is this youth ministry known for?

—What are its strengths?

—What areas need growth?

➤ Call youth pastors from churches in the area to get their perspectives. You may want to ask, "When you think of First Church, what comes to mind? How is First Church perceived by members in the community?"

When you've done your homework, prepare a list of questions based on what you've gleaned.

2. Familiarize yourself with the community.

Youth pastors on a job search generally take a look at the church with which they'll interview. But unless you're planning on living at the church 24/7, you need to check out the surrounding community. One of the easiest ways to do this is browsing local newspapers on the Internet. Along with checking out housing costs, get a feel for what's going on in the public schools, recreational opportunities, cultural offerings, the crime rate. If you're married, is this a place where your family will feel comfortable? If you're single, is this a place where you'll find like-minded people, or will you feel like "odd man out"? When you're single, you don't take your support system with you; rather, you have to start from scratch. That can be great in your 20s, but in your 30s or beyond, how will you feel about living at a great distance from your extended family and your friends? These are issues to consider as you look at the position.

FasTrack

75 Before your interview, get to know the organization and its community.

3. Prepare yourself.

➤ Before the interview, ask a friend to rehearse with you possible interview questions. For a sampling of typical interview questions, see the interviewing section.

➤ Don't hesitate to ask about interview dress code—then dress a step above. The more experienced you are, the less you have to worry about how formally you dress—your résumé and experience will carry you. But, if this is one of your first two jobs, compensate for your youth and inexperience by wearing a suit or a dress. Look at your purchases as an investment in your career.

➤ If you're "candidating" over a weekend, you'll probably want to make sure to bring casual Friday wear as well as your suit. You never know what they may ask you to do or where you might go. Rarely can you ever get away with wearing jeans—even when interviewing for a youth ministry position. Wear them only if you're going to be playing paintball with the board of deacons.

➤ Bring a prepared message with you. Again, you never know what they might ask you to do. What if the high school Sunday school teacher gets sick at the last moment? Guess what? You're now the guest speaker. Plan on it.

➤ Bring breath mints. Stick a couple loose ones in your pockets so they're easy to reach.

➤ Be careful what you eat before you interview. Butterflies don't mix with nachos. Let's just leave it at that.

The interview

An interview can bring on many of the same emotions as a first date. You feel nauseated as well as excited. You can't wait for it to come; you can't wait for it to be over. You want to impress, at the same time, you want to be yourself. And the big question… do you attempt a goodnight kiss? Following these practical tips can make the interview go a little more smoothly:

- **Arrive alone**. Nothing screams *insecure* more than bringing an uninvited friend or even a spouse. Don't bring your husband or wife unless specifically invited to do so.

- **Arrive on time**. A good saying to remember is, "To be early is to be on time; to be on time is to be late. To be late is not to be!" Get to the church about 15 minutes early. Walk around and get a feel for the place. Pick up any brochures you haven't seen yet. Check in with the receptionist about five minutes early.

- **Use the "Magic 4" hello**. Smile at the interviewer; make direct eye contact; say, "Hi, I'm (first name) (last name). It's a pleasure to meet you."; offer a firm but gentle handshake. Focus on coming across in a warm, professional manner.

- **Listen for and remember names**. Call members of the interview team by name. This communicates that you are interested in people.

- **Let the interviewer initiate the first part of the interview**. Just follow their lead in the pacing and the direction of the interaction.

Questions you'll be asked at an interview

- How and when did you become a Christian?
- Why do you feel called to youth ministry?
- What is your philosophy of youth ministry?
- Why do you feel called to this church or ministry?
- What do you know about our church? *(In the corporate world, this question is a test to see if you've done your homework. It's the same way in the ministry world. At one church I know of, this is the defining question. If you don't have something to say, the interview is over—no matter how strong your résumé is. No church wants someone who's just looking for a job. It wants someone who can be committed to the place.)*
- What are your strengths?
- In what areas do you need to grow?
- What would you do in a situation like this? *(This question provides huge clues to what's been issues in the past. If you're asked you questions about discipline or punctuality or communication, odds are that was a problem for the previous youth pastor.)*
- What are your views on—? *(This could be anything from homosexuality to the Palestinian/ Israeli conflict. It all depends on the church and the agenda of the interviewers.)*
- Where do you see youth ministry going in the future?
- What does a successful youth ministry look like?
- What would you do in your first three months at our church?
- What is your style of teaching?
- What is your current salary package?
- What is your view on mission trips (retreats, camps)?
- Why do you want to leave your current situation? *(By the way, when you're asked about your present or past employer, say only positive things. The interviewers don't want to know the dirt, and if you're too negative, they'll begin to wonder if they'd be hiring someone divisive.)*

➤ **Exhibit these seven attributes**: Enthusiasm, confidence, energy, dependability, loyalty, honesty, and a strong work ethic.

➤ **Use the Final 4**. When the interview is coming to a conclusion, smile…make direct eye contact…say, "It sounds like a great opportunity. I look forward to hearing from you"…and offer a firm but gentle handshake.

Critical questions you need to ask

Y ou need to get clear answers to the following questions before you ever agree to take a position:

➤ **How are raises determined?** You'll find out if you'll be locked into your starting salary for the rest of your tenure or if can you negotiate a raise. Are raises based on merit or on life circumstances (someone gets married, has kids, buys a house)? Are raises based on gender or marital status? (it still happens) Veteran advice: Negotiate the salary you want up front; don't plan on making up the difference in a raise. If the church starts you at a certain amount but promises to raise you to a higher amount within the first two years, get it in writing. Promises fade quickly once you're hired.

More career-limiting moves

- Unapproved expenditures involving lost of digits.

- Using live animals in the sancutary to boost attendance at the Christmas musical.

- Permanently canceling Sunday school.

- Making architectural changes to the facility on the basis of "better to ask forgiveness than permission".

- Purchasing equipment or services with the money budgeted for another purpose.

➤ **If the ministry is considered successful in three months, what will that look like? In six months? In one year?** This tells you more about the church's philosophy of ministry than any Web site ever will. It may deny being about numbers, but if your interviewers describe a successful ministry as being "packed out," "crammed with kids," or language like that, you know immediately how you'll be evaluated.

➤ **Why did the last youth pastor leave?** If this raises the least bit of suspicion, reframe this question and ask it again. For example: "Talk to me about staffers who didn't make it here and why." or "Tell me who has been a staff hero in the past and why." ("Is the former youth pastor one of them? Why or why not?")

➤ **Are you hiring me to be the pastor to every kid or to train and equip the adults?** In other words, will your primary focus be building relationships with students or building a team of adults? The answer you seek will be different based on your season of life.

➤ **What has been the youth ministry budget? How do you see that changing in the future? Is the youth pastor's salary included in that?** Listen for what the youth ministry receives from the total budget and listen for the reasoning. It may be that there were no adolescents up until a year ago when the church experienced huge growth. It may also be that the increased budget is due to the youth pastor's proposed salary. You may take the job—but have only $800 a year to work with.

► **What are the church's expectations for numerical and spiritual growth?** Listen for which piece they focus on. Which seems to be a priority and why?

► **How often are job reviews done? Who conducts them? What happens to the results?**

► **Who will supervise me and how much time will I spend with this person?** This is especially important if you are expecting to be mentored by the senior pastor or someone else. You may be interested in the position because it would mean being able to spend time with him or he may only expect to see you on the platform Sunday morning and at church meetings.

► **If someone were to ask you about me a year from now, and you responded that I've exceeded expectations, what would I be doing?**

► **If someone were to ask you about me a year from now, and you responded that I'm barely surviving, what would I have done or not done?** This question may be the way to get at the heart of why the last youth pastor left.

► **What's the process for determining and approving what the youth ministry does?** a) Does everything get approved by a youth committee? b) Does the senior pastor approve everything? or c) Do you have sole authority to make decisions?

► **What other expectations are there outside of youth ministry?** Does the church expect you to preach on a regular basis? Do nursing home visits? Perform weddings and funerals? Fill in when the nursery hits overload?

► **Has the staff ever had a paycheck withheld because the church was short of money?** If so, when? And how was that communicated to the church?

► **What happens when the church is behind budget?** Again, how is that communicated to the congregation?

► **What does a typical week look like?** If you're expecting to work 45 hours a week and they're expecting 60, you're headed for a major confrontation. Get it out in the open before you start.

► **What about outside speaking engagements?** Find out their policy for staff speaking to groups and camps outside the church. Are you allowed a certain number of days per year for that? Does it come out of your vacation time? What about honorariums—can you keep them or do you need to turn them over to the church?

► **Where will my office be located?** This isn't about having a corner office with huge windows. It's about having a place that's easily accessible to the public and won't isolate you from people. Because of the amount of counseling that goes on, your office should be in a central location with a window in the door, not tucked under the basement stairs where people need a map to find it.

Questions you should never ask:

• So, how much are you paying?

• How can I get fired?

• Got any good gossip?

• Do the pastors ever go out for happy hour?

• Do I get my name on the church sign by the street?

► **What computer equipment will I have?** Now's the time to ask for what you want. If possible, choose what you prefer using. Also inquire about software and Internet access.

► **Will I have an administrative assistant?** How many hours a week? With whom am I sharing this person? Who has priority? What is the assistant's base of computer knowledge?

► **What are the three most important qualities a staff member can possess?**

► **What does this church do well?**

► **What is this church known for in the community?**

► **In five years, what will the church look like?**

► **In five years, how do you hope the youth ministry looks?**

► **What is this church really about? What is important here?**

Responding to inappropriate questions

C hurches are notorious for asking inappropriate, and sometimes illegal, questions: *Have you ever committed a huge moral sin? Have you ever smoked pot and, if so, did you inhale? What's your ethnic heritage? What year did you graduate from high school? Who's going to take care of your children if you're hired for this position?* You may choose to answer the questions or respond with one of the following statements:

► "I'm willing to answer your question, but before I do, I'd like to know why you're asking it." This alerts the interviewer that they've crossed a boundary, but that you're willing to cooperate (if you are).

► "I'll answer your question, but you need to know that I'm uncomfortable in doing so." Wait and see what their response is before you continue.

► "I'm not sure I understand the question. Help me understand what you're getting at."

► "I'm sorry. I don't feel I can answer that question. Is there something else you'd like to ask?" You leave them wondering why you won't answer, and risk not getting the job. But if they're really that out of line, do you really want to serve there?

What if it's a phone interview?

Phone interviews can be tricky if more than two people get on the extensions. Some churches believe it's great to have the whole search committee at the phone interview. Sometimes you can be on the phone with seven other people.

As the unfortunate candidate, you have no way to avoid this chaos. Just be prepared for several people talking at once (to each other and to you) and for awkward periods of silence. Make the best of the situation by finding out who's on the other end and what their roles are (take notes!). Be sure to answer the questions you're asked. Make your answers concise. Don't ramble. Ask for feedback ("Do you need me to clarify that?"). Frequently use their names in the discussion.

Follow-up

Within a day after the interview, follow up with a handwritten thank-you note (an e-mail or a phone call is *not* okay). Make sure to thank the interviewer for his or her time, as well as express your continued interest in the position (if that is indeed the case). If you decide that you are no longer interested in the position, let them know your decision either by letter or phone call (again, e-mail is not acceptable).

People wonder how long they should wait to hear from the church about the next step. If you have not heard from the church after a week to 10 days, it's perfectly acceptable to call and ask about the status of the process. In fact, persistent (not annoying) follow-up usually communicates that you're eager and a self-starter.

Churches want people who don't just see their position as another "job" but will be as enthusiastic about being a part of their community as they are. Just watch your tone. Persistently communicate with a positive attitude until the outcome is clearly stated.

Recommended resources

An excellent resource for the legalities involved in hiring church workers is *Selecting and Screening Church Workers*. It is published by Church Law and Tax Report, a division of Christian Ministry Resources, 704/821-3845. This company specializes in the legal side of ministry and has many excellent, user-friendly resources.

The offer

If you remember nothing else, remember this: *Get everything in writing.*

Chapter preview

▶ Negotiating the offer
▶ Negotiating the compensation package
▶ Negotiating professional expenses
▶ Negotiating taxes and days off
▶ If you don't like the offer

Negotiating the offer

T he interviews have gone well. You like the church, it likes you. It looks like there's going to be a wedding. But before you say, "I do," negotiate the prenuptial very carefully. Does it feel awkward? Yes, but as uncomfortable as it feels to talk about money and ministry in the same breath, you live with the reality of paying for a roof and food and utilities, among other necessities. Your best plan is to negotiate for what you want at the beginning. Once you've taken the position, you can't go back and ask for more. The good news is that the more ministry experience you have, the easier it gets to negotiate the initial package.

The job offer can include several different elements—at least base salary and benefits (insurance, retirement). Beyond that, it can include housing, continuing education, auto allowance, and more. It depends on everything from your education and experience to the church's philosophy, experience, and financial soundness. If this is your third job and the church's fifth youth pastor, it's going to be much easier to negotiate an offer than if this is the first for both of you. Take some time to find out what you're really worth. Talk to youth ministry veterans to get a feel for what the going salary rate is for someone with your education and experience. Try not to sell yourself too high or too low. And spend some time clarifying your expectations of the job and putting it in writing before you sit down to negotiate. If your requests are acceptable to the hiring board, have them written into your contract. Youth pastor after youth pastor has echoed this advice: *If you don't have it in writing, you don't have it.*

When is it appropriate to bring up salary expectations?

Salaries in youth ministry vary widely. Don't waste your time or the time of the church if the suggested salary isn't even close to your expectations. If you're a veteran and the church is looking for a veteran, you'll probably be fairly close in expectations. But, the earlier you are in your career, the earlier in the interview process you need to bring up salary to discover any mismatch right away.

If the church contacts you, during the initial contact, ask these three questions: What's the greatest strength of the church? Where do you see it going in the future? Can you tell me the salary range?

If you contact the church, don't bring up salary. You may end up wasting some time, but that's better than being perceived as only interested in the money.

The compensation package

In a nutshell, *compensation* is what you get paid—either through actual dollars or through benefits. Your compensation package will be influenced by whether you are licensed or ordained. If the following elements of a compensation package are foreign concepts to you, talk with your denominational offices or with a tax advisor who is familiar with churches or faith-based organizations.

FACTOR   Base Salary

Your education. If you have a M.Div., your salary should be higher than an employee with only a Bachelor of Arts or an Associate of Arts. If it's not, it tells you that the church doesn't value educational experience. Is that a warning for you? The reality of increased student loans to repay goes with the increased degree.

Your experience. If you come with only a B.A., but you bring the benefit of eight years of experience, negotiate a salary that compensates for experience. Other professions do; so should the church.

Community cost-of-living. How much will it cost to live in this community? Renting a house in Red Oak, Iowa, for instance, costs less than renting an apartment in the Silicon Valley. Too often, youth pastors eager to get a job underestimate how much it will cost to live in a given area, and they end up working extra jobs just to pay the bills.

Several Web sites can do a cost-of-living analysis for you: datamasters.com or monster.com

Comparable salaries. It's helpful to put your position into perspective by comparing it with other professions with similar job requirements. A rule of thumb for recent college graduates is to find out what the area's first-year high school teachers are paid. The school system knows the cost of living for the community. If you have an advanced degree and experience, find out what counselors, principals, and medical personnel in the area are paid. You may also want to call your denominational offices to request salary guidance.

Evaluate

Compare your annual salary expectations with one denomination's base salary ranges for youth pastors:

✔ Bachelor's (of Arts or Sciences) with no experience: $18,000-$23,000

✔ BA with some experience: $22,000-$28,000

✔ Master of Arts in Christian Education (M.A.C.E.) or Master of Divinity (M.Div.): $28,000-$32,000

✔ M.A.C.E. or M.Div. with experience: $35,000-$55,000

FACTOR   ## Housing

It's rare but not unheard of for churches to include housing in youth pastors' compensation packages. They may have an old parsonage or apartment that they add into the arrangement. If that is part of the offer, find out these facts:

➤ Is this considered nontaxable income?

➤ How does the fact that you are (or are not) licensed affect your taxes in this sphere? (You need to discuss this with your tax advisor.)

➤ What housing costs does the church pay for, and what are you responsible for? You may need to pay the utility bills, which sounds like a great deal until you see that it costs $350 a month to heat the behemoth.

➤ Who is responsible for the upkeep? Usually, it's you. Do you have time to spend repaving driveways, painting shutters, and fixing screens and leaky pipes on a 75-year-old house? And who pays for the repairs?

The church may want to consider giving you the option of home ownership with a housing allowance or a parsonage with an equity allowance. Again, talk over these issues with your tax advisor.

FACTOR   ## Cost-of-living increases and bonuses

Ask how much of an increase the staff receives each year. If they do not give cost-of-living increases, you are, in effect, losing money each year. Inquire if bonuses are given when ministry goals are exceeded. Also ask if merit-based raises are given, and if so, how often and how are they determined?

Real Life

I had been on the job for two months and was planning to head home for the holidays. At staff meeting I reminded everyone that I would be gone until after the New Year. After the meeting the senior pastor called me into her office to correct me—I could only take 3 days of vacation, she explained, since I had had only a week of vacation coming to me my first full year (the same amount as the church secretaries), and hadn't been there the full year yet.

I went to my files and found the original job posting that said "two weeks of vacation a year." When I showed it to the pastor, she was mildly surprised but quickly agreed. Saving that piece of paper gave me the extra week I was due.

FACTOR   **Employee Benefits**

Retirement. Some churches have mandatory pension plans if you are licensed or ordained. Others have matching plans—they will match your retirement contributions up to, say, five percent of your salary. If you're a recent college graduate and still paying off student loans, investing in your retirement can seem like the last thing you need to consider. But, you should start investing immediately. The money you invest in your twenties will increase far beyond the money you invest in your thirties and forties. Find a trustworthy financial advisor and have a long conversation with her about your future.

Insurance. Find out which insurance, among all the different types, is covered by the church's plan.

- Medical. If you have a family, are they covered? Do you need to pay any extra for their coverage? Is dental included?
- Disability insurance.
- Life insurance.
- Liability insurance.
- Accidental death and dismemberment.

Taxes and days off

FICA. A youth pastor, like a senior pastor, often qualifies as self-employed. If you are considered self-employed, it's your responsibility to make quarterly tax payments to the government (both state and federal). Some churches pay the employer's share of the youth pastor's Social Security payments. Check to see your church's policy.

> ### Smart Tip
>
> A youth pastor asked a board member why a new staff person with less experience was getting paid more. "Because you didn't ask for enough when you started," said the board member. Whatever you think about that board's salary-setting policies, the point is clear: the time to ask is before you accept.

Time off.

▸ *Days off.* Expect a minimum of one full day off a week—the norm is two. Don't accept partial days off—like being off on Friday afternoon and Tuesday. A person needs a full day to be able to disengage and relax.

▸ *Vacation.* The length of your first year's vacation depends on when you start. If you start in June, you usually get half the number of day written into your contract. A piece of advice—don't even touch a position that offers less than two weeks of annual vacation. Ministry is such a time- and energy-intensive profession that you need that time to recuperate. Find out when your vacation is increased. An example is receiving an additional week of vacation—up to five weeks a year—for every three years on staff. For an experienced youth pastor, four paid weeks a year is appropriate. Sometimes churches that can't afford a large base salary offer more vacation time. If that seems to be the case of the interviewing church, you may negotiate more vacation time in lieu of the higher salary.

▸ *Compensation time.* Ask what the church's policy is on giving you time off after a time-intensive event, such as a mission trip or weekend retreat. If they blink rapidly and mumble, "Whazzat?" run…fast. Some churches expect you to show up at the 8 a.m. staff meeting despite the fact you were gone all weekend with the senior highers. These churches usually don't keep youth pastors for long.

> ## FasTrack
>
> **77** Resist the urge to sign the contract right away. Always take time to think through how it will affect you.

Reasonable comp time would be one extra day off (not to be confused with your regular days off) for every weekend retreat, and three extra days off for every week-long event. You also need to ask if can you store up comp time and use it later in the year, or if they expect you to use that time the week after you get back.

▸ *Holidays.* Typically holidays are some of the most heavily scheduled times of the year in youth ministry. Is holiday time off for the staff scheduled in light of this?

▸ *Sabbatical.* What is the church's policy on staff sabbaticals? Do pastors get three-month sabbaticals every five years? Do they ever get longer sabbaticals? Do they have to be used for certain purposes (study, continuing education) or can they be used for special projects (spending time with missionaries overseas, pursuing your desire to be a NASCAR driver)?

▸ *Sick days.* Can these be stored up for future use or are they "erased" at the end of the year?

▸ *Continuing education.* Anywhere from three days to two weeks is appropriate for study leave. This allows you to attend a conference or take an intensive course at a local seminary.

Professional expenses

These are expenses that should be included in the job but should not be factored into your compensation package.

➤ *Car allowance.* You should be reimbursed for the use of your car for ministry purposes. This can come as a monthly sum or as a per-mile reimbursement. If it's the latter, retain all receipts as well and keep a mileage log that includes date, destination, miles driven, and purpose of trip. Any drugstore or discount store will have a small notebook for this purpose in their stationery section.

➤ *Continuing education.* One way a church can honor its staff is to encourage them to continually sharpen their professional skills. They should offer enough money to cover at least a weeklong conference (registration, airfare, and food and lodging). The church may offer tuition and textbook reimbursement. If it expects you to get a seminary degree, will it cover those expenses (either partially or totally)? Will you still have money to attend youth-worker conferences?

➤ *Subscriptions.* They can be used for books or magazines to help you in ministry.

➤ *Hospitality.* There's a certain expectation that you will entertain people involved in your ministry, or even just the larger church, in your home or meet them at restaurants. Will the church reimburse you for these expenses?

➤ *Denominational gatherings.* If you are attending a denominationally affiliated church, you may be expected to attend certain denominational events. The church should pick up those related expenses.

➤ *Counseling stipend.* Ministry is one of the most stressful careers you can enter. More and more churches understand the importance of regular counseling for their pastoral staffs. They view it as part of overall healthcare. Does the church provide an annual stipend for counseling? Do they provide a special fund? Do they have a relationship with a local therapist who provides counseling on a sliding fee scale to the church?

If you don't like the offer

Don't be surprised or dismayed if you don't like the first offer. That's all it is, an offer. It's perfectly acceptable to come back with a counteroffer. Just make sure you can articulate why you want the changes.

Here are some helpful tips in negotiating—

▶ **Find out who's your advocate.** Is there a pastor or someone on the search committee who can go to bat for you in asking for an increase? It's always better to have someone other than you be the advocate.

▶ **Be clear and respectful.** Some churches have the philosophy that you're serving God so you should be poor. Others have sacrificed to get the money for this position and are paying what most of the people in the congregation make. Respect their sacrifice, but also be very clear about what you need and why you need it.

▶ **Don't spiritualize it**. Don't assume that it's God's will that you take what you're offered. God probably doesn't want you to eat tuna fish and macaroni and cheese for years. Just come back with a statement like, "I don't think I can make that work. Thank you for considering me. I've appreciated getting to know your congregation. Should circumstances change, please feel free to contact me again." Your response may cause them to reevaluate the offer and get you what you need.

FasTrack

78 You're making what could be a long-term commitment. Be sure the compensation package and job requirements are a fit for you.

Salary

Circle the answer most appropriate to your current frame of mind:
a. Your salary is never enough.
b. Consider yourself lucky for getting paid to play.
c. At least you know what to negotiate for at your *next* job.

Taken from *A Youth Ministry Crash Course* by Rick Bundschuh and E.G. Von Trutzschler (Zondervan/Youth Specialties 1996)

Leaving well

The way you leave a ministry is just as important as the way you come into it.

Chapter preview

- Leaving well
- If it's your decision
- Resignation letter
- Chain of notification
- If it's not your decision
- When you go…

Leaving well

In just about every ministry, there comes a time to move on. The motivation for the move can be your sense of God's call, changing life circumstances, a desire to be closer to family, or stock options. Research shows that the average person will hold down three careers and 12 jobs in a lifetime.

You can be moving toward something (a better offer, more challenge) or away from something (conflict between you and the senior pastor). So, in your excitement to move on to new ventures, take some time to think about how you're going to close this chapter of your career.

One youth pastor's resignation schedule

Wednesday—tell the senior pastor

Friday afternoon—notify associate staff at a meeting called by the senior pastor

Friday night—notify the volunteer staff at a special meeting

Saturday morning—notify the parent advisory team at a regularly scheduled meeting

Sunday morning—announce it to the youth ministry

If it's your decision

If you're the one who is deciding to move on, there are several aspects you need to consider:

▶ **Time frame**

Once you decide to leave a place, you'll generally give at least two weeks' notice—stay no more than 30 days. "But there's no way they can replace me in 30 days!" you say—and you're right. But, after 30 days you become a lame-duck youth pastor. You'll be excluded from certain conversations and meetings. And rightly so. ("You don't need to be at the planning day because, after all, you're not going to be around.") You've chosen to move on, and so will the church.

By choosing to stay *less* than two weeks, you don't allow the ministry or the church to say goodbye. Both sides will need time to tie up loose ends and to mourn and celebrate together. The only reason where it would be appropriate to leave with less than two-weeks' notice is if there are extreme matters of integrity at stake (for example, the church is choosing to overlook the fact that the pastor is in an extramarital affair). Even then, prayerfully consider staying for two weeks for the sake of the youth ministry.

▶ **Attitude**

This job may have been the worst ever. If truth were told, you think it should be called "The First Church of Purgatory." But now is not the time to act on those feelings. Dramatic resignations where you walk into the elder meeting and announce in no uncertain terms that they're instruments of Satan and swagger out as they sit there stunned and weeping play well only in your imagination.

▶ **Reason for leaving.**

People are always excited to support someone who's leaving to follow a dream or pursue the next step in his development. If you emphasize that you're leaving because of something going on in the organization, church members feel awkward and even rejected

Moving on

Here are the Youth Worker General's warning signs that indicate it may be time for you to move on:

• The senior minister starts to distance himself from you. He offers no shelter when the women's ministry wants to hang you for allowing kids to put Dr. Pepper in the church coffee pot.

• There is little or no communication with leadership; for example, they go to a leadership retreat to Maui and don't tell you about it.

• They keep you out of the public eye. You aren't even trusted with announcements.

• Leadership shows little or no interest in what's going on in youth ministry. A hundred street kids have become Christians this year, and does anyone up there care?

• Your budget is cut—past the marrow. Now you have to pay for everything yourself. You say you already do.

• Rumblings and criticism against the youth program are entertained—like when the deacon chairman finally snaps and accuses you of being a communist infiltrator.

• You return from vacation and your office has been turned into the tape library

• The rubber chicken has pins in it.

Taken from *A Youth Ministry Crash Course* by Rick Bundschuh and E.G. Von Trutzschler (Zondervan/Youth Specialties 1996)

because they are choosing to stay. You may choose to disclose the whys your inner circle, but the congregation won't know the story—and probably shouldn't.

Now is not the time to air dirty laundry or to blast the church. Quite honestly, it will have very little impact and will only associate a bitter taste with your time of ministry. Determine not to say anything negative about anyone to anyone else in the church. Even if rumors start flying, choose to be a person of integrity. If there are issues that need to be dealt with, go to the appropriate person or people. Resolve to follow Matthew 18:15-17, and have your personal board of directors or close personal friends hold you accountable.

FasTrack

79 Leave *for* something, not because *of* something.

Realize that the church will continue on.
Early in our ministry careers, we tend to believe that the ministry will fall apart without us. We are also convinced that we need to have a voice in our replacement. The harsh truth is that we are replaceable and that, generally, we have no right to have a say in who will be our successor.

Deal with your emotions.
If this is a pleasant parting of the ways, you'll experience the normal paradox of sadness and excitement. However, if you're leaving amid anger and frustration, you'll need to figure out how to vent those emotions in a constructive manner. This may mean visiting a therapist for a session or two, getting out your journal and writing, or sitting with your network of local youth workers who have proven that they can keep their mouths shut. This is not the time to let the students or the volunteer team in on the dark side of this decision. Remember that they're staying there.

Be careful not to overspiritualize.
If you truly sense God is leading you on, you can say that. But don't put it all on God if that's not the case. Students can always detect a snow job. Figure out a way to communicate your resignation clearly and honestly.

FasTrack

80 If leaving is your decision, set a definite departure timeline and maintain a constructive attitude.

Never leave without having something to go to.
It's very difficult to search for a job when you're unemployed. Unless circumstances are extremely difficult where you are, wait to resign until you have somewhere else to go.

Resignation letter

Make it short and to the point. This is not the time to write your Oscar acceptance speech or crucify the senior pastor and the board. Address it the senior pastor or your supervisor and send copies to the chair of the board, head elder, or the appropriate parties in your organization (if in doubt, ask the senior pastor).

If you're leaving on good terms, say how much you enjoyed your time at the church and how they will remain in your prayers and in your heart. Cite the fact that you're resigning effective on such-and-such date. (Some people recommend that you leave the date blank until you've discussed it with your senior pastor.)

If you're leaving on strained terms, just include a statement that you're resigning and the date that it is effective. If at all possible, bless the church in some fashion (for example, "My prayers will be with you during this time of transition."). Remember, once it's written and delivered, it's over. You can't edit it or take it back, and you won't have control over who sees it.

Chain of notification

STEP 1

▶ **Talk with the senior pastor or your direct supervisor.**

The ministry world is small and word travels fast. Your senior pastor needs to hear it from you, not someone else. Set up a meeting in a private place (not the church lobby as she's heading out the door to pick up her kids). Your church's policy manual may spell out how resignations are handled—or not handled.

If you have a close relationship with your pastor or supervisor, consider bringing him into the loop prior to your resignation. Maybe let him know when you start to seriously consider a change. It may feel like a slap in the face to learn of it after the fact. Each situation is different, but if you can risk being honest you may save the relationship over the long term. Also, your sharing may open up discussion of issues in your present ministry situation. It may even lead you to reconsider looking somewhere else.

FasTrack

81 Let your supervisor or senior pastor know within a few days of your acceptance of a call or position elsewhere.

If you have written your resignation letter, bring it with you. If not, discuss what should be your last day and when you will formally submit the letter.

Ask her how she wants to handle the process. More than likely, she will not have a plan. You should. Suggest how you would like it handled and get her agreement. Usually, she will concur with your suggestion.

STEP 2

► **Meet with the associate pastors and staff.**

Although your colleagues should know of your decision (preferably through you telling everyone in a meeting), caution them that you aren't making your resignation public for several days and ask that they keep the news confidential until you can tell the necessary parties yourself. And don't expect them to keep quiet for more than a week. After seven or eight days, the news gets filed in the brain's general info folder and easily becomes public knowledge.

STEP 3

► **Meet with key leaders and parents.**

Again, caution them that your resignation must remain confidential because you want to announce it to the students yourself. After telling them, answer questions they may have. You will need to lead them through the process. Don't expect them to know what to do. They'll probably sit stunned and feeling a little betrayed. This is especially true if you're leaving them for another youth ministry. For whatever reasons, it's easier for parents and ministry teams to accept your resignation if you are heading to adult ministries, missions, or something outside of youth work.

FasTrack

82 After telling the senior pastor that you're leaving, notify other paid staff, leaders in the youth ministry, and finally the students.

STEP 4

► **Announce it to the students.**

Tell students about your resignation at a time when they will naturally be together, either on a Sunday morning or at a Bible study. Make sure you tell them before it's announced at a church service. Be ready for the emotion you may face. Kids handle news like this in different ways. If your ministry has experienced a lot of changes, don't be surprised if they are angry, cold, or unresponsive. Some may actually get up and walk out while others sit quietly.

If you are the third youth worker for a high school junior, be ready for some anger. Students may feel like you've betrayed them. If you've been at the church for a longer period of time, students may be deeply saddened (or relieved). It may be hard for them to understand how they will go on. This is especially true of junior highers. For them, the ministry is over. You need to help them see that God still loves them. That even though *you* are abandoning them, God isn't (okay, don't say that). Also, let students know that you're available in the next few weeks to talk if they want. They may not take you up on it, but it provides a certain sense of security for them to know you're available.

If it's not your decision

It's always painful when it's not your choice to leave a position. But how you depart in these circumstances will say a lot about your character. Take the high road. Determine not to speak negatively about the church or anyone in the church, except to your therapist, journal, or trusted friend or accountability group.

It's normal for churches to include the phrase "at will" in an employment contract. It means that they can let you go whenever they want to. Unfair? Sometimes. Unfortunate? Always. Is it the norm? Thankfully, no. Caveat: If you feel that you've been unjustly discriminated against (perhaps because of race, gender, marital status, or age), seek legal counsel immediately. Do not accept the offer to resign (in lieu of being fired) or a severance check without first talking to a lawyer. By choosing to resign rather than be fired, you can make your case harder to prove in court.

Make sure you ask when your last day is, how students and staff will be notified of your departure, and what kind of severance package there will be. Hopefully, the church will provide some kind of financial assistance until you can get on your feet.

Be cautious of a sudden meeting where someone demands an immediate decision (unless you know why he or she is asking for your resignation). Don't be forced into a hair-trigger choice. Ask for a day (or two) to consider how you should respond. Then go and seek wise counsel. One youth worker was released from his church and was given no concrete reason when he asked why. He asked the church for severance pay for six months or until he found a new position, whichever was shorter. The church debated, then agreed to his request.

No matter what the circumstances of your leaving, it will be stressful for you. Make sure you have a support team to walk you through this—people who will pray for you and with you, who will listen to you, and who will give you wise counsel.

FasTrack

83 If leaving is not your decision, confirm with your supervisor a departure timeline and a proper order of notification of others affected by your leaving.

When you go . . .

▶ **What can you take with you?**

—Copies of fliers, management notebooks, computer files—leave the originals.

—Books that the ministry bought for your professional library. (You may want to verify this with your senior pastor or church administrator.)

—Personal items.

—Leftover pizza.

▶ **What should you leave behind?**

—Originals of fliers, management files, and notebooks.

—The computer and ministry files. Make sure you delete any personal files and e-mail accounts. Rule of thumb: Don't use a ministry computer for personal use. Technically, the church owns anything on the computer.

—Ministry-specific books like curriculum, training resources, Ideas books…

—Make sure you give all personnel files, confidential computer files, counseling files, medical history forms, and other confidential information to someone who will keep them locked in a restricted area.

—Computer back-up disks.

—Archives: photos, T-shirts, posters, brochures.

Do a good job of leaving things in order. You should leave your files and office in better shape than you found them.

> **Real Life**
>
> One of the most helpful things my predecessor did was to leave me a note that profiled all the volunteers with their quirks and preferences, as well as observations on how to best work with them. I felt like I was ahead of the game before I even met with the team.

Forms 4

Before you use any forms or tips or checklists or any other piece of advice in this book, evaluate them for their suitability to your own church and youth group and for any potential risks, safety precautions, or advance preparation that may be required. Neither Youth Specialties, Zondervan Publishing House, TCS Software, nor the authors are responsible for, nor have any control over, the use or misuse of any information published in this book and CD-ROM. Neither are these resources a substitute for your own legal counsel.

Note: The forms in this section are photocopyable and ready for you to use! But if you want to work with forms that you can change and tailor to your own needs, they're also available on the Youth Assistant / Special Edition CD-ROM in a simpler Microsoft Word® format.

Microsoft Word is a registered tradmark of the Microsoft Corporation.

Alphabetical list of forms

Intern

Job Search

Leadership

Risk Management

Student Data

Volunteer / Youth Ministry

Emergency numbers

- Counseling centers (including pager numbers and people's specialties)

- Crisis pregnancy centers

- Crisis referral numbers

- Drug rehabilitation centers

- Emergency contact numbers for coworkers, staff members, and families active in the ministry

- Hospitals (surgery center, emergency room number, as well as the name and number of the chaplain)

Schools

- Booster Club

- Head of the PTA

- Key teachers and coaches

- Local schools (and their Web sites)

- Principals

- School board members

- Superintendents

Rental companies

- Bus and van rental companies (contact person, great drivers you have used)

- Rental centers (large popcorn poppers, carnival games, tents, climbing equipment, folding chairs, etc.)

Services

- Bowling alleys (when you've used them, what event)

- Coffee shops

- Graphic artists (and what projects you used them for)

- Insurance agent

- Lawyer

- Local restaurants (Do they deliver? Can you get a copy of their menu?)

- Office supply stores (and Web site)

- Party supply stores (and Web site)

- Printing companies (and what projects you used them for)

- T-shirt companies (and what projects you used them for)

Ministries

- Camps you frequently use (and the contact person's name and rates)

- Churches in your area

- Missions organizations

- Music resources / bands

- Parachurch ministries

- Resource ministries

- Speakers

The National Network of Youth Ministries releases the *Youth Ministry Yellow Pages* each year. See them online at YouthWorkers.Net

Resources and organizations—catalogs, brochures on organizations (blue)

Abstinence training	Crisis	Crisis: Violence
Bible study	Crisis: Substance abuse	Crisis pregnancy centers
Camps	Crisis: Addictions	Curriculum & publishers
Campus ministry	Crisis: Depression	Curriculum & publishers: Cook
Choir music	Crisis: Eating disorders	Curriculum & publishers: Gospel Light
College	Crisis: Family issues	Curriculum & publishers: Group
Computer	Crisis: Runaways	Curriculum & publishers: Other
Confirmation	Crisis: Suicide	Curriculum & publishers: Standard

Resources and organizations—catalogs, brochures on organizations (blue)

Curriculum & publishers: Youth Specialties	**Leadership:** Committees / teams	**Miscellaneous**
Ice breakers	**Leadership:** Staff training	**Outreach**
Discipleship	**Leadership:** Follow-up materials	**Outreach:** Evangelism materials
Drama	**Leadership:** Student	**Parachurch ministries**
Evangelism training organizations	**Magazines**	**Parachurch ministries:** Fellowship of Christian Athletes
Games	**Missions**	**Parachurch ministries:** Other
Internet resources	**Music**	**Parachurch ministries:** Student Venture
Leadership	**Networking**	**Parachurch ministries:** Young Life

Resources and organizations—catalogs, brochures on organizations (blue)

Parachurch ministries: Youth for Christ	**Special events**	
Prayer	**Stewardship**	
Rental companies	**Urban ministry**	
Retreat centers	**Video**	
Rural ministry	**Worship**	
Seminary	**Youth-worker training organizations**	
Service organizations		
Speakers		

Topical—teaching resources (yellow)

Adolescent development: Emotional	**Adol. dev.—physical:** Sexual behaviors of teens	**Adol. dev.—seminar:** Handouts
Adolescent development: Mental	**Adolescent development:** Social	**Boys ministry**
Adol. dev.—mental: ADD / ADHD	**Adol. dev.—social:** Peer pressure	**Camping**
Adolescent development: Physical	**Adolescent development:** Spiritual	**Counseling**
Adol. dev.—physical: Reproductive issues	**Adol. dev.—spiritual:** Moral	**Counseling—abuse:** Physical, mental, sexual, verbal
Adol. dev.—physical: Health & body image	**Adolescent development:** Seminar	**Counseling—abuse:** Child abuse
Adol. dev.—physical: Homosexuality	**Adol. dev.—seminar:** Age group characteristics	**Counseling—abuse:** Chemical & substance
Adol. dev.—physical: Sexuality	**Adol. dev.—seminar:** Overheads	**Counseling:** Depression / suicide

Topical—teaching resources (yellow)

Counseling: Eating disorders	**Communication:** Teaching tips	**Family—parents:** Fliers, calendars, etc.
Counseling: Miscellaneous	**Discipleship**	**Family—parents:** Parenting articles
Counseling: Peer counseling	**Encouragement**	**Family—parents:** Parent ministry
Counseling: Resources	**Evangelism**	**Family—parents:** Seminars & talks given
Communication	**Family**	**Generational research**
Communication: Styles, tests, & explanations	**Family:** Blended families	**Generational research:** Gen-X
Communication: Patterns	**Family:** Death	**Generational research:** Gen-Y
Communication: Ways people communicate	**Family:** Divorce	**Girls' ministry**

Topical—teaching resources (yellow)

Justice system & youth	**Missions:** Articles	**Race, ethnicity & culture:** Racism
Leadership	**Missions:** Theology	**Relationships**
Leadership: Articles	**Missions:** Training	**Relationships:** Dating
Leadership—ministry: Expectations	**Models of youth ministry**	**Relationships:** Divorce
Leadership—ministry: Mission and vision	**Programming**	**Relationships:** Friendships
Leadership—ministry: Values	**Race, ethnicity & culture**	**Relationships:** Marriage
Missions	**Race, ethnicity, & culture:** Articles	**Relationships:** Miscellaneous
Missions: Activities / simulations	**Race, ethnicity, & culture:** Forgiveness	**Relationships:** Singleness

Topical—teaching resources (yellow)

Relationships: Sex / sexuality	**Spiritual issues**	**Youth culture:** Cluster groups
Small groups	**Spiritual issues:** Fasting	**Youth culture:** Drugs
Small groups: Activities	**Spiritual issues:** Other disciplines	**Youth culture:** Gangs
Small groups: Community building	**Spiritual issues:** Prayer	**Youth culture:** Media / music
Small groups: Expectations	**Spiritual issues:** Worship	**Youth culture:** Violence
Small groups: Forms	**Spiritual issues:** Warfare	**Youth worker:** Personal
Small groups: Ideas	**Spiritual issues:** Witchcraft & occult	**Youth worker—personal:** Growth plans
Spiritual formation	**Youth culture**	**Youth worker—personal:** Reviews

Topical—teaching resources (yellow)

Youth worker: Professional		
Youth worker—prof.: Continuing education		
Youth worker—prof.: Salary research		

Monthly Contact Summary Chart

Staff member _____ Due _____

Student's name	Phone number	Weekly call					Comments
1. _____							
2. _____							
3. _____							
4. _____							
5. _____							
6. _____							
7. _____							
8. _____							
9. _____							
10. _____							
11. _____							
12. _____							

Special concerns_____

_____

Group activity (1 every month) _____ Date_____

Brief description _____

_____

Is there anything the pastoral staff should be aware of? _____

_____

How can we encourage and pray for youth over the next month? _____

_____

Month of _____

Goals / priorities

_____

_____

_____

_____

Ideas

_____

_____

_____

_____

Phone calls / people to see

_____

_____

_____

_____

_____

_____

_____

_____

Letters & notes to write

_____

_____

_____

_____

_____

_____

_____

_____

Things to plan

_____

_____

_____

_____

Other things to do

_____

_____

_____

New people

_____

_____

_____

_____

Staff Contact List Monthly

Staff Contact List Monthly

P - Personal appointment   **T** - Telephone   **L** - Letter   **C** - Card   **E** - E-mail

Name	Phone number	1	2	3	4	5	6	7	8	9	10	11	12	Important dates
1.														
2.														
3.														
4.														
5.														
6.														
7.														
8.														
9.														
10.														
11.														
12.														
13.														
14.														
15.														
16.														
17.														
18.														
19.														
20.														

Week of _____

Goals / priorities

_____
_____
_____
_____

Ideas

_____
_____
_____
_____

Phone calls / people to see

_____
_____
_____
_____
_____
_____
_____
_____
_____

Letters & notes to write

_____
_____
_____
_____
_____
_____
_____
_____
_____

Things to plan

_____
_____
_____
_____
_____

Other things to do

_____
_____
_____

New people

_____
_____
_____
_____

One of the challenges of building a ministry calendar is providing diverse opportunities in which a variety of kids, ranging in stages of spiritual growth, can all feel excited about being involved. How can you reach and challenge the wide variety of students that have been entrusted to you?

Don't rush the process of designing an appropriate ministry calendar. And don't try to take a shortcut by developing the calendar on your own. Allow adult leaders, parents, your pastor, and key student leaders to agonize over this process with you.

❏ Begin with a blank calendar.

❏ These are out of your control, so place them on the calendar first:

1. Church / ministry mandated dates
Ask the pastor to be specific on his expectations regarding the participation of you or students in things like the following:
- Special worship and prayer services
- Choir and musical performances (especially Easter and Christmas)
- Church membership classes
- Church staff retreats
- Holiday services
- Missions conferences
- VBS
- All-church picnics
- Denominational events and retreats

2. Community / school conflicts to avoid
School—ask in particular about these important dates:
- captain's practices
- homecoming
- fall break (in some areas)
- Christmas break
- Spring break
- President's Day and Martin Luther King Weekend
- state or city holidays
- major testing periods
- school start and end dates
- sports and band schedules (beginning in the summer)
- agricultural or livestock events
- prom
- major concerts, drama performances, debates
- graduations, baccalaureate services
- SAT, ACT, and PSAT tests

3. Significant sports or cultural events, in the area and nationally
Events and concerts—
- Christian music festivals
- City-wide Christian events—including event training for your staff

Sports—
- Tournament weekends
- Men's, women's, and recreational sports schedules
- College and professional sports, like Superbowl, World Series, Final Four, World Cup, Stanley Cup, NASCAR Racing, X-Games, and the Olympics.
- Use sporting events as a theme for your programming. Instead of avoiding placing activities on these dates, you might capitalize on them.

4. Family dates: birthdays, anniversaries, vacations, et cetera.

5. Holiday and seasonal considerations

Events may need to be planned around weather and culturally supported seasons.

• Does the expected weather support your ministry event? It's hard to play broomball when it's 40 degrees outside, and picnics are no fun when it's cold and rainy.

• Based on your ministry environment and the culture in which you minister, determine what times of year are best for initiatives in specific areas. September and January, for instance, are months when students in the United States are more open to new things, fresh starts. Some churches use the following timeline:

—Summer is for relationship building.

—Late summer suits volunteer recruitment.

—Fall supports outreach and making new relationships.

—Winter is the season for personal growth, for building deeper relationships, and for student leadership development.

—Spring is a good time of year for celebration and preparations for summer missions activities.

❑ Examine your purpose, values, and goals, as created by your ministry team and approved by the church leadership, senior pastor first.

❑ Establish the *why* behind all the events you're considering doing.

❑ Examine your tentative plan for good balance among the following activities:

—outreach and evangelistic events

—service projects (including local tasks, missions events, and trips)

—opportunities for students to develop relationships and have fun together

—opportunities for growth (Bible studies, small groups, teaching, et cetera.)

—leadership development opportunities

—worship and prayer events

—staff meetings and training

—parent meetings

❑ Study your community. Meet with a diverse group of representative students. Ask about popular social hangouts, radio stations, music preferences, the way they experience peer relationships—including sexual standards, local rites of passage, perceptions of illegal substances—their views of local churches, work habits, and family relationships. Effective ministry strategy aligns with the needs of your community.

Event Budget

Event title _____ Event date _____

Formula: All expenses divided by the *least* number of participating students = the break even point.

Description	Total
Staff cost	
Number of staff= Food: Housing: Transportation: Misc. staff expenses **A: Subtotal**	
General event expenses	
Programming: Promotional materials: Transportation: Speaker Teaching materials Sports and activities Rental equipment: **B: Subtotal**	
Students and paying adults cost formula	
Food: Housing: Other misc. per-person expenses: **C: Subtotal**	
Total A + B + C = D: Total event cost	
D: Total event cost	
E: Student per-person cost divided by number of students (Round number up to nearest even number or go back and cut expenses.)	
Student per-person price:	

San Carlos Mission Trip   December 29, 2002
Formula: All expenses divided by the *least* number of participating students = the break even point.

Description	Total
Staff Cost	
Number of staff = 14	
Food: Apx. B = $6, D = $8 (2 days = $36 x 14 = $504)	$ 504
Housing: ($30 per person per night x 2 nights x 14 people)	$ 840
Transportation: (Two vans at $50 per van = $100)	$ 100
Misc. staff expenses: ($200 for incidentals)	$ 200
A: Subtotal	**$1,644**
General event expenses	
Programming: (lights, stage, sound, music, backdrop, props, et cetera)	$ 450
Promotional materials: (brochures, paper, postage, et cetera)	$ 175
Transportation: (100 students / paying staff = 2 buses x $200 each)	$ 400
Speaker (fee, transportation, housing, food, et cetera)	$ 500
Teaching materials	$ 50
Sports activities	$ 100
Rental equipment: (trailer, et cetera)	$ 75
B: Subtotal	**$1,875**
Students & paying adults cost formula	
Food: Apx. B = $4, L = $6, D = $8 (2 days = $36x100)	$ 3600
Housing: ($15 per person per night x 2 nights x 100 people)	$ 3000
Other misc. per-person expenses: (Rock climbing $5 x 100)	$ 500
C: Subtotal	**$7,100**
Total A + B + C = D: Total event cost	**$10,619**
D: Total event cost divided by number of students	**$10,619**
E: Student per-person cost	**$106.19**

(Round number up to nearest even number or go back and cut expenses.)

Student per-person price:	**$110.00**

Checklist for Staff Assignments

Event name_____Dates _____

Time / schedule_____

Location _____Maximum number of attendees _____

Accounting:

Per-person price for attendees _____Total anticipated income_____

Total anticipated expenses _____

$ break for early registration? _____By what date? _____Refunds given? _____

Deadline for forms or money to be turned in?_____

Other specific rules or regulations? _____

---

* Beside the asterisk, write the name of the individual who's responsible for the listed task.

❑ **Folder setup**   *_____
❑ **Database setup**   *_____
❑ **Special equipment**   *_____
                               *_____
❑ **Room reserved**   *_____
❑ **Promotional materials:**
   (Include registration form, permissions, medical releases, emergency #'s)

   Brochure / invitation / fliers   *_____
   Postcards or posters   *_____
   Need content by? _____ *_____
   How many?_____Mail? _____Bulk? _____
   By what date? _____Mail to whom?_____
   Production: in-house or printer? _____

Advertising media
❑ Posters   *_____
   Dates _____
❑ Church news   *_____
   Dates _____
❑ Worship folder   *_____
   Dates _____
❑ Pulpit announcement   *_____
   Dates _____
❑ Church communities   * Which one(s)?
   Dates _____
❑ Pastoral staff   *_____
❑ Radio   *_____
❑ Local newspapers   * Which one(s)?
   Dates _____
❑ Mail to churches   * Which one(s)?
   Dates _____
❑ E-mails   * To whom?
❑ Other   * To whom?

❑ **Schedule / booklet**   *_____
   How many? _____Date content needed?_____
❑ **Nametags**   *_____
❑ **What-to-bring list**   *_____
   List_____
   _____
❑ **Meals or food**   *_____
   Menu _____
   _____
   Budget _____Cost_____
❑ **Transportation**   *_____
   What? _____Company _____
   Budget _____Cost_____
❑ **Accommodations**   *_____
   Where? _____
   Budget _____Cost_____
❑ **Special purchases**   *_____
   What?_____
   _____By what date? _____
   Budget _____Cost_____
❑ **Adult chaperones**   *_____
   How many? _____Who?_____
   _____
   _____By what date? _____
❑ **Any special forms to fill out?** *_____
   If yes, which forms? _____
   _____
   _____By what date? _____
❑ **Other** _____   *_____

To: Team leaders
From: H20 steering committee
RE: Evaluation
Date: October 20, 2000

Thank you for the awesome job you've done with H20. We need your help evaluating the effectiveness of H20, and making suggestions for improving it for next year. Please answer the following questions in detail, and return this memo to the event director. Thanks.

1. Did you have enough information to effectively lead your team over the course of the event? If not, what more could we have provided for you?

2. Did you have enough statistical information—event goals, status of pledge achievement, et cetera? If not, what other statistics could we have provided for you?

3. What was your biggest challenge in leading your team?

4. Do you think that the insight stuff give-aways motivated the students? Which items got the most enthusiastic response from the students?

5. How did the teams respond to the incentives?

6. On a scale of 1 to 10 (ten being the highest), how would you rate your team's enthusiasm for H20?

7. How many students did you have on your team? Of that number, how many of the students actually participated in H20?

8. What could we do to improve student enthusiasm and involvement in H20?

9. How was your job site (the work, the site contact, et cetera)?

10. What one thing about H20 would you change for next year?

Event
Evaluation Worksheet

Event_____Date_____

Group_____Leader_____

Purpose

Goals

Attendance
Students_____
Staff _____
Total _____

Evaluation	Comments or recommended changes or suggestions for improvement:
1 **Promotion:** Was it quality work? Timed appropriately? Did we promote enough? Any changes?	
2 **Staffing:** Did we have enough staff? Any problems? What was their evaluation of the event?	
3 **Budget:** Did the results justify the effort and money spent? Attach completed **Event Budget**.	
4 **Program:** Describe its effectiveness. Attach an actual schedule.	
5 **Benefits:** What were the PROS for this activity?	

Evaluation	Comments or recommend changes or suggestions for improvement:
6 **Problems:** What were the CONS for this activity?	
7 **Materials needed:** What items, supplies, equipment, et cetera, did we forget that we need to bring next time?	
8 **Repetition:** Should we do this activity again? Why or why not?	
9 **Guest performance:** Evaluate how well the speaker or musicians related to and connected with our students.	
10 **Contact list:** Write out names, phone numbers, addresses, or directions that we need for next time.	
11 **Discipline:** Any discipline problems with students? Action taken? Attach any **Incident Report** filed.	
12 **Spiritual results:** What difference did this activity make in the lives of our students? Decisions made? Evidence of spiritual growth that occurred?	
13 **Other comments?** Next time, make sure...	

Financial Accountability Worksheet

Event name _____Event date_____

Attendance

Cost per student _____

Students_____

Staff _____

Total _____

Deposit 1: amount and date _____

Deposit 2: amount and date _____

Deposit 3: amount and date _____

Deposit 4: amount and date _____

Deposit 5: amount and date _____

Student income total $

Attach registration forms with list of students and payment amounts.
Indicate on registration form whether money collected is cash or check.

Student income total divided by total number of students attending should equal cost per student.

_____ divided by _____ = _____
   (income)   (students)   (cost / student)

Difference / shortage explanation _____

_____

_____

_____

_____

_____

_____

_____

_____

6:30 - 6:45 pm	Sound check in general session auditorium
6:50 - 7:00 pm	Background music
7:00 - 7:05 pm	Solo by Chris Smith
7:05 - 7:15 pm	Welcome by emcee - Introduce himself - Purpose for the retreat
7:15 - 7:25 pm	Worship and praise
7:25 - 7:30 pm	Video clip
7:30 - 7:33 pm	Speaker introduction
7:33 - 8:05 pm	Main speaker
8:05 - 8:10 pm	Closing song
8:10 - 8:15 pm	Closing announcements and prayer
8:15 - 8:30 pm	Walk-out music

Target marketing

Target marketing is a way to find groups of people who may be interested in your event—groups you wouldn't have thought of otherwise—and then to rate these groups according to how seriously you want to pursue them. The markets on the "A" list are given the most attention. The markets on the "B" and "C" lists receive attention only if resources and time are available.

Define your audience (for example, high school boys who don't regularly attend, but who have shown some interest in spiritual things)**:**

_____

_____

With your audience in mind, list all possible advertising options, regardless of expense:

_____

_____

_____

_____

_____

Prioritize your markets: Your *A-list groups* are those you most want to come to the event; it's designed for them (for example, middle schoolers at your church who are going into high school and might be a little nervous about it). *B-list groups* are your next target market if you've covered all of A and have more time and resources (for instance, middle schoolers who go to the nearest school). *C-list groups* are of lesser importance. (If you've covered A and B markets and have time and resources left, market your event to middle schoolers who go to the three local schools).

A-list groups	B-list groups	C-list groups

Sample target marketing for an event

For Move into High School, an event that helps middle schoolers successfully transition from middle school to high school, you might target your marketing like this:

A-list suggestions *(students attending your church who are entering high school in the fall)*
- Live announcements—in Sunday school, during church worship services, at regular weekly youth activities
- Videotaped promotions—a series of clips to show on Sundays, priming the youth group for the event
- Audiotape mailer sampling the musicians and speakers at the event
- A cover letter and a registration brochure to each student on the mailing list
- Newsletter announcements that build up to the event
- Phone invitations to key students in the ministry
- A Web presence—on the church page, the youth group page, or a page dedicated solely to the event
- Informed and inspired staff who can pump the event (Meet with the staff, send them frequent update memos or E-mail, and call them to keep them energized.)
- E-newsletters and event updates by E-mail
- Poster at the church information table or lobby bulletin board
- Registration brochures at the church information table
- Letters to parents and church families

B-list suggestions *(middle schoolers at the school next door to the church)*
- With appropriate permissions, place brochures at other churches
- With appropriate permissions, place brochures at the school
- Send a postcard to the home of every graduating middle school student
- Invite the youth ministry down the street to participate. Meet with the youth staff to explain the event and to deliver promotional materials—fliers, videotape, brochures, registration forms

C-list suggestions *(middle schoolers at other area middle schools)*
- Mail fliers, letters, brochures, other promotional items to area youth pastors. Invite them to participate in the leadership as well.
- Provide the local paper with a press release
- Take out an advertisement in the local paper, or request they list your event in the religion section of the paper
- Invite the press to come and photograph the event if the event is newsworthy
- Promote at local Christian colleges and seminaries when suitable
- Promote through local Christian bookstores using posters or brochures
- Send press releases to local Christian radio or TV stations. Include a media packet and request a public service announcement

Target marketing worksheet

What groups of people do you want to attract to your event? List them according to how seriously you want to pursue them—

A-list = must attend

B-list = those to whom you market your event if you're confident your A-list will attend, and as long as your time and resources last

C-list = market to these groups if your A- and B-lists are in the bag, and you have time and resources left

A-list

-
-
-
-
-
-
-

B-list

-
-
-
-
-
-
-
-

C-list

-
-
-
-
-
-
-

Event Marketing Packet

In an attractive folder or a 9" x 12" envelope, send advertising information announcing an event that is open to the public. Distribute press packets primarily to your C markets and media outlets, such as the local paper, radio stations, and maybe even television. Free public service announcements for local events are common. The media may even be interested in interviewing participants or performers at your event. Your job is to convince the media, through written and oral presentation, that your event is worth talking about to viewers and listeners.

Remember—

• Professional-looking and official press packets should be sent at least four to six weeks prior to the event. One or two weeks after sending the packet, follow up with a personal phone call to the organization.

• Network to find a personal contact within the radio or TV station. You don't want to be merely one of the many requests for airtime. If you can't uncover a personal contact, find out the name of the individual in charge of public service announcements and ask to speak to her. Let her know your packet is coming in the mail, or ask if you can deliver it in person. Without the personal contact, your press packet will likely be thrown away without a second look. Then follow up the press packet with another contact. The main ingredient of marketing success is follow-up, follow-up, follow-up (a perfect job for a motivated and articulate volunteer).

A press packet should include—
• Personal cover letter from the event director
• Event brochure
• List of notable achievements (in résumé style) of your group (social service projects make the most impact)
• Press release of no more than 500 words (one page)
• A short classified advertisement

Following are examples of a press release and a classified ad in the appropriate format.

Press Release
For immediate release
Contact: Chris Pattersby
Phone: (218) 223-0110
Page 1

450 words

Teens Spend Summer Serving Seniors

The Crew, 23 teenagers from Murray Hill Presbyterian Church, are paying money to spend six weeks of their summer renovating the local senior citizens' center. "Senior Summer" is their motto, and youth leader Chris Pattersby has helped them convince building supply and paint stores near their church to donate lumber, drywall, paint, and other supplies to put a new face on the building where senior citizens gather in the summer to stay cool, play bingo, talk, have a nourishing lunch, get regular medical assistance, and learn how to use the Internet.

Center manager Alex Stuart invited The Crew to make plans with the seniors who use the center. The church's youth staff and the center's staff are working with some of the seniors to repair walls—inside and out—and paint murals representing intergenerational relationships. Contractor Bill Hamaan is donating the time of one of his crew members each of the two weeks of work to supervise the project. "I've seen The Crew in action refurbishing the youth room at our church," Hamaan says. "They're hard workers, but there are building codes to follow and permits to get from the city, et cetera."

The efforts of The Crew and the transformation of the Senior Center will pop-up in the pre-show slides at local movie theaters, and a local printer has donated the printing of paper bags for local merchants. Shoppers will carry home the message "Senior Summer: A neighborhood project of The Crew, Murray Hill Presbyterian Church, 2134 SW Franklin Rd. We care, but Jesus cared first! Call 223-0110 to find out about God's TLC for you."

The Senior Center has served residents of the surrounding neighborhoods for 42 years. "Seventy or 80 seniors find their way here every day," Stuart said. "The fix-up and murals these kids are planning will draw even more." If it does, an ad hoc citizens' group will approach the mayor to purchase the empty building next door for a full-fledged medical center that focuses on senior health care. "These seniors have given a lot to our community," said Ellen Davies, a Hillview Community College professor who tutors computer learning at the center once a week. "It's time we serve them. And it's good to see kids investing in another generation. We have to work at building bridges between generations. We hope kids will get as much out of this as our seniors will."

If you have professional skills, time, or money to donate, or a relative who uses the center, come to the renovation planning meeting on May 3, 7:30 p.m., at the Senior Center, 8475 First St. For more information, contact Chris Pattersby at 223-0110.

# # #

The Crew
2134 SW Franklin Rd.
Chicago, IL, 07324
(218) 223-0110

April 15, 2000

Record Eagle
ATT: Maria Lopez
101 Sonport Express
Chicago, IL 07324

Dear Ms. Lopez:

The Crew, the high school-age youth at Murray Hill Presbyterian Church, want to make a difference for the elderly by renovating the nearby Senior Citizens' Center.

Staff from our church and the center, building contractors, and donations are making it possible for us to repair walls, replace broken fixtures, and paint positive, intergenerationally oriented murals. The folks who use the center are providing artistic talent and volunteering their wisdom, expertise, and even their labor to improve the place where they spend their free time.

We need your help to get the word out to businesses and families who can attend a meeting to list the tasks that need to be done and help us get the remaining supplies. We request that you put our press release or advertisement in your paper sometime during the weeks of April 20 to May 3. Also, we would like to invite you to come and join us for this kickoff event on May 3 at 7:30 p.m.

Sincerely,

The Crew
Murray Hill Presbyterian Church

Classified advertisement   30 words
For immediate release
Contact:
Phone:

Be part of renovating the Senior Citizens' Center with teens and adults from the Murray Hill Presbyterian Church. Saturday, May 3, at 7:30 p.m. at the Senior Center, 8475 First St. For more information, contact Chris Pattersby at (218) 223-0110.

The Crew
2134 SW Franklin Rd.
Chicago, IL 07324
(218) 225-0072

Mission statement: The Crew is part of the youth ministry of Murray Hill Presbyterian Church. We are dedicated to making a difference in our community. Every year we research ways to use part of our summer to make something better for others.

Vision: The Crew is a model for Christian outreach that is used in seven churches in the Chicago area. We teach church youth groups, and now non-church youth groups, how to get kids excited about making a difference. We talk to the kids themselves about how to solicit donations and supplies, and how to find professionals to oversee whatever jobs they want to do.

Projects:
- 1995 Painted playground equipment at a preschool
- 1996 Developed donors for supplies and professional skills to repair a home with Habitat for Humanity
- 1997 Wrote our plan for another church to use in starting up their own Crew. Helped them scrape and paint two halfway houses where young offenders get a fresh start.
- 1998-1999 Presented workshops for six churches and worked a little on each of their sites

Board of Directors: The committee that oversees the ministry of The Crew is made up of the youth pastor, six adult church members, and three members of the youth group. Every year different teens make up The Crew, but some stay with it all through high school.

Six months to one year out:

- ❏ Start your event notebook (**Event Notebook Checklist**)
- ❏ Determine a rough schedule for the event—how many days, arrival and departure times (**Event Checklist for Staff Assignments**)
- ❏ Location site inspection and booking (**Site Inspection**)
- ❏ Sign contract for the location site
- ❏ Develop a rough budget and student prices (**Event Budget**)
- ❏ Develop a rough timeline of what needs to get done by when (**Event Task Master**)
- ❏ Reserve transportation

Three months to six months out:

- ❏ Determine the event purpose (**Event Planning Worksheet**)
- ❏ Choose a theme
- ❏ Firm up the timeline and assign tasks to individuals in the areas of programming, speaker, games, transportation, promotion, Top Dog, and housing and registration
- ❏ If possible, take staff to the location to assist with planning
- ❏ Firm up budget and student prices. Make a system for recording all event expenses and income. (**Event Financial Accountability Worksheet**; **Student Data Single-Event Registration**)
- ❏ Start developing the registration brochure and promotional materials, and determine cutoff date. Confirm the date with the facility to make sure there's enough time for the final count. (**Medical Permisson and Release**)
- ❏ Develop the promotional strategy (**Event Marketing Strategy**)
- ❏ Keep in touch with the facility and send them any information they need. Also, plan the meals and reserve all the appropriate meeting spaces.

One to three months out:

- ❏ Start promoting the event and send out brochures
- ❏ Meet with the programming team to determine the details of the general sessions and breakout sessions
- ❏ Determine a detailed schedule, and let all staff and other appropriate individuals know what's expected of them while they're at the event
- ❏ Develop any handouts that are needed for the event
- ❏ Meet with each of the committee heads and find out where they are in the planning process. Assist where needed.
- ❏ Outline emergency procedures with Top Dog and come up with any contingency plans needed.
- ❏ Have each committee make a list of all equipment and supplies needed and authorize any purchases
- ❏ Reserve any rental equipment needed
- ❏ Secure needed volunteers and assign jobs

Two weeks out:

- ❏ Cutoff date for registration is one to two weeks out
- ❏ After the cutoff date, place students and leaders in housing
- ❏ Meet with staff to go over every aspect of the event, giving enough detail so that they are informed: Bible study information, small group questions, detailed schedule, expectations, emergency procedures, driving directions, student policies and rules, etc.
- ❏ Develop a parent handout sheet with retreat address, phone number, contact person, and any other pertinent information

- ❏ Gather any supplies and equipment
- ❏ Organize the registration process
- ❏ Make all signs and decorations
- ❏ Get petty cash, and request financial officer to cut any checks that you'll need

Two days out:

- ❏ Confirm facility, transportation, and any rental equipment
- ❏ Have all registration forms and permission slips in alphabetical order and available to Top Dog
- ❏ Check in with all committee leaders to see if they have any needs
- ❏ Get extra sleep, if possible

Day of event:

- ❏ Pack up, load up, get ready to roll
- ❏ Prepare registration area
- ❏ Instruct any last-minute volunteers
- ❏ Troubleshoot as different situations arise
- ❏ Keep your event notebook with you at all times. Try to keep at least one step ahead of the group so you can make eleventh-hour changes as needed.
- ❏ Encourage where needed
- ❏ Instruct when necessary
- ❏ Step in if you have to
- ❏ Keep on schedule
- ❏ Implement your plan
- ❏ See God work
- ❏ Go home and collapse

As soon as humanly possible after the event (within a week and before moving on to the next crisis):

- ❏ Finish any paperwork
- ❏ Pay all your bills
- ❏ Complete your entries on your budget and see how you did. Panic, if necessary, and make an appointment with the senior pastor to confess.
- ❏ Thank those who need to be thanked
- ❏ Praise those who deserve to be praised
- ❏ Fill out **Event Evaluation Worksheet**
- ❏ File any **Incident Reports**
- ❏ Reorganize your event notebook and put it on the shelf until you start planning next year's event

Good job. You survived!

Event

Medical Release Form

Please print in ink   **Effective dates:** _____ to _____   Page 1 of 2

Name: _____ Age _____ Birthday _____
         LAST   FIRST   MIDDLE

Year in school _____   ☐ Male ☐ Female   E-mail _____

Address_____ City _____ State _____ Zip _____

Phone _____ Pager / cell _____

Medical insurance company_____ Policy # _____

Mother's name_____ Phone: Home _____ Work_____

Father's name_____ Phone: Home _____ Work_____

Emergency contact _____ Phone: Home _____ Work_____

Physician_____ Office phone _____

Dentist _____ Office phone _____

Medical History

If necessary, describe in detail the nature and severity of any physical and / or psychological ailment, illness, propensity, weakness, limitation, handicap, disability, or condition to which your child is subject and of which the staff should be aware, and what, if any, action of protection is required on account thereof. Submit this notification in writing and attach it to this form. Include names of medications and dosages that must be taken.

Check the following areas of concern for this student. If necessary, add another page with details:

1. For your student's safety and our knowledge, is your student a—
   ☐ good swimmer   ☐ fair swimmer   ☐ non-swimmer

2. Does your student have allergies to—
   ☐ pollens   ☐ medications   ☐ food   ☐ insect bites

3. Does your child suffer from, or has ever experienced, or is being treated currently for any of the following:
   ☐ asthma   ☐ epilepsy / seizure disorder   ☐ heart trouble   ☐ diabetes
   ☐ frequently upset stomach   ☐ physical handicap   ☐ other

4. Date of last tetanus shot: _____

5. Does your student wear   ☐ glasses   ☐ contact lenses

6. Please list and explain any major illnesses the student experienced during the past year:

   Additional comments:

   Should this student's activities be restricted for any reason? Please explain:

299

For your information, we expect each student to confirm to these rules of conduct

No possession or use of alcohol, drugs, or tobacco

No students can drive

No fighting, weapons, fireworks, lighters, or explosives

No offensive or immodest clothing

No boys in girls' sleeping quarters and no girls in boys' sleeping quarters

Participation with the group is expected

Respect property

Respect one another, staff, and adult leaders

Respect and comply with event schedules

Students who fail to comply with these expectations may be sent home at their parents' expense.

I, the student, have read the rules of conduct and the above evaluation of my health and permission to participate in youth group activities. I agree to abide by the stated personal limitations and code of conduct.

Student signature: _____Date:_____

Activities may include, but are not limited to, the following: cookouts, boating, water skiing, swimming, basketball, roller skating, rollerblading, games in the park, soccer, broomball, ice skating, volleyball, softball, baseball, camping, downhill skiing, snowboarding, hiking, biking, concerts, Bible studies, golfing, miniature golf, hayrides. *Note: If you desire to limit your child's participation in any event, please submit your wishes in writing to the church youth pastor prior to that event.*

_____has my permission to attend all
NAME OF STUDENT

youth activities sponsored by _____ (hereinafter the
NAME OF ORGANIZATION

"Church") from _____ to _____.
DATE   DATE

This consent form gives permission to seek whatever medical attention is deemed necessary, and releases the Church and its staff of any liability against personal losses of named child.

I / We the undersigned have legal custody of the student named above, a minor, and have given our consent for him/her to attend events being organized by the Church. I / We understand that there are inherent risks involved in any ministry or athletic event, and I / we hereby release the Church, its pastors, employees, agents, and volunteer workers from any and all liability for any injury, loss, or damage to person or property that may occur during the course of my/our child's involvement. In the event that he / she is injured and requires the attention of a doctor, I / we consent to any reasonable medical treatment as deemed necessary by a licensed physician. In the event treatment is required from a physician and / or hospital personnel designated by the Church, I / we agree to hold such person free and harmless of any claims, demands, or suits for damages arising from the giving of such consent. I / We also acknowledge that we will be ultimately responsible for the cost of any medical care should the cost of that medical care not be reimbursed by the health insurance provider. Further, I / we affirm that the health insurance information provided above is accurate at this date and will, to the best of my/our knowledge, still be in force for the student named above. I / we also agree to bring my/our child home at my/our own expense should they become ill or if deemed necessary by the student ministries staff member.

Parent / guardian signature: _____Date:_____

For each room you use in your hotel or retreat center, you'll need to answer these questions—both for general sessions and breakouts.

1. Do you require staging? If so, what size and what height?

2. Do you want chairs? How many? Set up in which way?
    —*Theater:* chairs in rows, all facing front.
    —*Classroom:* narrow tables with chairs behind them, all facing front.
    —*Rounds:* round tables for 6-10 people each (good for discussions; bad for lectures).
    —*Cocktail rounds:* round tables for 3-4.
    —*Table square:* Four or eight tables set in a square. Participants sit around the outer edge of the table facing each other.

3. How many tables and where? Do you need numbers on the tables to indicate where students sit?

4. Do you need information tables?

5. Do you want the tables skirted?

6. Do you want water service in the meeting rooms?

7. What audio-visual equipment do you need?

8. Is there a Green Room off of the staging area for the musicians and speakers?

(Print on cardstock, hole punch, and place as the first page in your event notebook.)

Planning

- ☐ **Event Master Timeline**
- ☐ **Event Planning Worksheet**
- ☐ **Event Staff Assignment Checklist**
- ☐ Agendas and minutes from planning meetings
- ☐ **Event Task Master**
- ☐ To-do list

Finances

- ☐ **Event Budget**
- ☐ **Event Financial Accountability Worksheet**
- ☐ Actual event income and expense

Schedule

- ☐ Projected schedule
- ☐ Actual schedule

Promotion

- ☐ Event brochure / registration form
- ☐ Flyers
- ☐ E-mails
- ☐ Internet promotion copy
- ☐ **Event Marketing Packet**
  Press release
  Classified ads
  Public service announcements

Registration

- ☐ Student participants
  (copy of information on **Student Data Single-Event Registration** form)
- ☐ Staff
  (names, payment information, other pertinent information)

Facility, housing, and meals

- ☐ Signed contract (keep a copy in your office)
- ☐ General information flier
- ☐ **Site Inspection** form (filled out)
- ☐ Facility guidelines (rising time, lights out, snack bar hours, lake front hours, et cetera)
- ☐ Names and phone extensions for facility staff (meeting planner, facilities manager, banquet manager, et cetera)
- ☐ Facility map(s) (of the whole campus, as well as sleeping room floor plans)
- ☐ Menu plan
- ☐ Meeting space
- ☐ Sketch of room layouts
- ☐ Schedule of dates and times for room use and setup types
- ☐ Requests and schedules for AV equipment (if you're renting from the facility)

Transportation

- ☐ Signed contract (keep a copy in your office)
- ☐ Name(s) and phone number(s) of transportation provider(s)
- ☐ Map from home base to the facility

Printed materials

- ☐ Simplified event schedules
- ☐ Study notes
- ☐ Brochure, logo, other PR originals

Evaluation

- ☐ Notes taken during event
- ☐ Any **Incident Report** that was filed
- ☐ **Event Evaluation**

Planning Worksheet

Event name_____Event date(s)_____

Event manager _____Event time(s)_____

Audience description

Projected attendance

Students_____

Staff _____

Event goals and objectives

Total _____

Weekend event schedule

Hours	Thursday	Friday	Saturday	Sunday	Monday

Facility name _____ Contact person_____

Phone number _____

Housing needs

Meals needed

General session room

	Setup required	Equipment needs
Session 1	-	
Session 2		
Session 3		
Session 4		
Session 5		

Break-out rooms: setup options—theater, classroom, rounds, et cetera

Date and time	Topic	Teacher	Setup	Equipment needed

General session speaker name _____ Phone _____

Date contract signed _____

Topic_____Equipment needed _____

Program development meetings

Dates	Location	Attendees	Tentative agenda

Publicity and promotion

What type or piece	Who is in charge	Date implemented	Instructions

Budget: What are your rough budget estimates? Place a copy of the budget with this information. Track expenses on a spreadsheet. (see **Event Budget** sample).

Checks needed and when:

Housing needs: How many students and how many staff? What is the facility layout? Where do staff stay if they bring their family? Bedding needs?

Transportation requirements: Distance? Type of vehicles needed? Cost?
　　　　Company
　　　　Contact person
　　　　Vehicles reserved

Office setup: What office and administrative items need to be brought to the event site? Computer, printer, paper, stapler, pens, tape, etc.

First-aid requirements: What type of first-aid setup is needed? Who is coordinating the supplies?

Promotion strategy:
Flier design—date due: _____Flier mailing date: _____
Other plans for promotion—
　　　　Church publications
　　　　Community papers
　　　　Posters

Event approval from ministry leadership: Placed on master church / ministry calendar

Program planning: (securing people and resources)
　　　　Speaker
　　　　Musician
　　　　Multimedia
　　　　Miscellaneous needs / equipment

The Crew Retreat
Confirmation

You are about to experience a retreat full of challenge and fun that will alter the way you look at God and yourself.

We're excited that you're coming! The Crew retreat will be Friday through Sunday, September 9-11. Get ready for an incredible weekend of mind-blowing worship, in-your-face talks, small-group discussions that will get your out of your comfort zone, lots of laughter, and some new friendships!

Retreat info (read this before you go!)

Beginning
Meeting at the south door of the church at 6:32 p.m. on Friday night. Check in at registration. Find a seat on the yellow, luxury limo (a.k.a. school bus) for a two-hour drive up to Mission Lodge. *Be sure to eat dinner before you come.*

Ending
We're back at the south door of the church at 2:30 p.m. on Sunday afternoon. Make arrangements for a ride home *before* you leave home on Friday. The church phone will only be available for emergencies.

Staying
Mission Lodge, nestled in the beautiful mountains of southern Iowa, has log cabins, a sandy lake (bring your swimsuit for our traditional early morning polar-bear swim), trail riding ($5), a small skate park, and two full basketball courts. Each cabin sleeps ten and has its own bathroom. Mission Lodge serves tasty food and we'll be eating three meals on Saturday and two on Sunday. They also have a snack shop.

Bringing
Sleeping bag, pillow, Bible, pen & notebook, personal stuff (soap, shampoo, towels, toothbrush, and so on), flashlight, jacket or rain poncho, spending money, and any medications you may need.

Leaving
Leave these things at home—or we'll send you home with them: CD players, tape players, Walkmans, etc., knives, guns or other weapons, fireworks, alcohol, illegal chemical substances (this means drugs), and matches / lighters.

Office details—We've received your ☒registration   ☒permission slip   ☒medical release form

☛ We still need your **balance of payment.** You can bring it with you to registration.

If you have any questions or need assistance, please contact Chris at the church office by phone (218/223-0110) or E-mail (Chris@ourchurch.org).

We look forward to seeing you!

Day of Prayer

Setting: Youth Rooms—darkened, candles

6:45	Preshow—meditative music; quotes on prayer		
7:00	Opening Prayer		Becca and Zach
7:02	Scriptures on the Promises of Prayer		
		Psalm 34:4-6	Brian
		Jeremiah 33:3	Maggie
		Matthew 7:7-8	Kristina
		Psalm 62:7-8	Heather
7:04	Song: "Be Still" by Steven Curtis Chapman		
7:08	Worship		Worship Team
7:20	Personal Prayer—Confession		
		Luke 18:9-12	Sheree
		Luke 18:13-14	Tyler

Write out confession   Quiet Music—2 min.   I John 1:9   Michael
Kneel to Confess   Quiet Music—1 min.   "Close the Door"   Barb

7:30	Verses on Thanksgiving		
		Psalm 34:1-3	Chris
		James 1:17	Kyle
		Colossians 3:15-17	Ken
7:32	Large Group Prayer—Thanksgiving		
	Reading on Thankfulness		Heather
	Open mike sentence prayers of thanksgiving		
7:40	Worship		Worship team
7:52	Guided Personal Prayer		
	Major themes		
8:00	Small Group Prayer—groups of 6		
8:15	Closing Verse	Ephesians 3:14-19	CT

Closing Song—"Open the Eyes of My Heart"

6 months to one year ahead

Determine event
Seek approval
Reserve location for event
Publish dates (after checking for all possible conflicts)
Get it on master church calendar
Design budget

3 months ahead

Design and mail event flier
Reserve transportation
Line up staff and students to help
Determine best promotion strategy

1 month ahead

Visit event location (take camera!)
Begin major announcements and promotion begins
Finalize schedule for event
Determine supplies needed
Begin event sign-up (have system to register and collect money)

1 week ahead

Confirm all event details
Request needed checks
Meet with parents and staff who will be helping
Send E-mails to all you are inviting
Phone to secure final sign-ups

Think backward through your event—from final cleanup to early planning stages. Be sure to include the following tasks, many of which are often forgotten until the last moment:

- **Event cleanup** (Do you really want to do that job one more time—alone?)
- **Staff responsibilities the day of event** (Show your staff their significance to the event success by giving them a real job to do in advance, giving them a staff shirt or cool ID tag, etc.)
- **Transportation** (Do you know how best to get there and back—plane, train, bus, van car? Do you have copies of an accurate map and directions, and how long the trip really takes?)
- **Checks needed for event** (What cash and checks will you need on the day of the event that must come through your organization's financial officer? Change for a snack stand? Payment for performers or speakers? Vendor checks?)
- **Promotion** (Fliers, promoting it on your web site, call students, E-mail registration, community announcements)
- **Staff** (When you contact people in advance, it's amazing how many will make time to help out.)
- **Supplies** (What do you need and who can shop for them besides you?)
- **Reserving the site of the event** ('Nuff said!)

Facility distance from your home base
- Can you get to it within the time you have for travel?
- What type of transportation will you need to arrange?
- What potential stops along the way: restrooms, food, et cetera?
- What's the best route to get there?

General facility accessibility
- Is there access for your mode of transportation?
- Where will transporters drop off and pick up students?
- Is there parking to accommodate the vehicles?

General facility maintenance
- Is it clean?
- Is it in good repair?
- Is the facility inspected yearly, and when was the last inspection?
- For recommended camps, see Christian Camping International's Web site (www.cci.org.au)

General facility safety
- Is there anything that might be unsafe for students to be around?
- Are there exposed electrical or other maintenance problems?
- Is there anything that you could not afford to replace if one of your students broke it?
- What injury has occurred most often at the site?

General facility flexibility
- Is the management helpful?
- Does the management seem flexible and able to work with your group's needs?
- Will there be other groups at the facility, or will you be the only group?
    - —Is the facility staffed well enough to meet the needs of both groups?
    - —Which group has priorities in which area?
    - —Will both groups be eating together?
- Is there staff on duty 24/7? If not, what are their hours and in an emergency how can you contact them?
- Is there a certain time for lights out?
- Do you have access to the office area? Phone, fax, E-mail? Photocopying?
- Sleeping room size, conditions:
    - —Number of beds per room?
    - —Quality of beds?
    - —Number of bathrooms?
    - —Mirrors in the bathrooms?
    - —Are there areas that can be designated by gender, and how far apart are they?
    - —What ratio of staff to students can be used in these sleeping areas?
    - —Are the sleeping rooms in an area that might disturb other guests not in your party?
    - —Are there rooms available for program staff, speakers, and musicians? Linens available?

General session room size, condition, and usability
- What options are there for room set up?
- How many people can fit comfortably in the room?
- Is the room too big or too small?
- Is there permanent staging? What type of staging is available for the room?
- How are the acoustics?
- How will the room feel for your event?

- What do you need to do decoratively to make the room feel like you want it to feel?
- If there are other groups at the facility what possible disturbances might there be in the general session room? Sound? Smoke?
- Is there a foyer that is usable for materials or information tables?
- Is there a room that you can use as a holding room or Green Room prior to performances? If so, is it large enough and accessible?
- What is available for sound and AV needs? Do you have access to all equipment?

Seminar rooms
- Room sizes?
- How many are available?
- What condition are they in?
- How accessible are they?
- Will sound or other guests be a conflict for the rooms?

Eating area
- Food quality and quantity?
- Eating area space availability?
- Can they effectively feed all the attendees at one time, or do you need to eat in multiple sessions?
- Will you be eating a predetermined menu, from a buffet, or ordering whatever you want?
- What are the seating options?
- Are there designated meal times?
- Can special dietary needs be accommodated?

Activities or sports area
- What inside and outside areas are available?
- If weather is poor, what are other options?
- Are you the only group using the sports area?
- Is the sports area within walking distance of the sleeping and meeting areas?
- Are there any safety hazards on the fields or at the lakefront?
- Will lifeguards be available if needed?

Prices
(Retreat centers generally quote a per-person price that includes all meals. Hotels generally price per room for sleeping and per person for food.)
- When is their biggest season and when is their off-season?
- What is the pricing structure during each of the seasons?
- Are the meeting spaces extra or are they based on the number of rooms used?
- Are tax and gratuity included in the pricing?
- Will they exempt the ministry from any taxes?
- What type of payment schedule does the facility require? What down payment amount will put a hold on your dates, and when do you have to pay it?
- What is their cancellation policy and the penalty fees?
- What if there is a last-minute cancellation due to inclement weather or other large unforeseen complication?

Surrounding area
- What other facilities are available in the surrounding areas (stores, fast food, et cetera)? Take maps and flyers.
- If relevant, what other type activities are available within a short drive from the facility?
- How would the students be transported to those areas?
- Note the address, phone number, and directions to the closest hospital or medical facility. When is it open?

November / December

Housing—

Task	Start	Due	Whom	Progress
Hotel site inspections				
Hotel contract negotiation				
Contracts signed				

January / February

Event management—

Task	Start	Due	Whom	Progress
Preliminary calendar / timeline				
Theme chosen				
Mission statement defined				
Director job descriptions developed				
Organizational flow chart developed				
Budget developed				
Take directors and select staff to event				

Programming—

Task	Start	Due	Whom	Progress
Director job descriptions developed				
Organizational flow chart developed				
Budget developed				
Speaker / performers chosen and contracted				
Take programming staff to event				

Housing—

Task	Start	Due	Whom	Progress
Ministry housing assignments				
Hotel hosts job description				

March

Event management—

Task	Start	Due	Whom	Progress
Director meetings scheduled				
Detailed timeline				
Division leaders to event				
Child care strategy developed				
Directors chosen				
Directors recruited and assigned tasks				
Logo developed				
Giveaways chosen				

Progress keys—Not started (leave blank), In **P**rocess, **N**ear Completion, **C**ompleted, Needs **H**elp

Communications—

Task	Start	Due	Whom	Progress
Director appointed				
Determine needed communication—written materials				
Develop marketing plan				
Develop schedule of printed materials and sign-off procedure				

Registration / data processing—

Task	Start	Due	Whom	Progress
Scholarship management—detailed				
• Policies and procedures				
• Determine the ministry needs				
• Track appropriated scholarships				
• Coordinate with registration to document scholarships				
• Contingency plan for on-site troubleshooting of scholarships				

Residents hall / dorm—

Task	Start	Due	Whom	Progress
Determine space usage, room setups and room assignments for the following:				
• Registration				
• Operations room				
• Equipment storage				
• Communion preparation				
• Counting the offering				
• Volunteer Central and hospitality				
• Registration solutions				
• Lunch				
• Exhibits				
• Production / Green Room				

Housing—

Task	Start	Due	Whom	Progress
Hotel host's job description				

Key meetings—

Task	Start	Due	Whom	Progress
Executive committee				
Area leaders				

Progress keys—Not started (leave blank), In **P**rocess, **N**ear Completion, **C**ompleted, Needs **H**elp

Task Master

November / December

Housing—Laura

Task	Start	Due	Whom	Progress
Hotel site inspections	Nov. 97	Dec. 97	Laura +	C
Hotel contract negotiation	Nov. 97	Dec. 97	"	C
Contracts signed	Dec. 97	Jan. 98	"	C

January / February

Event management—Dawn

Task	Start	Due	Whom	Progress
Preliminary calendar / timeline	Feb.	March	Dawn	C
Theme chosen	Feb.	March	Exec.	C
Mission statement defined	Feb.	March	?	
Director job descriptions developed	Feb.	March	Dawn	C
Organizational flow chart developed	Feb.	March	Dawn	C
Budget developed	Feb.	March	Dawn	C
Take directors and select staff to Milwaukee	Feb.	June	John	P

Programming—Jim

Task	Start	Due	Whom	Progress
Director job descriptions developed	Feb.	March	Jim	C
Organizational flow chart developed	Feb.	March		P
Budget developed	Feb.	March		C
Speaker / performers chosen and contracted	Feb.	May	Exec. / Dawn	P
Take programming staff to Milwaukee	Feb.	June		P

Housing—Laura

Task	Start	Due	Whom	Progress
Ministry housing assignments	Feb.			C
Hotel hosts job description	March			C

March

Event management—Dawn

Task	Start	Due	Whom	Progress
Director meetings scheduled	March		John	
Detailed timeline	March	April	Dawn	C
Division Leaders to Milwaukee	March	April	By Req.	C
Child care strategy developed	March	April	Dawn	C
Directors chosen	March	April	Dawn	P
Directors recruited and assigned tasks	March	April	Dawn	N
Logo developed	March	June 10	Dawn	P
Giveaways chosen	March	June	Dawn	P

Progress keys: Not started (leave blank), In **P**rocess, **N**ear Completion, **C**ompleted, Needs **H**elp

Communications—Bill & Tari

Task	Start	Due	Whom	Progress
Director appointed	March		Dawn	P
Determine needed communication—written materials	March		Team	C
Develop marketing plan	March	April	Tari	P
Develop schedule of printed materials and sign-off procedure	March	April	Dawn	P

Registration / data processing—TBD

Task	Start	Due	Whom	Progress
Scholarship management - detailed	March	May		
• Policies and procedures				
• Determine the ministry needs				
• Track appropriated scholarships				
• Coordinate with registration to document scholarships				
• Contingency plan for on-site troubleshooting of scholarships				

Residents hall / dorm—Paul

Task	Start	Due	Whom	Progress
Determine space usage, room setups and room assignments for the following:	March	June	Dawn Paul / Laura	P
• Registration				
• Operations room				
• Equipment storage				
• Communion preparation				
• Counting the offering				
• Volunteer Central and Hospitality				
• Registrations Solutions				
• Lunch				
• Exhibits				
• Production / Green Room				

Housing—Laura

Task	Start	Due	Whom	Progress
Hotel hosts job description	March			C

Key meetings—

Task	Start	Due	Whom	Progress
Executive committee	March	Weekly	Marni	P
Area leaders	March	Monthly	John	C / P

Progress keys: Not started (leave blank), In **P**rocess, **N**ear Completion, **C**ompleted, Needs **H**elp

Job description

Visionary, director, and administrator of the event

Responsibilities

1. General vision for the event: location, direction, quality, et cetera.

2. Overall finances: budget, accounting, honorariums.

3. Arrange insurance or CCLI licensing if needed.

4. Assign and follow through with the event logistics.

5. Quality control manager for the event.

6. Work in conjunction with the meeting planner for specific site inspection and selection and dates, according to speaker availability.

7. Collaborate with the meeting planner for menus, number of rooms needed, and other logistical details.

8. Develop brochures and promotional material with graphic designer.

9. Coordinate the programming and scheduling with the speaker representative.

10. Steering committee selection, recruitment, orientation, appointment of a chairperson, and quality control for the committee.

11. Make sure that the steering committee has the materials needed: media packet, fundraising information, speaker bios, et cetera.

12. Negotiate and contract the musicians, performers, sound crew, and tape individuals (from steering committee's recommendations).

13. Make the travel and shuttle arrangements for the speakers.

14. Prepare final program schedule for the confirmation packets.

15. Insure delivery of cassettes to the event site (if you're recording the speakers and selling the tapes).

16. Be the on-site representative at the event.

17. Conduct the final evaluation with the committee and faculty on site.

18. Prepare a final evaluation.

19. Send thank-you notes and gifts to the appropriate individuals.

Job description

Work with the Director for the selection of the event site
Contract and manage the physical facilities for the ministry

Responsibilities

1. Inspect the site.

2. Select and contract with the hotel.

3. Act as on-site liaison for the director and the hotel / event location.

4. Arrange for the physical requirements for the event: meeting space, staging, platforms, podiums, screens, white boards, markers, tables, banquet facilities, et cetera.

5. Plan menus with the conference director and the steering committee.

6. Reserve lodging for the speakers and other contracted individuals.

7. Arrange for a site inspection for the steering committee members.

8. Review publicity materials.

9. Manage the event with the conference director and property representative.

10. Attend the post-event evaluation.

11. Review all charges posted to the event account.

Sound Engineer

Job description

To equip the event with adequate audio and lighting for the general sessions
To record all sessions (when needed) and produce good quality, salable cassette tapes

Responsibilities

1. Negotiate and finalize contract with the director.

2. Equip the general sessions with sound, lights, microphones, and any other contracted equipment.

3. Arrive and set up the equipment according to the time scheduling determined by the director.

4. Work with the director to acquire the necessary tapes for the event.

5. While on site, work with the director to meet the audio needs of the performers and speakers.

6. Arrive 30 minutes before the start of each general session for a sound check with the performers and speakers.

7. Tape all the general sessions and all of the seminar sessions the first time they are given.

8. Duplicate the tapes for purchase by the event attendees.

9. Label and prepare the tapes for sale, available by the end of the event.

10. Assist the sales table volunteers with any tape questions or difficulties.

Speakers / Artists Representative

Job description

Represent and be the contact person for an event's speakers, artists, et cetera. Be the mentor (shepherd), advocate, and team leader for these people.

Responsibilities

1. Work with the speakers / artists and conference director to develop the overall vision for the conference.

2. Work with the conference director concerning scheduling of the conference and topic and programming coordination.

3. Contact the speakers for prayer requests, special instructions, biographies, deadlines for notes, and any other special announcements or arrangements.

4. Organize meals for speakers / artists during the event.

5. Conduct any meetings or prayer times for speakers / artists during the event.

6. Relay any messages to the speakers / artists during the event concerning scheduling and announcements.

7. Debrief with the speakers / artists and steering committee members.

8. Write evaluation of the overall conference and submit to the conference director.

9. Send thank-you notes to the speakers / artists.

Event Staff
Steering Committee

(Six or seven members)

General job description

To be the local individuals that attend to the logistics of the event for their region in conjunction with the director and meeting planner

To be the primary marketing agents for the event

To create a unique environment facilitating growth, warmth, and comfort

General responsibilities

1. Meet together regularly prior to the event.

2. Determine each committee member's area of responsibility.

3. Map out a marketing strategy including letters, phone calling, press releases, advertisements, and radio.

4. Attend the post-event evaluation.

Offices of the Steering Committee (descriptions follow)

1. Chairperson

2. Registration coordinator

3. Decorations coordinator

4. Volunteer coordinator

5. Program coordinator

6. Secretary / treasurer

7. Special projects coordinator

Job description

The committee coordinator

The liaison between the director and the committee

Bring enthusiasm, direction, and vision to the committee and volunteers

Responsibilities

1. Oversee all aspects of the Steering Committee's involvement with the event, and lead the team.

2. Meet regularly with the director (by phone), keeping him or her apprised of registration numbers, finances, progress on the event, et cetera.

3. Brief the director about any peculiarities of the region.

4. Assign tasks to the committee and check on follow through.

5. Arrange for the steering committee to visit the event facilities.

6. Implement the marketing strategy developed by the Steering Committee.

7. Raise funds with the assistance of the secretary / treasurer (a minimum of $_____).

8. Determine the event schedule with the event director.

9. Host the visiting faculty and staff with a welcome meal.

10. Register the committee members with the meeting planner to receive their tuition discount.

11. Arrange an appropriate individual to be the emcee for the event.

12. Attend the event evaluation.

13. Submit a final evaluation and all financial records and other requested materials to the director.

14. Write thank-you notes to all committee members.

Decorations coordinator

Job description

To develop, implement, and install the decorations at the event

Responsibilities

1. Develop general session staging, table arrangements, signs for seminar rooms, signs for facility, et cetera.

2. Work with the committee to establish a decorative theme for the event.

3. Establish a team of volunteers: designers, artists, and set-up crew.

4. Work with the volunteer coordinator to develop a clean-up crew for the event.

5. Submit decorations for the steering committee's approval.

6. Acquire the necessary materials (with prior financial approval from the chairperson and treasurer).

7. Develop the products.

8. Decorate the facility prior to the event in accordance to the schedule.

9. Arrange to sell the centerpieces and turn in a written report and the funds to the treasurer, if appropriate.

10. Remove all signs and clean up all decorations after the event.

11. Attend the event evaluation.

12. Submit a report to the chairperson.

13. Write thank-you notes to all the decoration contributors and volunteers.

Steering Committee

Job description

Develop the special touches to make the program unique and effective

Create an environment conducive to worship, learning, growth, and warmth

Responsibilities

1. Nominate and investigate appropriate singers, musicians, song leaders, and performers.

2. Submit the nominations, *with a tape* and written material about them, to the director for review.

3. Communicate any specific needs of the performers to the chairperson who will let the event director know.

4. Work with the decorations coordinator for the appropriate decorations for the staging.

5. Work with the committee and the event director for song selection.

6. Prepare the overheads for the songs for the general sessions with large bold letters (a minimum of 14 points depending on the length of the song).

7. Acquire overhead projectors and *sturdy* music stands for use in the general sessions and in each of the seminar sessions and have them delivered to each of the rooms during set-up time (a small self-standing podium would be helpful for the general sessions, preferably light-weight wood or acrylic).

8. Arrange time for rehearsals with the performers pre-event if necessary.

9. Host and assist the performers upon arrival and during set-up.

10. Assist the sound technician and the performers to perform *complete* sound checks.

11. Meet performers / speakers 30 minutes before each general session to perform a sound check and to check any other stage props.

12. Communicate to the sound technician any special needs that the performers might have.

13. Oversee prop changes and adjustments during the session (adjusting the microphone, moving equipment or scenery, keeping in mind that the goal is to help the audience receive the clearest possible presentation without distraction).

14. Prepare the stage for the next session after the general session.

15. Tidy up the general session room and rearrange the chairs if necessary.

16. Assist the performers with the tear-down of their equipment after the event.

17. Attend the event evaluation.

18. Write thank-you notes to your volunteers.

Registration coordinator

Job description

To take the participants' registration applications from the inquiry stage to check participants in at the event

Responsibilities

1. Contact individuals from each of the local area churches.

2. Develop a cover letter to send out with the registration information.

3. Send the information (using a not-for-profit bulk rate indicia permit).

4. Process the registrations as they come in and forward the funds to the treasurer.

5. Develop a registration packet with all applicable information in it to be sent to each of the registered individuals: location and map, schedule, available local restaurants, hotel arrangement suggestions, et cetera.

6. Submit weekly registration summary to the chairperson or directly to the director.

7. Make name tags for attendees and special name tags with the appropriate designations for speakers, committee members, and other volunteers.

8. Coordinate the on-site registration with a team of volunteers.

9. Submit registration funds to the treasurer with written documentation.

10. Attend the event evaluation.

11. Work with the treasurer to submit final records and numbers to the event director.

12. Write thank-you notes to all registration volunteers.

Job description

Assist the committee with the secretarial and financial matters of the event

Responsibilities

1. Take minutes for all steering committee meetings.

2. Assemble a phone and address list of the committee members for the event director.

3. Assemble a notebook for the director with all correspondence and minutes taken during the event preparation.

4. Submit a copy of all outgoing correspondence for final approval to the director before distribution (allow enough time for the director to respond).

5. Make supplemental marketing tools such as a brochure, fliers, et cetera.

6. Keep all the financial records, including all expenses (and the book and tape table).

7. Work within the predetermined budget for the finances.

8. Open a checking account if necessary.

9. Make weekly deposits as registrations start arriving.

10. Write checks when necessary with approval of the chairperson.

11. Give weekly financial updates to the chairperson.

12. Assist the chairperson with the fundraising.

13. Distribute the evaluation forms and the faculty notes to the appropriate individuals (faculty assistants, ushers, et cetera).

14. Count the offering and fill out appropriate forms (store in a safe place).

15. Collect and recount the funds from the tape and book tables, initial the appropriate form.

16. Attend the event evaluation and take notes.

17. Arrange for the extra books and tapes to be shipped.

18. Distribute a list of the names and addresses of all event volunteers and steering committee members to the director at the evaluation.

19. Make the final deposit of all the funds received at the event.

20. Reimburse outstanding bills to committee members.

21. Write a final check to the event manager with a full accounting of the financial records after the final accounting.

22. Close the checking account.

Job description

To enthusiastically recruit, equip, and instruct volunteers to fill the assigned positions (possibly drawing from a variety of churches in the area)

Responsibilities

The key responsibility is to see that each volunteer team has a *clear* understanding of its positions and responsibilities, and to monitor the team on site—which may include meeting with them prior to the event

The teams / individuals needed are as follows:

1. Faculty assistant: One for each speaker

Job description

- A. Contact speakers prior to the event to pray together.
- B. Communicate any regional information appropriate for the speakers' preparation.
- C. Meet the speakers at the beginning of the event.
- D. Provide guides for the speakers at the facility.
- E. Provide escorts for the speakers to their seminar room to help arrange the room as needed.
- F. Be available if any errands need to be run (snacks, drinks, etc.) and submit receipts for reimbursement to the treasurer.
- G. Escort the speaker to the reception if needed and introduce to others.
- H. Check on speaker occasionally to make sure that he is comfortable.
- I. Get the speaker's handouts from the chairperson and put them in the speaker's seminar room.
- J. Introduce the speaker in her seminar (then you can go to another seminar if you wish).
- K. Help the speaker to gather supplies and prepare the room for the next seminar.
- L. Assist the speaker when needed.
- M. Escort the speaker to his next scheduled event if needed.
- N. Be sensitive to the speaker to allow her to meet the needs of those asking questions after the seminar.

2. Tape sales: Two volunteers to set up and manage the tape table

Job description

- A. Develop and set up an attractive table display for tape sales.
- B. Work with the sound engineer to bring the tapes from the taping room to the sales table.
- C. Assist customers in tape selection.
- D. Fill out the appropriate forms.
- E. Bundle the tapes.
- F. Take the money for the tapes—cash or check (with phone number).
- G. Give all the receipts, funds, and a completed report to the treasurer at completion of event.
- H. Box extra tapes and bring them to the registration table.
- I. Disassemble table display.

Event Staff

3. Assistants: For the meeting planner, director, the chairperson, and steering committee

Job description:

Be available to the individuals to be helpful with any logistical details necessary throughout the event. Specific _____ instructions will be given by each individual.

4. Book table: Two volunteers to set up and manage the book table (Help volunteers become acquainted with the sale books *prior to the event*.)

Job description

A.   Develop and set up an attractive table display for book sales.

B.   Assist customers with any questions.

C.   Fill out the appropriate forms.

D.   Take the money for the books / cash or check (with phone number).

E.   Give all the receipts and funds to the treasurer, with a written report of the amount of books sold and income accounting at completion of event.

F.   Box extra books and bring them to the registration table.

5. Ushers: For the general session

Job includes

A.   Head usher arranges for appropriate containers for the offering and assigns stations for the other ushers.

B.   Arrive 15 minutes prior to each general session.

C.   Know the locations of emergency exits, telephones, restrooms, and lost and found (generally located at the registration table).

D.   Keep the doors closed during the sound check until the head usher says that the doors can be opened to let attendees in.

E.   Assist individuals with seat selection, filling in seats from the front.

F.   Do not let individuals block the doorways.

G.   Be attentive to any individuals needing special attention.

H.   Distribute handouts when necessary.

I.   Deliver messages to the general session performers and speakers if necessary.

J.   Close the doors five minutes after the session starts and have latecomers remain in the back of the room until the appropriate time to be seated.

K.   Manage the doors to the room so they are closed quietly and minimize hallway noise when people come and go.

L.   Do not seat attendees during special music, drama, or prayers.

M.   Take the offering and bring the funds to the head usher, who counts the money with the treasurer in a private place.

N.   Collect evaluation forms from the event participants.

O.   Deliver evaluation forms to the head usher, then to the registration table.

6. **Hostesses:** For the seminar sessions

   Job includes

   A. Arrive 15 minutes early to the seminar room.

   B. Make sure there is a glass of water for the speaker in the front of the room.

   C. Welcome the participants into the seminar room and ask them to fill the seats in the front of the room first, filling in all the empty seats.

   D. Distribute any handouts.

   E. Turn on the tape player just *before* the faculty assistant introduces the speaker, if requested by the sound engineer.

   F. Turn over the tape if needed.

   G. Stay in the back of the room during the session and assist anyone who needs to go in or out.

   H. Cue the speaker five minutes before the session is over.

   I. Stop the tape when the session is finished and leave the tape in the machine.

   J. Collect the evaluation forms and bring to the registration table after the session.

   K. Straighten the room and pick up any leftover handouts.

   L. Prepare the room for the next session.

   M. Return leftover handouts to the speaker or to the registration table after the session.

7. **Photographer:** Of the event

   Job includes

   A. Purchase the film (two rolls of 35 mm, color, print film, ASA 400).

   B. Take several photographs during each phase of the event.

   C. Take mostly *close-ups* of small groups of people (2-3 people at a time).
       Also photograph individual participants, the speakers, and the steering committee members.

   D. Leave the used film at the registration table after the event.

Budget—Asking the Right Questions

It's time to reevaluate the current budget and make some changes. That means you need to articulate the philosophy of financial management for both the youth ministry and the larger organization. The budget should reflect the philosophies, not drive them.

Allocation of ministry money is directly linked to your values and goals. When you develop the budget, you and your team determine where to allocate money by answering questions like the following.

What does the church value?

• Where does the church invest its resources? (Find out by browsing the last few annual reports.)

• What is the church's spending philosophy? Do they buy the best of a particular item knowing that will last a long time, or do they get the cheapest possible item that will do the job because they don't have a lot of cash on hand? Is youth ministry spending in line with the philosophy of the larger organization?

• Is youth ministry a critical part of the church or is it a small part? (Find out by examining the percent of the total budget dedicated to youth ministry. If it's less than the sandbox allotment for the preschool, you're likely to be in for a struggle if you wish to increase your budget.)

• What has the financial committee approved in the past for youth ministry programs and equipment? You'll get an idea of how flexible they are—how open to ideas new to the church.

What does the youth ministry value?

• Of all the good things on which we can spend ministry money, which things, programs, and people do we value most? How will our spending reflect those values?

• How important is environment to your ministry? Do you need to appropriate funds to make your ministry area more student-friendly?

• How important is staff and staff development?

• Do you have experienced staff, or do they need a lot of training and development?

• Do your staff members need a lot of encouragement? A lot of resources?

What is the financial history of the youth ministry?

- What was the annual budget?

- Where does that money come from?

- Where has the majority of money gone (outreach events, small group materials, van rentals)?

- What brought in the most money (fundraisers, mission trips, service or work projects)?

- Have you inherited any debt? What debt can be carried over, and what debt must you immediately clear up?

- What budget items need to be carried on, and what can be disposed of?

- Are there any annual events you need to finance—denominational gatherings, the annual junior high / senior citizen putt-putt golf tournament?

What are the mechanics of the financial process?

- Does your church tell you to get what you need when you need it, or does it require you to work the purchase into next year's budget and to make do with what you have for this year?

- Are there predetermined vendors for curriculum, sound equipment, retreat sites? Or do you determine who to purchase from?

- Do you get parental financial support, or are you solely dependent on money allocated from the church general budget? What role do your ministry fundraisers play?

- When do you need to turn in your budget proposal to the administration?

- When is the budget decided, and are midyear changes allowed? If so, what's the procedure?

- Can you raise additional funds if needed? Do you need approval for that?

What financial standards are in harmony with your community?

- In what socioeconomic area is the church located, and in what way is that population reflected in your group? (If your church is primarily populated by upper-middle-class members, you can probably request a bigger budget. If your congregation is financially strapped, you will have less available financing resources. Study how your church's socioeconomic makeup affects your ministry finances.)

- Do you have transportation available to you for ministry outings, or do you have to rent vehicles?

- What needs upgrading over the course of the next year—for student safety?

- What do you need to make the ministry student-friendly?

- What items need to be purchased in order for you to continue the development of your ministry? List in order of priority, and find out the approximate cost of each item.

What to Include in Your Budget

SALARY AND BENEFITS

YOUTH ADMINISTRATION
- Professional books
- Magazines / periodicals / newsletters
- Continuing education
- Training / seminars / workshops
- Dues
- Office expenses

PROGRAM (listed alphabetically)
- Activities
  - *Fall*
  - *Winter*
  - *Spring*
  - *Summer*
- Banquets
- Camps and retreats
  - *Honorariums*
  - *Programming*
  - *Scholarships*
  - *Miscellaneous*
- Campus ministry
  - *Bible clubs*
  - *"See You at the Pole"*
- Curriculum
- Fundraising
- Gifts
- Honorariums
- Insurance
- Leadership development / discipleship
- Library / resource center
  - *Books*
  - *Magazines*
- Ministry teams
  - *Drama*
  - *Music*
    - Sunday / Wednesday program
    - Teen choir
    - Groups
    - Other
- Office supplies
- Photography / video
- Promotion / publicity / advertising
- Recreation equipment
- Senior recognition
  - *Graduation gifts*
  - *Banquet / reception*
- Special events
- Transportation
- Travel
- Miscellaneous

POSTAGE
- Mass mailings
- Weekly communications / monthly newsletter / personal letters
  - *Teens*
  - *Volunteers*
- United Parcel Service / R.P.S. / other
- Miscellaneous

PRINTING
- Class notes / lessons
- Calendars
- Fliers
- Class newspaper
- Letters / mass mailings
- Transparencies / overheads
- Daily use
- Other

TRANSPORTATION
- Activities
  - *Fall*
  - *Winter*
  - *Spring*
  - *Summer*
  - *Miscellaneous*
- Camps and retreats
- Youth administration
  - *Visitation*
  - *Hospital visitation*
  - *Miscellaneous*

Adapted from "What I Include in My Budget" by Kevin Winningham, *Youthworker*, Spring 1994.

Budget & Monthly Report

Fiscal Year _____

Accounts	Category	Budget	Year-to-date actual	Over / under	Aug.	Sep.	Oct.	Nov.	Dec.	Jan.	Feb.	Mar.	Apr.	May	Jun.	Jul.
Income																
	Church support															
	Donations															
	Fundraisers															
	Other income															
	Total income															
Expense																
	Administration															
	Advertisement															
	Books and materials															
	Dues and subscriptions															
	Facilities															
	Finance charges															
	Fundraising expenses															
	Gifts															
	Insurance															
	Mailings															
	Office expenses															
	Payroll															
	Postage															
	Transportation															
	Travel															
	Miscellaneous															
	Total expenses															
	Net income															

(income − expenses = net income)

Finance
Budget & Monthly Report

sample

Budget & Monthly Report

Fiscal Year

Accounts	Category	Budget	Year-to-date actual	Over / under	Aug.	Sep.	Oct.	Nov.	Dec.	Jan.	Feb.	Mar.	Apr.	May	Jun.	Jul.
Income																
	Church support		$10,000.00													
	Donations		$2,000.00													
	Fundraisers		$1,500.00													
	Other income		$600.00													
	Total income		**$14,100.00**													
Expense																
	Administration		$150.00													
	Advertisement		$75.00													
	Books and materials		$250.00													
	Dues and subscriptions		$25.00													
	Facilities		$2,500.00													
	Finance charges		$15.00													
	Fundraising expenses		$98.00													
	Gifts		$200.00													
	Insurance		$250.00													
	Mailings		$350.00													
	Office expenses		$125.00													
	Payroll		$8,000.00													
	Postage		$150.00													
	Transportation		$455.00													
	Travel		$209.00													
	Miscellaneous																
	Total expenses		**$12,852.00**													
	Net income		**$1,248.00**		(income - expenses = net income)												

(Place on church letterhead)

October 15, 2000

David Martinez
6475 Lake Lamont
San Diego, CA 92118

Dear David,

Thank you for your thoughtful gift of (amount of money, description of item or service given). Your generosity allows us to continue our mission to (insert your adjusted mission statement here).

May God return to you the blessing you have so generously given to us. We appreciate your continued prayers for our ministry among adolescents. The staff depends on the Lord's strength and provision every day.

Sincerely,

Your name

Organization name _____

Address _____

City _____ State _____ Zip _____

Phone _____

Received from _____
Donor name

Date _____ **Donation amount** _____

Organization name _____

Address _____

City _____ State _____ Zip _____

Phone _____

Received from _____
Donor name

Date _____ **Donation amount** _____

Organization name _____

Address _____

City _____ State _____ Zip _____

Phone _____

Received from _____
Donor name

Date _____ **Donation amount** _____

Organization name _____

Address _____

City _____ State _____ Zip _____

Phone _____

Received from _____
Donor name

Date _____ **Donation amount** _____

Organization name _____

Address _____

City _____ State _____ Zip _____

Phone _____

Received from _____
Donor name

Date _____ **Donation amount** _____

Organization name _____

Address _____

City _____ State _____ Zip _____

Phone _____

Received from _____
Donor name

Date _____ **Donation amount** _____

How to Begin a Budget

Step 1

See that youth ministry becomes a budget item.

Step 2

Check out the budgets of other youth ministries to learn what your budget may need to include. Start with ministries in your own area, then network with other ministries in your region and even across the country. Pay particular attention to budgets of ministries similar in size to yours.

Step 3

Determine what should and shouldn't be included in your budget, based on last year's check disbursements and purchase orders, this year's check disbursements and purchase orders, and old budgets (if there are any).

Step 4

Keep a file of your research. Include articles on budgets from youth magazines and denominational and secular publications, as well as actual budgets researched in Steps 2 and 3 above.

Step 5

Propose a budget. Present yourself as a professional—distribute handouts, use an overhead projector, flipchart, or presentation software, and respond with detailed rationale for each item you propose. Preface your presentation with a persuasive talk about why youth ministry should be part of the budget. Buttress your requests by sharing information gleaned from networking (in Step 2, above). Conclude your presentation with a brief overview of your proposed youth ministry.

Step 6

Keep good records for the next year, including income (from activities, camps, retreats, fundraisers) and all expenses.

Step 7

Be a good steward of your ministry resources. Let your use of resources be guided by prayer and accountability to one or more individuals who support the youth ministry.

Reprinted by permission from *Youthworker*, Spring 1994.

Monthly Expense Report

Fiscal Year

Account #	Category	Budget	Year-to-date actual	Over / under	Aug.	Sep.	Oct.	Nov.	Dec.	Jan.	Feb.	Mar.	Apr.	May	Jun.	Jul.
	Total expenses															

Monthly Expense Report

sample

Fiscal Year 1999

Account #	Category	Budget	Year-to-date actual	Over / under	Aug.	Sep.	Oct.	Nov.	Dec.	Jan.	Feb.	Mar.	Apr.	May	Jun.	Jul.
1001	Staff dev.	$125	$100	$ 25	$10		$10	$10	$10	$10	$50					
1002	Operations	$200	$ 60	$140		$25		$10		$25						
1003	Materials	$150	$ 50	$100		$25					$25					
1004	Transportation	$20	$-	$ 20												
1005	Food	$100	$250	$(150)	$50		$25	$25		$25		$75		$25	$25	
1006	Misc.	$75	$ 75	$-		$25		$25				$25				
Total expenses		$670	$535	$135	$60	$75	$35	$70	$10	$60	$75	$100	$-	$25	$25	$-

Petty Cash Receipt

Date _____ / _____ / _____

To_____
NAME OF RECIPIENT

Amount $_____

To use for—

Return date—

_____ / _____ / _____

Petty Cash Receipt

Date _____ / _____ / _____

To_____
NAME OF RECIPIENT

Amount $_____

To use for—

Return date—

_____ / _____ / _____

Petty Cash Receipt

Date _____ / _____ / _____

To_____
NAME OF RECIPIENT

Amount $_____

To use for—

Return date—

_____ / _____ / _____

Petty Cash Receipt

Date _____ / _____ / _____

To_____
NAME OF RECIPIENT

Amount $_____

To use for—

Return date—

_____ / _____ / _____

Petty Cash Receipt

Date _____ / _____ / _____

To_____
NAME OF RECIPIENT

Amount $_____

To use for—

Return date—

_____ / _____ / _____

Petty Cash Receipt

Date _____ / _____ / _____

To_____
NAME OF RECIPIENT

Amount $_____

To use for—

Return date—

_____ / _____ / _____

Petty Cash Receipt

Date _____ / _____ / _____

To_____
NAME OF RECIPIENT

Amount $_____

To use for—

Return date—

_____ / _____ / _____

Petty Cash Receipt

Date _____ / _____ / _____

To_____
NAME OF RECIPIENT

Amount $_____

To use for—

Return date—

_____ / _____ / _____

Profit & Loss Statement

From _____ to _____
        DATE   DATE

Income

Church support

Donations

Fundraisers

Other income
_____

Total income

Expense

Administration

Advertisement

Books and materials

Dues & subscriptions

Facilities

Finance charges

Fundraising expenses

Gifts

Insurance

Mailings

Office expense

Payroll

Postage

Transportation

Travel

Total expense

Net income
(Total income minus total expense)

Reimbursement

Name _____

Whose money _____

Address (optional) _____

_____

Account name _____

Explanation _____

_____

Receipt total

Deduct

Tax & personal expenses

Reimbursement total

Division leader's approval

Reimbursement

Name _____

Whose money _____

Address (optional) _____

_____

Account name _____

Explanation _____

_____

Receipt total

Deduct

Tax & personal expenses

Reimbursement total

Division leader's approval

Reimbursement

Name _____

Whose money _____

Address (optional) _____

_____

Account name _____

Explanation _____

_____

Receipt total

Deduct

Tax & personal expenses

Reimbursement total

Division leader's approval

Reimbursement

Name _____

Whose money _____

Address (optional) _____

_____

Account name _____

Explanation _____

_____

Receipt total

Deduct

Tax & personal expenses

Reimbursement total

Division leader's approval

Retreat Budget

	Quantity	Cost	Projected	Actual	Projected	Actual
Expenses						
Brochure printing	1	$ 65	$ 65	$ -		
Postage	1	$ 50	$ 50	$ -		
T-shirts	125	$ 8	$ 1,000	$ -		
Student camp fees	100	$ 49	$ 4,900	$ -		
Bus rental	2	$200	$ 400	$ -		
Bus mileage	1	$100	$ 100	$ -		
Speaker	1	$450	$ 450	$ -		
Late vehicle	1	$120	$ 120	$ -		
Fuel	1	$150	$ 150	$ -		
Band	1	$800	$ 800	$ -		
Truck rental	1	$200	$ 200	$ -		
Equipment rental	1	$225	$ 225	$ -		
Supplies / props	1	$300	$ 300	$ -		
Dinner	1	$250	$ 250	$ -		
Program staff	8	$ 59	$ 472	$ -		
Staff expense	10	$ 49	$ 490	$ -		
Total Expenses			**$9,972**	$ -		
Revenue (not including student fees)						
Program budget	1	$1,000	$ 1,000	$ -		
Staff payment	8	$ 25	$ 200	$ -		
Revenue			**$1,200**	$ -		
					Projected	Actual
Total expenses					$9,972	$ -
Minus total revenue					$1,200	$ -
Equals Net Cost					**$8.772**	$ -
Student fees						
Net cost (same as total student fees)			$8,772			
Divided by number of students attending			$100			
Cost per student			$87.72			
					Projected	Actual
Revenue					$1,200	
Plus total student fees					$8,772	
						$9,972
Minus total expenses					$9,972	
NET (+ \ -)						$0

Summary Balance Sheet

As of _____
DATE

Assets

Checking / savings $

Other current assets $ (include all assets)

Total current assets $

Liabilities and equity

Current liabilities $ (include all outstanding bills)

Total liabilities $

Net income $

Summary Balance Sheet

sample

As of July 31, 2002

Assets

Checking / savings	$ 2,000	
Other current assets	$ 248	(include all assets)

Total current assets $ **2,248**

Liabilities and equity

Current liabilities	$ 1,000	(include all outstanding bills)

Total liabilities $ **1,000**

Net income $ **1,248**

Tips for the Newcomer

"It's my first day on the job. What do I do now?"

First week

- Request a copy of the current budget and last year's budget.
- Schedule a meeting with the person familiar with the youth ministry budget.
- Ask for training on the current procedures for tracking income and expenses.
- Ask what ways of handling finances have worked in the past and what trouble spots you should be aware of. (Keep an eye on the trouble spots during the next few weeks.)
- Unless the finances are in crisis, keep to the system currently in place. Change and improvements can come when you have more knowledge of and experience with the ministry.

First month

- Study and understand the budget. Get a feel for how it's been used in the past—what worked and what didn't.
- Talk to anyone who's had experience working with the youth ministry budget.
- Talk to the current church treasurer to see what has worked well with the youth ministry and what hasn't. Also ask if there's anything that could be done differently to be helpful to the treasurer.
- Work on patching the financial holes. If necessary, call a temporary spending freeze until you get a handle on the finances.
- Meet with the pastor and / or treasurer to discuss
    — the church's philosophy on spending, on corporate and personal fundraising, and on ministry money management.
    — what things are in stone and what things are negotiable.
    — what the current systems are set for bill paying and reimbursements, and when you have to submit the paperwork to receive timely payment.
- Investigate how youth ministry petty cash, donations, fees, and expense reimbursement is currently handled and evaluate if it's successful or not. Try to assign someone else to handle the petty cash (administrative assistant, financial volunteer, et cetera). If needed, change the system so that every bill, check, donation, petty cash receipt, and dollar goes across your desk. You need to know how every penny is being collected and spent. That's the only way you'll ever get a handle on the ministry finances.

First six months

- After understanding, observing, and personally monitoring the budget for at least six months, you can delegate to a staff person or trusted (experienced) volunteer some of the routine procedures. Request weekly or monthly reports from your volunteer so you can monitor any major income or expenses (perhaps more than $25 or $100, depending on the size and scope of your ministry).
- Reevaluate the current budget and adjust it according to your ministry needs.
- Never assume. Always check and double check numbers.
- If at any time you creep into the financial danger zone—overspending a monthly budget, losing money on an event, unable to account for some expenses or the reason for some checks or cash you find in a drawer—notify the church's treasurer or CFO and get assistance ASAP. CFO's don't like surprises and are more forgiving if you come forward sooner rather than later.

Trip _____ Date_____

Price of room per night	$			
Divided by—number of people per room	/			
Equals—price per person	$			
Multiplied by—number of nights	x			
		=	**Per-person lodging cost**	$

• Transportation package				
Price of round trip to event	$			
Divided by—number of participants	/			
		=	**Per-person cost with package**	$
• Vehicle rental and gas				
Miles we're traveling				
Miles per gallon in rental vehicle			**Use only *one* calculation:**	
Total gallons needed =			Per-person cost with package	
Multiplied by—average price per gallon	x $		**OR**	
Total gas cost =	$		Per-person cost with vehicle rental and gas	
Plus—total vehicle rental cost =	$			
Total of gas and rental =	$			
Divided by—number of riders	/			
		=	**Per-person cost with vehicle rental and gas**	$

Food				
Number of breakfasts per person				
Multiplied by—average price for breakfast	x $			
Total for breakfasts (A)	$			
Number of lunches per person				
Multiplied by—average price for lunch	x $			
Total for lunches (B)	$			
Number of dinners per person				
Multiplied by—average price for dinner	x $			
Total for dinners (C)	$			
(A)	$			
Plus (B)	+ $		Per-person cost for all lodging	$
Plus (C)	+ $		Per-person cost for all travel	$
		=	Per-person cost for all meals	$
		=	**Total per-person cost for trip**	$

sample

San Carlos Mission Trip   December 29, 2002

Lodging

Price of room per night	$ 85.95			
Divided by—number of people per room	/ 4			
Equals—price per person	$ 21.49			
Multiplied by—number of nights	x 3			
	=	**Per-person lodging cost**		$ 64.49

Transportation

• Transportation package			
Price of round trip to event	$ 400.00		
Divided by—number of participants	/ 13		
	=	**Per-person cost with package**	$ 30.75
• Vehicle rental and gas			
Miles we're traveling	850		
Miles per gallon in rental vehicle	13	**Use only *one* calculation:**	
Total gallons needed =	66	Per-person cost with package	
Multiplied by—average price per gallon	x $ 1.75	**OR**	
Total gas cost =	$ 115.50	Per-person cost with vehicle rental and gas	
Plus—total vehicle rental cost =	$ 250.00		
Total of gas and rental =	$ 365.50		
Divided by—number of riders	/ 13		
	=	**Per-person cost with vehicle rental and gas**	$ 28.12

Food

Number of breakfasts per person	3		
Multiplied by—average price for breakfast	x $ 4.00		
Total for breakfasts (A)	$ 12.00		
Number of lunches per person	4		
Multiplied by—average price for lunch	x $ 6.00		
Total for lunches (B)	$ 24.00		
Number of dinners per person	4		
Multiplied by—average price for dinner	x $ 8.00		
Total for dinners (C)	$ 32.00		
(A)	$ 12.00		
Plus (B)	+ $ 24.00	**Per-person cost for all lodging**	$ 64.46
Plus (C)	+ $ 32.00	**Per-person cost for all travel**	$ 28.12
=		**Per-person cost for all meals**	$ 68.00
=		**Total per-person cost for trip**	**$ 160.50**

In theory, having an intern would lighten your workload and enhance the youth ministry. In practice, however, having a intern can be a drag on your energy as you bring the intern up to speed and contribute to the intern's development. Ask yourself questions like these before you take the step of proposing a youth ministry internship to your supervisor:

- *Do I have a clear job description with measurable goals?* What exactly would you hire an intern to accomplish in the youth ministry?

- *Am I clear on what I expect from an intern?* Is church membership an expectation? What meetings must they attend on a regular basis? What meetings should they attend once or twice for the experience? When do you expect them to be in the office? What about days off? What is acceptable dress in the church? What about when they're with students? How does the intern access resources—secretarial help, church vehicles, et cetera.?

- *How long will the internship last?* Is it full-time during the summer? Part-time for a year? Does it run concurrently with school, or does the intern commit a block of time (for example, one year before starting seminary)?

- *How many hours a week will the intern work?* Does the internship pay enough to live on, or will the intern need a part-time job to supplement her income? If the internship runs concurrently with school, how many hours a week is it feasible for the intern to work? Is the church willing to be flexible when finals roll around?

- *What age group will the intern work with?* Middle school? High school? College-age?

- *What program will the intern work with?* Vacation Bible School, day camp, small groups, worship ministry?

- *Who will be her supervisor? Do I have enough experience to develop another youth worker? Does anyone else on staff?* What will an aspiring youth worker learn from spending time with you and this ministry?

- *Do I have the time to develop and guide another youth worker?* Youth pastors quickly realize that supervising an intern to do a task always takes more of their time than doing it themselves. How will having an intern affect your ability to do your job?

- *Is my church or organization supportive of it?* Have they hired an intern before? Have any of the leadership done an internship as part of their professional development? Who would you need to clear the idea with?

- *Does the church staff understand the job description of a youth ministry intern?* Or will the church secretary expect an intern to stuff envelopes? Might the janitor expect he can delegate the Sunday school room set up to the intern?

- *Is my church willing to provide compensation to the intern?* If his compensation is room and board, with whom will he live? If it's a small stipend, tuition credit, or cash, out of which budget will it come? Based on what you're looking for in an intern, what do you think would be the best form of compensation?

- *What will she use for transportation?* Will the organization loan her a car? Reimburse her for travel and job expenses?

- *Does my church's insurance cover an intern? How about Workers' Compensation?*

- *Does my church believe in developing future leaders for ministry, and are they willing to take on the accompanying risks?* The internship is a step in the intern's discernment process. It may be that during the internship, it becomes clear that ministry is not the right direction for this person. Is the church willing to take that risk? Have you written out a description of those actions that would terminate an internship?

- *Is my church willing to let this person fail as well as succeed?* Interns are rookies. As they try out their ministry legs, there are bound to be messes as well as successes. In what areas is the church willing to extend grace? In what areas can there be no mess-ups?

- *Am I ready to take appropriate and decisive action if conflict arises with an intern or about the intern?* How can you be proactive in conflicts involving the intern? Can you confront based on early recognition of potential problems, or are you inclined to let things slide until you're forced to react?

- *How can the relationship be terminated if things don't work out as planned?*

Along with the details covered above, you'll need to decide what elements will form a basis for the learning contract between your church and the intern. Once the internship begins, you can invite the intern to add to your contract things he wants to accomplish or experience by the end of the internship. Talk together about how both parties will be different because of the internship experience. You'll want to develop goals in the areas of knowledge, skill, and character qualities, keeping in mind each party's time, abilities, motivations, available resources, and so on.

- What *knowledge* objectives will she achieve by the end of the internship? Here's some ideas:

By the end of this internship, the intern should be able to—

—Begin to formulate and articulate a philosophy of youth ministry

—Identify the key characteristics of adolescence, as well as the impact on adolescents of family, society, and church

—Explain the rationale behind the model of youth ministry the church uses

—Articulate the demographics of the community and the services available through the local community

—Describe the importance of the youth minister, whether professional or volunteer, in effective leadership of adolescents and their families

- What *skills* will he achieve by the end of the internship? Include goals like these in the learning contract:

By the end of this internship, the intern should be able to—

—Write and lead a Bible study appropriate for senior high students

—Initiate exploratory conversations with parents and with several subcultures of adolescents

—Develop and produce a worship service

—Put together a three-month program that includes a variety of events and topics geared towards adolescents' felt and real needs. It may include Sunday school, confirmation, and weekly activities

—Develop and manage a youth ministry budget

—Run an effective meeting

—Recruit and interview potential volunteers

- What *areas and tasks* will the intern be exposed to?

By the end of this internship, the intern will have experienced—

—Weekly church staff meetings in order to better understand how the whole church operates

—A weekly Bible study as both an observer and a leader

—Participating in the organization and leadership of a week-long missions trip

—Producing a variety of communication tools: fliers, church and youth ministry announcements, calendars, permission slips

—Participation in planning and strategy meetings

- What can the intern expect from you and the church?

During this internship, the intern can expect—

—Weekly or bi-weekly meetings with the supervisor

—Exposure to the full scope of the ministry, including administrative areas (budget development, hiring and development of volunteer staff, church staff meetings, congregational meetings, and counseling appointments when appropriate).

—Timely payment of a salary or stipend

—Medical insurance

—Conference registration for a professional seminar for youth workers

- What can the church expect from the intern?

During this internship, the church can expect that the intern will—

—Show up on time to all meetings or responsibilities

—Dress appropriately for the ministry situation

—Maintain a model lifestyle during the internship

—Immediately inform the supervisor of any areas of concern or conflict

- How will success be determined?

At the end of the internship, the intern will be evaluated—

—By means of a formal self-evaluation and a written evaluation by the supervisor (see **Intern Self-Evaluation** and **Intern Supervisor Evaluation**)

—Based on the intern's completion of the learning contract written out at the start of the internship (This should be the conclusion of an on-going discussion and shouldn't have any surprises.)

—Through discussing—both informally and at a designated meeting—with the supervisor and other activity leaders and participants the level of excellence achieved in various areas (the results, or what happened) and discussing what they learned from the experiences (why it happened the way it did)

A successful internship requires clear definition—identifying a specific type of intern and specific tasks to achieve. Once you know what you're looking for, where will you search?

- **Look within.** Is there a student within the larger ministry who is trying to discern his or her call to ministry?

- **Look at local colleges and seminaries.** Christian colleges with youth ministry majors or minors usually post job descriptions. Send yours to the chair of the department, as well as to the career counseling office. (Often students interested in going into youth ministry major in another field.) You may even want to post your internship with local community colleges or universities.

- **Look at your denominational seminary.** If you have a strong denominational affiliation and are looking for several interns, sometimes it helps to actually recruit live on a campus. "Cold call" students are more likely to consider your ministry's internship if they have a conversation with you.

- **Look at other youth ministries.** Are there colleagues who have students that might be potential interns in your ministry? I advise students to avoid doing an internship at their home church—it's usually too difficult to be seen as an adult. Perhaps some intern swapping might work in your local network.

Applicant's name_____

The person named above is applying for a 12-month youth ministry internship with _____
Church name

The applicant has been instructed to give you this form. Please complete it to the best of your knowledge. It will become part of the application and will be used to help determine the applicant's suitability for the desired ministry. No single reference will determine acceptance or refusal, so frank appraisal will be appreciated both by the applicant and the selection committee. Thank you for your time on behalf of the applicant.

Please send the completed form to: _____
Church name   Address   City   State   Zip

1. How long have you known the applicant?

2. What is your relationship to the applicant?

3. In each category, check the characteristics that to your knowledge best describe the applicant. Add brief comments if necessary.

Physical health
- ❏ somewhat below par
- ❏ fairly healthy
- ❏ good health

Personality
- ❏ avoided by others
- ❏ tolerated by others
- ❏ accepted by others
- ❏ liked by others
- ❏ sought after by others

Achievement
- ❏ starts but often does not finish
- ❏ does only what is assigned
- ❏ meets average expectation
- ❏ resourceful and effective
- ❏ superior creative ability

Teamwork
- ❏ frequently causes friction
- ❏ prefers to work alone
- ❏ knows how to follow
- ❏ works well with others
- ❏ most effective in teamwork

Spiritual maturity
- ❏ immature faith
- ❏ has made basic commitment
- ❏ somewhat rigid beliefs
- ❏ active and growing faith
- ❏ exceptional insight and discipline

Intelligence
- ❏ learns and thinks slowly
- ❏ average mental ability
- ❏ alert, has good mind
- ❏ intelligent, makes thoughtful analysis
- ❏ brilliant, exceptional capability

Responsiveness
- ❏ slow to sense how others feel
- ❏ reasonably responsive
- ❏ understanding and thoughtful
- ❏ accurately aware of others
- ❏ responds with unusual insight

Leadership
- ❏ makes no attempt to lead
- ❏ tries but lacks ability
- ❏ has some leadership skills
- ❏ unusual, exceptional leadership

Emotional stability
- ❏ somewhat over-emotional
- ❏ inclined to be apathetic
- ❏ rapidly shifting moods
- ❏ usually well balanced
- ❏ good control in difficult situations

Knowledge of the Bible
- ❏ sketchy, limited
- ❏ basic, but improving
- ❏ well established
- ❏ superior grasp

Adapted with permission from: First Presbyterian Intern Committee, 1840 Niagara, Montrose, CO 81401 (970/249-4732)

Letter of Reference for Internship Applicant

Applicant's name _____

Please use the scale indicated below to further describe the applicant.
Rating scale: 1 = Outstanding, 2 = Good, 3 = Satisfactory, 4 = Fair, 5 = Poor, U/K= Unknown

1. Self-understanding

ability to identify his/her own personal strengths	1	2	3	4	5	U/K
ability to identify his/her own weaknesses	1	2	3	4	5	U/K
ability to see self as others see him/her	1	2	3	4	5	U/K
openness to growth and change	1	2	3	4	5	U/K

2. Emotional strength

ability to deal constructively with personal feelings	1	2	3	4	5	U/K
ability to receive constructive criticism	1	2	3	4	5	U/K
ability to be flexible in the face of change	1	2	3	4	5	U/K
ability to persevere through difficulties	1	2	3	4	5	U/K

3. Interpersonal relationships

ability to listen accurately to others	1	2	3	4	5	U/K
ability to respond to feelings and needs of others	1	2	3	4	5	U/K
ability to initiate friendships and care for others	1	2	3	4	5	U/K
willingness to resolve interpersonal conflicts	1	2	3	4	5	U/K

4. Motivation for ministry

desire to serve out of genuine love for Christ	1	2	3	4	5	U/K
desire to serve out of genuine love for others	1	2	3	4	5	U/K
willingness to do humble tasks joyfully	1	2	3	4	5	U/K
ability to take risks and respond to challenges	1	2	3	4	5	U/K

Working in a team, working with children, youth, or people older than oneself, experiencing new ways of handling things, and getting to know new people—while all these things make being an intern exciting, they're stressful as well. Such stress may sometimes exaggerate some personality traits such as those listed below. Please check any that you feel apply to the applicant.

❑ Impatient   ❑ Perfectionist

❑ Argumentative   ❑ Critical of others

❑ Domineering   ❑ Easily embarrassed

❑ Sullen   ❑ Easily discouraged

❑ Cocky   ❑ Withdrawn

❑ Irritable   ❑ Anxious

❑ Easily offended   ❑ Lacking a sense of humor

If there is anything else you feel would be important for us to know regarding the applicant, please respond on a separate page. Or if you prefer, check this box, and we will call you. ❑

Your name (print) _____ Day phone _____

Address _____

Occupation _____

Signature _____ Date _____

Sincere thanks!

Name _____ Date of evaluation _____

Description of internship _____

_____

Please circle the number that describes you.
  1 is a solid yes
  2 is a tentative yes
  3 is a tentative no
  4 is a solid no

1	2	3	4	I feel good about my overall internship experience.
1	2	3	4	I have helped set the pace in developing the ministry's identity, enthusiasm, momentum, and unity / teamwork.
1	2	3	4	My internship prepared me well for ministry.
1	2	3	4	I believe I have been able to use my gifts at my internship.
1	2	3	4	I have grown as a Christian as a result of my internship experience.
1	2	3	4	I believe that my internship experience allowed me to grow in being a leader in ministry.
1	2	3	4	I was open to evaluation and feedback from my supervisor.
1	2	3	4	I fulfilled the responsibilities of my internship in an effective manner.
1	2	3	4	I related well to other staff / coworkers.
1	2	3	4	I feel fairly comfortable helping people grow.
1	2	3	4	I was open to new ideas.

As a result of your internship, rate the following, as you now see yourself, by checking the appropriate box:

JOB DESCRIPTION CATEGORIES	Never did it	Feel hesitant	Feel okay	Feel good about it
Contacting new persons				
Introducing person to Jesus				
Counseling				
Leading a Bible study				
Long-range planning: theme development, vision, and mission				
Publicity				
Budget preparation and management				
Equipping leaders (volunteer)				
Working with a board				
Working with a committee				
Recreation				
Retreats				
Service projects / mission trips				
Teaching Sunday school				
Leading youth meetings				
Giving a youth talk				

Please answer the following questions.

What was a highlight of your internship for you?

What did you do well in your internship?

What area(s) need improvement in your ministry?

What area(s) need improvement in our ministry?

What was the most challenging aspect of your internship for you?

How did you balance your time between your ministry and your personal time?

How has your relationship with God grown as a result of your internship?

What do you consider the most helpful aspect of the time spent as an intern?

Was there any time in which your time as an intern was a disappointment? If so, please describe.

Would you recommend other people to serve in this internship in the future? Why or why not?

Any other comments:

Name _____ Phone _____

Name of Intern _____ Date of evaluation _____

Description of internship _____

_____

_____

Please evaluate the following competencies of the intern as you have observed them in ministry.
Circle the number that best describes the intern.

1 is a solid yes
2 is a tentative yes
3 is a tentative no
4 is a solid no

Competencies	**Additional comments**

1 2 3 4   Appeared enthusiastic about ministry

1 2 3 4   Was prepared to fulfill their responsibilities

1 2 3 4   Related well to the students

1 2 3 4   Related well to other staff and co-workers

1 2 3 4   Took the initiative with projects and assignments

1 2 3 4   Was open to constructive criticism from me

1 2 3 4   Shared ideas without insisting implementation

1 2 3 4   Recognized when they needed help and sought it

1 2 3 4   Demonstrated a loving, patient spirit

1 2 3 4   Reached out to persons on the fringe

1 2 3 4   Arrived on time

1 2 3 4   Organized effectively

1 2 3 4   Was resourceful

1 2 3 4   Demonstrated gifts for ministry

What areas of strength did you observe in this intern? (List, and be specific.)

What areas for further growth did you observe in this intern?

Did you meet regularly with the intern? If so, what did you discuss or do in those meetings?

Describe the interaction between the other staff members and / or the congregation:

Did the intern display the maturity level needed for ministry?

Additional comments:

You need to get clear answers to the following questions before you ever agree to take a position:

• **How are raises determined?** You'll find out if you'll be locked into your starting salary for the rest of your tenure or if can you negotiate a raise. Are raises based on merit or on life circumstances? (someone gets married, has kids, buys a house) Are raises based on gender or marital status? (It still happens.) Veteran advice: Negotiate the salary you want up front; don't plan on making up the difference in a raise. If the church starts you at a certain amount but promises to raise you to a higher amount within the first two years, get it in writing. Promises fade quickly once you're hired.

• **If the ministry is to be considered successful in three months, what will that look like? In six months? In one year?** This tells you more about their philosophy of ministry than any Web site ever will. They may deny being about numbers, but if they describe a successful ministry as being "packed out," "crammed with kids," or language like that, you know immediately what you'll be evaluated on.

• **Why did the last youth pastor leave?** If this raises the least bit of suspicion, reframe this question and ask it again. For example: **Who have been some staff who didn't make it here and why?** or **Tell me who has been a staff hero in the past and why?** (Is the former youth pastor one of them? Why or why not?)

• **Are you hiring me to be the pastor to every kid or to train and equip the adults?** In other words, will your primary focus be building relationships with students or building a team of adults? The answer you seek will be different based on what season of life you're in.

• **What has been the budget for youth ministry? How do you see that changing in the future? Is the youth pastor's salary included in that?** Listen for what percentage it gets out of the total budget and listen for the reasoning. It may be that there were no adolescents up until a year ago when the church experienced a huge growth surge. It may also be that the increase in budget is due to the youth pastor's proposed salary. You may take the job, but have only $800 a year to work with.

• **What are the church's expectations for numerical and spiritual growth?** Listen for which piece they focus on. Which seems to be a priority and why?

• **How often are job reviews done? Who does them? What happens to the results?**

Critical Questions You Need to Ask at Your Interview

• **Who am I going to report to and how much time per week will I spend with them?** This is especially important if you are expecting to be mentored by the senior pastor or someone else. You may be interested in the position because it would mean being able to spend time with them. They may only expect to see you on the platform Sunday morning and at church meetings.

• **If someone were to ask you about me one year from now and you would respond that I have exceeded expectations, what would I be doing?**

• **If someone were to ask you about me one year from now and you would respond that I am barely surviving, what would I have done or not done?** This question may be the way to get at the heart of why the last youth pastor left.

• **What's the process for determining and approving what the youth ministry does?** a) Does everything get approved by a youth committee? b) Does the senior pastor approve everything? c) Do you have sole authority to decide what is done?

• **What other expectations are there for me outside of youth ministry?** Does the church expect you to preach on a regular basis? Do nursing home visits? Perform weddings and funerals? Fill in when the nursery hits overload?

• **Has the staff ever had a paycheck withheld because the church was short of money?** If so, when was that and how was that communicated to the church?

• **What happens when the church is behind budget?** Again, how is that communicated to the congregation?

• **What does a typical week look like?** If you're expecting to work 45 hours a week and they're expecting 60, you're headed for a major confrontation. Get it out in the open before you start.

• **What about outside speaking engagements?** Find out their policy for staff speaking to groups and camps outside the church. Are you allowed a certain number of days per year for that? Does it come out of your vacation time? What about honorariums—can you keep them or do you need to turn them over to the church?

- **Where will my office be located?** This isn't about having a corner office with huge windows. It's about having a place that is easily accessible to the public and that does not isolate you from people. Because of the amount of counseling that goes on, your office should be in a central location with a window in the door, not tucked under the basement stairs where people need a map to find it.

- **What computer equipment will I have?** Now is the time to ask for what you want. If possible, choose what you prefer using. Also inquire about software and Internet usage.

- **Will I have access to an administrative assistant?** How many hours a week? With whom are you sharing his or her time? Who has priority on their time? What is their base of computer knowledge?

- **What are the three most important qualities for a staff member at this church to possess?**

- **What does this church do well?**

- **What is this church known for in the community?**

- **In five years, what will the church look like?**

- **In five years, how do you hope the youth ministry looks?**

- **What is this church really about? What is important here?**

Prepare yourself for your job interview.

Familiarize yourself with that particular church or organization.

• Find out as much as you can about the ministry with which you're interviewing. That way, you walk in primed to ask key questions and to explore the significant issues.

❑ Request annual reports, denominational information, mission statements, and informational brochures.

❑ Check out their web site, if they have one. Look not only for what they say, but what they omit. How often does the youth ministry get mentioned? What percentage of the whole church budget is dedicated to the youth ministry?

❑ Use your discretion to determine how best to talk with former youth pastors, counselors, the church secretary (a gold-mine of information), or students in the group. Ask What is this youth ministry known for? What are its strengths? What areas need growth?

❑ Call other churches in the area to get their perspective. You may want to ask, "When you think of First Church, what comes to mind? How is First Church perceived by members in the community?"

Based on what you learn, prepare a list of questions to put to your interviewer.

Familiarize yourself with the community.

❑ Browse local newspapers on the Internet.

❑ Check out housing costs.

❑ Look up Web sites of the local schools.

❑ Look up the city's Web site to learn about recreational opportunities, cultural offerings, the crime rate.

❑ If you're married, is this a place where your family will feel comfortable?

❑ If you're single, is this a place where you'll find like-minded people? (When you're single, you don't take your support system with you; rather, you have to start from scratch.)

Prepare yourself.

• Ask a friend to rehearse with you answers to possible interview questions. (See **Critical Questions to Ask at Your Interview** and **Questions You May Be Asked at Your Interview**)
• Ask what dress code you should follow for the meetings you'll attend—then, dress a step above. (If this is one of your first jobs, compensate for your youth and inexperience by wearing a suit or dress. Look at your purchases as an investment in your career.)
• If you're candidating over a weekend, ask what activities you'll observe or participate in, and bring appropriate clothing.
• Bring a prepared message with you.
• Bring breath mints. Stick a couple loose in your pockets so they're easy to reach.
• Be careful what you eat before you interview. Butterflies don't mix with nachos. Let's just leave it at that.

Negotiate your job offer very carefully. As uncomfortable as it feels to talk about money and ministry in the same breath, you live with the reality of paying for a roof and food and utilities, among other necessities. Negotiate for what you want at the beginning—once you've taken the position, you can't go back and ask for more.

Try not to sell yourself too high or too low. And spend some time clarifying your expectations of the job and putting it in writing before you sit down to negotiate. If your requests are acceptable to the hiring board, have them write it into your contract—if you don't have it in writing, you don't have it.

Salary expectations

• **If the church contacts you**, during the initial contact, ask these three questions: What's the greatest strength of the church? Where do you see it going in the future? Can you tell me the salary range?
• **If you contact the church**, don't bring up salary. You may end up wasting some time, but that's better than being perceived as only interested in the money.

The compensation package

• **Your base salary will be affected by—**

Your education. If you have a M.Div., your salary should be higher than an employee with only a Bachelor of Arts or an Associate of Arts. If it's not, it tells you that the church doesn't value educational experience. Is that a warning for you? The reality of increased student loans to repay goes with the increased degree.

Your experience. If you come with only a B.A., but you bring the benefit of eight years of experience, negotiate a salary that compensates for experience. Other professions do; so should the church.

Community cost-of-living. How much will it cost to live in this community? Renting a house in Red Oak, Iowa, for instance, costs less than renting an apartment in the Silicon Valley. Too often, youth pastors eager to get a job underestimate how much it will cost to live in a given area. They end up working extra jobs just to pay the bills. Several web sites can do a cost-of-living analysis for you: datamasters.com or monster.com

Comparable salaries. It's helpful to put your position into perspective by comparing it with other professions with similar job requirements. A rule of thumb for recent college graduates is to find out what the area's first year high school teachers are paid. The school system knows the cost of living for the community. If you have an advanced degree and experience, find out what counselors, principals, and medical personnel in the area are paid. You may also want to call your denominational offices to request salary guidance.

• **Find out if the package includes housing. If so—**
  — Is this considered nontaxable income?
  — How does the fact that you are (or are not) licensed impact your taxes in this sphere? (You need to discuss this with your tax advisor.)
  — What costs of housing does the church pay for, and what are you responsible for? You may need to pay the utility bills, which sounds like a great deal until you see that it costs $350 a month to heat the behemoth.
  — Who is responsible for the upkeep? Usually, it will be you. Do you have time to spend repaving driveways, painting shutters, and fixing screens and leaky pipes on a 75-year-old house? And who pays for the repairs?
  — Does the church offer the option of home ownership with a housing allowance or a parsonage with an equity allowance? Again, talk over these issues with your tax advisor.

• **Ask if your compensation includes cost-of-living increases and bonuses.**
  — How much of an increase does the staff receives each year? (If they don't give cost-of-living increases, you are, in effect, losing money each year.)
  — Are bonuses given if ministry goals are exceeded?
  — Are merit-based raises are given? (If so, how often and how are they determined?)

• **Find out what employee benefits come with your package.**

Retirement. Some churches have mandatory pension plans if you are licensed and / or ordained. Others have matching plans—they will match your retirement contributions up to, say, 5 percent of your salary.

Insurance. Which insurance, among all the different types, is covered by the church's plan?

Medical. If you have a family, are they covered? Do you need to pay any extra for their coverage? Is dental included?
  Disability insurance
  Life insurance
  Liability insurance
  Accidental death and dismemberment

Taxes and days off

• **FICA.** If you are considered self-employed, it is your responsibility to make quarterly tax payments to the government (both state and federal). Some churches pay the employer's share of the youth pastor's social security payments. Check to see your church's policy.

• **Time off.**

Days off. Expect a minimum of one full day off a week—the norm is two. Don't accept partial days off— like being off on Friday afternoon and Tuesday. A person needs a full day to be able to disengage and relax.

Vacation. The length of your first year's vacation depends on when you start. If you start in June, you usually get half the number of day written into your contract. A piece of advice—don't even touch a position that offers less than two weeks of vacation. Ministry is such a time and energy intensive profession that you need that time to recuperate. Find out when your vacation is increased. An example is receiving an additional week of vacation, up to five weeks a year, for every three years on staff. For an experienced youth pastor, four paid weeks a year is appropriate. Sometimes, churches that can't afford a large base salary offer more vacation time. If that seems to be the case of the interviewing church, you may negotiate more vacation time in lieu of the higher salary.

Compensation time. Ask what the church's policy is on giving you time off after a time-intensive event, such as a mission trip or weekend retreat. If they blink rapidly and mumble, "Whazzat?" run…fast. Some churches expect you to show up at the 8:00 a.m. staff meeting despite the fact you were gone all weekend with the senior highers. They usually don't keep a youth pastor for long.

Reasonable comp time would be one extra day off (not to be confused with your regular days off) for every weekend retreat, and three extra days off for every weeklong event. You also need to ask if can you store up comp time and use it later in the year, or if they expect you to use that time the week after you get back.

Holidays. Typically, holidays are some of the most heavily scheduled times of the year in youth ministry. Is holiday time off for the staff scheduled in light of this?

Sabbatical. What is the church's policy on staff sabbaticals? Do pastors get a three-month sabbatical every five years? Do they ever get a longer sabbatical? Does it have to be used for a certain purpose (for example, study, continuing education), or can it be used for a special project (for example, spending time with missionaries overseas, pursuing your desire to be a NASCAR driver)?

Sick days. Can these be stored up for future use or are they erased at the end of the year?

Continuing education. Anywhere from three days to two weeks is appropriate for study leave. This allows you to attend a conference or take an intensive course at a local seminary.

Professional expenses that are paid for by the organization, but not factored into your compensation package

• **Car allowance.** You should be reimbursed for the use of your car for ministry purposes. This can come as a monthly sum or as a per mile reimbursement. If it's the latter, retain all receipts as well and keep a mileage log that includes date, destination, miles driven, and purpose of trip. Any drug store or discount store will have a small notebook for this purpose in their stationery section.

Continuing education. One way a church can honor its staff is to encourage them to continually sharpen their professional skills. They should offer enough money to cover at least a weeklong conference (registration, airfare, and food and lodging). They may offer tuition and textbook reimbursement. If the church expects you to get a seminary degree, will they cover those expenses (either partially or totally)? Will you still have money to attend youth worker conferences?

Subscriptions. This can be used for books or magazine subscriptions to help you in ministry.

Hospitality. There's a certain expectation that you will entertain people involved in your ministry,. or even just the larger church, in your home or meet them at restaurants. Will the church reimburse you for these expenses?

Denominational gatherings. If you are at a denominationally affiliated church, you may be expected to attend certain denominational events. The church should pick up those related expenses.

Counseling stipend. Ministry is one of the most stressful careers you can enter. More and more churches understand the importance of regular counseling for its pastoral staff. They view it as part of overall health care. Does the church provide an annual stipend for counseling? Do they provide a special fund? Do they have a relationship with a local therapist who provides counseling on a sliding fee scale to the church?

Questions You May Be Asked at Your Interview

• How and when did you become a Christian?

• Why do you feel called to youth ministry?

• What is your philosophy of youth ministry?

• Why do you feel called to this church / ministry?

• What do you know about our church? (Note: in the corporate world, this question is a test to see if you've done your homework. It's the same way in the ministry world. At one church I know of, this is the defining question. If you don't have something to say, the interview is over—no matter how strong your résumé is. No church wants someone who's just looking for a job. They want someone who can be as committed to the place as they are.)

• What are your strengths?

• In what areas do you need to grow?

• What would you do in this situation—(fill in the blank)? (This question is a huge clue to what has been an issue in the past. If they ask you questions about discipline or punctuality or communication, odds are, that was a problem for the previous youth pastor.)

- What are your views on (fill in the blank)? (This could be anything from homosexuality to the Palestinian / Israeli conflict. It all depends on the church and the agenda of the interviewers.)

- Where do you see youth ministry going in the future?

- What does a successful youth ministry look like?

- What would you do in your first three months at our church?

- What is your style of teaching?

- What is your current salary package?

- What is your view on mission trips (retreats, camps)?

- Why do you want to leave your current situation? (By the way, when you're asked about your present or past employer, say only positive things. The interviewers don't want to know the dirt, and if you're too negative, they'll begin to wonder if they'd be hiring someone divisive.)

CHRIS SMITH
1234 Third Ave.
Second City, SD 60625
123/555-5555
CSmith@freemail.com

Ministry address (if appropriate)
Second Church
2323 Second Ave.
Second City, SD 60625
123/ 555-5555

MISSION STATEMENT

To help adolescents and their families become committed followers of Christ and to teach them how to minister to others.

LEADERSHIP / MANAGEMENT POSITIONS

SECOND CHURCH, Second City, SD
Director, High School Ministry, 1998 - present
Responsible for selecting, developing, and evaluating volunteer leaders in a high school ministry that serves over 75 adolescent students and their families. Coordinate idea development, planning efforts, and leadership training. Develop on-going youth development experiences such as student leadership teams, outreach events, retreats, service projects, and camps and missions trips. Other responsibilities also include: creating and maintaining the youth ministry budget, some individual and family counseling, speaking in the public schools, overseeing a part-time administrator, and curriculum development for confirmation and Wednesday night Bible studies.

SECOND CITY COMMUNITY SERVICE BUREAU, Second City, SD
Consultant, 1999 - present
Perform workshops and consultations that assist churches, schools, and community groups in building relationships with adolescents and their families. Some crisis counseling and intervention work as well. Currently, developing a team of consultants for neighboring towns.

THIRD CHURCH, Third Town , NJ
Middle School Director, 1992 - 1998
Organized and carried out a variety of events, including retreats, camps, training conferences, and service projects for middle school adolescents and their families. Selected and developed a team of adult volunteers. Public speaking opportunities included public and private schools as well as church functions.

VOLUNTEER LEADERSHIP POSITIONS

SECOND CITY NETWORK OF YOUTH WORKERS, Second City, SD
Network coordinator, 1999 - present
Coordinate monthly meetings for a group of local youth workers. Provide training, support, and community events to supplement individual ministries.

PRESENTATIONS AND SEMINARS

• SECOND CHURCH'S YOUTH WORKERS FORUM, 2000 & 2001
Various seminars on the topics of middle school ministry, community ministry, and team building.

FORMAL EDUCATION

SECOND SEMINARY, Second City, SD
Master of Divinity degree with an emphasis in Youth Ministries, 2004
SECOND COLLEGE, Second City, SD
Bachelor of Arts, May,1994
Major: Youth Ministry. Minors: Biology and Philosophy.

ADDITIONAL EDUCATION

• YOUTH SPECIALTIES YOUTH WORKERS' CONVENTION, *FALL*, 2000
• YOUTH SPECIALTIES ONE DAY RESOURCE SEMINARS, 1999 – 2001

CHRIS SMITH
1234 Third Ave.
Second City, SD 60625
123/555-5555
CSmith@freemail.com

School address (from September to May)
Second College
2323 Second Ave.
Second City, SD 60625
123/ 555-5555

VOCATIONAL OBJECTIVE

To find a full-time ministry position ministering with high school students in a church or para-church setting.

FORMAL EDUCATION

SECOND COLLEGE, Second City, SD
Bachelor of Arts candidate, May, 2005
Major: Youth Ministry. Minors: Biology and Philosophy.
Courses include: Leadership and Management in Youth Ministry, Child and Adolescent Psychology, Truth, Beauty, and Curriculum Development, and Creative Teaching.

LEADERSHIP POSITIONS / WORK EXPERIENCE

SECOND CAMP, Second City, SD
Program Director, Summers, 2002 - 2003
Oversaw the summer camp program for age groups ranging from grade schoolers through college-age, and including one week of family camp. Responsibilities included: creating and developing the theme for the summer, directing staff meetings, overseeing summer staff, organizing various special events and games, maintaining the morale and the safety of the camp, and leading daily staff devotions.

SECOND COLLEGE, Second City, SD
Resident Assistant, 2001- 2002
Leader of 24 college students in the Second Memorial Dormitory. Responsibilities included: building relationships with every resident on the floor, developing community-building programs, implementing disciplinary procedures, facilitating weekly Bible studies, counseling residents as needed, and working with other Resident Assistants, the Resident Director, the Campus Counseling Center and the college administration.

SECOND GROCERY STORE, Second City, SD
Head Grocery Bagger, 1998 - 2000
Responsible for accurately and carefully bagging customers' groceries, greeting customers, and initiating community-building activities among other baggers, as well as leading a bagger Bible study.

VOLUNTEER LEADERSHIP POSITIONS

SECOND CHURCH, Second City, SD
Bible Study Leader, 2000 - current
Organized a Bible study for a group of high school students that met weekly throughout the school year. Responsibilities included: creating new curriculum, coordinating social activities, developing individual and community relationships.

HONORS AND OTHER ACTIVITIES

• Winner of the National Grocery Bag Scholarship, 2000.
• Contributing writer, National Grocery Bag Newsletter, 1999 - 2000
• Campus Bible study leader at Second City High School, 1998

REFERENCES

Available upon request

Prayerfully consider the descriptions that you hope characterize your ministry or the students' in the next three years. Write down stand-out goals. In the appropriate columns list action steps that will move your group toward each goal, sketch a potential timeline for taking the steps, name barriers you'll likely need to overcome to reach the goal, and identify people to involve in the process.

Vision / Goal	Action Steps	Dates	Potential Barriers	Potential Partners

Defining a Personal Vision

Prayerfully consider the descriptions of yourself and your ministry that you hope to grow into in the next three years. Dream about—

- **What you would like to *be***. Patient under stress, valuing solitude, a licensed social worker
- **What you would like to *do***. Administrate a recovery camp, work on a master's degree, write an article
- **What you would like to *have***. Control of your schedule, a gas barbecue, a reliable van

Write down your stand-out goals. In the appropriate columns, list action steps to move yourself toward each goal, then prioritize them and attach a goal date. Name barriers you'll likely need to overcome, and identify people to involve in the process of achieving your goals. Work a little bit each week on one or two goals at a time.

Vision / Goal	Action Steps	Dates	Potential Barriers	Potential Partners

U sing these questions, tune up your next meeting a step or two above the last couple meetings you've led. With each meeting, add extra elements of purpose, design, participation, and prayer. And have some fun while you're all at it.

Determining goals—purposeful planning

What is the goal of the meeting? *(example—to brainstorm a theme for the winter retreat)*

What is the desired meeting outcome? *(That we come away with the theme for the retreat, Bible passages that illuminate the theme, ideas for games and speakers)*

Who will participate? How many?

How long does it need to last? *(Remember, all meetings don't have to end on the half hour. Keep people only as long as needed.)*

Where is the best place to meet? *(Is there room to work? To gather in breakout groups? To write on butcher paper or a whiteboard?)*

When is the best time for this meeting *(based on above answers)*?

What resources will I contribute to the meeting?

Do I need to receive anything from the participants (either before or during the meeting)?

Designing details—coordinated details

How are my goals best accomplished? (example—brainstorming, feedback groups, surveys, discussion, a potluck for parents)

When and how do I deliver the meeting agenda to participants?

Will there be any costs?

What do I need to do ahead of time to secure and make the most of the location of the meeting?

What food shall I offer to attendees?

What materials do I need to prepare ahead to bring to the meeting? (handouts, posters, magazines to cut up for brainstorming or get-acquainted game, et cetera)

Getting out the word—inform and energize participants
(Tailor promotion to the group size and make up and the personality of the occasion.)
- Phone calls
- Memos
- E-mail or snail mail invitations
- Pulpit announcements
- One-on-one invitations
- Other:

Purpose-driven content—focused programming
(Be accountable to yourself—check off these guidelines as you complete each one. Attach a copy of the agenda, handouts or game instructions and props, action points assigned at the meeting, and your follow-up notes.)

- ❑ Provide the agenda in advance
- ❑ Start on time
- ❑ Define meeting etiquette or protocol (example—keep an open mind, listen for understanding, honor each other's comments, have fun, et cetera)
- ❑ Keep things moving
- ❑ Use creativity to make meetings fun
- ❑ Define action points
- ❑ End on time
- ❑ Provide follow-up notes

Prayer—trust in God
(List your prayer requests regarding the meeting, and list prayer requests generated at the meeting.)

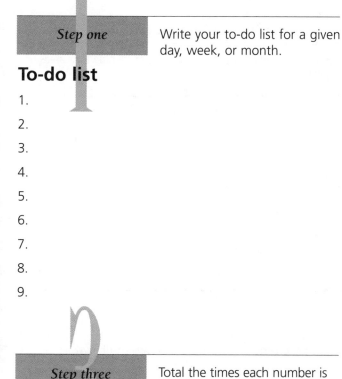

Step one

Write your to-do list for a given day, week, or month.

To-do list

1.
2.
3.
4.
5.
6.
7.
8.
9.

Step two

Using the numbers in column 1, compare item 1 with item 2 in your to-do list. Next compare 1 with 3; 1 with 4, et cetera, all the way through item 9. With each comparison, circle the number of the item that is the highest priority. Then do the same to columns 2-8.

Column	1	2	3	4	5	6	7	8
	1							
	2							
	1	2						
	3	3						
	1	2	3					
	4	4	4					
	1	2	3	4				
	5	5	5	5				
	1	2	3	4	5			
	6	6	6	6	6			
	1	2	3	4	5	6		
	7	7	7	7	7	7		
	1	2	3	4	5	6	7	
	8	8	8	8	8	8	8	
	1	2	3	4	5	6	7	8
	9	9	9	9	9	9	9	9

Step three

Total the times each number is circled and record here.

1's	2's	3's	4's	5's	6's	7's	8's	9's

Step four

Based on the totals from step three, reorder your to-do list.

Top priorities

1.
2.
3.
4.
5.
6.
7.
8.
9.

Step five

Complete your top priorities one after the other. What you don't finish on one day becomes the first item on your list for the next day.

Spiritual Gifts and Areas of Interest

Many tools for discerning spiritual gifts are currently in use in churches. Find out right away if your church offers workshops or adult classes on spiritual gifts. Prospective volunteers who have taken the classes may already know that youth ministry suits their interests and abilities. You can use the following questions to help volunteers identify their areas of interest and discern the most appropriate arena in which they might serve.

Area of service

Find out what triggers a person to dream and plan and take action. That arena is where they'll find most satisfaction and where you'll get their best work.

- What keeps you awake at night (besides too much coffee)?
- What do you find yourself pounding the table over?
- What would your friends say is a reoccurring theme in your conversations?
- What topics do you find yourself drawn to read about?
- What Web trail do you find yourself following—music, movies, youth culture, counseling?

Spiritual gifts and natural abilities

Sometimes these overlap; sometimes not.

- When you look back on your life, what activities brought you joy, energy, and / or success in early childhood? In grade school? Middle school? High school? College? As a young adult?
- What are the reoccurring themes of your memories?
- What verbs do you find yourself using—organizing, creating, discussing, building, performing, writing?
- What patterns do you discern?
- What insight have you gained in any spiritual gifts workshops (like Network or Life Keys) or from sermons or Christian teaching?
- From the following list, choose those spiritual gifts you feel you already use. (Some of these gifts are alluded to rather than named in the Bible.)

❑ Administration	❑ Hospitality
❑ Creative communication	❑ Leadership
❑ Counseling	❑ Listening
❑ Discernment	❑ Mediation
❑ Encouragement	❑ Mercy
❑ Evangelism	❑ Shepherding
❑ Helps	❑ Teaching

- In what ways have those close to you (who are honest with you) affirmed those gifts?

Day of the week _____ Date _____

Where does the time go? Here's your chance to find out. Log activities at 30-minute intervals.
As inconvenient as it may be to note what you're doing every 30 minutes, what you find out about how you use your time is worth the effort. The clock notations will give you a sense of what you're most likely to be doing at different times of the day and on different days of the week. The Quadrant notations help you evaluate your use of working hours. (See chapter 2 of *Youth Ministry Management Tools* for a refresher on Stephen Covey's time-management quadrants.) Armed with the knowledge you gather, you can plan more effectively.

Activity	Clock Start	Clock Stop	Time Spent	Quadrant

Instructions:
Document all vital information about the damaged items.

Date report is filed?

Date the damage occurred?

Person filing the report?

What was your involvement with the damage?

What happened and how did the damage occur?

Who, if anyone, was involved with the damage?

Where is the damaged item now?

What action was taken?

What do you believe is the reason the damage occurred?

Additional comments?

Every youth leader should have a written emergency procedure policy for all general ministry activities.

- Provide each staff member with a written manual, including emergency procedures.

- Verbally explain procedures at new staff orientation.

- At each event, assign an emergency or crisis manager (you or another staff person) who knows procedures. Larger ministries who retain a doctor, nurse, or emergency medical technician (EMT) may place that professional in the manager position.

- Staff and leadership need to know specifically who is the crisis manager on duty (sometimes called the Top Dog or point person). In an emergency, speed is important, clarity is critical, and teamwork is essential.

- Make sure that several members of your staff have taken basic CPR and first-aid training courses. Clear thinking in a medical crisis comes with proper medical training.

- Keep a well-stocked medical kit easily accesible.

- Retain additional staff who have received advanced first-aid training, if possible.

- Get to know doctors, nurses, Certified First Reponders, and EMTs in your ministry. In case you have an emergency, however, do not rely on them as substitutes for calling 911. Instead, rely on them to provide assistance until help arrives. Make yourself aware of liailities related to using off-duty medical personnel.

- Be sure that a certified lifeguard is on duty or available to watch your group whenever swimming is part of an activity.

Incident Report

Date of incident _____

Date report is filed _____

Person filing the report _____

Instructions:

As close as possible to the time the incident occurred, a copy of this report is to be filled out by the person in charge. Other eyewitnesses to the incident (preferably adults) may also fill out additional copies of this form.

Your involvement in the incident

Describe the incident

Where the incident occurred (location)

Individuals who were injured and a description of the injuries

Describe action taken on behalf of the injured

Names of others involved in the incident

Name of the adult in charge at time of incident

Names of other witnesses

Cause of incident (in your opinion)

Additional comments

What coverage does your ministry provide for those who volunteer? For those participating in events? For automobile accidents? Get answers to these critical volunteer insurance questions from your church's insurance agent.

- Who do I ask when I have questions about our church's insurance coverage?

- Who is the insurer for off-site events, on-site use of facilities, transportation?

- Who is covered by our insurance? What kind and amount of insurance coverage does our organization offer to volunteers?

- Does our policy include medical reimbursement, personal liability insurance, or excess automobile insurance?

- Do we have a commercial general liability (CGL) policy? If so, can we add volunteers as additional insureds?

- Does the CGL include or exclude travel between home and the church or event?

- What level of driver training does our policy require of volunteer drivers?

- Do we have accident insurance and what does it cover *(in case a volunteer is injured during the course of a ministry event).*

- Do we have volunteer liability? *(If a volunteer causes damage or is negligent, he or she may be sued. This protection helps if there is a financial judgment rendered.)*

- Do we have excess auto liability? *(This is coverage over and above the volunteer's own coverage as required by state law.)*

- Do we have coverage for volunteer/employee dishonesty *(to protect the ministry in case a volunteer steals money or destroys property)*?

- Is it a good idea to include our volunteers in our workers' compensation program?

- What crisis procedures does our insurance company use?

- What kind and amount of insurance is in effect at the facility to which we're going?

This isn't a complete list—so during your conversation find out any other information your agent believes would be helpful to you. Do not assume that insurance questions and needs are being taken care of by another staff person at the church. *And don't stop asking until you have an answer.*

(For more insurance information, call The CIMA Companies, Inc., at 800/468-4200, or go to their Web site at cimaworld.com, and click on "Volunteers Insurance." CIMA specializes in insurance coverage for nonprofit organizations and volunteer workers.)

Assuming you call an EMT immediately when you have a serious injury—and a hospital is readily accessible—your medical kit should be filled with these medical supplies:

- ❑ Band-Aids
- ❑ Instant ice packs
- ❑ Hydrogen peroxide
- ❑ Rubbing alcohol
- ❑ Tweezers
- ❑ Aspirin or nonaspirin medication such as Tylenol (you and other adult leaders don't give to students without written permission)
- ❑ Surgical (rubber) gloves
- ❑ Thermometer (the small, plastic disposable ones are handy)
- ❑ Antibiotic ointment or cream (such as Neosporin)
- ❑ Antibacterial or antiseptic spray (such as Bactine)
- ❑ Bug bite cream or lotion (such as Cortaid or Cortizone 10)
- ❑ Gauze
- ❑ Medical tape

You may also need to have a biohazard kit on hand in case of bleeding (available in janitorial supply catalogs or visit **www.safetyonline.com** for links to suppliers). In addition to surgical gloves and medical supplies, you'll need a chemical that absorbs blood spills and sanitizes the area.

If you need a more extensive medical kit (remote location, international travel, special-needs student, et cetera), consult with trained medical personnel.

Steps toward preventing sexual abuse

1. Selection and screening
- Requiring church membership
- Clearing the applicant's name with the pastoral staff
- Requiring thorough staff application, references that we actually call
- Conducting an application interview with two staff
- Enforcing a probationary period
- Accepting only those applicants willing to let the ministry do a background check with local law enforcement
- Accepting only those applicants willing to let the ministry check them with central abuse registry

2. Supervision
- New volunteers are paired with veterans for a time and are not alone with students.
- New volunteers are specifically evaluated at 30, 60, and 90 days.
- All volunteers receive at least yearly evaluations based on supervisory observation.
- Two adults must be present with a student or group of students.
- One-on-one meetings are conducted in a public place or in a room with an open door where there's regular, human traffic.

3. Specific reporting process
Basic steps to be followed in possible abuse cases:
- All efforts to handle the incident will be well documented immediately.
- The incident will immediately be reported to ministry supervisors and, very likely, our attorney.
- We will contact the proper civil authorities—they, not our ministry, will handle the investigation.
- We will notify the parents.
- We will take allegations seriously; reach out to the victim and his or her family; and treat the accused with dignity and support.
- If the accused is a church worker, that person will be relieved temporarily of his or her duties until the investigation is finished.
- We will use the text of a prepared public statement to answer the press and convey news to the congregation. Safeguarding the privacy and confidentiality of all involved will be our priority.

4. The following are reporting procedures for volunteer staff
- If a child or student is observed to have signs of physical abuse (bruises caused by hitting, unexplainable injuries, et cetera), volunteer staff should call these things to the attention of a pastoral staff member immediately.
- If a child or student verbally accuses a family member or other person of abusing them in some way, the volunteer staff member should ask appropriate questions in an attempt to determine the veracity of the claims and the imminence of danger. If the truth of the claims seems clear, the matter should be immediately brought to the attention of a pastoral staff member. If the truth of the claims seems questionable, the claims should still be brought to the attention of a pastoral staff member on the same day that the claims are expressed.
- Whether clearly true or questionable in the estimation of the volunteer staff member, the allegations or observations should be put in writing on the day of the incident, including a verbatim / exact account of the observation and / or accusation. Every detail of the events—including date, time of day, names of persons involved, et cetera—should be included in this report. The person making the report should keep one copy, and one copy should be given to the pastoral staff member who oversees that area of ministry. These reports must be kept safe and confidential. The pastoral staff member will be responsible for making a determination as to the appropriate actions to be taken as follow-up to these observations / accusations.

5. Defining sexual abuse

A. Touching

1. Fondling—touching the body on private parts
2. Inappropriate kissing
3. Intercourse (consensual or non-consensual)
4. Oral or anal intercourse

B. Non-touching

1. Sexual remarks
2. Showing pornography
3. Watching any sexual activity
4. Exhibitionism

6. Detecting sexual abuse

- Most cases of sexual abuse go undetected. There may be no apparent physical signs, or there may be physical signs detected only through medical examination.
- The cases that are reported are generally reported by abused children to their parents, siblings, or other caretakers—often in the form of casual remarks that lead the listener to query further.
- Most children say nothing. They may not realize that what was done to them was wrong. Or they may be too embarrassed or frightened to speak up. They may not want to get the offender in trouble—especially if a friendship has developed between offender and victim.
- In some cases, telltale physical or emotional signs may arouse your suspicion. In its publication *The Educator's Role in the Prevention and Treatment of Child Abuse and Neglect*, the National Center on Child Abuse and Neglect outlines certain indicators of sexual abuse.

Physical indicators

Difficulty in walking or sitting
Torn, stained, or bloody underclothing
Pain or itching in the genital area
Bruises or bleeding in external genitalia, vaginal or anal area
Venereal disease, especially in preteens
Pregnancy

Behavioral indicators

Unwilling to change for gym or participate in physical education class
Withdrawal, fantasy or infantile behavior
Bizarre, sophisticated, or unusual sexual behavior or knowledge
Poor peer relationships
Delinquency or running away
Reports sexual assault by caretaker

These signs can be indicative of other problems and are not exclusively tied to sexual abuse. But the repeated occurrence of an indicator or the presence of several indicators warrants further investigation.

When you're considering doing an activity or event that you haven't done before, run the idea through this set of questions.

1. What could possibly go wrong?

2. If something goes wrong, do I know what to do?

    • Emergency phone numbers for the event site and type of potential emergencies

    • How to get the proper help

    • Directions to closest medical facility

    • Evacuation plan

    • A way to account for every student in case of large-scale emergency

3. How much could this mistake cost (medical bills, repair, liability, legal bills, et cetera)?

4. Has someone done this successfully and safely before?

5. What is the safety record of the organization/person you are hiring to lead the event?

6. Are protections in place to lessen the risk to the safety of students? Is the value of the experience worth the risk to students and to your career?

7. If your senior pastor knew you were doing this, what would she think? Would you still be employed?

Sample guidelines for a camping event

- Bring staff experienced in outdoor camping.
- Require a member of your camp staff to become trained in first aid and CPR.
- Designate a contact person at home who knows where you're camping and when you'll return.
- Find out how to get help when you're at your destination camp site.
- Obtain current road and trail maps.
- Bring supplies necessary for the kind of camping—tent, cabin, wilderness.
- On your **Medical Release** form, specifically ask about special medical needs of students relevant to the kind of camping—poison oak allergies, hay fever, bee stings—especially those needs that affect their level of participation in selected activities.
- Ask a professional outfitter to review your route, supplies, and meal plans.
- Bring a weather radio to warn you of significant weather threats, such as thunderstorms and tornadoes.
- Well ahead of the camping event, provide training program for adult leaders for preventing sexual abuse.
- No swimming without a qualified lifeguard.
- No use of the ropes course without trained staff supervising.
- Male and female students and staff will not share the same sleeping facilities.
- Youth will not share tents with an adult other than their own parent.
- Coed overnight activities require both male and female leadership from qualified members of your staff who are over 21 years of age.
- No alcohol, tobacco, or controlled substances permitted (applies to students and adults).
- Set a curfew—all campers in their sleeping quarters by 11 p.m.
- Preview the camping facility to be sure you planned for adequate supervision. Note places and situations where supervision is difficult, and prep your staff.
- Provide the camp director with a list of students participating in an event, accompanied by a **Medical Release** form. Be certain that the form tells you who are to contact in case of an emergency. It must contain all important medical information about the student.
- Only those adult leaders who have completed the driver screening process may provide transportation to the event.

Sample guidelines for water events

Swimming—
- Is there a certified lifeguard watching your group?
- Is the diving area deep enough?
- Have you assigned a buddy to each swimmer?

Boating—
- Are there enough Coast Guard approved life preservers?
- Is the boat driver qualified to drive the boat? To haul skiers?
- Have you limited the number of boat riders to what the boat safely holds?
- Have you confirmed that the weather is safe for boating?
- Have you confirmed that the boat is equipped with other safety measures?
    - whistle
    - drinking water
    - paddles
    - fire extinguisher
    - two-way radio
- Have you informed your contact person on shore where you're going and when you'll return?

Sample guidelines for travel

When you are away from home with your group, do you know—
- How to provide safe food and water for your group?
- The location, phone number, and directions to the closest emergency medical facility?
- Dangers that you may face in a given location (such as, flash flooding, animals, insects)?
- How to contact family members?
- How to facilitate an emergency medical evacuation?
- Do you have accurate bus or van lists and know which vehicle people are in?

Travel considerations—
- Are the vehicles you're driving safe? How do you know?
- Do you have a back-up plan for dealing with worse case scenarios?
- Have you enlisted a staff person to handle issues like kids who come late, get sick, have discipline needs?
- Do you have a vehicle to transport your group in case of a sudden need? Who has the keys? If you only have the church bus or van, your options are limited.
- Do you have access to a cell phone or radio for communication?
- Have you trained your staff how to respond in the event of an emergency? What if you were injured?

Sample guidelines for retreats

When using a retreat facility or hotel, do you know—
- Where everyone is (room assignments)?
- How to evacuate everyone safely in the event of a fire?
- How to make sure everyone is accounted for in the event of an emergency?
- How to summon medical or police help, and how long it will take for them to arrive?

High-risk events
Does your church allow and your insurance company cover the activities listed below? (Your insurance policy generally spells out exclusions. Read the policy carefully.) If you are free to choose the following types of activities, carefully evaluate the fun in context with the accompanying risks. Also provide qualified adults to supervise your group's event. Consult with your supervisor and insurance agent first. Safety is the number-one priority.

Bungee jumping
Trampolines
Spelunking
Scuba diving
Boating events
Rock climbing
Parasailing
Skiing and snowboarding
Hayrides
Snowmobiling
Whitewater rafting
Drag racing in the church parking lot

Sexual Abuse / Molestation Checklist

How good are your current screening processes?
Check off the formal employee / volunteer screening programs you have below.

Screening & training

❑ Verification of educational background and degree

❑ Checking at least three past references

❑ Taking a photo I.D.

❑ Interviews by at least three individuals

❑ Obtaining a police records check which includes fingerprinting and verification on state and national levels

❑ Maintaining employee personnel files that document all screening records

❑ Keeping a checklist for each employee that documents all training

❑ Guided supervision of new staff members during the first three months on the job

❑ Orientation of new workers or employees, including a review of the organization's policy on abuse / molestation incidents

❑ Release form signed by potential volunteers / employees, informing them that there will be extensive screening of applicants through background checks, personal references, and criminal checks specifically geared toward controlling the problem of abuse and molestation.

❑ In-service training for all staff members, including specific information about abuse / molestation and its indications and effects

❑ Regular written performance appraisals of all staff members

Policies & observations

❑ If a student is injured and requires first aid, at least two adults will be present at the examination of the injuries.

❑ At least two staff members are assigned supervisory responsibility over a student.

❑ Students are only released to their legal guardian or someone designated in writing by the guardian.

❑ Students may not be touched on areas of their bodies that would be covered by swimming suits.

❑ Administrators interview students periodically to hear about their experiences in the program.

❑ Staff must immediately report any signs of injury or possible child abuse to the program administrator.

❑ Supervisors make frequent and unannounced visits to observe staff as they work with students, including (for 24-hour programs) late night visits and shower times.

❑ Staff may not use physical punishment, verbally abusive comments, or denial of necessities of care in dealing with a student.

Adapted with permission from nonprofitcoverage.com

- **Experience in successful crisis management.** The Top Dog (TD) needs to be a trained and accomplished leader who has shown the ability to act when a crisis arises. Use a trainee TD in an apprentice role with a current TD. Only after proving themselves should trainees be appointed sole Top Dog. Although the job is a "hurry up and wait" type position, when they are needed, Top Dogs must always be at their best. It's a bummer to find out in the middle of a problem that someone doesn't handle crisis well.

- **Equipped with basic medical training.** TDs need at least a certification in first aid and CPR—not that the job of the TD is to diagnose or treat the injured, but rather to assess what the next course of action should be and to lead the team in that direction.

- **Calm and cool-headed.** Even though most injuries are minor and only minimal treatment is necessary, the TD needs to be able to be calm under pressure.

- **Availability.** The TD needs to be accessible and available. On a retreat or extended event, several people may act as the TD at different times. That way your crisis manager is always ready and refreshed. You may equip the TD with a communication tool to make the TD more accessible. At a retreat use a walkie-talkie, a pager, or an air horn. Try different things to see what works.

- **Supported by the rest of the leadership team.** Once the TD determines the course of action, the staff needs to support the decision. A crisis is not the time to debate issues; it's the time for the leader to lead and the followers to follow. If the stakes are high, the lines of authority must be clear and everyone has to do his job.

  The TD shouldn't accompany the injured to the hospital, if hospitalization is required. The TD needs to stay with the group in case there are any other incidents. The TD should pick a staff person or two to accompany the student at the hospital until the parents arrive. The accompanying staff should be a responsible person, preferably of the same gender, and with whom the student feels comfortable.

- **Good adult communicator.** The TD discusses the incident with the staff member who accompanied the injured person and reviews their written incident report.

- **Perform appropriate emergency procedures.**

  1. One staff person attends to the injured party's needs.

  2. Another staff person immediately contacts the TD. (In a dire emergency, if the TD can't be located expediently, the staff in charge proceeds with the next steps while sending someone to find the TD.)

  3. TD assesses the situation.

  4. TD determines if the individual can be assisted locally. If so, the TD assigns an appropriate adult to assist the injured. The TD also determines at this point whether to notify the parents or apply a Band-Aid and call it good.

  5. If the situation requires trained medical assistance or transportation to the hospital, TD asks a leader to call 911 to request paramedics and an ambulance. The caller needs to know the status of the injured person and the specific the street address or location of the injured. The caller needs to remain on the phone to assist the dispatcher as long as necessary.

  6. TD sends a staff member to the entrance to guide the paramedics.

  7. TD assigns another, calm staff person to contact the individual's parents and advise them of the situation. If the person is being transported to the hospital, the parents should meet them at the hospital.

  8. The TD and any other needed staff member stays with the injured individual. All other staff assist the TD by keeping students and other onlookers away from the victim and out of the emergency team's way.
  9. A staff member brings the student's **Medical Release** form to the TD.

10. The TD appoints a staff member to accompany the student to the hospital and gives her the form.

11. After the student is transported, the TD assigns someone to clean up the accident site. If there is blood involved, use a biohazard kit for cleanup.

12. The TD determines what, if any, explanation needs to be given to the remaining students, or if the scheduled activities need to be adjusted or cancelled.

13. The staff person who accompanies the student to the hospital checks in with the TD once they arrive at the medical facilities, and again when any news is known. (Remember that cellular phones cannot be used inside hospitals.)

14. The TD and the leaders involved fill out an **Incident Report** and, if necessary, a **Damage Report**.

15. The following day, or as soon as possible, the TD distributes copies of the reports to the appropriate recipients.

- **Have access to the following information.**

  —Location of phones and how to dial out

  —How and where to find trained medical help (especially if the group is in a remote location)

  —Address, directions, and phone number of the nearest medical center

  —Location of the first-aid kit

  —Where staff and students are rooming

  —How to reach the facility director (camp, hotel, retreat center, et cetera)

  —Location of medical release forms

  —Where a designated emergency vehicle is parked and who has the keys

  —Special medical / physical conditions of the participants as recorded on the medical release forms. (The TD must communicate these special needs to the rest of the staff.)

Authorization for Medical Treatment

Conformed as to California law

I, _____, am the parent or legal guardian of
NAME OF PARENT OR GUARDIAN

_____, hereinafter, "my child", who was born on _____, _____.
NAME OF MINOR

My child is attending and participating in activities at _____
NAME OF ORGANIZATION

(hereinafter, "this camp," "church," "school," etc.), located at _____
ADDRESS

in the city of _____, county of _____, and state of

_____, beginning on the day of _____.

I hereby authorize the _____ and his/her officers, agents,
SUPERVISOR / PASTOR / DIRECTOR

servants, or employees who are 18 years of age or older, who supervise the activities at this

_____ into whose care my child has been entrusted, to consent to medical
CAMP / CHURCH

care or dental care, or both, for my child under Sections 6901, 6902, and 6910 of the California Family Code.

The authority granted by this authorization includes the authority to consent to any x-ray examination, anesthetic, medical, or surgical diagnosis or treatment and hospital care under the general or special supervision and upon the advice of or to be rendered by a physician and surgeon licensed under the Medical Practice Act for my child. This authority also extends to any x-ray examination, anesthetic, dental or surgical diagnosis or treatment and hospital care by a dentist licensed under the Dental Practice Act for my child.

I further authorize the _____ and his/her officers, agents, servants, or
SUPERVISOR / PASTOR / DIRECTOR

employees who are 18 years of age or older, who supervise the activities at the _____ to receive
CAMP / CHURCH

physical custody of my child, under Section 1283 (a) of the California Health and Safety Code, upon completion of any treatment, and I specifically instruct any treating health facility to surrender physical custody of my child

to the _____ and his/her officers, agents, servants, or employees who are
SUPERVISOR / PASTOR / DIRECTOR

18 years of age or older who supervise the activities at this _____.
CAMP / CHURCH

It is understood that this authorization is given in advance of any special diagnosis, treatment, or hospital care being required, but is given to provide authority and power on the part of the supervisor and his/her authorized designee, to exercise his/her best judgment on what is advisable for my child's care, upon advice of such physician, dentist, and surgeon.

Dated _____, _____

_____
SIGNATURE OF PARENT OR LEGAL GUARDIAN

Additional information

PARENT / GUARDIAN

ADDRESS

CITY · STATE · ZIP

HOME PHONE · WORK PHONE

MEDICAL / HEALTH INSURANCE COMPANY · INSURANCE POLICY NO.

IN CASE OF EMERGENCY, NOTIFY PARENT OR GUARDIAN · RELATIONSHIP TO MINOR

ALLERGIES / ALLERGIC REACTION OF MY CHILD

MEDICINE BEING TAKEN BY MY CHILD

OTHER INFORMATION REGARDING MY CHILD'S HEALTH THAT A DOCTOR SHOULD KNOW

This form was researched and drafted by the law firm of
McKay, Byrne, & Graham
3250 Wilshire Blvd., Ste. 603
Los Angeles, CA 90010-1578
213-386-6900
jmckay@mbglaw.com

It is made available as a sample form with their permission. Neither McKay, Byrne, & Graham nor Church Mutual Insurance (churchmutual.com) warrant that it is appropriate for use by any of our insureds. The form was drafted as a sample document and may not be appropriate for the specific needs of a particular organization. This form will protect any facility that chooses to use it. Before using this sample document or any documents like it, you should consult with your own attorney to make certain that the document you eventually use is correct and current under the law of your particular jurisdiction and that the document meets your needs for your particular situation.

Multiple-Event Registration

Event name / date	Turned in medical release	Date paid	Check# (or cash)	Amount	Participant's name
1.					
2.					
3.					
4.					
5.					
6.					
7.					
8.					
9.					
10.					
11.					
12.					
13.					
14.					
15.					
16.					
17.					
18.					
19.					
20.					
21.					
22.					
23.					
24.					
25.					
26.					
27.					
28.					
29.					
30.					

Scholarship Application

Confidential

Please complete the following and return to the youth ministry office.

Student's name _____

Parent's name(s)_____

Address_____

City_____State _____Zip _____

Home phone _____Grade_____

I am applying for assistance for_____
EVENT

The total cost of this event is $ _____, and I am requesting help with_____% of the cost (normal maximum is 50%).

Please describe your student's involvement at _____
CHURCH NAME

_____

_____

_____

Why do you believe that it is important for your son / daughter to attend this event? _____

_____

_____

_____

Please describe the situation that causes your need at this time in as much detail as possible. _____

_____

_____

_____

Staff use only

Approved amount _____

Staff name_____

Single-Event Registration

Group _____ Event _____ Date_____ Per-person cost _____

Name	Deposit	Check #	Balance	Check #	Permission	Shirt Size	Med. Form
1							
2							
3							
4							
5							
6							
7							
8							
9							
10							
11							
12							
13							
14							
15							
16							
17							
18							
19							
20							
21							
22							
23							
24							
25							
26							
27							
28							
29							
30							
31							
32							
33							
34							
35							
36							
37							
38							
39							
40							

Student Data
Student Profile
Page 1 for student to fill out, pages 2 & 3 for office use only.

Confidential   Page 1 of 3

Today's Date _____

Personal Information

Student's Name _____ Phone _____

❑ Male   ❑ Female   E-mail address_____ _____

Address _____ City _____ State _____ Zip _____

Birthday_____ School _____ Graduation year _____

Family information

Father's name_____ Step-father's name_____

Mother's name _____ Step-mother's name_____

Whom do you live with? _____

Parent's phone _____ Parent's E-mail address _____

Do parents attend this church? ❑ Yes ❑ No   Do parents attend an adult education class? ❑ Yes ❑ No

If yes, which one?_____

Brothers/Sisters: Name _____ Age/Grade _____

Name _____ Age/Grade _____

Name _____ Age/Grade _____

Name _____ Age/Grade _____

Interests check all that apply

Sports: ❑ Basketball   ❑ Baseball   ❑ Football   ❑ Soccer   ❑ Volleyball   ❑ Hockey

❑ Golf   ❑ Broomball   ❑ Snow skiing   ❑ Water skiing   ❑ Golf   ❑ Tennis

❑ Swimming   ❑ Gymnastics   ❑ Other _____

Music   ❑ Likes to sing! ❑ Instruments _____

Hobbies   ❑ Drama   ❑ Computer   ❑ Reading   ❑ Other _____

Page 1 for student to fill out, pages 2 & 3 for office use only.

Student's name

Last _____ First _____ Middle _____

Preferred name or nickname _____ Birthday _____

School _____ Graduation year _____ Gender _____

Current church _____ Membership status _____ Brought by _____

Student's Address

Street Address _____ City _____ State_____ Zip _____

Alternate Address _____ City _____ State_____ Zip _____

Home phone _____ Student's personal phone _____ Cell phone _____

Beeper / pager _____ Fax _____ E-mail _____

Emergency contact _____ Phone _____

Emergency contact (not parents) _____ Phone _____

Peer sponsor _____ Sponsor _____

Primary Guardian

Last _____ First_____

Relationship _____

Address _____

City _____ State_____ Zip _____

Phone _____ Fax _____

Beeper / cell phone _____

E-mail _____

Employer _____ Phone_____

Secondary Guardian

Last _____ First_____

Relationship _____

Address _____

City _____ State_____ Zip _____

Phone _____ Fax _____

Beeper / cell phone _____

E-mail _____

Employer _____ Phone_____

School activities (list)

_____

Small groups (list)

_____

Spiritual gifts (list)

_____

Sports and hobbies (list)

_____

Notes

_____

Events (list)

Student Data

Student Profile

Confidential   Page 3 of 3

Page 1 for student to fill out, pages 2 & 3 for office use only.

| Ministry involvement | | | |

Sunday ❑ New attender ❑ Active ❑ Inactive

Wednesday (or other day) ❑ New attender ❑ Active ❑ Inactive

Retreats attended:

Missions trips attended:

Spiritual gifts:

Church membership ❑ Yes ❑ No
Baptism ❑ Yes ❑ No

Describe this student's faith journey:

Describe any other areas of ministry involvement:

Checklist for Applicant's File

Once potential youth ministry volunteers receive application packets, you should start files on them. Use this form to track their progress.

- **Date that the application packet is sent or given out** _____

- **Date when each item is returned**

  Application _____

  Reference 1_____

  Reference 2_____

  Reference 3_____

  Background check permission _____

  Reading assignment statement
  (completion of statement of faith, child abuse policy, et cetera) _____

- **Fingerprinting completed**_____

  Results _____

- **Child registry completed**_____

  Results _____

- **Interview date**_____

  Notes placed in folder _____

- **Observation period started** _____

- **Observation completed**_____

- **Observation partner**_____

- **Talked to observation partner**_____

  Notes placed in folder _____

- **Final conversation**_____

  Decision_____

- **Welcome and introduction to students and leadership team** _____

Volunteer / Youth Ministry
Driver Application

Effective year _____

Driver's name_____
                 Last   First   MI

Driver's license number _____

State of issue_____ Expiration date _____

Current address_____

City _____ State _____ Zip_____

Home phone _____Cell phone _____

Birth date_____ Social Security no. _____

Type of license
- ❑ Operators
- ❑ Commercial (CDL)
- ❑ Chauffeur
- ❑ Other (please specify)

Describe any medical conditions that could affect your ability to safely transport students or adults.

Date of your last physical _____
List any medications you currently take that could potentially impair driving ability.

If you hold a CDL, please attach a copy of your current health form.
Please describe driver training that you have received:

Have you been convicted of any moving violations in the last five years?
❑ Yes   ❑ No   If yes, please describe each conviction.

Do you have any restrictions or endorsements on your driver's license?
❑ Yes   ❑ No   If yes, please list those restrictions or endorsements.

Have you been involved in any motor vehicle accidents in the last seven years?
❏ Yes ❏ No   If yes, please give date and briefly describe each accident.

Have you been convicted of a DUI, or had your license revoked or suspended in the past 10 years?
❏ Yes ❏ No   If yes, please provide complete details.

Do you carry personal auto insurance?
❏ Yes ❏ No   If yes, please identify the insurance company and policy #.

Does our church or ministry have any reason to be concerned about your ability to be a responsible and careful driver?
❏ Yes ❏ No   If yes, please briefly describe.

I certify that all of the information on this application is truthful and completely accurate. I agree to notify the church within 14 days of any changes in any of the above information. I authorize the church to verify this information with the Department of Motor Vehicles and to check references on my driving. I understand that false statements on this application will constitute grounds for immediate dismissal.

By signing, I agree to abide by safety procedures established by the church and abide by all laws.

Signature _____Date _____

Print name clearly_____

Please attach a photocopy of both sides of your current driver's license to this form.

Office Use Only

DMV check   ❏ Yes ❏ No   Date _____

Contact name_____

Cleared with insurance company   ❏ Yes ❏ No   Date _____

Contact name_____

❏ Approved to drive.

Date _____

Letter of Reference for Staff Applicant

Confidential

_____ is applying to become a volunteer youth worker with the student ministry

at _____ and has given your name as a personal reference.
Church name

The person in this staff position will be in close contact with students, and we want to ensure that these relationships will be healthy ones. Please complete the form below and use the enclosed envelope to send us your evaluation of this person's character and integrity. Your response will remain confidential.

1. Describe your relationship with this person.

2. How long have you known this person?

Please use the following scale to respond to questions 3 through 8:

1 - low   2 - below average   3 - average   4 - very good   5 - excellent

How would you rate his / her ability in the following:

3. Involvement in peer relationships?   1   2   3   4   5

4. Emotional maturity?   1   2   3   4   5

5. Resolving conflict?   1   2   3   4   5

6. Following through with commitments?   1   2   3   4   5

7. Ability to relate to students?   1   2   3   4   5

8. Spiritual maturity?   1   2   3   4   5

9. What are this applicant's greatest strengths?

10. Do you have any concerns about this person working with students? If so, please explain.

❑ Please check this box if you have concerns that you would prefer discussing in person.

Thank you for taking the time to fill this out. If you have any questions regarding this reference, please contact

_____ at _____.
Name of youth pastor   Phone

_____.
Your name (printed)   Daytime phone

_____.
Signature   Street address

_____.
City   State   Zip

Please forward this document to_____
Name and address of church

Parent Information

Student name(s) _____ Grade(s) _____

Mother's name _____ Father's name _____

Address _____ Address _____
STREET   STREET

_____ _____
CITY / STATE / ZIP CODE   CITY / STATE / ZIP CODE

Home phone _____ Home phone _____

Work phone _____ Work phone _____

Best time to reach you _____ Best time to reach you _____

Fax _____ Fax _____

E-mail _____ E-mail _____

Resources available for youth activities

❑ van or SUV   ❑ jet ski   ❑ boat   ❑ swimming pool   ❑ tent

❑ home   ❑ cabin   ❑ other _____

How many people can you host? _____maximum number you could host _____more in summertime

Helps

❑ miscellaneous administration (filing, copying, etc.) ❑ drive a follow car (to bring latecomers, etc.)

❑ computer   ❑ phone calls   ❑ staff information desk   ❑ art / decorations

❑ video   ❑ newsletter   ❑ shopping   ❑ crowd control

❑ transportation   ❑ serve food   ❑ provide scholarships   ❑ Web design

❑ photography   ❑ other _____

Leadership

❑ cell group leader   ❑ parent mentor   ❑ activities staff   ❑ Bible study leader

❑ service activity ldr./helper   ❑ student tracking   ❑ program planning   ❑ refreshment coordinator

❑ special projects   ❑ parent education   ❑ parent resource librarian   ❑ prayer team

❑ special topic speaker—*please list topic(s)* _____

Worship team: ❑ vocal ❑ instrumental ❑ drama ❑ other _____

Prospective Staff Interview Questions

■ f you're new to a youth ministry position, practice interviewing by asking some of the following questions of those who held down the fort until you got there. You could ask them in the past tense—"Why were you interested in working with the youth ministry?" Or you could phrase them with the future in mind—"Are you interested in continuing to work in your current role?" Comments about the purpose or value of the question is in parentheses at the end of each question.

The **Prospective Staff Interview Worksheet** includes these same questions and space for taking notes during an interview.

1. Church background

How did you hear about our ministry? (This gives you insight into which forms of recruiting bring good results.)

Why are you interested in working with us? (People's motives for joining a ministry vary. They may want to spend more time with their own kids who are in the ministry. They may want to stop teenagers from repeating the same mistakes they did. They may be bored and really like the music that the high school band plays.)

How long have you been going to our church? (Someone who's just started coming may be a church hopper, or even have a history of stirring up dissension wherever they go.)

What brought you here? (It's helpful to know if they've grown up in your denomination or if they were intrigued by the sermon topics advertised in the paper.)

Are you a member of the church? (What's your church's policy on membership and volunteering? More and more churches are leaning toward requiring volunteers to be church members, for more accountability.)

2. Spiritual background

Tell me about your faith journey. (The reason for asking the question this way is that it invites a more comprehensive story than if you ask, "Tell me about when you became a Christian." Instead of hearing "I was saved in July 1985 at Bible camp," you'll learn details that may trigger other questions or give you a feel for experiences that equip them for particular kinds of ministry.)

How long have you been a Christian? Talk to me about how you became a Christian. (If you feel the answer to any question is incomplete, reframe the question until you're satisfied with the answer.)

On a scale from one to ten, what's your relationship with Christ like now and why? (Sometimes you'll get people who have recently renewed their faith and are eager to get active in the church. You may want to give them some time to get grounded by attending a small group of their own rather than placing them in leadership. Question any extreme on the scale. If they're a one or two, find out if they expect the youth ministry to bolster their faith. If they're a nine or ten, how do they deal with the dry times in their walk?)

What do you do to keep your spiritual life sharp? (Are they active in a Bible study or small group? Do they practice spiritual disciplines like devotions and prayer? You're trying to get a sense of how they nurture their own faith. If they aren't maturing themselves, they can't help someone else.)

Are you or have you ever been discipled or been in a small group? (This is especially appropriate if the person is applying to be a small group leader. If they've never experienced a successful small group, they'll have difficulty leading a group. You may want to suggest that, before they volunteer in the youth ministry, they take some time to ground themselves. A tough call? Yes, but it communicates that you're more interested in their spiritual growth than in their being a body serving in the youth ministry. Don't worry, they'll come back.)

3. Ministry experience

Are you serving with any other ministries? (Typically, youth ministry is one of the most time-intensive ministries of the church. Unless they're helping out in a nonrelational capacity—for example, putting together newsletters for you or entering data in the database—they won't have time or energy to serve in other ministries at the same time.)

Have you served in another ministry in the past? If so, why did you stop serving? (You're listening for patterns here. Does the person have a track record of leaving when things get tough? Do they cause conflict and leave? Do they leave if they don't get their own way? If you have a corresponding section in your application, you can do some comparing. Word of experience: if someone left their last ministry because of unresolved conflict, you can bet that conflict will follow them into this ministry.)

What do you believe your spiritual gifts are? What do you love doing? What have other people told you you're good at? (Do their gifts fit the needs of the job for which they're applying? They may have been "guilted" into volunteering with the youth ministry, when their talents really lie with the senior citizens or the justice and mercy committee. You're also looking to see if other people have affirmed their gifts. Often we'll hear the phrase, "God's leading me to work with the students." Don't be satisfied merely with their assertion. Ask, "Who else has seen you in action and affirmed this leading?" Probe for details.)

Have you ever worked with our ministry before? (If you're relatively new to the church—and especially if you know there was divisiveness in the ministry before you came—you'll protect the ministry by asking the question. If this person left because of your predecessor and now wants to come back, is that a good thing or a bad thing? Investigate this one.)

4. Personal information

Introduce this section by saying something like this: "It's important that we have a handle on the personal lives of our leadership team because seasons of life and relational dynamics can greatly impact our ministry. This information is strictly confidential, unless we get your permission to talk about it with a third party. Please tell what you feel we should know and what you are comfortable with sharing, with the understanding that we need to know anything that would influence or impact your ministry with students and the ministry as a whole."

(Optional) What is your home situation? Are you married? Are there children? Do you have a roommate(s)? (You're listening for issues dealing with their personal relationships. Are they divorced, separated, living with someone of the other gender? What is your ministry's and your church's stance on these issues? If they are divorced or widowed, how long has it been, and have they worked through the grieving and other issues affiliated with those kind of losses?)

(Optional) If married, are your spouse and / or kids supportive of your commitments? (You're trying to avoid putting this person in conflict. If they're not being supported, their ministry can be hindered.)

Where do you work? (Be listening for jobs that may affect the applicant's fit with the ministry. For example, if she's a CPA, she may be out of commission from January until April. If she / he teaches high school or middle school, will she flame out if she serves students after hours as well?)

Are you reasonably content with your job? (Discontent is a yellow flag only; job satisfaction may or may not impact their effective ministry.)

(Optional) Tell me about your relationship with your family growing up. (You're listening for unresolved issues here. Although you're not a therapist, you may learn you need to recommend one. Again, people get into ministry with mixed motives. How they dealt with (and continue to relate to) their family of origin affects how they do ministry.)

Students with whom you are in relationship pick up not only what you teach, but also what you model. What one thing in your life would you like them to learn from you? On the flip side, what one thing would you rather they didn't learn from you?

Each of us struggles with a character weakness or a stubborn bad habit. What would you say yours is? (Compare this response to the previous one. Are they similar? If not, why not?)

Is there anything in your past or current life that may adversely affect your ministry to young students? (Alcoholism, drug use, family concerns, child abuse, depression, et cetera)

What are your views on the legal use of alcohol, tobacco, et cetera? (This question may be related to certain views they expressed on their application or that the church holds.)

1. Church background

How did you hear about our ministry?

Why are you interested in working with us?

How long have you been going to our church?

What brought you here?

Are you a member of the church?

2. Spiritual background

Tell me about your faith journey.

How long have you been a Christian? or Talk to me about how you became a Christian.

On a scale from one to ten, what's your relationship with Christ like now and why?

What do you do to keep your spiritual life sharp?

Are you or have you ever been discipled or been in a small group?

3. Ministry experience

Are you serving with any other ministries?

Have you served in another ministry in the past? If so, why did you stop serving?

What do you believe your spiritual gifts are? Or what do you love doing? What have other people told you you're good at?

Have you ever worked with our ministry before?

4. Personal information

(Optional) What is your home situation? Are you married? Are there children? Do you have a roommate(s)?

(Optional) If married, are your spouse and / or kids supportive of your commitments?

Where do you work?

Are you reasonably content with your job?

(Optional) Tell me about your relationship with your family growing up.

Students with whom you are in relationship pick up not only what you teach, but also what you model. What one thing in your life would you like them to learn from you? On the flip side, what one thing would you rather they didn't learn from you?

Each of us struggles with a character weakness or a stubborn bad habit. What would you say yours is?

Is there anything in your past or current life that may adversely affect your ministry to young students? (alcoholism, drug use, family concerns, child abuse, depression, et cetera)

What are your views on the legal use of alcohol, tobacco, et cetera?

Staff Application 1

Ministry code_____

This application is to be completed by all applicants for any volunteer or compensated position involving the supervision or custody of minors. This is not an employment application. Persons seeking a position in the church as paid employees will be required to complete an employment application in addition to this screening form. Thank you for helping our church provide a safe and secure environment for children and youth who participate in our programs and use our facilities.

General information

Date_____

Name_____ Spouse's name _____

Address _____ City _____ State _____ Zip _____

Home phone ( ) _____ Work phone ( ) _____

Date of birth_____ Social Security no. _____

Background information

Do you regularly attend our weekend services? ❑ Yes ❑ No If yes, since when: Month _____Year _____

Do you regularly attend a small group? ❑ Yes ❑ No If yes, since when: Month _____ Year _____

In what church ministries are you presently involved? _____

In what church ministries are you currently serving? _____

Have you personally accepted Jesus Christ as your Lord and Savior, and are you committed to having the character of Jesus live through you?   ❑ Yes   ❑ No

Tell us about your spiritual journey to date.

Tell us why you have chosen to work with youth at our church.

If there has been alcohol abuse, drug abuse, or physical or sexual abuse in your family background, what steps have you taken to minimize the impact that those issues create for you?

References

List three adults you've known for at least one year, who are not related to you and have a definite knowledge of your character and ability to work with adolescents.

1. A staff member, leadership team member, small group, or ministry leader from our church

Name _____ Nature of association _____

Occupation _____ Length of time known _____

Address _____ City _____ State _____ Zip _____

Home phone ( ) _____ Work phone ( ) _____

2. Employer or fellow employee

Name _____ Nature of association _____

Occupation _____ Length of time known _____

Address _____ City _____ State _____ Zip _____

Home phone ( ) _____ Work phone ( ) _____

3. Friend or neighbor

Name _____ Nature of association _____

Occupation _____ Length of time known _____

Address _____ City _____ State _____ Zip _____

Home phone ( ) _____ Work phone ( ) _____

Previous address

If you have lived at your current address for less than seven years, provide information on all addresses during that period.

Address _____ City _____ State _____ Zip _____

Dates _____ - _____

Address _____ City _____ State _____ Zip _____

Dates _____ - _____

Employment history

If you have been employed at this position for less than two years, provide information on each job during that period.

Present employer _____ Supervisor _____

Address _____ City _____ State _____ Zip _____

Position(s) held _____ ❑ Full-time ❑ Part-time

Employment dates: Starting _____ Ending _____

Previous employer _____ Supervisor _____

Address _____ City _____ State _____ Zip _____

Position(s) held _____ ❑ Full-time ❑ Part-time

Employment dates: Starting _____ Ending _____

Military service

Branch _____ Enlist date _____ Discharge date _____

Check desired ministry area: ❏ **Middle school** ❏ **Senior high** ❏ **College-age**

Basic information

Name _____
First   MI   Last

Street address _____
City   State   Zip

Phones _____
Home   Pager   Cell   Work

(It's okay to call me at work ❏ Best times to reach me at home are _____

Employer _____ Employer address _____

Position at work _____ Years at current job _____

E-mail _____ Social Security no. _____

Driver's license (state and number) _____

Church membership: ❏ Member   ❏ Regular attendee

How long have you regularly attended this church? _____

Emergency contact _____ Emergency phone _____
Name and relationship

Family information (optional)

Marital status (check one):   ❏ Single   ❏ Married (anniversary date _____)   ❏ Divorced

If married, spouse's name _____

If you have children, their names and ages:

1. _____   4. _____

2. _____   5. _____

3. _____   6. _____

Education

High school _____ City _____ State _____ Grad year _____

College / trade school _____ City _____ State _____ Grad year _____

Degree and major _____ Minor _____

Other education, training, or licenses _____

Ministry Experience (list most recent first)

Church (name, city, state, and zip)	Dates	Area of service	Contact	Phone
1.				
2.				
3.				

Tell us about yourself

1. When and how did you become a Christian?

2. What have you been doing to grow spiritually in the past year?

3. What would you do to maintain your spiritual growth as a volunteer?

4. What are your expectations of the youth ministry team?

5. Explain your background in student ministry at this church or elsewhere.

6. What special qualities or qualifications would you contribute as a volunteer staff member?

7. What is your belief concerning the following issues:

   a. The authority of the Bible

   b. Use of tobacco, drugs, alcoholic beverages

   c. Premarital / extramarital sex

   d. Homosexuality

Staff Application 2

References

Please provide three character references (other than family members) who can identify your strengths and weaknesses and describe your background. (Please mail one copy of the **Letter of Reference for Staff Application** and an addressed, stamped envelope to each of these references and ask them to mail it back to the church office.)

1. _____
      Name   Address   Home / work phone   Relationship

2. _____
      Name   Address   Home / work phone   Relationship

3. _____
      Name   Address   Home / work phone   Relationship

Self-description

Please circle the words that best describe you. Cross out words that least describe you.

trustworthy	dependable	active	compassionate	reliable	self-starter	punctual	flexible	laid-back
quick thinker	spontaneous	decisive	teachable	team player	humorous	thoughtful	solitary	leader
cautious	risk taker	patient	reflective	honest	organized	creative	disciplined	faithful

What are your spiritual gifts?

Please list any personal weaknesses, areas where you need to grow, or special concerns that could affect your ministry with students.

1. _____

2. _____

3. _____

Medical information

Have you had any prior injuries that might be aggravated by working in youth ministry?

Are you currently taking any medication prescribed by a doctor for physical or other conditions that would affect your ministry?

Do you have any medical conditions(s) that might be hazardous to others?

If you answered yes to any of the questions above, please attach another page and explain completely.

Background information

Have you, at any time, been involved in or accused, rightly or wrongly, of sexual abuse, maltreatment, or neglect?   ❏ yes   ❏ no

Have you ever been accused or convicted of possession / sales of controlled substances or of driving under the influence of alcohol or drugs?   ❏ yes   ❏ no

Are you using illegal drugs?   ❏ yes   ❏ no

Have you been arrested or convicted for any criminal act more serious than a traffic violation?   ❏ yes   ❏ no

Have you ever been involved romantically or sexually with any student in the youth ministry or had sexual relations with any minor after you became an adult?   ❏ yes   ❏ no

Have you ever been a victim of any form of child abuse?   ❏ yes   ❏ no

If yes, would you like to speak to a counselor or pastor?   ❏ yes   ❏ no

Have you ever gone through treatment for alcohol or drug abuse?   ❏ yes   ❏ no

Have you ever been asked to step away from ministry or work with students or children in any setting, paid or volunteer?   ❏ yes   ❏ no

Is there anything in your past or current life that might be a problem if we found out about it later?   ❏ yes   ❏ no

I have read the church's statement of faith, **Staff Expectations**, and **Reducing the Risk of Physical and Sexual Abuse** enclosures and agree to be bound by them. ❏ yes ❏ no _____
INITIALS

If the answer to any of the above questions is yes, please attach another page and write a full explanation. These issues will be discussed confidentially during your interview.

Waiver / release

I, the undersigned, give my authorization to _____ (church name) representatives—hereinafter referred to as The Church—to verify the information on this form. The Church may contact my references and appropriate government agencies as deemed necessary in order to verify my suitability as a church youth / student ministry worker. I am willing to request and submit to The Church background reports on myself from the (state) Department of Social Services central registry.

The information contained in this application is correct to the best of my knowledge. I authorize any references or churches listed in this application to give you any information (including opinions) that they may have regarding my character and fitness for student ministry. In consideration of the receipt and evaluation of this application by The Church, I hereby release any individual, church, youth organization, charity, employer, reference, or any other person or organization, including record custodians, both collectively and individually, from any and all liability for damages of whatever kind or nature that may at any time result to me, my heirs, or family, because of compliance or any attempts to comply with this authorization. I waive any right that I may have to inspect any information provided about me by any person or organization identified by me in this application.

Should my application be accepted, I agree to be bound by the constitution, statement of faith and policies of The Church, and to refrain from conduct unbecoming to Christ in the performance of my services on behalf of The Church. If I violate these guidelines, I understand that my volunteer status may be terminated. By signing this application, I state that all of the information given about myself is true.

I further state that **I HAVE CAREFULLY READ THE FOREGOING RELEASE AND KNOW THE CONTENTS THEREOF, AND I SIGN THIS RELEASE AS MY OWN ACT**. This is a legally binding agreement which I have read and understand.

Print Name _____

Signature _____

Witness _____ Date _____

Items to include in an application packet

❑ **Staff Application Process Letter** explaining the process

❑ **Staff Application (1 or 2)**

❑ **Staff Expectations**

❑ Church's statement of faith

❑ Church's constitution

❑ **Reducing the Risk of Physical and Sexual Abuse**

❑ **Letter of Reference for Staff Applicant** form (3 copies)

❑ Health (medical) form

❑ Handouts on—

  ❑ Child registry

  ❑ Fingerprinting

❑ Optional items (depending on your church policy and state law)

Dear future youth worker,

Thanks for your interest in working with our students. We're excited that you want to make a difference in the lives of our students.

We work hard to provide an environment for spiritual growth in a context of healthy, positive relationships with adults. We take seriously our responsibility to shield our students from sexual abuse, to protect our adult leaders from accusations of sexual abuse, and to limit the exposure of the church to legal risk and liability. To accomplish this, we ask that all paid staff, as well as those volunteers who'll be working with anyone under the age of 18, complete our application process. Since you're looking into working with students under the age of 18, we need you to carefully and thoughtfully fill out the attached application and return it as quickly as possible.

So, you might be asking…

What's involved in the volunteer application process?

When you fill out the application, you authorize us to check personal references and to request a background check for criminal records. Please thoroughly and honestly complete all forms. Send out your reference forms, including return envelopes addressed to the church, and complete the background check authorization form.

On what basis does the church approve someone to work with students?

We invite into ministry only those applicants a) who have no previous conviction for sexual or physical abuse of children; b) for whom we receive positive responses from their personal and professional references; and c) who meet the qualifications of the position for which they are applying.

If background checks raise any questions, the individual will be asked to meet with the appropriate pastor to clarify the questionable issues prior to being placed in a position relating to students.

Who will see this application?

The completed application and any subsequent information you will be available only to the pastoral staff and church board. Once the approval process has been completed, your application and references will be maintained in a secure file.

Please attach a photocopy of your current, valid driver's license with the application.

Thanks for understanding that this paperwork is about protecting you and our students. We appreciate your willingness to help us achieve our mission to students!

❑ Appearance

"People look on the outward appearance but God looks on the heart."
The first phrase is not the heart of the verse, but it's the truth. Students and adults will base their impression of our ministry on their impression of us. For this reason we wear appropriate clothing (1 Corinthians 9:19-23).

- The activity should dictate the type of clothing worn.
- All of our clothing should be clean, communicating personal discipline and recognition of self-worth, and be modest, protecting the reputation and image of the Holy Spirit (1 Timothy 2:9, 1 Corinthians 8:27, 1 Thessalonians 4:6a), and avoid masking our inner qualities (I Peter 3:1-8).

❑ Student relationships

Discretion in staff members' personal lives is fundamental to both spiritual integrity and to continuing to do spiritual ministry among students and their families (Ephesians 5:1-12, 15-16). To live wisely and without any hint of sexual misconduct we keep the following standards:

- Any verbal or nonverbal sexual interaction with any student is inappropriate.
- Dating or going out with any junior or senior high student is forbidden.
- Discretion must be used in physical contact with any students. Innocent behavior can be misinterpreted. A hug around the shoulders is not sexual abuse, but a full body-to-body hug, stroking, massaging, or affectionate kissing raises questions. Any overt display of affection, appropriate hugging, for example, should be made in a public setting in front of other group members.
- Sexual gestures or overtures to a staff member by a student should be reported to one of the ministry directors or the student ministries pastor so that discussion can be held with the student.
- Staff should form male / female ministry teams whenever possible.
- One-on-one counseling with a student should always occur in a public place, never alone in a car or a private place. As a general rule, when counseling a member of the other gender, invite a member of the same gender as the counselee to be the observing staff.
- When a situation arises where you are alone with a student of the other gender, quickly move that situation to a public setting. Make the meeting as brief as necessary to accomplish God's purpose.
- Driving alone with a student of the other gender should be avoided at all times.
- Romantic or sexual attraction for a student by an adult leader should be brought up and discussed with the ministry director for prayer and guidance.
- All suspicions of child or sexual abuse must be reported to the ministry director who will report it to the mandated reporter in the organization. That person will notify the appropriate agency.
- Any knowledge or suspicion of any youth ministry staff having an inappropriate relationship with a student must be reported promptly to the youth ministry leader. If the person in question is the leader, the report should be made to that person's supervisor.
- No wrestling or physical horseplay should ever occur between staff and students of the opposite sex.
- Church staff or volunteers should obtain the consent of the student's parent or guardian before going out with that student or spending time with the student in an unsupervised situation.

❑ Dating

Acknowledging that one of the most fulfilling relationships in Scripture and life is the one that a man and woman share, we recognize that a staff member may establish a relationship with a staff member of the other gender. We also recognize the greatest visible destroyer of ministries is moral impurity. The following policies should be understood in that light.

- No staff member will date a student in junior high or high school.
- Staff members involved in a dating relationship should model appropriate behavior. Particularly during church functions, our focus is to be on the Lord as well as students.
- In the case of premarital sex, extramarital sex, or a homosexual incident, immediate suspension from staff will occur.
- Remember as you date another member of the staff or church that if the relationship ends, that person will still be around to testify to your behavior and character.

❑ Character expectations

- **To keep our integrity:** the motives, attitude, and actions of staff should be completely transparent to any observer. Our honesty should be testable by Luke 16:10-12.
    1. *Faithfulness in little things*—being on time, keeping our word, filling requests on time, following through with students and other responsibilities.
    2. *Faithfulness in money*—turning in receipts, being very cautious with event cash and petty cash, remembering people have sacrificially given that dollar.
    3. *Faithfulness in that which belongs to another*—treating all the church equipment and property with utmost respect.
- **To be teachable:** None of us must claim to have arrived at infallibility. We must continually attend sessions, conferences, worship services, read, and observe with a teachable spirit, continually seeking to grow.
- **To be an appropriate role model:** Staff responsibilities naturally require frequent interaction with students and their families, as well as the community. Youth staff members come into Christian ministry from a variety of backgrounds and beliefs—especially in the gray areas of Christianity. Because staff are leaders and role models, they must use careful discretion when choosing movies, music, et cetera, for ministry activities. The use of R-rated movies is prohibited with junior high students and parental permission is required with senior highers. Use PG-13 movies with extreme caution. In all cases preview a movie you're considering showing at a youth activity. When in doubt, check with parents or a ministry director.

    Along with entertainment choice, substances used by staff model behavior to students. Since the number one substance abused by teenagers is alcohol, staff will abstain from the use of alcoholic beverages in the presence of students.
- **To develop a servant's heart:** "Let nothing be done through strife or vain glory; but in lowliness of mind let each esteem others better than themselves. Look not every man on his own things, but every man also on the things of others. Let this mind be in you, which was also in Christ Jesus...who made Himself of no reputation and took upon Him the form of a servant...He humbled Himself, and became obedient...even the death of the cross." (Phil. 2:3-8).

We aren't concerned about rank or position; the one in the pulpit is of no greater importance in God's eyes than the one leading a small group or driving the buses. As we faithfully serve one another within the ministry, the Lord expands our outreach and provides opportunities to serve those outside of the ministry. In homes, at church, and in the community, others should remember us by our willingness to serve them. "Humble your-selves in the sight of the Lord, and He will lift you up" (James 4:10 and Luke 17:10).

Staff Orientation Process

Name _____ Phone _____

Address _____ Work phone _____

City _____ State _____ Zip _____ E-mail _____

Process Steps	Date	Comments
Initial contact	_____	_____
Run name by pastoral staff	_____	_____
Interest letter sent	_____	_____
First meeting w/ _____ STAFF NAME	_____	_____
Application sent	_____	_____
Application returned	_____	_____
Background check filed	_____	_____
Background check completed	_____	_____
References checked 　1. _____	_____	_____
2. _____	_____	_____
3. _____	_____	_____
Church membership	_____	_____
Membership seminar	_____	_____
Membership interview	_____	_____
Membership reception	_____	_____
Welcome card sent	_____	_____
Youth ministry interview _____ STAFF NAME	_____	_____
Assigned role	_____	_____
Assigned role	_____	_____
Assigned mentor	_____	_____
Training plan	_____	_____
Follow up 　30 day _____ 　　STAFF NAME	_____	_____
60 day _____ 　　STAFF NAME	_____	_____
90 day _____ 　　STAFF NAME	_____	_____

Staff Reference Check

Use one **Staff Reference Check** sheet per reference to record notes from your conversations with the applicant's references.

Confidential

Reference check

Applicant name _____ Social security no. _____

Name of reference _____ Phone ( ) _____

Interviewer's name _____

Date/time of interview _____ ❑ In person ❑ By phone

Qualify the reference

Qualify the applicant

- Social interaction / emotional maturity—

- Experience with adolescents—

- Responsible to commitment—

- Special problems—

- Criminal offenses—

- Trustworthiness with adolescents—

- Other comments—

Resources from Youth Specialties

Youth Ministry Programming

Camps, Retreats, Missions, & Service Ideas (Ideas Library)

Compassionate Kids: Practical Ways to Involve Your Students in Mission and Service

Creative Bible Lessons from the Old Testament

Creative Bible Lessons in 1 & 2 Corinthians

Creative Bible Lessons in John: Encounters with Jesus

Creative Bible Lessons in Romans: Faith on Fire!

Creative Bible Lessons on the Life of Christ

Creative Bible Lessons in Psalms

Creative Junior High Programs from A to Z, Vol. 1 (A-M)

Creative Junior High Programs from A to Z, Vol. 2 (N-Z)

Creative Meetings, Bible Lessons, & Worship Ideas (Ideas Library)

Crowd Breakers & Mixers (Ideas Library)

Downloading the Bible Leader's Guide

Drama, Skits, & Sketches (Ideas Library)

Drama, Skits, & Sketches 2 (Ideas Library)

Dramatic Pauses

Everyday Object Lessons

Games (Ideas Library)

Games 2 (Ideas Library)

Good Sex: A Whole-Person Approach to Teenage Sexuality & God

Great Fundraising Ideas for Youth Groups

More Great Fundraising Ideas for Youth Groups

Great Retreats for Youth Groups

Holiday Ideas (Ideas Library)

Hot Illustrations for Youth Talks

More Hot Illustrations for Youth Talks

Still More Hot Illustrations for Youth Talks

Ideas Library on CD-ROM

Incredible Questionnaires for Youth Ministry

Junior High Game Nights

More Junior High Game Nights

Kickstarters: 101 Ingenious Intros to Just about Any Bible Lesson

Live the Life! Student Evangelism Training Kit

Memory Makers

The Next Level Leader's Guide

Play It! Over 150 Great Games for Youth Groups

Roaring Lambs

So What Am I Gonna Do with My Life? Leader's Guide

Special Events (Ideas Library)

Spontaneous Melodramas

Spontaneous Melodramas 2

Student Leadership Training Manual

Student Underground: An Event Curriculum on the Persecuted Church

Super Sketches for Youth Ministry

Talking the Walk

Videos That Teach

What Would Jesus Do? Youth Leader's Kit

Wild Truth Bible Lessons

Wild Truth Bible Lessons 2

Wild Truth Bible Lessons—Pictures of God

Wild Truth Bible Lessons—Pictures of God 2

Worship Services for Youth Groups

Professional Resources

Administration, Publicity, & Fundraising (Ideas Library)

Dynamic Communicators Workshop for Youth Workers

Equipped to Serve: Volunteer Youth Worker Training Course

Help! I'm a Junior High Youth Worker!

Help! I'm a Small-Group Leader!

Help! I'm a Sunday School Teacher!

Help! I'm a Volunteer Youth Worker!

How to Expand Your Youth Ministry

How to Speak to Youth...And Keep Them Awake at the Same Time

Junior High Ministry (Updated & Expanded)

The Ministry of Nurture: A Youth Worker's Guide to Discipling Teenagers

Postmodern Youth Ministry

Purpose-Driven Youth Ministry

Purpose-Driven Youth Ministry Training Kit

So That's Why I Keep Doing This! 52 Devotional Stories for Youth Workers

Teaching the Bible Creatively

A Youth Ministry Crash Course

Youth Ministry Management Tools

The Youth Worker's Handbook to Family Ministry

Academic Resources

Four Views of Youth Ministry & the Church

Starting Right: Thinking Theologically about Youth Ministry

Discussion Starters

Discussion & Lesson Starters (Ideas Library)

Discussion & Lesson Starters 2 (Ideas Library)

EdgeTV

Get 'Em Talking

Keep 'Em Talking!

Good Sex: A Whole-Person Approach to Teenage Sexuality & God

High School TalkSheets

More High School TalkSheet

High School TalkSheets from Psalms and Proverbs

Junior High TalkSheets

More Junior High TalkSheets

Junior High TalkSheets from Psalms and Proverbs

Real Kids: Short Cuts

Real Kids: The Real Deal—on Friendship, Loneliness, Racism, & Suicide

Resources from Youth Specialties (continued)

Real Kids: The Real Deal—on Sexual Choices, Family Matters, & Loss

Real Kids: The Real Deal—on Stressing Out, Addictive Behavior, Great Comebacks, & Violence

Real Kids: Word on the Street

Unfinished Sentences: 450 Tantalizing Statement-Starters to Get Teenagers Talking & Thinking

What If...? 450 Thought-Provoking Questions to Get Teenagers Talking, Laughing, and Thinking

Would You Rather...? 465 Provocative Questions to Get Teenagers Talking

Have You Ever...? 450 Intriguing Questions Guaranteed to Get Teenagers Talking

Art Source Clip Art

Stark Raving Clip Art (print)

Youth Group Activities (print)

Clip Art Library Version 2.0 (CD-ROM)

Digital Resources

Clip Art Library Version 2.0 (CD-ROM)

Ideas Library on CD-ROM

Youth Ministry Management Tools (CD-ROM)

Videos & Video Curricula

Dynamic Communicators Workshop for Youth Workers

EdgeTV

Equipped to Serve: Volunteer Youth Worker Training Course

Good Sex: A Whole-Person Approach to Teenage Sexuality & God

The Heart of Youth Ministry: A Morning with Mike Yaconelli

Live the Life! Student Evangelism Training Kit

Purpose-Driven Youth Ministry Training Kit

Real Kids: Short Cuts

Real Kids: The Real Deal—on Friendship, Loneliness, Racism & Suicide

Real Kids: The Real Deal—on Sexual Choices, Family Matters, & Loss

Real Kids: The Real Deal—on Stressing Out, Addictive Behavior, Great Comebacks, & Violence

Real Kids: Word on the Street

Student Underground: An Event Curriculum on the Persecuted Church

Understanding Your Teenager Video Curriculum

Student Resources

Downloading the Bible: A Rough Guide to the New Testament

Downloading the Bible: A Rough Guide to the Old Testament

Grow For It Journal

Grow For It Journal through the Scriptures

So What Am I Gonna Do with My Life? Journaling Workbook for Students

Spiritual Challenge Journal: The Next Level

Teen Devotional Bible

What (Almost) Nobody Will Tell You about Sex

What Would Jesus Do? Spiritual Challenge Journal

Wild Truth Journal for Junior Highers

Wild Truth Journal—Pictures of God